Beginning
C# Databases

From Novice to
Professional

JAMES HUDDLESTON,
RANGA RAGHURAM, SCOTT ALLEN,
SYED FAHAD GILANI,
JACOB HAMMER PEDERSEN, JON REID

Lead Editor: Dominic Shakeshaft

Editorial Board: Steve Anglin, Dan Appleman, Ewan Buckingham, Gary Cornell, Tony Davis, Jason Gilmore, Chris Mills, Dominic Shakeshaft, Jim Sumser

Project Manager and Production Editor: Laura Cheu

Copy Edit Manager: Nicole LeClerc

Copy Editor: Kim Wimpsett

Production Manager: Kari Brooks-Copony

Compositor: Linda Weidemann, Wolf Creek Press

Proofreader: Linda Marousek

Indexer: Kevin Broccoli

Artist: April Milne

Cover Designer: Kurt Krames

Manufacturing Manager: Tom Debolski

Distributed to the book trade in the United States by Springer-Verlag New York, LLC, 233 Spring Street, 6th Floor, New York, NY 10013 and outside the United States by Springer-Verlag GmbH & Co. KG, Tiergartenstr. 17, 69112 Heidelberg, Germany.

In the United States: phone 1-800-SPRINGER, fax 201-348-4505, e-mail orders@springer-ny.com, or visit http://www.springer-ny.com. Outside the United States: fax +49 6221 345229, e-mail orders@springer.de, or visit http://www.springer.de.

For information on translations, please contact Apress directly at 2560 Ninth Street, Suite 219, Berkeley, CA 94710. Phone 510-549-5930, fax 510-549-5939, e-mail info@apress.com, or visit http://www.apress.com.

The source code for this book is available to readers at http://www.apress.com in the Downloads section.

To Jared, Quinn, and Tess.
I love you.
—Jim Huddleston

Contents at a Glance

Contents

About the Authors

JAMES HUDDLESTON has worked with computers since 1974, specializing in database design and development since 1980. He has a bachelor's degree in Latin and Greek from the University of Pennsylvania and a juris doctor degree from the University of Pittsburgh. A technical reviewer of dozens of computer books, including *Beginning C# Objects* (Apress, 2004), he finds databases an endlessly fascinating area of work and almost as intellectually rewarding as his hobby, translating Homer's *Iliad* and *Odyssey* from the original Greek.

RANGA RAGHURAM has a bachelor's degree in engineering from Birla Institute of Technology and Science in Pilani, India, and a master's degree from Virginia Tech in Virginia.

SCOTT ALLEN has a master's degree in computer science from Shippensburg University. He's a Microsoft Certified Solution Developer. He regularly serves as an adjunct faculty member at various colleges in Maryland and Pennsylvania.

SYED FAHAD GILANI has more than fifteen years of experience in computing. He sold his first program at the age of ten.

JACOB HAMMER PEDERSEN started programming in the early 1990s, moving gradually from Pascal to C++ to Visual Basic. In the summer of 2000, he discovered C# and has explored it happily ever since.

JON REID was editor for the C++ and Object Query Language components of the Object Data Management Group standard and has coauthored several C# books.

Acknowledgments

I'd like to thank Dominic Shakeshaft of Apress for asking me to bring this book up-to-date and for his confidence I could do it well. I'd also like to thank Laura Cheu of Apress for her consistently helpful editorial support and Kim Wimpsett of Apress for her thorough and expert copyediting. No author could possibly find a more professional team. Whatever flaws remain are entirely my fault, not theirs.

Thank you, too, Nicholas Andrea, Laurie Apgar, Tiffany Armstrong, Elizabeth A. Baker, Roy Beatty, Wesley R. Bowman, W. Truxton Boyce, Robert Chodoroff, Wydell Conley, Liam Curkin, Chip Deaton, Rebecca Doeltz, Melissa Dupre, Elrod S. Ferreira, Justin Finucan, Francoise Friedlaender, David Gaines, Milo Gibbons, Michael Green, Judith Gregory, Lania Herman, Sarah James, Jackie Jones, Renee L. Kane, Cary Kerrigan, Gil Lachance, Jeff Lee, Joel Lipman, Darren R. Lloyd, Ron Maguire, Jason B. Majewski, Edna Ocampo, Susan Paul, Jax Pierson, Paul Preiss, John Reda, Helen Rei, Eric Robson, Michael P. Small, Teri Small, Michael Thompson, Susan Tussey, James Tuzun, and Paul Yip.

—Jim Huddleston

Introduction

Every program manipulates data. Most real-world programs use data stored in relational databases, so every programmer needs to know how to access relational data. This book explains how to do this with C# and ADO.NET.

We'll start at the beginning with the installations you need, and then we'll cover ADO.NET 1.1, SQL, and relational databases. Then we'll go on to more advanced topics. Finally, we'll close with a brief look ahead to ADO.NET 2.0. By the end of this book, you'll be equipped to tackle the core topics in C# database programming.

Who Is This Book For?

This book is for anyone interested in how to access relational data with C#. This book is targeted at programmers, managers, and even students, since only basic knowledge of C# is assumed and no prior experience with relational databases or the relational database language SQL is required. We've done our best to provide comprehensive, clear descriptions of concepts and to demonstrate them with straightforward programs you can use as the basis for your own code.

What Does This Book Cover?

This book covers all the fundamentals of relational database and ADO.NET that every C# programmer needs to know and understand.

Getting Started

The first three chapters explain how to install Microsoft SQL Server Desktop Engine (MSDE), demonstrate how to build a database application using Visual Studio .NET wizards, and introduce SQL.

Learning ADO.NET Basics

Chapters 4 to 8 introduce ADO.NET and describe how to use its most fundamental features to connect to databases and query and update data.

Building ADO.NET Applications

Chapters 9 to 11 describe how to build Windows Forms and ASP.NET applications that access databases.

Learning More About SQL and Relational Databases

Chapters 12 to 16 cover a variety of database-specific topics, expanding your knowledge of SQL and MSDE. You'll learn how to code more complex queries; how to create tables, views, indexes, constraints, and stored procedures; and how to provide for database security.

Using Advanced Features

Chapters 17 to 21 cover how ADO.NET supports XML, exception handling, transactions, events, and large data objects.

Introducing ADO.NET 2.0

Chapter 22 demonstrates how to convert ADO.NET 1.1 programs to ADO.NET 2.0 and also modifies three applications developed earlier in the book to use alternative features new in ADO.NET 2.0.

What Do You Need to Use This Book?

You can code and run many of the examples using only the command-line C# compiler provided with the .NET Framework 1.1, but Visual Studio .NET 2003 is the development environment we used and the one that can run all the examples. However, Visual C# .NET Standard Edition is adequate for almost all the examples.

Although you can use ADO.NET with any relational database, we base our examples on MSDE, because it's just as powerful as SQL Server and it's available without charge from Microsoft. In Chapter 1 we show you how to download and install both MSDE and SQL Server documentation.

In Chapter 5 we show you how to connect to Access, DB2, Oracle, and MySQL, so you can use any of these relational database systems instead of MSDE. Of course, what data you work with will depend on which database you use, so your output will differ from the MSDE sample table data we display, but you should use whatever relational database system you prefer.

How to Download the Sample Code

The source code for this book is available to readers at http://www.apress.com in the Downloads section. Please feel free to visit the Apress Web site and download all the code there. You can also check for errata and related titles from Apress.

■ ■ ■

Installing MSDE

Chances are that you're already familiar with the term *data* and have some understanding that data can be stored in many formats. You can store data in a text file as a comma-separated list, or you can store it in a database such as SQL Server or Oracle. You can even store data as Extensible Markup Language (XML) documents, which is probably the biggest innovation in data storage in recent years. You can then work with this data and present it to end users in many different ways, from an application running on a local machine to a Web application viewed with a browser.

Throughout this book we'll discuss how to work with data using C#, and in order to have a common set of samples to work with, you need to set up a database. We'll therefore start by showing how to set up a database server and a sample database, both provided free by Microsoft.

In this chapter, we'll cover the following topics:

- Installing Microsoft SQL Server Desktop Engine (MSDE)

- Installing the sample databases

- Installing the Microsoft SQL Server documentation

- Authentication modes

- Connecting with Server Explorer

Obtaining and Installing MSDE

We've chosen MSDE as our relational database management system (RDBMS) since it's available for free. MSDE is an exciting and powerful product that can be embedded in and redistributed with applications. It's the server component of SQL Server 2000, but it's limited to 25 concurrent users and doesn't include visual tools for database management and development. It includes the SQL Server 2000 relational engine and storage engine. Databases and applications developed with it can be easily migrated to SQL Server 2000. If you already have SQL Server 2000 installed, feel free to use it instead of MSDE, but look through the upcoming section "Installing the Sample Databases" to see how to install the sample databases if they're not installed.

MSDE is provided with a number of Microsoft products, including the following:

- Microsoft Office XP (Developer Edition)

- Microsoft Visual Studio .NET (Architect, Developer, Professional Editions)

- SQL Server 2000 (Standard, Enterprise, Developer Editions)

You can also download MSDE as a separate product, and that's what we'll assume you'll do. We'll also install the latest sample databases and SQL Server documentation, which also applies to MSDE. We downloaded the MSDE version used in this book from `http://www.microsoft.com/sql/msde/downloads`. We downloaded the sample databases from the *Northwind and pubs Sample Databases* link at the same uniform resource locator (URL). We downloaded the documentation (SQL Server 2000 Books Online) from `http://www.microsoft.com/sql/techinfo/productdoc/2000/books.asp`.

To install MSDE, perform the following steps:

1. Download `MSDE2000A.exe` from `http://www.microsoft.com/sql/msde/downloads`.

2. Run `MSDE2000A.exe`, which extracts the MSDE installation files. The License Agreement window appears (see Figure 1-1).

Figure 1-1. *MSDE installation's License Agreement window*

3. Read the license agreement, and then click I Agree. The Installation Folder window appears. Specify the folder for the extracted files, and then click Finish (see Figure 1-2).

Figure 1-2. *MSDE installation's Installation Folder window*

4. When the PackageForTheWeb message box appears, click Yes (see Figure 1-3).

Figure 1-3. *MSDE installation's PackageForTheWeb message box*

5. A progress window appears. When the message "The package has been delivered successfully" appears, click OK (see Figure 1-4).

Figure 1-4. *MSDE installation package delivered*

6. The installation files are now in C:\MSDERelA (or wherever you put them). Open a command prompt window, and go to this directory. Run the following command, using whatever password you prefer if you don't want to use sa (see Figure 1-5):

```
setup instancename="netsdk" sapwd="sa"
```

A progress window will display until the setup is complete. If all goes well, a Windows service named MSSQL$NETSDK will be created that will start automatically at Windows startup. This service is an MSDE server instance known as (local)\netsdk for connection purposes. By default, we chose Windows Authentication, so any user who can log onto Windows can connect to it.

To start up the server, from any command prompt, enter the following (see Figure 1-5):

```
net start mssql$netsdk
```

To shut it down, enter the following (see Figure 1-5):

```
net stop mssql$netsdk
```

Figure 1-5. *Creating the* NETSDK *MSDE server instance*

That's it! MSDE is installed, and you can now install the sample databases.

Installing the Sample Databases

To install the Northwind sample database, perform the following steps:

1. Download SQL2000SampleDb.msi after following the *Northwind and pubs Sample Databases* link at http://www.microsoft.com/sql/msde/downloads.

2. Open `SQL2000SampleDb.msi`, which extracts the sample database installation files. A welcome window appears. Click Next (see Figure 1-6).

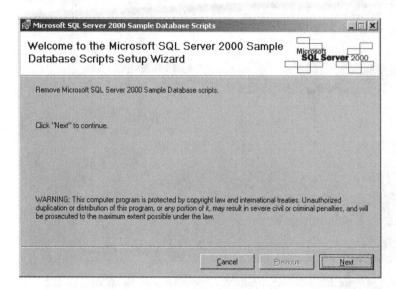

Figure 1-6. *Sample database installation's welcome window*

3. A License Agreement window appears. Read the license agreement, and then click the I Agree radio button. When the Next button is enabled, click it (see Figure 1-7).

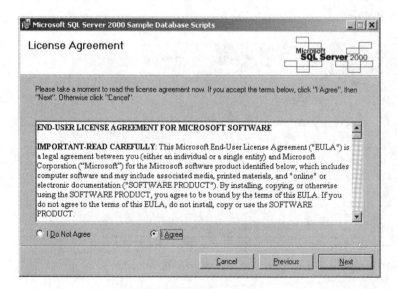

Figure 1-7. *Sample database installation's License Agreement window*

4. When the Choose Installation Options window appears, click Next (see Figure 1-8).

Figure 1-8. *Sample database installation's Choose Installation Options window*

5. When the Confirm Installation window appears, click Next (see Figure 1-9).

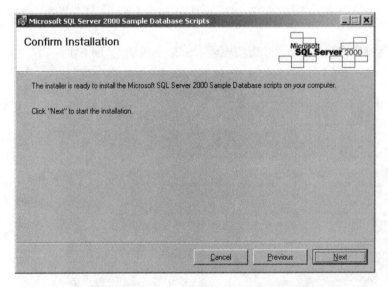

Figure 1-9. *Sample database installation's Confirm Installation window*

6. A progress window may briefly appear, followed by the Installation Complete window. Click Close. The installation files have been extracted to (no, we're not kidding) `C:\Program Files\Microsoft SQL Server 2000 Sample Database Scripts` (see Figure 1-10). Note that the sample databases haven't yet been created. Only the installation files that create them have been "installed."

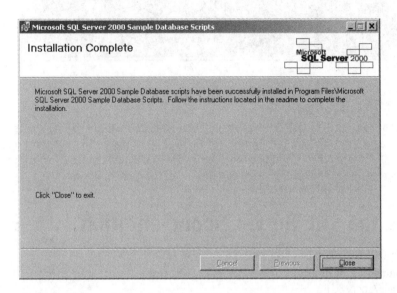

Figure 1-10. *Sample database installation's Installation Complete window*

7. To create (or re-create, whenever you like) the `Northwind` sample database, make sure the `MSSQL$NETSDK` service is started (refer to Figure 1-5), open a command prompt window, and then go to whatever directory contains the `instnwnd.sql` file (for convenience, we copied ours to `C:\BegCSharpDb`, but that's not necessary). Then enter the following, paying attention to case (see Figure 1-11):

```
osql -E -S (local)\netsdk -i instnwnd.sql
```

Figure 1-11. *Creating the* Northwind *sample database*

A lot of largely unintelligible output will display, eventually ending with the screen shown in Figure 1-12.

Figure 1-12. Northwind *sample database created*

The Northwind sample database is now installed in the MSDE instance (local)\netsdk. You can install the pubs sample database similarly with osql by using the instpubs.sql file. Note that in step 7 you used the -E option to connect to the MSDE instance (server) using a trusted connection and the -S option to specify the server to which to connect.

Installing the SQL Server Documentation

To install the SQL Server documentation, perform the following steps:

1. Download sqlbolsetup.msi from http://www.microsoft.com/sql/techinfo/productdoc/2000/books.asp.

2. Open sqlbolsetup.msi, which extracts the documentation files. A welcome window appears. Click Next (see Figure 1-13).

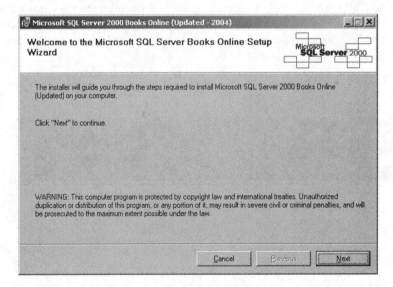

Figure 1-13. *SQL Server documentation's welcome window*

3. A License Agreement window appears. Read the license agreement, and then click the I Agree radio button. When the Next button is enabled, click it (see Figure 1-14).

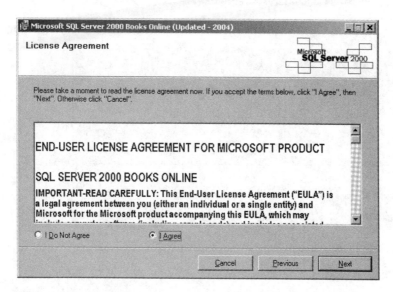

Figure 1-14. *SQL Server documentation's License Agreement window*

4. When the Choose Installation Type window appears, click the Install Microsoft SQL Server Books Online to a separate directory radio button and then click Next (see Figure 1-15).

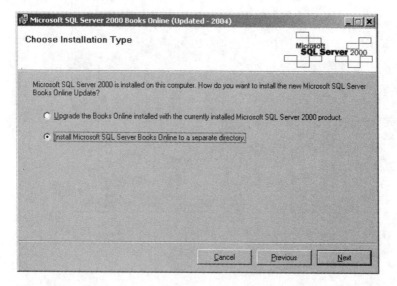

Figure 1-15. *SQL Server documentation's Choose Installation Type window*

5. When the Select Installation Folder window appears, click Next (see Figure 1-16).

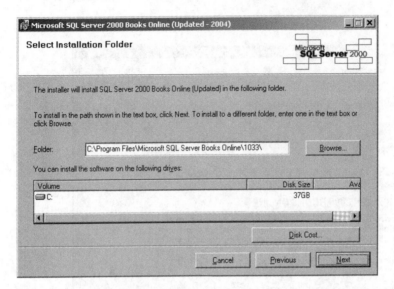

Figure 1-16. *SQL Server documentation's Select Installation Folder window*

6. When the Confirm Installation window appears, click Next (see Figure 1-17).

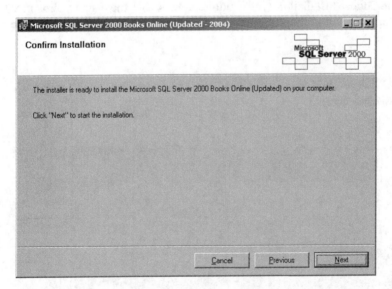

Figure 1-17. *SQL Server documentation's Confirm Installation window*

7. A progress window appears, followed by the Installation Complete window (see Figure 1-18). Click Close. The documentation files have been installed.

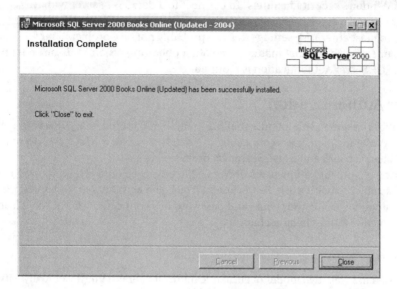

Figure 1-18. *SQL Server documentation's Installation Complete window*

Microsoft SQL Server 2000 Books Online is now installed. You can run it from its shortcut on the Start ➤ Programs submenu, or, for convenience, copy the shortcut to your desktop. Now you're ready to work with MSDE!

Introducing Authentication Modes

Before you start playing with MSDE, we'll talk a bit about who can play with it. SQL Server, and therefore MSDE, has two distinct modes for authenticating users.

- Windows Authentication

- SQL Server Authentication

Tip When we installed MSDE, we defaulted to Windows Authentication, since it's the more flexible and secure mode. As a rule, you should use SQL Server Authentication only when you're not connecting over a network.

Windows Authentication

When a database uses Windows Authentication, SQL Server validates user names and pass-words through Windows security facilities. To connect to a database server with this type of authentication (known as a *trusted connection*), you must be logged onto Windows XP or Windows 2000. In most enterprise settings this will probably not be a problem, but for users on Windows 98 or earlier (or for that matter, some other operating system) this isn't possible. For such users, SQL Server Authentication is required.

SQL Server Authentication

SQL Server Authentication uses accounts that are created and stored in SQL Server itself. With SQL Server Authentication, users connecting to a database server will have two accounts: an operating system account and a SQL Server account.

With this kind of authentication, users don't need to be logged onto just Windows XP or Windows 2000, so any user with a SQL Server account can gain access. Another benefit is that a program can supply a specific user name and password in a connection string. You'll learn more about connection strings in later chapters.

Mixed Mode

What's this? We said there are two modes of authentication, and here's a third? Not really. Mixed Mode means the database server can use both Windows Authentication and SQL Server Authen-tication. The benefit is that applications can connect using Windows Authentication, if available, or use SQL Server Authentication, if necessary.

Connecting with Server Explorer

You connected to your MSDE server with osql when you installed the sample databases. Now let's look at one way to connect with Visual Studio .NET, with Server Explorer.

When you open Visual Studio .NET, Server Explorer is collapsed on the left (if not, press Ctrl+Alt+S to view it). Server Explorer displays a tree from which you can control just about anything on the local computer and any remote computers to which you have access. (In Visual C# Standard Edition, you can't connect to remote servers.)

Figure 1-19 shows Visual Studio .NET 2003's Server Explorer. The Visual C# Standard Edition Server Explorer displays only local data connections, but that will do just fine for our purposes.

Figure 1-19. *Visual Studio .NET 2003 Server Explorer tree*

■Note A big difference between Visual Studio .NET and Visual C# Standard Edition is that Visual C# supports only connecting to databases and viewing database details. In Visual Studio .NET you can create new databases, tables, views, stored procedures, and so on. MSDE users without Visual Studio .NET can use a tool such as Microsoft Access for visual database management. However, SQL, executed through command-line utilities or ADO.NET code, can achieve the same results. You'll eventually be comfortable enough to perform such tasks even without visual tools.

You're interested in the Data Connections node. Using this node, you can create and manage connections to any number of databases, located on any number of servers.

Let's create a connection to the Northwind database. Follow these steps:

1. Right-click the Data Connections node in the tree, and select Add Connection....

2. Enter the information in Table 1-1 on the Connection tab of the Data Link Properties dialog box (see Figure 1-20).

Table 1-1. *Connection Properties*

Property	Value
Server name	(local)\netsdk
Authentication	Use Windows NT Integrated Security
Database	northwind

Figure 1-20. *Specifying connection properties*

3. Click the Provider tab. On this tab you can select which provider to use to connect to a database server. The default provider is Microsoft OLE DB Provider for SQL Server, which isn't an ADO.NET data provider (introduced in Chapter 4) but can connect to MSDE (see Figure 1-21).

Figure 1-21. *Selecting Microsoft OLE DB Provider for SQL Server*

4. Click OK. If the SQL Server Login window appears, check Use Trusted Connection and then click OK (see Figure 1-22).

Figure 1-22. *Logging into SQL Server*

5. Expand the Database Connections node, if necessary, and you'll see the node for the new connection. Click the plus sign in front of the new node to expand it. Click the plus sign in front of the Tables node to view the tables in the Northwind database (see Figure 1-23).

Figure 1-23. Northwind *tables in Server Explorer*

6. Double-click the Employees table to view its data (see Figure 1-24).

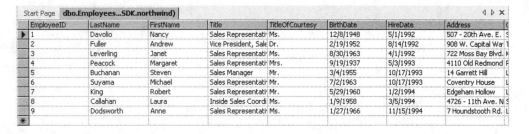

EmployeeID	LastName	FirstName	Title	TitleOfCourtesy	BirthDate	HireDate	Address	
1	Davolio	Nancy	Sales Representati	Ms.	12/8/1948	5/1/1992	507 - 20th Ave. E.	S
2	Fuller	Andrew	Vice President, Sale	Dr.	2/19/1952	8/14/1992	908 W. Capital Wa	T
3	Leverling	Janet	Sales Representati	Ms.	8/30/1963	4/1/1992	722 Moss Bay Blvd.	K
4	Peacock	Margaret	Sales Representati	Mrs.	9/19/1937	5/3/1993	4110 Old Redmond	R
5	Buchanan	Steven	Sales Manager	Mr.	3/4/1955	10/17/1993	14 Garrett Hill	L
6	Suyama	Michael	Sales Representati	Mr.	7/2/1963	10/17/1993	Coventry House	L
7	King	Robert	Sales Representati	Mr.	5/29/1960	1/2/1994	Edgeham Hollow	L
8	Callahan	Laura	Inside Sales Coordi	Ms.	1/9/1958	3/5/1994	4726 - 11th Ave. N	S
9	Dodsworth	Anne	Sales Representati	Ms.	1/27/1966	11/15/1994	7 Houndstooth Rd.	L

Figure 1-24. Employees *data from Server Explorer*

Summary

In this first chapter you installed MSDE, the sample Northwind database, and Microsoft SQL Server Books Online. You learned about authentication modes and saw how to connect to an MSDE database with osql and with Visual Studio .NET's Server Explorer.

You're now ready to develop a simple application against the Northwind database. You'll do that in the next chapter.

CHAPTER 2

■ ■ ■

Creating a
Simple Database Application

Now that you've installed your database server and had a look at what's in the Northwind database, we'll walk through the steps needed to create a basic database application, using some of the powerful functionality provided by Visual Studio .NET. You're not going to look too hard at what's going on behind the scenes; instead, you'll concentrate on getting comfortable using Visual Studio .NET's rapid application development (RAD) features. In later chapters we'll discuss the code that's generated for you by Visual Studio .NET and how to work with it to improve and refine your applications.

In this chapter, you'll see the following:

- How to build a Windows Forms application that connects to the Northwind database and displays data from it

- How to update the database with edited data

Creating the Application

The application will perform some simple but common tasks on a single table from the Northwind database. Once complete, you'll be able to do the following:

- Display a list of last names of employees in the Northwind database.

- Display and edit information for an employee selected from the list.

- Update the edited information in the database.

So, it's time to get started! In the following sections, you'll just create the project, adding to it as you progress.

Try It Out: Creating the Foundations

You'll be creating a Windows Forms application, so open Visual Studio .NET and follow these steps:

1. Create a new blank solution by clicking the *New Project* link on the Start page and then selecting the Visual Studio Solutions project type and the Blank Solution template. Alternatively, you can select File ➤ New ➤ Blank Solution... from the main menu. Name your solution Chapter2_Examples, specify its location (we used C:\BegCSharpDb), and click OK (see Figure 2-1).

Figure 2-1. *Creating a new solution*

■**Note** We'll use this solution structure throughout the book for the examples and in the code download. The code for each chapter will consist of one or more example projects, each contained within one chapter solution. You can obtain the code from the Downloads section of the Apress Web site (http://www.apress.com).

---

2. Not a lot appears to happen when you click OK. However, if you hover your mouse over Solution Explorer (normally found on the right in Visual Studio .NET), you'll see your solution listed there. Right-click the solution, and select Add ➤ New Project... from the context menu. Create a new application by selecting Visual C# Projects and selecting Windows Application. Name it Employees, and click OK.

3. In Solution Explorer, click the Show All Files icon at the top, and then expand all the nodes. You should see something like Figure 2-2.

Figure 2-2. *Solution Explorer tree*

How It Works

The simple action of creating a new project has created several default files and directories. Inside the files, Visual Studio .NET has inserted some starter code.

The items in the list you'll become most acquainted with include the following:

- The Form1.cs file, which is the default file for a Windows form. This is where the form code resides.

- The References item, which lists namespaces. By default, Visual Studio .NET decided that you may need namespaces relating to graphical elements and data applications, because these are common parts of Windows Forms applications. As your needs become more complex, you may have to add to this list.

These two items—along with the project and solution—are the ones you use most when creating a Windows Forms application. Other types of applications create slightly different files. For example, a Web Forms application will include files that relate to configuration details, global application settings, and references to namespaces with the word *Web* in them (System.Web, System.Web.UI, and so on). In contrast, when creating a console application, you see fewer items in Solution Explorer, since you're not concerned with a visual front end.

Let's continue with the application and see how to connect to your database. (You actually connect to the *database server*, but it's simpler to say just *database*.)

Establishing a Database Connection

To work with a database, you need to connect to it from your Windows Forms application. In Chapter 1, you saw how to create a connection to the Northwind database with Server Explorer, but that's not the same as creating a connection programmatically.

Try It Out: Creating a Connection

To access a database, you must first establish a connection to it.

1. Click the form to select it, and then examine the Properties window on the right. Find (DataBindings). Expand it by clicking the plus sign (+) on the left (see Figure 2-3).

Figure 2-3. *Windows form* (DataBindings) *property*

2. Leaving the (Advanced) property for later, you can see two properties of the form, Tag and Text, that can be bound to data. However, if you try to assign something to them, you can't. The reason is because currently no reference to any data exists since you haven't yet connected your application to your database.

3. In Server Explorer, drag the connection to the Northwind database (that you created in Chapter 1) onto the form (see Figure 2-4). Rather than placing the connection on the form itself, Visual Studio .NET opens a tray below the form and places the connection in the tray.

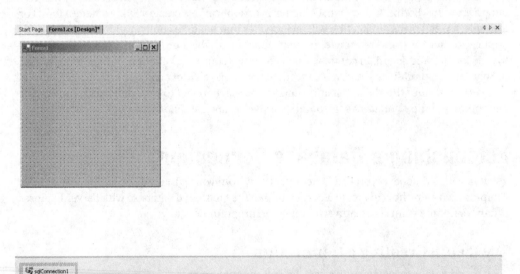

Figure 2-4. *Adding a database connection to a form*

4. Right-click the sqlConnection1 object in the tray, and select Properties (see Figure 2-5).

Figure 2-5. *Database connection properties*

5. Change (Name) to sqlConnectionNorthwind.

Tip One of the other properties in the list is ConnectionString. A *connection string* provides parameters for establishing a database session. For now don't concern yourself too much with this, as Server Explorer generates it for you, and you'll see how to write your own connection strings in Chapter 5.

---

6. The next step is to specify which data to get from the database. Open Server Explorer, and expand the Tables node of the connection. Select and drag the Employees table onto the form. This adds a sqlDataAdapter to the tray. Select it, and change its (Name) to sqlDataAdapterEmployees. A *data adapter* specifies how to select, edit, and update data. It doesn't, however, hold the data itself—this job is performed by another ADO.NET component, namely, a *dataset*.

7. Just below the properties list you'll see three links (see Figure 2-6).

Figure 2-6. *Data adapter links*

These links are as follows:

- *Configure Data Adapter...*: Click this link to configure how the data adapter accesses the database. This was done for you when you dragged the table onto the form, so you'll leave this option alone.

- *Generate Dataset...*: This is the option in which you're interested. It will allow you to generate a dataset, which is the object that will actually contain the data from the table.

- *Preview Data...*: Clicking this link displays a window where you can preview the data.

8. Click the *Generate Dataset...* link.

9. In the dialog box, change the name from DataSet1 to DataSetEmployees and click OK (see Figure 2-7). The dataset will be added to the tray.

Figure 2-7. *Generate Dataset window*

How It Works

All you appear to have done so far is a lot of clicking and a bit of dragging and dropping, but don't worry, Visual Studio .NET has actually been busy writing code for you with each step. You now have the ability to connect to a database, select specific data, and work with that data using a dataset. You'll look more at data adapters and datasets in Chapter 8, where you'll learn how to code and use them.

Note that although you named the dataset DataSetEmployees, the designer named it DataSetEmployees1, so when you refer to this dataset later, you'll use DataSetEmployees1.

Introducing Data Binding

Now let's take some data from the database and display it using controls on a Windows form—this is what we mean by *data binding*. You have two ways to bind data to controls: *complex* and *simple* data binding. Complex data binding is supported by only a few Windows Forms controls, such as `DataGrid` and `ListBox`, and allows the control to display lists of data. Simple data binding is supported by most other Windows Forms controls, and, unlike complex data binding, it allows the control to bind to only a single value at a time.

You'll use complex data binding only once in this application—to bind the data for a list of names. The rest of the controls are text boxes that use simple data binding. Let's start putting the form together.

Try It Out: Creating a User Interface

You need to create the front end for the database application, which involves a certain amount of dragging and dropping. You also need to specify what data to display in the interface controls.

1. You should have a blank form displayed in Forms Designer. To the left is a tab for the Toolbox. The Toolbox contains a list of controls that you can place on the form. You'll use five text boxes, one label, and one list box. Figure 2-8 shows the layout of the form.

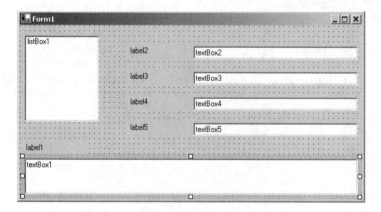

Figure 2-8. *User interface layout*

The large box is the list box. The other controls are text boxes. The text next to each text box is in a corresponding label. Add and position the controls according to Figure 2-8 by dragging and dropping them from the Toolbox onto the form.

2. Using the Properties window, set the properties of the text boxes as in Table 2-1.

Table 2-1. *Text Box Properties*

Number	Property	Value
1	(Name)	textBoxNotes
1	MultiLine	True
2	(Name)	textBoxFirstName
3	(Name)	textBoxLastName
4	(Name)	textBoxBirthDate
5	(Name)	textBoxHomePhone

3. For each of the text boxes, clear the Text property.

4. For each of the labels, set the Text property to match the text box data.

5. Set the properties of the list box as in Table 2-2.

Table 2-2. *List Box Properties*

Property	Value	Description
(Name)	listBoxNames	The name of the control.
DataSource	dataSetEmployees1.Employees	Identifies the dataset and table containing the data to display.
DisplayMember	LastName	The control will display the value of the LastName column.
ValueMember	EmployeeID	When selecting data, the control will use EmployeeID rather than LastName.

6. Select `textBoxNotes`, and look at the top of the Properties window (see Figure 2-9). There you'll find (`DataBindings`).

Figure 2-9. *Data bindings for* textBoxNotes

7. Expand this entry, and then open the `Text` property. Expand the `dataSetEmployees1` node and then the `Employees` node (see Figure 2-10). Scroll down, and select the `Notes` column.

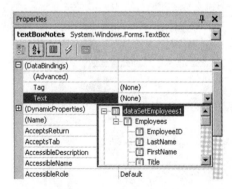

Figure 2-10. *Binding a column to a text box control*

8. Repeat steps 6 and 7 for the remaining text boxes, assigning columns to the appropriate text boxes as in Table 2-3.

Table 2-3. *Other Text Box Data Bindings*

Number	Property	Value
2	DataBindings.Text	FirstName
3	DataBindings.Text	LastName
4	DataBindings.Text	BirthDate
5	DataBindings.Text	HomePhone

9. Right-click the form, and select View Code.

10. Locate the Form1 constructor, and insert the following bold code:

```
InitializeComponent();

sqlDataAdapterEmployees.Fill(dataSetEmployees1);
```

11. Run the application, and you should see the Northwind data displayed in your Windows form, as shown in Figure 2-11.

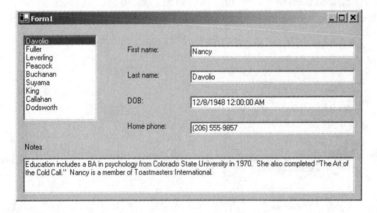

Figure 2-11. *Displaying employee data*

How It Works

You started by adding the following three ADO.NET components to the application by dragging and dropping them onto the form from Server Explorer (see Figure 2-12):

- Connection (sqlConnectionNorthwind)

- Data adapter (sqlDataAdapterEmployees)

- Dataset (dataSetEmployees1)

Figure 2-12. *ADO.NET objects in component tray*

You'll see these components a lot during the course of the book, so in later chapters we'll go into much more detail about them.

Note that ADO.NET uses the prefix *Sql* (for example, SqlConnection) for each type name. These prefixes indicate that you're working with the .NET Framework data provider for SQL Server. Had you performed all of the previous steps with an Access database as the back end, the type names would have been prefixed with *OleDb* (for example, OleDbConnection). You'll learn more about the different data providers in Chapters 4 and 5. Aside from the way they connect to databases, and their prefixes, the components are essentially interchangeable.

After a lot of cosmetic steps where you added controls to the form and set some of their properties, you bound the list box to the LastName column in the Northwind Employees table.

First, you set the DataSource property. This tells the list box where it should look for its data. Remember that dataSetEmployees1 is the ADO.NET object that stores the data. Second, you set the DisplayMember property, which tells the list box which column to use to fill itself. The third property you set was ValueMember, which was bound to the table's primary key, EmployeeID. This means that when you ask the list box for the selected item in the list, you want the value of the EmployeeID column rather than that of the LastName column. (More than one employee can have same last name, but every employee must have a unique employee ID).

Next, you set the data binding properties for all the text boxes. Since these controls use simple data binding, they're rather easy to set. You set the Text property of the DataBindings collection to the column of the data you want the text box to display.

Finally, you added a single line of code to the Form1 instance constructor.

```
sqlDataAdapterEmployees.Fill(dataSetEmployees1);
```

A data adapter accesses the data, but a dataset holds the data. To get the data into the dataset, you call the Fill method on the data adapter, passing the dataset as an argument. When the application runs, the list box displays the last names of the employees in the Employees table, and the text boxes display the detail information—all achieved with one line of code!

When you run the application, you see the expected results: the details for the employee selected in the list box (Davolio) are displayed in the text boxes on the right. However, when you select another employee from the list box, nothing happens! The reason for this is that you have no link between the information displayed in the list box and what's displayed in the text boxes. You need to add this link to your code.

Try It Out: Making the Form Dynamic

To add the link, follow these steps:

1. Return to Design view. Go to the Properties window for the list box, and click the yellow lightning icon at the top to display the available event handlers for the control. Locate the SelectedValueChanged event, give it the value listBoxNames_SelectedValueChanged, and then hit Enter.

2. The event handler method should automatically be displayed in Code view. Enter the code shown in Listing 2-1 in the event handler.

Listing 2-1. *Event Handler Code*

```
// Clear the data bindings on the text boxes
textBoxBirthDate.DataBindings.Clear();
textBoxFirstName.DataBindings.Clear();
textBoxHomePhone.DataBindings.Clear();
textBoxLastName.DataBindings.Clear();
textBoxNotes.DataBindings.Clear();

// Add a new binding, with a new data source: the selected row.
textBoxBirthDate.DataBindings.Add(
    "Text",
    dataSetEmployees1.Employees.Rows[listBoxNames.SelectedIndex],
    "BirthDate"
);

textBoxFirstName.DataBindings.Add(
    "Text",
    dataSetEmployees1.Employees.Rows[listBoxNames.SelectedIndex],
    "FirstName"
);

textBoxHomePhone.DataBindings.Add(
    "Text",
    dataSetEmployees1.Employees.Rows[listBoxNames.SelectedIndex],
    "HomePhone"
);

textBoxLastName.DataBindings.Add(
    "Text",
    dataSetEmployees1.Employees.Rows[listBoxNames.SelectedIndex],
    "LastName"
);

textBoxNotes.DataBindings.Add(
    "Text",
    dataSetEmployees1.Employees.Rows[listBoxNames.SelectedIndex],
    "Notes"
);
```

Run the application again. When you select an item in the list box, the values in the text boxes change, as shown in Figure 2-13.

Figure 2-13. *Displaying a selected employee's data*

How It Works

You created an event handler for the SelectedValueChanged event of the list box. This is triggered whenever the active selection in the list box is changed by a user clicking it.

The event handler may look complex, but it contains only two kinds of C# statements. These are repeated for each of the text boxes on the form.

```
textBoxAddress.DataBindings.Clear();
textBoxAddress.DataBindings.Add(
    "Text",
    dataSetEmployees1.Employees.Rows[listBoxNames.SelectedIndex],
    "Address"
);
```

The first statement tells the text box to remove any current data bindings. The second statement then adds a new data binding, this time with data for the currently selected row. The first parameter of the Add method is the name of the property you want to bind data to, namely, the Text property. The second parameter is the actual data the control should use. You know that the index of the selected item in the ListBox is the same as the row you're interested in, and so you use this index to retrieve a row from the Employees table. The third and final parameter is the name of the column the control should use.

Editing Data

Now that you're able to display and move around in the data, you have one last task: to edit the data and update it in the database. The editing part is simple since you're using text boxes. You'll update the database every time the Validated event is fired by one of the text boxes. This happens whenever a text box loses focus to another control that has the CausesValidation property set to true. This is the default for all the controls you've used in this chapter.

Try It Out: Adding Edit Functionality

To add the edit functionality, follow these steps:

1. In Design view, select the text box named textBoxNotes. In the Properties window, click the lightning icon, and select the Validated entry. Give it the value TextBox_Validated, and hit Enter.

2. Repeat this for the remaining text boxes.

3. Add the following bold code to the TextBox_Validated event handler:

```
private void TextBox_Validated(object sender, System.EventArgs e)
{
    // Open the connection
    sqlConnectionNorthwind.Open();

    // Update
    sqlDataAdapterEmployees.Update(dataSetEmployees1, "Employees");

    // Refresh the data in the dataset
    sqlDataAdapterEmployees.Fill(dataSetEmployees1);

    // Close the connection
    sqlConnectionNorthwind.Close();
}
```

4. Run the application, select the third name in the list, and change the last name of that employee as shown in Figure 2-14.

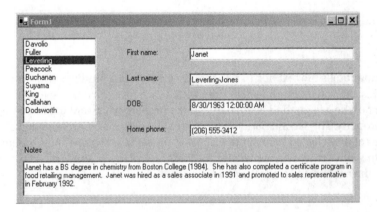

Figure 2-14. *Updating an employee's last name*

5. Hit the Tab key. This will update the database (see Figure 2-15).

Figure 2-15. *Updated employee's last name*

How It Works

You created a single event handler, TextBox_Validated, which is triggered for all the text boxes whenever the Validated event is fired. The first line opens the connection to the database.

```
sqlConnectionNorthwind.Open();
```

You may be surprised to learn that the connection to the database has actually been closed ever since you first called the Fill method on the data adapter in the instance constructor of Form1. The data is said to be *disconnected* from the database. This has a number of advantages over connected data, and you'll look at this in more detail in later chapters. For now, you simply reconnect to the database in order to be able to transmit the changes to it.

The second line updates the data in the database.

```
sqlDataAdapterEmployees.Update(dataSetEmployees1, "Employees");
```

You call Update on the data adapter. The first parameter of the Update method is the dataset containing the data you want to update, and the second parameter specifies the table you want to update.

The third line refreshes the data in the dataset, which keeps the list box refreshed in case a last name was changed.

```
sqlDataAdapterEmployees.Fill(dataSetEmployees1);
```

Finally, you close the connection.

```
sqlConnectionNorthwind.Close();
```

Using the Data Form Wizard

Notice in Figure 2-15 that once the Tab key was pressed, the focus moved to the next text box and the list box selection was lost. Coordinating such things is beyond the scope of this simple example but is certainly needed for a robust application. Notice also that to keep the exercise short, we used only five of the thirteen Employees columns.

Visual Studio .NET has a wizard that will automatically make all columns available, provide for inserting and deleting as well as updating, and do it all in a coordinated way.

Try It Out: Creating a User Interface with the Data Form Wizard

You need to create the front end for the database application, which involves a certain amount of dragging and dropping. You also need to specify what data to display in the interface controls.

1. Create a new blank solution named Chapter2_Wizard. Add a C# Windows application named DataFormWizard to it. Select Project ➤ Add Component ..., click the Data Form Wizard template, and click Open (see Figure 2-16). This starts Data Form Wizard (see Figure 2-17). Click Next.

Figure 2-16. *Creating a data form with the wizard*

Figure 2-17. *Data Form Wizard's Welcome window*

2. In the next window, name the new dataset DataSet1 (see Figure 2-18). Click Next.

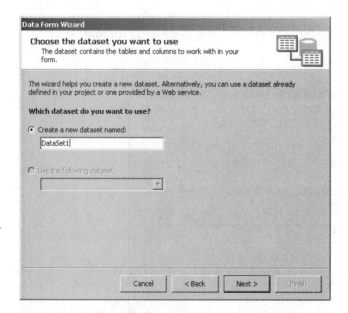

Figure 2-18. *Creating a new dataset with the wizard*

3. The connection to the Northwind database should be selected in the next window (see Figure 2-19). Click Next.

Figure 2-19. *Selecting a connection with the wizard*

4. In the next window, double-click the Employees node, and then click Next (see Figure 2-20).

Figure 2-20. *Selecting a table with the wizard*

5. In the next window, click Next to select all the columns in the Employees table (see
Figure 2-21).

Figure 2-21. *Selecting columns with the wizard*

6. In the Choose the Display Style window, select the Single Record in Individual Controls radio button and click Finish (see Figure 2-22). The wizard exits, and the data form appears in Design view.

Figure 2-22. *Choosing the display style with the wizard*

7. A data form doesn't include a Main method (although you could add one to it), so something has to be done to display it. You have several possibilities, but the easiest for now is just to add the following line to the Form1 constructor:

```
new DataForm1().ShowDialog();
```

8. Run the application with F5. When the form opens, click the Load button; the display should look like Figure 2-23.

Figure 2-23. *Data form for* Employees

■Tip Notice that the address for employee 1 (Davolio) has a strange character in it. This isn't a bug in the data form but bad data in the database! (And it isn't the only place the data is unclean.) If you look at the instnwnd.sql file you used in Chapter 1 to create the Northwind database, you'll find a linefeed embedded between the street number and the apartment. A word to the wise: make sure your data is clean before debugging your programs.

Summary

In this chapter you built a simple application without looking in detail at how the code works. Instead, you relied heavily on the rapid application development (RAD) features of Visual Studio .NET. With just a few clicks and a minimal amount of coding, you created some quite powerful functionality. As you worked through the chapter, you learned the following:

- How to create a blank solution and add a Windows Forms project to it

- What Visual Studio .NET creates for you when you create a C# Windows Forms application

- How to add data connectivity to your application using Server Explorer, and by a similar process, how to create a data adapter and dataset

- How to create a user interface with controls and bind data to them

- How to get your application to update the database dynamically

- How to use the Data Form Wizard

You'll learn much more about ADO.NET components starting with Chapter 4, but before you dive in, you'll look at the most important tool in the database application developer's toolkit, the international standard database language SQL.

■■■

Introducing SQL

In the previous chapter you saw how easy it is to build a simple application using C# and Visual Studio .NET that displays and modifies database data. In this chapter, we'll step away from applications and cover SQL.

You'll learn about some of the most common elements of SQL.

- Queries

- INSERT statements

- UPDATE statements

- DELETE statements

- Data types

What Is SQL?

If you've ever worked with relational databases, you've probably seen some SQL. SQL is the international standard database language. You can use SQL to create, retrieve, change, or delete data.

The formal definition of SQL comes from the American National Standards Institute (ANSI). It's the same as the international standard specified by the International Organization for Standardization (ISO). Transact-SQL is the dialect of SQL provided by SQL Server. Since we're using MSDE, we focus on Transact-SQL rather than standard SQL, but unless we're discussing a feature not found in standard SQL we'll refer to both simply as *SQL*. We'll use *standard SQL* when referring specifically to the ISO/ANSI version of the language. Each database vendor offers its own implementation of SQL, which conforms at some level to the standard but typically adds to it. Transact-SQL does just that, and some of the SQL used in this book may not work if you try it with a database server other than SQL Server.

■**Tip** Relational database terminology is often confusing. For example, neither the meaning nor the pronunciation of *SQL* is crystal clear. IBM invented the language some 30 years ago and called it Structured English Query Language (SEQUEL), changing it shortly thereafter to Structured Query Language (SQL) to avoid conflict with another vendor's product. SEQUEL and SQL were both pronounced *sequel*. When the ISO/ANSI standard was adopted, it referred to the language simply as *database language SQL* and was silent on whether this was an acronym and how it should be pronounced. Today, two pronunciations are used. In the Microsoft and Oracle worlds (as well as many others), it's pronounced *sequel*. In the DB2 and MySQL worlds (among others), it's pronounced *ess cue ell*. (How one properly pronounces the name of the standard language is unclear.) We'll follow the most reasonable practice. We're working in a Microsoft environment, so we'll pronounce SQL as *sequel*. When in Rome....

Let's briefly look at the application of the previous chapter to see how it handled SQL.

If you display the properties of sqlDataAdapterEmployees, you'll see four of them named: DeleteCommand, InsertCommand, SelectCommand, and UpdateCommand (see Figure 3-1).

Figure 3-1. *Data adapter command properties*

The four *commands* (not a standard SQL term but an ADO.NET one) mentioned here represent a *query* and DELETE, INSERT, and UPDATE *statements*. (In Chapter 2 you retrieved and updated data with the data adapter but didn't insert or delete any.) In this chapter you'll look at SQL queries, data modification statements, and data types.

Using SQL

To execute SQL, you need a way to pass it to the database manager. Various techniques are available.

- Visual Studio .NET's built-in SQL tool

- The osql command-line utility

- SQL Server Query Analyzer

- Custom tools

Since the minimum requirements for this book are MSDE and Visual C# Standard Edition, you'll look at all of these except SQL Server Query Analyzer. The custom tool you'll look at is one we supply with the code download and implement step-by-step in Appendix A. (Though you aren't yet familiar with all its coding techniques, working through Appendix A now, before using the custom tool later in this chapter, should be both fun and enlightening.)

Executing SQL from Visual Studio .NET

Both Visual Studio .NET and Visual C# Standard Edition have a tool that you used in Chapter 1 to execute SQL. Let's learn more about it.

Try It Out: Executing SQL from Visual Studio .NET

To execute SQL from Visual Studio .NET, follow these steps:

1. Open Visual Studio .NET, and navigate to Server Explorer. In Chapter 1 you created a connection to the Northwind database, so let's look at that connection now. Expand the Tables node, and double-click the Employees table (see Figure 3-2).

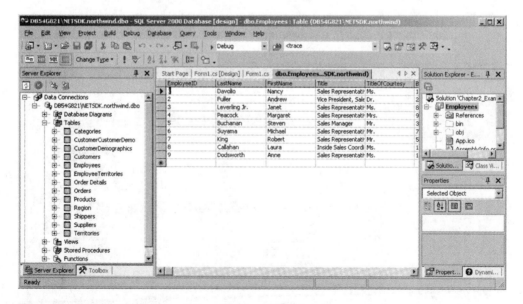

Figure 3-2. *Displaying database data with Server Explorer*

2. If you position your cursor anywhere within the data grid, the Show SQL Pane button (the one with *SQL*) on the toolbar becomes enabled, so click this button; you should see the pane shown in Figure 3-3. You should now see a window above the data grid, which displays the query generated to retrieve the data.

Figure 3-3. *Displaying the SQL pane*

3. To test the window, change Employees to Products, and click the Run Query icon (the one with *!*) on the toolbar to run the query, as shown in Figure 3-4.

Figure 3-4. *Executing a query from the SQL pane*

How It Works

This Visual Studio .NET facility is quite powerful and lets you execute all kinds of queries and statements using SQL. Since you haven't yet looked at how SQL works, we won't cover this in detail here, but it's worth remembering that this facility exists.

Executing SQL from the Command Line

If you need to use SQL without a visual tool, you can use the osql utility that comes with MSDE. You can enter SQL one line at a time in a command prompt window, or you can input it from a text file. The osql utility is a simple but useful tool.

To use osql, open a command prompt window and enter osql followed by appropriate arguments that specify osql options. Figure 3-5 lists the options, which you can obtain by running osql /? on a command line.

Figure 3-5. osql *options*

It's not our intention to describe all these options; however, we'll demonstrate the ones essential for using SQL in this book.

Try It Out: Executing SQL Using osql

To execute SQL using osql, follow these steps:

1. To connect to the local MSDE server, use the -E option to connect using a *trusted connection* (in other words, Windows Authentication) and the -S option followed by your server name.

   ```
   osql -E -S (local)\netsdk
   ```

■**Caution** Option names are case sensitive, but their arguments aren't. For example, -S isn't the same option as -s, but -S (local)\netsdk is equivalent to -S (LOCAL)\NETSDK.

■**Tip** You can enter options in any order. You can use either a hyphen or a slash as an option indicator. Option names are case sensitive, but values associated with options aren't.

To connect to a server other than one on the local machine, simply change (`local`) to the name of the remote server. You'll find out more about connections in Chapter 5.

---

2. Now that you're connected to the server, you can enter SQL one line at a time delimited by pressing the Enter key. Once all the SQL is entered, simply type go on a separate line to execute it. Enter the following line by line:

```
osql -E -S (local)\netsdk
use northwind
set rowcount 2
select * from products
go
```

You should see the output shown in Figure 3-6.

Figure 3-6. *Executing a query with* osql

3. To close the connection and exit osql, type quit and press Enter.

How It Works

Although it isn't exactly the prettiest tool, and the output isn't necessarily the easiest to read, osql allows you to quickly interrogate (and, in fact, do virtually anything with) a database. You can direct output to a file using the -o option.

In this brief example, you used osql to connect, using Windows Authentication, to the MSDE instance (`local`)\NETSDK created for this book. You then executed some simple SQL to retrieve just two rows from a table in the Northwind database. Don't worry about the actual SQL now, since it merely demonstrates the tool; we'll cover most of this code soon.

To execute SQL from a file, use the -i option. You'd do this for more complex or repetitive operations. For example, you could have placed the four lines of code from step 2 into a file named selectsql.sql and then run the following:

```
osql -E -S (local)\netsdk -i selectsql.sql
```

Using the Custom Query Tool

As an additional exercise in working with C# and databases, we've created a custom query application that you can use to execute the queries in this chapter. The code and an explanation of how to create this application are in Appendix A, but the working application is available in the Chapter 3 code download. Once you've worked through more of this book and feel more comfortable writing C# to work with databases, you may want to revise this code and create your own version of the application.

You can execute all the SQL in this chapter, of course, with any of the tools we've mentioned, but we'll use the custom tool for the rest of the examples in this chapter.

Retrieving Data

In the previous chapter you used a data adapter to retrieve data from the database. The data adapter uses SQL behind the scenes. If you look again at the properties for the data adapter and expand SelectCommand, you'll see an entry named CommandText (see Figure 3-7).

Figure 3-7. *Data adapter* CommandText *property*

This property contains the query that was used in the application to retrieve all the Employees data. Let's look at this query in more detail.

Using Queries

A query retrieves data from a database. In its simplest form, it consists of two parts.

- A select list where the columns to be retrieved are specified

- A FROM clause, where the table or tables to be accessed are specified

---

Tip We've written FROM in capital letters, simply to indicate it's a SQL *keyword*. SQL isn't case sensitive, and keywords are typically written in lowercase in code.

In Transact-SQL, queries are called *SELECT* statements, but the ISO/ANSI standard clearly distinguishes queries from statements. The distinction is conceptually important: A query is an operation on a table that produces a table as a result; statements may (or may not) operate on tables and don't produce tables as results, so we'll call queries *queries* instead of *SELECT* statements. Call queries whatever you prefer, but keep in mind that queries are special elements of SQL.

Using the two keywords, SELECT and FROM, you write the simplest possible query that will get all the data from the Employees table.

```
select
    *
from
    employees
```

The asterisk (*) means you want to select all the columns in the table. If you run this query against the Northwind database, you'll get all the rows and columns in the Employees table.

Tip Although most of the SQL you'll see in this book is short and sweet, statements, and especially queries, can be complex and require many lines (in extreme cases, hundreds) of code. Formatting SQL as carefully as you format C# code is an excellent coding practice.

Try It Out: Writing a Simple Query

To try this query, open the Chapter3_Examples solution that comes in the code download. Hit F5 to run the SQL Tool application, and you're now ready to enter the query.

    1. In the RichTextBox control at the top of the dialog box, enter the following:

```
select
    *
from
    employees
```

2. To execute the query, press F5 or select Actions ➤ Execute.

3. The result should look something like Figure 3-8.

Figure 3-8. *Query result in SQL Tool*

Select the Format statements command by hitting F12. This colors the SELECT and FROM keywords, as well as converts them to uppercase, as in Figure 3-9.

Figure 3-9. *SQL* Tool Format *statements command*

How It Works

You asked the database to return the data for all columns, which is exactly what has happened. If you scroll to the right, you'll find all the columns in the Employees table.

Most of the time you should limit queries to only relevant columns. When you select columns you don't need, you place unnecessary strain on the network and database. To explicitly select columns, enter the column names after the SELECT keyword, like so:

```
select
    employeeid,
    firstname,
    lastname
from
    employees
```

This query selects all the rows from the Employees table but only the EmployeeId, FirstName, and LastName columns. (Use the splitter between the query and result areas to expand/contract them.)

Try It Out: Selecting Specific Columns

To select specific columns, follow these steps:

1. Run the SQL Tool application, and enter the following query:

   ```
   select
       employeeid,
       firstname,
       lastname
   from
       employees
   ```

2. Hit F5 to execute the query (see Figure 3-10).

Figure 3-10. *Selecting specific columns*

> **Tip** If you still have the application running and have some text in the `RichTextBox` control, you don't have to delete it. Instead, enter the new text below the old text. Then select the new text, and hit F5. Only selected text is sent to the database. If nothing is selected, everything in the `RichTextBox` control is sent to the database.

How It Works

Figure 3-10 shows the application after the query has been run. Note that only the three columns `EmployeeId`, `FirstName`, and `LastName` are displayed.

Using the WHERE Clause

Queries may have `WHERE` clauses. The `WHERE` clause allows you to specify criteria for selecting rows. This clause can be complex, but we'll stick to a simple example for now. The syntax is as follows:

```
WHERE <column1> <operator> <column2>
```

where `<operator>` is a comparison operator (for example, =, <>, >, or <). Table 3-1, after this example, lists the comparison operators.

Try It Out: Refining Your Query

To refine your query, follow these steps:

1. Enter the following text into your application:

```
select
    firstname,
    lastname,
    country
from
    employees
where
    country = 'USA'
```

2. Run the query by pressing F5, and you should see the screen shown in Figure 3-11.

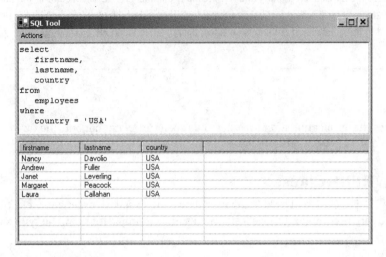

Figure 3-11. *Using the* WHERE *clause*

■**Caution** SQL keywords and table and column names aren't case sensitive, but string literals (enclosed in single quotes) are; hence, use USA, not usa, for this example.

How It Works

You could formulate the previous query as "Return the data for columns FirstName, LastName, and Country from the Employees table, but only for rows where the Country column equals *USA*."

Using the Operators of the WHERE Clause

You can use a number of different comparison operators in a WHERE clause (see Table 3-1).

Table 3-1. *Comparison Operators*

Operator	Description	Example
=	Equals	EmployeeID = 1
<	Less than	EmployeeID < 1
>	Greater than	EmployeeID > 1
<=	Less than or equal to	EmployeeID <= 1
>=	Greater than or equal to	EmployeeID >= 1=
<>, !=	Not equal to	EmployeeID <> 1
!<	Not less than	EmployeeID !< 1
!>	Not greater than	EmployeeID !> 1

■Tip As mentioned earlier, every database vendor has its own implementation of SQL. This discussion is specific to Transact-SQL; for example, standard SQL doesn't have the != operator and calls <> the *not equals operator.* In fact, standard SQL calls the expressions in a WHERE clause *predicates*; we'll use that term because predicates are either true or false, but other expressions don't have to be. If you work with another version of SQL, please refer to its documentation for specifics.

In addition to these operators, the LIKE operator (see Table 3-2) allows you to match patterns in character data. As with all SQL character data, strings must be enclosed in single quotes (').

Table 3-2. LIKE *Operator*

Operator	Description	Example
LIKE	Allows you to specify a pattern to search for	WHERE Title LIKE 'Sales %' selects all rows where the Title column contains a value that starts with the word *Sales* and a space.

You can use four different wildcards in the pattern (see Table 3-3).

Table 3-3. *Wildcard Characters*

Wildcard	Description
%	Any combination of characters.
_	Any one character. WHERE Title LIKE '_ales' selects all rows where the Title column equals *Aales, aales, Bales, bales,* and so on.
[ ]	A single character within a range [a-d] or set [abcd]. WHERE Title LIKE '[bs]ales' selects all rows where the Title column equals either the word *bales* or *sales.*
[^]	A single character not within a range [^a-d] or set [^abcd].

Sometimes it's useful to select rows where a value is unknown. When no value has been assigned to a column, the column is NULL. (This isn't the same as a column that contains the value 0 or blank.) To select a row with a column that's NULL, use the IS [NOT] NULL operator (see Table 3-4).

Table 3-4. IS [NOT] NULL *Operator*

Operator	Description	Example
IS NULL	Allows you to select rows where a column has no value.	WHERE Region IS NULL returns all rows where Region has no value.
IS NOT NULL	Allows you to select rows where a column has a value.	WHERE Region IS NOT NULL returns all rows where Region has a value.

> **■Note** You must use the IS NULL and IS NOT NULL operators (collectively called the *null predicate* in standard SQL) to select or exclude NULL column values, respectively. The following is a valid query but always produces zero rows: SELECT * FROM employees WHERE region = NULL. If you change = to IS, the query will return rows where regions have no value.

To select values in a range or in a set, you can use the BETWEEN and IN operators (see Table 3-5).

Table 3-5. BETWEEN *and* IN *Operators*

Operator	Description	Example
BETWEEN	True if a value is within a range.	WHERE extension BETWEEN 400 AND 500 returns the rows where Extension is between 400 and 500, inclusive.
IN	True if a value is in a list. The list can be the result of a subquery.	WHERE city IN ('Seattle', 'London') returns the rows where City is either Seattle or London.

Combining Predicates

Quite often you'll need to use more than one predicate to filter your data. You can use the logical operators shown in Table 3-6.

Table 3-6. *Logical Operators*

Operator	Description	Example
AND	Combines two expressions, evaluating the complete expression as true only if both are true	WHERE (title LIKE 'Sales%' AND lastname = 'Peacock')
NOT	Negates a boolean value	WHERE NOT (title LIKE 'Sales%' AND lastname = 'Peacock')
OR	Combines two expressions, evaluating the complete expression as true if either is true	WHERE (title = 'Peacock' OR title = 'King')

When you use these operators, it's often a good idea to use parentheses to clarify the conditions. In complex queries this may be absolutely necessary.

Sorting Data

After you've filtered the data you want, you can sort the data by one or more columns and in a certain direction. Since tables are by definition unsorted, the order in which rows are retrieved by a query is unpredictable. To impose an ordering, you use the ORDER BY clause.

```
ORDER BY <column> [ASC | DESC] {, n}
```

The <column> is the column that should be used to sort the result. The {, n} syntax means you can specify any number of columns separated by commas. The result will be sorted in the order in which you specify the columns.

The following are the two sort directions:

- **ASC**: Ascending (1, 2, 3, 4, and so on).

- **DESC**: Descending (10, 9, 8, 7, and so on). If you omit the ASC or DESC keywords, the sort order defaults to ASC.

Now that you've seen the following basic syntax for queries:

```
SELECT <column>
FROM <table>
WHERE <predicate>
ORDER BY <column> ASC | DESC
```

Let's use it in an example.

Try It Out: Writing an Enhanced Query

Let's code a query that uses all this. You'll want to do the following:

- Select all the orders that have been handled by employee 5.

- Select the orders shipped to either France or Brazil.

- Display only OrderID, EmployeeID, CustomerID, OrderDate, and ShipCountry.

- Sort the orders by the destination country and the date the order was placed.

Does this sound complicated? Let's try it. Follow these steps:

1. Run the SQL Tool application, and enter the following:

```
select
    orderid,
    employeeid,
    customerid,
    orderdate,
    shipcountry
from
    orders
where
    employeeid = 5
    and
    shipcountry in ('Brazil', 'France')
order by
    shipcountry asc,
    orderdate asc
```

2. Hit F5, and you should see output as in Figure 3-12.

Figure 3-12. *Enhanced query*

How It Works

Let's look at the clauses individually. The SELECT list specifies which columns you want to use.

```
SELECT
    orderid,
    employeeid,
    customerid,
    orderdate,
    shipcountry
```

The FROM clause specifies that you want to use the Orders table.

```
FROM
    orders
```

The WHERE clause is a bit more complicated. It consists of two predicates that individually state the following:

- EmployeeID must be 5.

- ShipCountry must be in the list Brazil and France.

As these predicates are combined with AND, they both must evaluate to true for a row to be included in the result.

```
WHERE
    employeeid = 5
    AND
    shipcountry IN ('Brazil', 'France')
```

The ORDER BY clause specifies the order in which the rows are sorted. The rows will be sorted by the ShipCountry first and then by OrderDate.

```
ORDER BY
    shipcountry ASC,
    orderdate ASC
```

Inserting Data

The second important task you need to be able to do is add data. You do this with the INSERT statement. The INSERT statement is much simpler than a query, particularly because the WHERE and ORDER BY clauses have no meaning when inserting data and therefore aren't used.

A basic INSERT statement has these parts:

```
INSERT INTO <table>
(<column1>, <column2>, ..., <columnN>)
VALUES (<value1>, <value2>, ..., <valueN>)
```

Using this syntax, let's add a new row to the Shippers table of the Northwind database. Before you insert it, let's look at the table. It has three rows (see Figure 3-13).

Figure 3-13. Shippers *data before inserting a row*

The first column, `ShipperID`, is an `IDENTITY` column, and as such you can't insert values into it explicitly—MSDE will make sure a unique value is inserted for you. Therefore, the `INSERT` statement will look like this:

```
insert into shippers
    (
    companyname,
    phone
    )
values ('We Shred Them Before You Get Them', '555-1234')
```

Executing this statement should produce a message box reporting "1 row(s) affected." After the insert, the query will return the results in Figure 3-14. (To see the full company name, double-click the separator between the `CompanyName` and `Phone` columns.)

Figure 3-14. `Shippers` *data after inserting a row*

Be careful to insert data of the correct data type. In the previous example, both the columns are the character type; therefore, you inserted strings. If one of the columns had been of integer data type, you would have inserted an integer instead. We'll describe the SQL data types in the "Using SQL Data Types" section.

Updating Data

The third important task you need to be able to do is change data. You do this with the `UPDATE` statement. In Chapter 2, database data was transparently changed by the data adapter, based on changes to the dataset, and you had no reason to be concerned when performing updates. When coding `UPDATE` statements, however, you must be careful to include a `WHERE` clause, or you'll update *all* the rows in a table. In fact, you must always code an appropriate `WHERE` clause, or you won't change the data you intend to change. So, be careful to enter all the text in the following example before hitting F5!

Tip Should you inadvertently change something in the `Northwind` database, remember that you can simply re-create it using the procedure described in the section "Installing the Sample Databases" in Chapter 1.

Now that you're aware of the implications of the UPDATE statement, let's take a good look at it. In essence, it's a simple statement that allows you to update values in one or more rows and columns.

```
UPDATE <table>
SET <column1> = <value1>, <column2> = <value2>, ..., <columnN> = <valueN>
WHERE <predicate>
```

As an example, let's imagine that the company you added earlier, We Shred Them Before You Get Them, has realized that, though (unfortunately) accurate, its name isn't good for business, and it's therefore changing its name to Speed of Light Delivery. To make this change in the database, you first need to locate the row with this name. More than one company could have the same name, so you shouldn't use the `CompanyName` column as the key. Instead, you locate the correct row in the result of the previous query and make a note of the `ShipperID` identity column (`ShipperID`) value.

The primary key of the row is 4, and you can now update its `CompanyName` column.

```
update shippers
set
    companyname = 'Speed of Light Delivery'
where
    shipperid = 7
```

Executing this statement should produce a message box reporting "1 row(s) affected." If you retrieve the row again, you'll see that `CompanyName` has changed, as in Figure 3-15.

Figure 3-15. Shippers *data after* UPDATE

When you update more than one column, you code the SET keyword only once. For example, the following statement would change both the name and the phone of the example company:

```
update shippers
set
   companyname = 'Speed of Light Delivery',
   phone = '555-9876'
where
   shipperid = 4
```

Deleting Data

The fourth important task you need to be able to do is remove data. You do this with the DELETE statement. The DELETE statement has the same implications as the UPDATE statement; it's all too easy to delete every row (or, at least, the wrong rows) in a table by forgetting the WHERE clause, so be careful. The DELETE statement removes entire rows, and it's therefore not necessary (or possible) to specify columns. Its basic syntax is as follows (remember, the WHERE clause is optional, but without it *all* rows will be deleted):

```
DELETE FROM <table>
WHERE <predicate>
```

If Speed of Light Delivery finally gives up and goes out of business, you'd need to remove it from the Shippers table. As with the UPDATE statement, you need to determine the primary key of the row you want to remove (or recall that it's 4) and use that in the DELETE statement, like so:

```
delete from shippers
where shipperid = 4
```

Again a message box should report "1 row(s) affected." If you retrieve all the data from the Shippers table now, you'll see that Speed of Light Delivery is no longer there (see Figure 3-16).

Figure 3-16. Shippers *data after deleting a row*

If you try to delete one of the three other shippers, you'll get a database error. A foreign-key relationship exists from `Orders` to `Shippers`, and MSDE enforces it, preventing deletion of `Shippers` rows that are referred to by `Orders` rows. You'll examine this in more detail in Chapter 12.

Sometimes you do need to remove every row from a table. In such cases the `TRUNCATE TABLE` statement may be preferable to the `DELETE` statement, since it performs faster. The `TRUNCATE TABLE` statement doesn't do any *logging* (saving each row in a log file before deleting it) to support recovery, but every row removed by `DELETE` is logged. See SQL Server Books Online for descriptions of both `TRUNCATE TABLE` and logging.

This concludes our introduction to basic SQL for retrieving, adding, changing, and removing data. Next you'll look at SQL data types.

Using SQL Data Types

In Chapter 2 you used the values of some of the columns in `Employees`. The reason you were able to do this relatively effortlessly is that Server Explorer had already mapped the data types of the columns in the database to types compatible with C#. You can find this mapping if you open the project again.

1. Open the `Chapter2_Examples` solution.

2. In Solution Explorer to the right, click the Show All Files icon.

3. Double-click `DataSetEmployees.xsd`. This opens a window showing the *elements* of the `Employees` table (see Figure 3-17).

Figure 3-17. `Employees` *elements*

In Figure 3-17 you can see how the data has types with which C# can work. These aren't, however, necessarily the same data types as the columns in the database. The following tables show the data types that are available in SQL Server and how they map to predefined C# types or to a .NET Framework type (usable by any .NET language, including C#).

Numeric Data Types

The eight SQL numeric data types map to C# simple types (see Table 3-7).

Table 3-7. *SQL Numeric Types*

SQL Data Type	C# Type	Description
bigint	long	32-bit signed integer
bit	bool	Unsigned number that can be 0, 1, or NULL
decimal	decimal	128-bit signed number
float	double	64-bit floating-point number
int	int	32-bit signed integer
real	float	32-bit floating-point number
smallint	short	16-bit signed integer
tinyint	byte	8-bit unsigned integer

Character String Data Types

All six SQL character string data types map to the C# string type (see Table 3-8).

Table 3-8. *SQL Character String Data Types*

SQL Data Type	C# Type	Description
char	string	Fixed-length string of 1 to 8,000 bytes
nchar	string	Fixed-length Unicode string of 1 to 4,000 bytes
text	string	Variable-length string of 1 to 2,147,483,647
ntext	string	Variable-length Unicode string of 1 to 1,073,741,823
varchar	string	Variable-length string of 1 to 8,000 bytes
nvarchar	string	Variable-length Unicode string of 1 to 4,000 bytes

Date and Time Data Types

Both SQL date and time types map to the .NET Framework type System.Data.SqlTypes.SqlDateTime (see Table 3-9).

Table 3-9. *SQL Date/Time Data Types*

SQL Data Type	C# Type	Description
datetime	SqlDateTime	Date and time data from Jan. 1, 1753, through Dec. 31, 9999, accurate to 1/300th of a second
smalldatetime	SqlDateTime	Date and time data from Jan. 1, 1900, through June 6, 2079, accurate to the minute

Using Binary Data Types

All three SQL binary data types map to C# byte arrays (see Table 3-10).

Table 3-10. *SQL Binary Data Types*

SQL Data Type	C# Type	Description
binary	byte[]	Fixed-length binary data of 1 to 8,000 bytes
image	byte[]	Variable-length binary data of 0 to 2,147,483,647 bytes
varbinary	byte[]	Variable-length binary data of 1 to 8,000 bytes

Using Money Data Types

Both SQL money data types map to a single C# type, decimal (see Table 3-11).

Table 3-11. *SQL Money Data Types*

SQL Data Type	C# Type	Description
money	decimal	Values from -922,337,203,685,477.5808 through 922,337,203,685,477.5807
smallmoney	decimal	Values from -214,748.3648 through 214,748.3647

Using Other Data Types

Three of the other five SQL data types map to types compatible with C#. Two of the SQL data types aren't accessible by C# (see Table 3-12).

Table 3-12. *Other SQL Data Types*

SQL Data Type	C# Type	Description
cursor		For internal SQL Server use only
sql_variant	object	Can hold other SQL data types
table		For internal SQL Server use only
timestamp	byte[]	8-byte database-unique integer
uniquridentifier	System.Guid	128-bit globally unique integer

Summary

In this chapter you saw how to use SQL to perform the four most common tasks against a database: SELECT, INSERT, UPDATE, and DELETE. You also looked at how to use comparison and other operators to specify predicates that limit what rows are retrieved or manipulated. You surveyed the SQL data types and saw how they map to C# or .NET types. Understanding these SQL language elements will be essential later when you retrieve and manipulate data with ADO.NET.

■ ■ ■

What's ADO.NET?

Now that you've used SQL, MSDE, and Visual Studio .NET to create simple database applications, let's look at the final piece in the puzzle: ADO.NET. When you created the simple application in Chapter 2, you used Visual Studio .NET controls to connect to your database and work with your data. What you didn't look at in detail was what Visual Studio .NET did for you behind the scenes. Underneath all the drag-and-drop functionality, Visual Studio .NET used ADO.NET objects to access and display your data. Understanding these objects is the key to building powerful database applications. Before you start building more sophisticated applications, you need to learn more about ADO.NET.

In this chapter, you'll learn the following:

- Why ADO.NET was developed

- What the core ADO.NET architecture comprises

- How to use .NET Framework data providers

- That the .NET Framework data provider is an API

Why ADO.NET?

Almost all applications require some data access. Before the .NET Framework, developers used data access technologies such as ODBC, OLE DB, and ADO. With the introduction of .NET, Microsoft created a new way to work with data, called ADO.NET. Before you concentrate on ADO.NET in future chapters, you'll briefly look at older data access technologies, since OLE DB and ODBC still have a place in the ADO.NET environment.

From ADO to ADO.NET

ActiveX Data Objects (ADO) may be familiar to those of you who've worked with Microsoft data access technologies before .NET. ADO is a collection of ActiveX objects that are designed to work in a constantly *connected* environment. It was built on top of OLE DB (which you'll look at later in the "OLE DB Data Provider" section). OLE DB provides access to non-SQL data as well as SQL databases, and ADO provides an interface designed to make it easier to work with OLE DB providers.

However, accessing data with ADO (and OLE DB under the hood) means you have to go through several layers of connectivity before you reach the data source. Just as OLE DB is there to connect to a large number of data sources, an older data access technology, Open Database

Connectivity (ODBC), is still there to connect to older data sources such as dBase and Paradox. To access ODBC data sources using ADO, you use an OLE DB provider for ODBC (since ADO only works directly with OLE DB), thus adding more layers to an already multilayered model.

Acknowledging the problems in maintaining continuous connections to data sources, a disconnected data access model was introduced, which was termed Remote Data Services (RDS). Although this works reasonably well in storing locally cached data, you're restricted to using Internet Explorer 4 or newer as RDS uses Dynamic Hypertext Markup Language (DHTML). Also, updating the original data source proved troublesome, and as a result many developers stuck with the connected data access model.

With the multilayered data access model and the connected nature of ADO, you could easily end up sapping server resources and creating a performance bottleneck. ADO served well, but ADO.NET has some great features that make it a far superior data access technology.

ADO.NET Isn't a New Version of ADO

ADO.NET is a completely new data access technology, with a new design that was built entirely from scratch. Let's first get this cleared up: ADO.NET *doesn't* stand for ActiveX Data Objects .NET. Why? It's because of many reasons, but the following are the two most important ones:

- ADO.NET is an integral part of the .NET Framework, not an external entity.

- ADO.NET *isn't* a collection of ActiveX components.

The name *ADO.NET* is analogous to ADO because Microsoft wanted developers to feel at home using ADO.NET and didn't want them to think they'd need to "learn it all over again," so it purposely named and designed ADO.NET to offer similar features implemented in a different way.

During the .NET Framework design, Microsoft realized that ADO wasn't going to fit in. ADO was available as an external package based on Component Object Model (COM) objects, requiring .NET applications to explicitly include a reference to it. In contrast, .NET applications are designed to share a single model, where all libraries are integrated into a single framework, organized into logical namespaces, and declared public to any application that wants to use them. It was wisely decided that the .NET data access technology should comply with the .NET architectural model. Hence, ADO.NET was born.

ADO.NET is designed to accommodate both connected and disconnected environments. Also, ADO.NET embraces the fundamentally important XML standard (more on this in Chapter 17), much more than ADO did, since the explosion in XML use came about after ADO was developed. With ADO.NET you cannot only use XML to transfer data between applications, but you can also export data from your application into an XML file, store it locally on your system, and retrieve it later when you need to do so.

Performance usually comes with a price, but in the case of ADO.NET, the price is definitely reasonable. Unlike ADO, ADO.NET doesn't transparently wrap OLE DB providers; instead, it uses *managed data providers* that are designed specifically for each type of data source, thus leveraging their true power and adding to overall application speed and performance.

ADO.NET also works in both connected and disconnected environments. You can connect to a database, remain connected while simply reading data, and then close your connection, which is a process similar to ADO. Where ADO.NET really begins to shine is in the disconnected world. If you need to edit database data, maintaining a continuous connection would be costly on the server. ADO.NET gets around this by providing a sophisticated disconnected model. Data is sent from the server and cached locally on the client. When you're ready to update the database, you can send the changed data back to the server, where updates and conflicts are managed for you.

In ADO.NET, when you retrieve data, you use an object known as a *data reader*. When you work with disconnected data, the data is cached locally in a relational data structure called a *dataset*.

ADO.NET and the .NET Framework

A dataset can hold large amounts of data in the form of tables (as DataTable objects), their relationships (as DataRelation objects), and constraints (as Constraint objects) in an in-memory cache, which can then be exported to an external file or to another dataset. Since XML support is integrated into ADO.NET, you can produce XML schemas and transmit and share data using XML documents (much more on this in Chapters 8 and 17).

Table 4-1 describes the namespaces in which ADO.NET components are grouped.

Table 4-1. *ADO.NET Namespaces*

Namespace	Description
System.Data	Classes, interfaces, delegates, and enumerations that define and partially implement the ADO.NET architecture
System.Data.Common	Classes shared by .NET Framework data providers
System.Data.Odbc	The .NET Framework data provider for ODBC
System.Data.OleDb	The .NET Framework data provider for OLE DB
System.Data.OracleClient	The .NET Framework data provider for Oracle
System.Data.SqlClient	The .NET Framework data provider for SQL Server
System.Data.SqlServerCe	The .NET Compact Framework data provider for SQL Server CE
System.Data.SqlTypes	Classes for native SQL Server data types

Since XML support has been closely integrated into ADO.NET, some ADO.NET components in the System.Data namespace rely on components in the System.Xml namespace. So, you sometimes need to include both namespaces as references in Solution Explorer.

These namespaces are physically implemented as assembly files, and if you create a new console application project in Visual Studio, references to the assemblies should automatically be created, along with the reference to the System assembly. However, if they're not present, simply perform the following steps to add the namespaces to your project:

1. Right-click the References item in Solution Explorer, and then click Add Reference....

2. A dialog box with a list of available references displays. Select System.Data.dll, System.XML.dll, and System.dll (if not already present) one by one (hold down the Ctrl key for multiple selections), and then click the Select button.

3. Click OK, and the references will be added to the project.

For those of you working from the command line, you can use the following compiler options to include the assemblies:

```
/r:System.dll /r:System.Data.dll /r:System.XML.dll
```

As you can see from the namespaces, ADO.NET can work with older technologies such as OLE DB and ODBC. However, the SQL Server data provider communicates directly with SQL Server (versions 7.0 and newer), the most efficient form of connection, so it accesses SQL Server faster than OLE DB or ODBC. Likewise, the Oracle data provider accesses Oracle directly.

ADO.NET is a data access technology that's likely to be *the* primary data access technology of .NET for a long time, so learning how to use it is a worthwhile investment.

Understanding ADO.NET Architecture

Figure 4-1 presents the most important architectural features of ADO.NET. We'll discuss them in far greater detail in later chapters.

Figure 4-1. *ADO.NET architecture*

ADO.NET has two central components: data providers and datasets.

A *data provider* connects to a data source and supports data access and manipulation. You'll play with three different ones later in this chapter.

A *dataset* supports disconnected, independent caching of data in a relational fashion, updating the data source as required. A dataset contains one or more data tables. A *data table* is a row-and-column representation that provides much the same logical view as a SQL table. For example, you can store the data from the Northwind database's Employees table in a data table and manipulate the data as needed. You'll learn about datasets starting with Chapter 8.

In Figure 4-1, notice the DataView class (in the System.Data namespace). This isn't a data provider component. Data views are used primarily to bind data to Windows and Web forms. We'll cover data views in Chapter 9.

As you saw in Table 4-1. each data provider has its own namespace. In fact, each data provider is essentially an implementation of interfaces in the System.Data namespace, specialized for a specific type of data source.

For example, if you use SQL Server version 7 or newer (SQL Server 2000 is actually version 8) as your database manager, you should use the SQL Server data provider (System.Data.SqlClient) because it's the most efficient way to work with these versions. This data provider communicates natively with SQL Server, bypassing the layers that OLE DB and ODBC connections have to use.

The OLE DB data provider supports access to older versions of SQL Server as well as to other databases, such as Access, DB2, MySQL, and Oracle. However, native data providers (such as System.Data.Oracle) are preferable for performance, since the OLE DB data provider works through two other layers, the OLE DB service component and the OLE DB provider, before reaching the data source.

Figure 4-2 illustrates the difference between using the SQL Server and OLE DB data providers to access a SQL Server (version 7.0 or higher) database.

Figure 4-2. *SQL Server and OLE DB data provider differences*

If your application connects to an older version of SQL Server (6.5 or newer) or to more than one kind of database server at the same time (for example, an Access and an Oracle database connected simultaneously), only then should you choose to use the OLE DB data provider.

No hard and fast rules exist; you can use both the OLE DB data provider for SQL Server and the Oracle data provider (System.Data.OracleClient) if you want, but it's important you choose the best provider for your purpose. Given the performance benefits of the server-specific data providers, if you use SQL Server or MSDE, 99 percent of the time you should be using the System.Data.SqlClient classes.

Before you look at what each kind of data provider does and how it's used, you need to be clear on their core functionality. Each .NET data provider is designed to do the following two things very well:

- Provide access to data with an active connection to the data source

- Provide data transmission to and from the independent datasets through data adapters

Database connections are established by using the data provider's connection class (for example, System.Data.SqlClient.SqlConnection). Other components such as data readers, commands, and data adapters support retrieving data, executing SQL statements, and reading or writing to datasets, respectively.

As you've seen, each data provider is prefixed with the type of data source it connects to (for instance, the SQL Server data provider is prefixed with *Sql*), so its connection class is named SqlConnection. The OLE DB data provider's connection class is named OleDbConnection.

Look now at the object model of these two providers in Figure 4-3. You'll work simultaneously with different databases (Access and SQL Server) so you can see how easy it is to switch between data providers and what, if any, their main visible differences are. Note that the two data providers support the same application and share a single dataset.

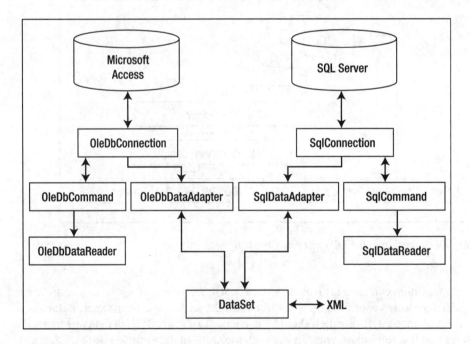

Figure 4-3. *ADO.NET concurrently using Access and SQL Server*

The OLE DB data provider belongs to the System.Data.OleDb namespace; the SQL Server data provider belongs to System.Data.SqlClient. Both data providers seem to have a similar architecture, though they're actually very different internally.

Let's see how you put the three data providers that can be used with SQL Server to work.

Using the SQL Server Data Provider

The .NET data provider for SQL Server (7.0 or newer) is located in the System.Data.SqlClient namespace. This data provider communicates directly with the server using its native network protocol instead of through a number of layers (the way OLE DB does).

Table 4-2 describes some important classes in the SqlClient namespace.

Table 4-2. *Commonly Used* SqlClient *Classes*

Classes	Description
SqlCommand	Executes SQL queries, statements, or stored procedures
SqlConnection	Represents a connection to a SQL Server database
SqlDataAdapter	Represents a bridge between a dataset and a data source
SqlDataReader	Provides a forward-only, read-only data stream of the results
SqlError	Holds information on SQL Server errors and warnings
SqlParameter	Represents a command parameter
SqlTransaction	Represents a SQL Server transaction

Another namespace, System.Data.SqlTypes, maps SQL Server data types to .NET types, both enhancing performance and making developers' lives a lot easier. We discussed this in Chapter 3.

Let's look at an example that uses the SQL Server data provider. It won't cover connections and data retrieval in detail, but will familiarize you with what you'll encounter in upcoming chapters.

Try It Out: Creating a Simple Console Application Using the SQL Server Data Provider

You'll build a simple console application that opens a connection and runs a query, using the SqlClient namespace against the MSDE Northwind database. You'll display the retrieved data in the console prompt window.

1. Open Visual Studio .NET, and create a new solution (as described in Chapter 2) named Chapter4_Examples.

2. Right-click the solution in Solution Explorer, select Add ➤ New Project..., create a C# console application, and name the application SqlServerProvider. Rename Class1.cs to SqlServerProvider.cs.

3. Since you'll be creating this example from scratch, select all the code in Code view and delete it. Enter the code in Listing 4-1.

   Listing 4-1. SqlServerProvider.cs

   ```
   using System;
   using System.Data;
   using System.Data.SqlClient;
   ```

```
class SqlServerProvider
{
    static void Main(string[] args)
    {
        // Set up connection string
        string connString = @"
            server = (local)\netsdk;
            integrated security = true;
            database = northwind
        ";

        // Set up query string
        string sql = @"
            select
                *
            from
                employees
        ";

        // Declare connection and data reader variables
        SqlConnection conn = null;
        SqlDataReader reader = null;

        try
        {
            // Open connection
            conn = new SqlConnection(connString);
            conn.Open();

            // Execute the query
            SqlCommand cmd = new SqlCommand(sql, conn);
            reader = cmd.ExecuteReader();

            // Display output header
            Console.WriteLine(
                "This program demonstrates the use of "
              + "the SQL Server Data Provider."
            );
            Console.WriteLine(
                "Querying database {0} with query {1}\n"
                , conn.Database
                , cmd.CommandText
            );
            Console.WriteLine("First Name\tLast Name\n");

            // Process the result set
            while(reader.Read()) {
                Console.WriteLine(
```

```
                            "{0} | {1}"
                            , reader["FirstName"].ToString().PadLeft(10)
                            , reader[1].ToString().PadLeft(10)
                        );
                    }
                }
                catch (Exception e)
                {
                    Console.WriteLine("Error: " + e);
                }
                finally
                {
                    // Close connection
                    reader.Close();
                    conn.Close();
                }
            }
        }
```

4. Save the project, and press Ctrl+F5 to run it. A console prompt window should appear, as shown in Figure 4-4.

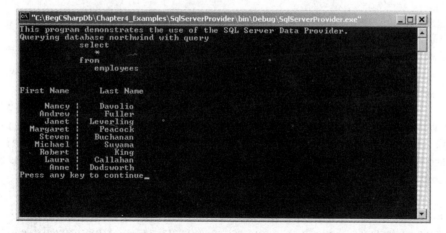

Figure 4-4. *Running the* SqlServerProvider *application*

How It Works

Let's take a look at how the code works, starting with the using directives.

```
using System;
using System.Data;
using System.Data.SqlClient;
```

The reference to System.Data is actually not needed in this small program, since you don't explicitly use any of its members, but it's a good habit to always include it. The reference to System.Data.SqlClient is, of course, necessary since you want to use the simple names of its members.

You specify the connection string with *parameters* (key-value pairs) suitable for an MSDE session.

```
// Set up connection string
string connString = @"
    server=(local)\netsdk;
    integrated security=true;
    database=northwind
";
```

The connection string contains this parameter:

```
integrated security=true;
```

which specifies Windows Authentication. The true value is equivalent to SSPI, which stands for *Security Support Provider Interface.*

You then code the query, like so:

```
// Set up query string
string sql = @"
    select
        *
    from
        employees
";
```

■**Tip** We use verbatim strings because it allows us to indent the source code conveniently. The connection string is actually parsed before it's assigned to the connection's ConnectionString property, so the new lines and extra spaces are inconsequential. SQL can contain extraneous new lines and spaces, so you can likewise format it to make it more readable and maintainable.

You next declare variables for the connection and data reader, so they're available to the rest of your code. You then create the connection, like so:

```
// Declare connection and data reader variables
SqlConnection conn = null;
SqlDataReader reader = null;

try
{
    // Open connection
    conn = new SqlConnection(connString);
```

You do this (and the rest of your database work) in a `try` block to handle exceptions, in particular exceptions thrown by ADO.NET in response to database errors, though in this simple example you're not interested in distinguishing them from other exceptions. Here, ADO.NET will throw an exception if the connection string parameters aren't syntactically correct, so you may as well be prepared. If you had waited until you entered the `try` block to declare the connection (and data reader) variable, you wouldn't have it available in the `finally` block to close the connection.

Creating the connection doesn't actually connect to the database. You need to call the `Open` method on the connection.

```
// Open connection
conn.Open();
```

To execute the query, you first create a command object, passing its constructor the SQL to run and the connection on which to run it. Next, you create a data reader by calling `ExecuteReader` on the command object. This not only executes the query but also sets up the data reader. Note that unlike most objects, you have no way to create a data reader with a `new` expression.

```
// Execute the query
SqlCommand cmd = new SqlCommand(sql, conn);
SqlDataReader reader = cmd.ExecuteReader();
```

You then produce a header for your output, using connection and command properties (`Database` and `CommandText`, respectively) to get the database name and query text.

```
// Display output header
Console.WriteLine(
    "This program demonstrates the use of "
  + "the SQL Server Data Provider."
);
Console.WriteLine(
    "Querying database {0} with query {1}\n"
    , conn.Database
    , cmd.CommandText
);
Console.WriteLine("First Name\tLast Name\n");
```

You retrieve all the rows in the result set by calling the data reader's `Read` method, which returns `true` if there are more rows and `false` otherwise. Note that the data reader is positioned immediately *before* the first row prior to the first call to `Read`.

```
    // Process the result set
    while(reader.Read()) {
      Console.WriteLine(
          "{0} | {1}"
        , reader["FirstName"].ToString().PadLeft(10)
        , reader[1].ToString().PadLeft(10)
      );
    }
}
```

You access each row's columns with the data reader's *indexer* (here, the `SqlDataReader.Item` property), which is overloaded to accept either a column name or a zero-based integer index. We use both to demonstrate the indexer's use, but using column numbers is more efficient than using column names.

Next you handle any exceptions, quite simplistically, but at least you're developing a good habit. We'll cover exception handling much more carefully in Chapter 18.

```
catch(Exception ex)
{
  Console.WriteLine("Error: " + ex.Message);
}
```

Finally, in a `finally` block, you close the data reader and the connection by calling their `Close` methods. As a general rule, you should close things in a `finally` block to be sure they get closed no matter what happens within the `try` block.

```
finally
{
  // Close active connection
    reader.Close();
    conn.Close();
}
```

Technically, closing the connection also closes the data reader, but closing both (in the previous order) is another good habit. A connection with an open data reader can't be used for any other purpose until the data reader has been closed.

Using the OLE DB Data Provider

Outside the .NET Framework, OLE DB is still Microsoft's high-performance data access technology. You can use it to access data stored in any format, so even in ADO.NET it plays an important role in accessing data sources that don't have their own ADO.NET data providers.

The .NET Framework data provider for OLE DB is in the namespace `System.Data.OleDb`. Table 4-3 describes some important classes in the `OleDb` namespace.

Table 4-3. *Commonly Used* `OleDb` *Classes*

Classes	Description
OleDbCommand	Executes SQL queries, statements, or stored procedures
OleDbConnection	Represents a connection to an OLE DB data source
OleDbDataAdapter	Represents a bridge between a dataset and a data source
OleDbDataReader	Provides a forward-only, read-only data stream of rows from a data source
OleDbError	Holds information on errors and warnings returned by the data source
OleDbParameter	Represents a command parameter
OleDbTransaction	Represents a SQL transaction

Notice the similarity between the two data providers, SqlClient and OleDb. Their difference is transparent, in their implementation, but the user interface is fundamentally the same.

The ADO.NET OLE DB data provider requires that an OLE DB provider be specified in the connection string. Table 4-4 describes some OLE DB providers. Note that MSDASQL, the OLE DB provider for ODBC, *isn't* available in ADO.NET, since ADO.NET has its own data provider (the namespace System.Data.Odbc) for ODBC.

Table 4-4. *Some OLE DB Providers*

Provider	Description
DB2OLEDB	Microsoft OLE DB provider for DB2
SQLOLEDB	Microsoft OLE DB provider for SQL Server
Microsoft.Jet.OLEDB.4.0	Microsoft OLE DB provider for Access (which uses the Jet engine)
MSDAORA	Microsoft OLE DB provider for Oracle
MSDASQL	Microsoft OLE DB provider for ODBC

Let's use the OLE DB data provider to access the MSDE database, making a few straightforward changes (shown in bold in Listing 4-2) to the code in Listing 4-1. (Of course, you'd use the SQL Server data provider for real work since it's more efficient.)

Try It Out: Creating a Simple Console Application Using the OLE DB Data Provider

Follow these steps:

1. Create a new C# console application named OleDbProvider in the Chapter4_Examples solution. Rename the Class1.cs file to OleDbProvider.cs. Replace the generated code with the code in Listing 4-2, which shows the changes to Listing 4-1 in bold.

    Listing 4-2. OleDbProvider.cs

    ```
    using System;
    using System.Data;
    using System.Data.OleDb;

    class OleDbProvider
    {
        static void Main(string[] args)
        {
            // Set up connection string
            string connString = @"
                provider = sqloledb;
                data source = (local)\netsdk;
                integrated security = sspi;
                initial catalog = northwind
            ";
    ```

```csharp
// Set up query string
string sql = @"
   select
      *
   from
      employees
";

// Declare connection and data reader variables
OleDbConnection conn = null;
OleDbDataReader reader = null;

try
{
   // Open connection
   conn = new OleDbConnection(connString);
   conn.Open();

   // Execute the query
   OleDbCommand cmd = new OleDbCommand(sql, conn);
   reader = cmd.ExecuteReader();

   // Display output header
   Console.WriteLine(
         "This program demonstrates the use of "
      + "the OLE DB Data Provider."
   );
   Console.WriteLine(
         "Querying database {0} with query {1}\n"
      , conn.Database
      , cmd.CommandText
   );
   Console.WriteLine("First Name\tLast Name\n");

   // Process the result set
   while(reader.Read()) {
      Console.WriteLine(
            "{0} | {1}"
         , reader["FirstName"].ToString().PadLeft(10)
         , reader[1].ToString().PadLeft(10)
      );
   }
}
catch (Exception e)
{
   Console.WriteLine("Error: " + e);
}
```

```
    finally
    {
        // Close connection
        reader.Close();
        conn.Close();
    }
  }
}
```

2. Since you now have two projects in your solution, you need to make this project the startup project so it runs when you hit Ctrl+F5. Right-click the project name in Solution Explorer, and then click Set As StartUp Project (see Figure 4-5).

Figure 4-5. *Setting the startup project*

3. Run the application with Ctrl+F5. A console prompt window should appear, as shown in Figure 4-6.

Figure 4-6. *Running the* OleDbProvider *application*

How It Works

This program does the same thing as the first example, so we'll discuss the only changes here. You replaced SqlClient with OleDb in the third using directive.

```
using System;
using System.Data;
using System.Data.OleDb;
```

The connection string required the most change, since the OLE DB data provider doesn't accept the same parameters as the SQL Server data provider. In addition, it requires a provider parameter.

```
// Set up connection string
string connString = @"
    provider = sqloledb;
    data source = (local)\netsdk;
    integrated security = sspi;
    initial catalog = northwind
";
```

Only four other lines had to change to use the OLE DB data provider classes for the connection, command, and data reader.

```
OleDbConnection conn = null;
OleDbDataReader reader = null;
```

```
try
{
    // Open connection
    conn = new OleDbConnection(connString);
    conn.Open();

    // Execute the query
    OleDbCommand cmd = new OleDbCommand(sql, conn);
    reader = cmd.ExecuteReader();
```

The final change was a semantic one and wasn't required by ADO.NET.

```
// Display output header
Console.WriteLine(
        "This program demonstrates the use of "
    + "the OLE DB Data Provider."
```

Using the ODBC Data Provider

ODBC was Microsoft's original general-purpose data access technology. It's still widely used for data sources that don't have OLE DB providers or .NET Framework data providers. ADO.NET includes an ODBC data provider in the namespace System.Data.Odbc.

The ODBC architecture is essentially a three-tier process. An application uses ODBC functions to submit database requests. ODBC converts the function calls to the protocol (*call-level interface*) of a *driver* specific to a given data source. The driver communicates with the data source, passing any results or errors back up to ODBC. Obviously this is less efficient than a database-specific data provider's direct communication with a database, so for performance it's preferable to avoid the ODBC data provider, since it merely offers a simpler interface to ODBC but still involves all the ODBC overhead. Table 4-5 describes some important classes in the OleDb namespace.

Table 4-5. *Commonly Used* Odbc *Classes*

Classes	Description
OdbcCommand	Executes SQL queries, statements, or stored procedures
OdbcConnection	Represents a connection to an ODBC data source
OdbcDataAdapter	Represents a bridge between a dataset and a data source
OdbcDataReader	Provides a forward-only, read-only data stream of rows from a data source
OdbcError	Holds information on errors and warnings returned by the data source
OdbcParameter	Represents a command parameter
OdbcTransaction	Represents a SQL transaction

Let's use the ODBC data provider to access the MSDE database, making the same kind of straightforward changes (highlighted in Listing 4-3) to the code in Listing 4-1 as you did in using the OLE DB data provider.

Before you do, though, you need to create an ODBC data source—actually, you configure a DSN for use with a data source accessible by ODBC—for the Northwind database, since, unlike the SQL Server and OLE DB data providers, the ODBC data provider doesn't let you specify the server or database in the connection string. (The following works on Windows 2000 and the process is similar for other versions of Windows.)

Creating an ODBC Data Source

To create an ODBC data source, follow these steps:

1. In the Control Panel, double-click Administrative Tools (see Figure 4-7).

Figure 4-7. *Selecting Administrative Tools*

2. In Administrative Tools, double-click Data Sources (ODBC) (see Figure 4-8).

Figure 4-8. *Selecting Data Sources (ODBC)*

3. When the ODBC Data Source Administrator window opens, click the User DSN tab
   and then click Add... (see Figure 4-9).

Figure 4-9. *Opening the ODBC Data Source Administrator window*

4. The Create New Data Source wizard starts. Follow its instructions carefully! First, select
   the SQL Server ODBC driver; second, click Finish (see Figure 4-10).

Figure 4-10. *Selecting the driver*

5. The next window prompts for the data source name and server. Fill the entries as in Figure 4-11, and then click Next.

Figure 4-11. *Setting up the server and data source*

6. Accept the defaults in the authentication window by clicking Next (see Figure 4-12).

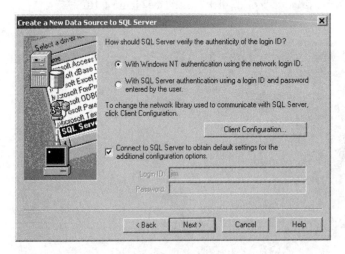

Figure 4-12. *Setting up authentication*

7. In the next window, check the Change the Default Database option, specify the Northwind database, and click Next (see Figure 4-13).

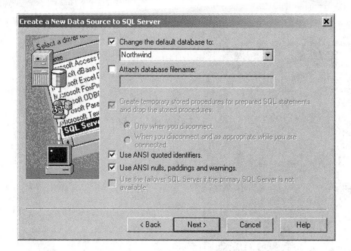

Figure 4-13. *Selecting the default database*

8. In the next window, simply click Finish (see Figure 4-14).

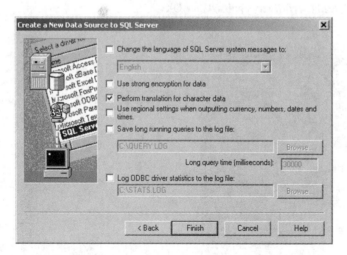

Figure 4-14. *Finishing the setup*

9. A confirmation window appears, describing the new data source. Click Test Data Source... (see Figure 4-15).

Figure 4-15. *Testing the connection*

10. A window reporting a successful test should appear (see Figure 4-16). (If it doesn't, cancel your work and *carefully* try again.) Click OK.

Figure 4-16. *A successful connection test*

11. When the confirmation window reappears, click OK. When the ODBC Data Source Administrator window reappears, the new data source will be on the list (see Figure 4-17).

Figure 4-17. *Data source creation: new data source created*

Now that you have an ODBC data source, you can get back to programming!

Try It Out: Creating a Simple Console Application Using the ODBC Data Provider

Follow these steps:

1. Create a new C# console application named OdbcProvider in the Chapter4_Examples solution. Rename the Class1.cs file to OdbcProvider.cs. Replace the generated code with the code in Listing 4-3, which shows the changes to Listing 4-1 in bold.

Listing 4-3. OdbcProvider.cs

```
using System;
using System.Data;
using System.Data.Odbc;

class OdbcProvider
{
    static void Main(string[] args)
    {
        // Set up connection string
        string connString = @"dsn=northwindodbc";
```

```csharp
// Set up query string
string sql = @"
   select
      *
   from
      employees
";

// Declare connection and data reader variables
OdbcConnection conn = null;
OdbcDataReader reader = null;

try
{
   // Open connection
   conn = new OdbcConnection(connString);
   conn.Open();

   // Execute the query
   OdbcCommand cmd = new OdbcCommand(sql, conn);
   reader = cmd.ExecuteReader();

   // Display output header
   Console.WriteLine(
       "This program demonstrates the use of "
      + "the ODBC Data Provider."
   );
   Console.WriteLine(
       "Querying database {0} with query {1}\n"
      , conn.Database
      , cmd.CommandText
   );
   Console.WriteLine("First Name\tLast Name\n");

   // Process the result set
   while(reader.Read()) {
      Console.WriteLine(
          "{0} | {1}"
         , reader["FirstName"].ToString().PadLeft(10)
         , reader[1].ToString().PadLeft(10)
      );
   }
}
catch (Exception e)
{
   Console.WriteLine("Error: " + e);
}
```

```
        finally
        {
            // Close connection
            reader.Close();
            conn.Close();
        }
    }
}
```

2. Make this project the startup by right-clicking the project name in Solution Explorer and then clicking Set As StartUp Project.

3. Run the application with Ctrl+F5. A console prompt window appears, as shown in Figure 4-18.

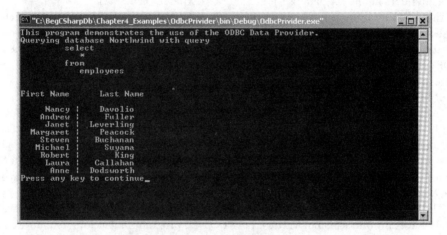

Figure 4-18. *Running the* OdbcProvider *application*

How It Works

This was easy! You simply changed *Sql* to *Odbc* in the namespace and class names (and, of course, the output header), just as you did to modify the program to work with OLE DB. The biggest change, and the only one really deserving attention, was to the connection string.

```
// Set up connection string
string connString = @"dsn=northwindodbc";
```

The ODBC connection string isn't limited only to the DSN, but it doesn't allow blanks or newlines anywhere in the string.

■**Tip** Each data provider has its own rules regarding both the parameters and syntax of its connection string. Consult the documentation for the provider you're using when coding connection strings.

Now that you've played with all the data providers that access SQL Server (the SQL Server CE data provider is beyond the scope of this book), let's make sure you clearly understand what a data provider is.

Data Providers Are APIs

The .NET Framework data providers, sophisticated as they are (and you'll learn plenty about exploiting their sophistication later), are simply APIs for accessing data sources, most often relational databases, in the .NET Framework. (ADO.NET is essentially one big API of which data providers are a major part.)

Newcomers to ADO.NET are often understandably confused by the Microsoft documentation. They read about `Connection`, `Command`, `DataReader`, and other ADO.NET objects, but they see no classes named `Connection`, `Command`, or `DataReader` in any of the ADO.NET namespaces. The reason is that data provider classes implement *interfaces* in the `System.Data` namespace. These interfaces define the data provider methods of the ADO.NET API.

The key concept is simple. A data provider, such as `System.Data.SqlClient`, consists of classes whose methods provide a uniform way of accessing a specific kind of data source. In this chapter you used three different data providers (SQL Server, OLE DB, and ODBC) to access the same MSDE database. The only real difference in the code was the connection string. Except for choosing the appropriate data provider, the rest of the programming was effectively the same. This is true of all ADO.NET facilities, whatever kind of data source you need to access.

The SQL Server data provider is optimized to access SQL Server and can't be used for any other RDBMS. The OLE DB data provider can access any OLE DB data source—and you used it without knowing anything about OLE DB (a major study in itself)! The ODBC data provider lets you use an even older data access technology, again without knowing anything about it. Working at such an abstract level enabled you to do a lot more, a lot more quickly, than you could have otherwise.

ADO.NET isn't just an efficient data access technology, but is also an elegant one. Data providers are only one aspect of it. The art of ADO.NET programming is founded more on conceptualizing than on coding. First get a clear idea of what ADO.NET offers, and then look for the right method in the right class to make the idea a reality.

Since conceptual clarity is so important, you can view (and refer to) connections, commands, data readers, and other ADO.NET components primarily as abstractions rather than merely objects used in database programs. If you concentrate on concepts, learning when and how to use relevant objects and methods will be easy.

Summary

In this chapter, you saw why ADO.NET was developed and how it supersedes other data access technologies in the .NET Framework. We gave an overview of its architecture and then focused on one of its core components, the data provider. You built three simple examples to practice basic data provider use and experience the uniform way data access code is written, regardless of the data provider. Finally, we offered the opinion that conceptual clarity is the key to understanding and using both data providers and the rest of the ADO.NET API.

CHAPTER 5

■ ■ ■

Creating Connections

Before you can do anything useful with a database, you need to establish a *session* with the database server. You do this with an object called a *connection*, which is an instance of a class that implements the System.Data.IDbConnection interface for a specific data provider. In this chapter, you'll use various data providers to establish connections and look at problems that may arise and how to solve them.

By the end of this chapter, you'll know how to do the following:

- Use connections

- Specify connection strings

- Use the most essential connection methods and properties

- Solve common connection problems

Introducing the Data Provider Connection Classes

As you learned in Chapter 4, each data provider has its own namespace. Each has a connection class that implements the System.Data.IDbConnection interface. Table 5-1 summarizes the data providers supplied by Microsoft.

Table 5-1. *Data Provider Namespaces and Connection Classes*

Data Provider	Namespace	Connection Class
ODBC	System.Data.Odbc	OdbcConnection
OLE DB	System.Data.OleDb	OleDbConnection
Oracle	System.Data.OracleClient	OracleConnection
SQL Server	System.Data.SqlClient	SqlConnection
SQL Server CE	System.Data.SqlServerCe	SqlCeConnection

As you can see, the names follow a convention, using *Connection* prefixed by an identifier for the data provider. Since all connection classes implement System.Data.IDbConnection, the use of each one is similar. Each has additional members that provide methods specific to a particular database. You used connections in Chapter 4. Let's take a closer look at one of them: SqlConnection in the namespace System.Data.SqlClient.

Connecting to MSDE with SqlConnection

In this example, you'll connect to the MSDE Northwind database.

Try It Out: Using SqlConnection

Follow these steps:

1. Create a new solution named Chapter5_Examples.

2. Add a C# console application named Connection_Sql. Rename the Class1.cs file to Connection_Sql.cs, and replace the generated code with the code in Listing 5-1.

Listing 5-1. Connection_Sql

```
using System;
using System.Data;
using System.Data.SqlClient;

namespace Connection_Sql
{
   class Connection_Sql
   {
      static void Main()
      {
         // Connection string
         string connString = @"
            server = (local)\netsdk;
            integrated security = sspi;
         ";

         // Create connection
         SqlConnection conn = new SqlConnection(connString);

         try {
            // Open connection
            conn.Open();
            Console.WriteLine("Connection opened.");
         }
         catch (SqlException e) {
            // Display error
            Console.WriteLine("Error: " + e);
         }
         finally {
            // close connection
            conn.Close();
            Console.WriteLine("Connection closed.");
         }
      }
   }
}
```

3. Run it with Ctrl+F5. If the connection is successful, you'll see the output in Figure 5-1.

Figure 5-1. *Connecting to SQL Server*

If the connection failed, you'll see an error message much like in Figure 5-2. (You can get this by shutting down MSDE first, with `net stop mssql$netsdk` entered at a command prompt.)

Figure 5-2. *Failed connection attempt*

Bear in mind that connections often fail for reasons that have nothing to do with your code. It may be because a server isn't started, a password is wrong, or some other configuration problem exists. You'll soon look at common problems in establishing database connections.

How It Works

Let's examine the code in Listing 5-1 to understand the steps in the connection process. First you specify the ADO.NET and the SQL Server data provider namespaces, so you can use the simple names of their members.

```
using System;
using System.Data;
using System.Data.SqlClient;
```

Next, you declare the namespace, class, and entry point (`Main` method) for the application.

```
namespace Connection_Sql
{
    class Connection_Sql
    {
        static void Main()
```

Because this example is so small, you do all of your work in the Main method; let's look at it line by line.

The first thing you do is create a *connection string*. A connection string consists of parameters—in other words, key=value pairs separated by semicolons—that specify connection information. Although some parameters are valid for all data providers, each data provider has specific parameters it will accept, so it's important to know what parameters are valid in a connection string for the data provider you're using.

```
// Connection string
string connString = @"
    server = (local)\netsdk;
    integrated security = sspi;
";
```

Next you create a connection (a SqlConnection object), passing it the connection string. This doesn't create a database session. It simply creates the object you'll use later to open a session.

```
// Create connection
 SqlConnection conn = new SqlConnection(connString);
```

Let's briefly examine each of the connection string parameters in this example. The server parameter specifies the SQL Server instance to which you want to connect.

```
server = (local)\netsdk;
```

■**Tip** If you installed the (local)\VSdotNET instance of MSDE that comes with Visual Studio .NET, then you should use that name in the server clause instead.

The next clause indicates that you should use Windows Authentication to log into SQL Server.

```
integrated security = sspi;
```

You could alternatively use true instead of sspi, as they both have the same effect. Other parameters are available. You'll use one later to specify the database to which you want to connect.

Now you have a connection, but you still need to establish a session with the database by calling the Open method on the connection. If the attempt to open a session fails, an exception will be thrown, so you use a try statement to enable exception handling. You display a message after calling Open, but this line will be executed only if the connection was successfully opened.

```
try {
    // Open connection
    conn.Open();
    Console.WriteLine("Connection opened.");
}
```

At this stage in the code, you'd normally issue a query or perform some other database operation over the open connection. However, you'll save that for later chapters and concentrate here on just connecting.

Next comes an exception handler in case the Open fails.

```
catch (SqlException e) {
    // Display error
    Console.WriteLine("Error: " + e);
}
```

Each data provider has a specific exception class for its error handling; SqlException is the class for the SQL Server data provider. Specific information about database errors is available from the exception, but here you're just displaying its raw contents.

When you're finished with the database, you call Close to terminate the session and then print a message to show that Close was called.

```
finally {
    // Close connection
    conn.Close();
    Console.WriteLine("Connection closed.");
}
```

You call Close within the finally block to ensure it *always* gets called.

Note Establishing connections (database sessions) is relatively expensive. They use resources on both the client and the server. Although connections may eventually get closed, through garbage collection or by timing out, leaving one open when it's no longer needed is a bad practice. Too many open connections can slow a server down or prevent new connections from being made.

Note that you can call Close on a closed connection, and no exception will be thrown. So, your message would have been displayed if the connection had been closed earlier or even if it had never been opened. See Figure 5-2, where the connection failed but the close message was still displayed.

In one typical case, multiple calls to both Open and Close make sense. ADO.NET supports offline processing of data, even when the connection to the data provider has been closed. The pattern looks like this:

```
try
{
    conn.Open(); // Open connection
    //
    // Online processing (e.g., queries) here
    //
    conn.Close(); // Close connection
```

```
    //
    // Offline processing here
    //

    conn.Open(); // Reopen connection
    //
    // Online processing(e.g., INSERT/UPDATE/DELETE) here
    //
    conn.Close(); // Reclose connection
}
finally {
    //Close connection
    conn.Close();
}
```

The `finally` block still calls `Close`, calling it unnecessarily if no exceptions are encountered, but this isn't a problem or expensive, and it ensures the connection will be closed. Although many programmers hold connections open until program termination, this is usually wasteful in terms of server resources. With *connection pooling*, opening and closing a connection as needed is actually more efficient than opening it once and for all.

That's it! You're finished with the first connection example. Since, however, you saw a couple possible errors, let's look at typical causes of these errors.

Debugging Connections to SQL Server

Writing the C# code to use a connection is usually the easy part of getting a connection to work. Problems often lie not in the code, but rather in a mismatch in the connection parameters between the client (your C# program) and the database server. All appropriate connection parameters must be used and must have correct values. Even experienced database professionals often have problems getting a connection to work the first time.

More parameters are available than the ones shown here, but you get the idea. A corollary of Murphy's Law applies to connections: If several things can go wrong, surely one of them will. Your goal is to check both sides of the connection to make sure all of your assumptions are correct and that everything the client program specifies is matched correctly on the server.

Often the solution is on the server side. If the SQL Server instance isn't running, then the client will be trying to connect to a server that doesn't exist. If the user name and password on the client don't match the name and password of a user authorized to access the SQL Server database, then the connection will be rejected. If the database requested in the connection doesn't exist, an error will occur. If the client's network information doesn't match the server's, then the server may not receive the client's connection request, or the server response may not reach the client.

For connection problems, using the debugger to locate the line of code where the error occurs usually doesn't help—the problem almost always occurs on the call to the `Open` method. The question is, why? You need to look at the error message.

A typical error is as follows:

```
Unhandled Exception: System.ArgumentException:
    Unknown connection option in connection string: user.
```

The most likely cause for this is a simple typographical error in one of the clauses in your connection string. Make sure you've entered what you really meant to enter.

Figure 5-3 shows probably the most common message when trying to connect to SQL Server.

Figure 5-3. *Failed connection attempt*

In this case, most likely SQL Server isn't running. Restart MSDE (as explained in Chapter 1) with `net start mssql$netsdk`.

Other possible causes of this message are as follows:

- The SQL Server instance name is incorrect—you used `(local)\netsdk`, but your machine may use the `(local)\VSdotNET` instance instead. It's also possible that SQL Server was already installed as `(local)` with no instance name or is on another machine (see the next section); correct the instance name if this is the case.

- The MSDE program hasn't been installed—go back to Chapter 1 and follow the instructions there for installing MSDE.

- A security problem—your Windows login and password aren't valid on the server. This is unlikely to be the problem when talking to a `(local)` SQL Server instance, unless you installed MSDE under a different Windows login from the one you're using to write C# programs.

- A hardware problem—again unlikely if you're trying to connect to a server on the same machine.

Security and Passwords in SqlConnection

As you saw in the first chapter, you have two ways of logging into SQL Server. The first, preferred way is to use Windows integrated security, as you did in the first example. SQL Server uses your Windows login to access the database. Your Windows login must exist on the machine where SQL server is running, and your login must be authorized to access the SQL Server database or be a member of a user group that has that access.

If you don't include the `"Integrated Security = SSPI"` (or `"Integrated Security = True"` parameter in the connection string, the connection defaults to SQL Server security, which uses a separate login and password within SQL Server.

How to Use SQL Server Security

If you really did intend to use SQL Server security because that's how your company or department has set up access to your SQL Server (perhaps because some clients are non-Microsoft), then you need to specify a user name and password in the connection string, as shown here:

```
thisConnection.ConnectionString = @"
    server = (local)\netsdk;
    user id = sa;
    password = x1y2z3
";
```

The sa user name is the default system administrator account for SQL Server. If a specific user has been set up, such as george or payroll, then specify that name. The password for sa is set when SQL Server is installed. If the user name you use has no password, you can omit the password clause entirely or specify an empty password, as follows:

```
password =;
```

However, a blank password is bad practice and should be avoided, even in a test environment.

Connection String Parameters for SqlConnection

Table 5-2 summarizes the basic parameters for the SQL Server data provider connection string.

Table 5-2. *SQL Server Data Provider Connection String Parameters*

Name	Alias	Default Value	Allowed Values	Description
Application Name		.Net SqlClient Data Provider	Any string	Name of application
AttachDBFileName	extended properties, Initial File Name	None	Any path	Full path of an attachable database file
Connect Timeout	Connection Timeout	15	0–32767	Seconds to wait to connect
Data Source	Server, Address, Addr, Network Address	None	Server name or network address	Name of the target SQL Server instance
Encrypt		false	true, false, yes, no	Specifies whether to use SSL encryption
Initial Catalog	Database	None	Any database that exists on server	Database name
Integrated Security	Trusted_ Connection	false	true, false, yes, no, sspi	Specifies the authentication mode

Table 5-2. *SQL Server Data Provider Connection String Parameters*

Name	Alias	Default Value	Allowed Values	Description
Network Library	Net	dbmssocn	dbnmpntw, dbmsrpcn, dbmsadsn, dbmsgnet, dbmslpcn, dbmsspxn, dbmssocn	Network .dll
Packet Size		8192	Multiple of 512	Network packet size in bytes
Password	PWD	None	Any string	Password if not using Windows Authentication
Persist Security Info		false	true, false, yes, no	Specifies whether sensitive information should be passed back after connecting
User ID	UID		None	User name if not using Windows Authentication
Workstation ID		Local computer name	Any string	Workstation connecting to SQL Server

The Alias column in Table 5-2 gives alternate parameter names. For example, you can specify the server using any of the following:

```
data source = (local)\netsdk
server = (local)\netsdk
address = (local)\netsdk
addr = (local)\netsdk
network address = (local)\netsdk
```

Connection Pooling

One low-level detail that's worth noting—even though you shouldn't change it—is *connection pooling*. Recall that creating connections is expensive in terms of memory and time. With pooling, a closed connection isn't immediately destroyed but is kept in memory in a pool of unused connections. If a new connection request comes in that matches the properties of one of the unused connections in the pool, then the unused connection is used for the new database session.

Creating a totally new connection over the network can take seconds whereas reusing a pooled connection can happen in milliseconds; it's much faster to use pooled connections. The connection string has parameters that can change the size of the connection pool or even turn off connection pooling. The default values (for example, connection pooling is on by default) are appropriate for the vast majority of applications. See the SQL Server 2000 Books Online for details.

Improving Your Use of Connection Objects

The code in the first sample program was simple so you could concentrate on how connections work. Let's enhance it a bit.

Using the Connection String in the Connection Constructor

You created the connection and specified the connection string in separate steps. Since you always have to specify a connection string, you can use an overloaded version of the constructor that takes the connection string as an argument.

```
// Create connection
SqlConnection conn = new SqlConnection(@"
   server = (local)\netsdk;
   integrated security = sspi;
");
```

This constructor sets the ConnectionString property when creating the SqlConnection object.

Displaying Connection Information

Connections have several properties that provide information about the connection. Most of these properties are read-only, since their purpose is to display rather than set information. (You set connection values in the connection string.) These properties are often useful when debugging, to verify that the connection properties are what you expect them to be.

Here, we'll describe the connection properties common to most data providers. The complete list of properties and methods is available in the SQL Server 2000 Books Online. Later, you'll see some of the properties specific to other data providers.

Try It Out: Displaying Connection Information

Follow these steps:

1. Add a C# console application named Display, and rename Class1.cs to Display.cs.

2. Replace the code in Display.cs with that in Listing 5-2.

Listing 5-2. Display.cs

```
using System;
using System.Data;
using System.Data.SqlClient;
```

```csharp
namespace Display
{
   class Display
   {
      static void Main()
      {
         // Connection string
         string connString = @"
            server = (local)\netsdk;
            integrated security = sspi;
         ";

         // Create connection
         SqlConnection conn = new SqlConnection(connString);

         try {
            // Open connection
            conn.Open();
            Console.WriteLine("Connection opened.");

            // Display connection properties
            Console.WriteLine("Connection Properties:");
            Console.WriteLine(
               "\tConnection String: {0}",
               conn.ConnectionString);
            Console.WriteLine(
               "\tDatabase: {0}",
               conn.Database);
            Console.WriteLine(
               "\tDataSource: {0}",
               conn.DataSource);
            Console.WriteLine(
               "\tServerVersion: {0}",
               conn.ServerVersion);
            Console.WriteLine(
               "\tState: {0}",
               conn.State);
            Console.WriteLine(
               "\tWorkstationId: {0}",
               conn.WorkstationId);
         }
         catch (SqlException e) {
            // Display error
            Console.WriteLine("Error: " + e);
         }
         finally {
            // Close connection
```

```
            conn.Close();
            Console.WriteLine("Connection closed.");
        }
    }
  }
}
```

3. Make it the startup project, and run it with Ctrl+F5. If the connection is successful, you'll see output like that shown in Figure 5-4.

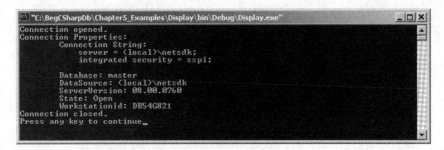

Figure 5-4. *Displaying SQL Server connection information*

How It Works

The ConnectionString property can be both read and written. Here you display it.

```
Console.WriteLine(
    "\tConnection String: {0}",
    conn.ConnectionString);
```

You'll see the value you assigned to it, including the whitespace, in the verbatim string.

What's the point? Well, it's handy when debugging connections to verify that the connection string really contains the values you thought you assigned. For example, if you're trying out different connection options, you may have different connection string parameters in the program. You may have commented out one intending to use it later but forgot about it. Displaying the ConnectionString property helps to see that a parameter is missing.

The next statement displays the Database property. Since each SQL Server instance has several databases, this property shows which one you're initially using when you connect.

```
Console.WriteLine(
    "\tDatabase: {0}",
    conn.Database);
```

In this program, it displays

```
Database: master
```

since you didn't specify a database in the connection string and were connected to the default database, which for this MSDE instance is master. If you wanted to connect to the Northwind database, then you'd need to specify the Database parameter, for example:

```
// Connection string
string connString = @"
    server = (local)\netsdk;
    database = northwind;
    integrated security = sspi;
";
```

Again, this is a handy property to display for debugging purposes. If you get an error saying that a particular table doesn't exist, often the problem isn't that the table doesn't exist but
that it isn't in the database to which you're connected. Displaying the Database property helps
you to find that kind of error quickly.

■Tip If you specify a database in the connection string that doesn't exist on the server, you may see the
error: "System.Data.SqlClient.SqlException: Cannot open database requested in login 'Northwind'. Login fails."
This can happen if you didn't run the script to create the Northwind sample database when installing MSDE.

You can change the database currently used on a connection with the ChangeDatabase
method. You'll see a good use for that method in Chapter 6.

The next statement displays the DataSource property, which gives the server instance
name for SQL Server database connections.

```
Console.WriteLine(
    "\tDataSource: {0}",
    conn.DataSource);
```

In this program it displays the same SQL Server instance name you've used in all the
examples so far.

```
DataSource: (local)\netsdk
```

The utility of this, again, is mainly for debugging purposes.

The ServerVersion property displays the server version information.

```
Console.WriteLine(
    "\tServerVersion: {0}",
    conn.ServerVersion);
```

It shows the version of MSDE you installed in Chapter 1. (Your version may differ.)

```
ServerVersion: 08.00.0760
```

The version number is useful for debugging. This information actually comes from the
server, so it indicates the connection is working.

The State property indicates whether the connection is open or closed.

```
Console.WriteLine(
    "\tState: {0}",
    conn.State);
```

Since you display this property after the Open call, it shows that the connection is open.

```
State: Open
```

You've been displaying your own message that the connection is open, but this property contains the current state. If the connection is closed, then the State property would be Closed.

The WorkstationId property is specific to SQL Server but is handy for debugging, so it deserves mention.

```
Console.WriteLine(
    "\tWorkstationId: {0}",
    conn.WorkstationId);
```

The workstation ID is a string identifying the client computer. It defaults to the computer name. Our computer is named DB54G821, but yours, of course, will be different.

```
WorkstationId: DB54G821
```

What makes this useful for debugging is that the SQL Server tools on the server can display which workstation ID issued a particular command. If you don't know which machine is causing a problem, you can modify your programs to display the WorkstationId property and compare them to the workstation IDs displayed on the server.

You can also set this property with the workstation ID connection string parameter as follows, so if you want all the workstations in, say, Building B to show that information on the server, you can indicate that in the program:

```
// Connection string
string connString = @"
    server = (local)\netsdk;
    workstation id = Building B;
    integrated security = sspi;
";
```

That completes the discussion of the fundamentals of connecting to SQL Server. Now let's look at connecting with other data providers.

Connecting to Microsoft Access with OleDbConnection

As you saw in the previous chapter, you use the OLE DB data provider to work with any OLE DB-compatible data store. Microsoft provides OLE DB data providers for SQL Server, Microsoft Access (Jet), Oracle, and a variety of other database and data file formats.

If a native data provider is available for a particular database or file format (such as the SqlClient data provider for SQL Server), then it's generally better to use it rather than the generic OLE DB data provider. This is because OLE DB introduces an extra layer of indirection between the C# program and the data source.

One common database format for which no native data provider exists is the Microsoft Access database (.mdb file) format, also known as the Jet database engine format, so in this case you need to use the OLE DB (or the ODBC) data provider.

Try It Out: Connecting to Access with the OLE DB Data Provider

Follow these steps:

1. Copy the Microsoft Access Northwind.mdb file to your development directory (use c:\begcsharpdb), or note the full path name to the file for use in the connection string.

2. Create a new C# console application named AccessConnect, and rename Class1.cs to AccessConnect.cs.

3. Replace the code in AccessConnect.cs with that in Listing 5-3. This is basically the same code as Display.cs, with the changed code in bold.

Listing 5-3. AccessConnect.cs

```
using System;
using System.Data;
using System.Data.OleDb;

namespace AccessConnect
{
    class AccessConnect
    {
        static void Main()
        {
            // Connection string
            string connString = @"
                provider = microsoft.jet.oledb.4.0;
                data source = c:\begcsharpdbs\northwind.mdb;
            ";

            // Create connection
            OleDbConnection conn = new OleDbConnection(connString);

            try {
                // Open connection
                conn.Open();
                Console.WriteLine("Connection opened.");

                // Display connection properties
                Console.WriteLine("Connection Properties:");
                Console.WriteLine(
                    "\tConnection String: {0}",
                    conn.ConnectionString);
                Console.WriteLine(
                    "\tDatabase: {0}",
                    conn.Database);
                Console.WriteLine(
                    "\tDataSource: {0}",
                    conn.DataSource);
```

```
                Console.WriteLine(
                    "\tServerVersion: {0}",
                    conn.ServerVersion);
                Console.WriteLine(
                    "\tState: {0}",
                    conn.State);
            }
            catch (OleDbException e) {
                // Display error
                Console.WriteLine("Error: " + e);
            }
            finally {
                // Close connection
                conn.Close();
                Console.WriteLine("Connection closed.");
            }
        }
    }
}
```

4. Make it the startup project, and run it with Ctrl+F5. If the connection is successful, you'll see output like that shown in Figure 5-5.

Figure 5-5. *Displaying Access connection information*

How It Works

We'll discuss only the differences between this example and the previous ones.

The first step is to reference the OLE DB data provider namespace, System.Data.OleDb.

```
using System.Data.OleDb;
```

Next, you specify the connection string. Instead of the server parameter, you use Provider and Data Source. You can't use the Integrated Security parameter with OLE DB.

```
// Connection string
string connString = @"
    provider = microsoft.jet.oledb.4.0;
    data source = c:\begcsharpdbs\northwind.mdb;
";
```

Next, you create an OleDbConnection object instead of a SqlConnection object.

```
// Create connection
OleDbConnection conn = new OleDbConnection(connString);
```

Note that you omitted the WorkstationId property in your display. The OLE DB data provider doesn't support it.

This is the pattern for accessing any data source with any .NET data provider. Specify the connection string with parameters specific to the data provider. Use the appropriate objects from the data provider namespace. Use only the properties and methods provided by that data provider.

Now let's access some other major RDBMSs. All can be used with the OLE DB and ODBC data providers, but all also have their own native data providers, which you'll use. You'll start with Oracle, since Microsoft supplies its own .NET data provider for Oracle as part of the .NET Framework.

Connecting to Oracle

Both Microsoft and Oracle supply a .NET Framework data provider for Oracle. You'll use System.Data.OracleClient, the Microsoft-supplied data provider.

Try It Out: Connecting to Oracle with System.Data.OracleClient

Follow these steps:

1. Add a C# console application named OracleConnect, and rename the Class1.cs file to OracleConnect.cs.

2. Replace the code in OracleConnect.cs with that in Listing 5-4. Change the connection string parameter values to reflect your server name, user ID, and password.

Listing 5-4. OracleConnect.cs

```
using System;
   using System.Data;
using System.Data.OracleClient;

namespace OracleConnect
{
   class OracleConnect
   {
      static void Main()
      {
         // Connection string
         string connString = @"
            server = o92;
            uid = scott;
            password = tiger;
         ";
```

```
            // Create connection
            OracleConnection conn = new OracleConnection(connString);

            try {
                // Open connection
                conn.Open();
                Console.WriteLine("Connection opened.");

                // Display connection properties
                Console.WriteLine("Connection Properties:");
                Console.WriteLine(
                    "\tConnection String: {0}",
                    conn.ConnectionString);
                Console.WriteLine(
                    "\tServerVersion: {0}",
                    conn.ServerVersion);
                Console.WriteLine(
                    "\tState: {0}",
                    conn.State);
            }
            catch (OracleException e) {
                // Display error
                Console.WriteLine("Error: " + e);
            }
            finally {
                // Close connection
                conn.Close();
                Console.WriteLine("Connection closed.");
            }
        }
    }
}
```

3. Add a reference to the Oracle data provider assembly (System.Data.OracleClient.dll)
   to the project. Right-click the References item. Click Add Reference.... Navigate to
   System.Data.OracleClient.dll, and double-click it. Click OK.

■**Note** The Microsoft data provider for Oracle isn't part of the .NET Framework core assembly file, so you
must explicitly reference it. Also, Oracle supplies different data providers for Oracle9*i* and Oracle 10*g*.
They're backward, but not forward, compatible and, of course, must be explicitly referenced.

---

4. Make this the startup project, and run it with Ctrl+F5. If the connection is successful, you'll see output like that shown in Figure 5-6.

Figure 5-6. *Connecting to Oracle with the* System.Data.OracleClient *data provider*

How It Works

Except for the connection string and use of Oracle as the type name prefix, this code is basically like the earlier examples.

Note that you omitted the Database and WorkstationId properties in the display. The OracleClient data provider doesn't support them.

■**Tip** From the command line, use the compiler option -r:System.Data.OracleClient.dll.

Connecting to DB2

IBM supplies a .NET Framework data provider for DB2 in namespace IBM.Data.DB2.

Try It Out: Connecting to DB2 with IBM.Data.DB2

Follow these steps:

1. Add a C# console application named Db2Connect, and rename the Class1.cs file to Db2Connect.cs.

2. Replace the code in Db2Connect.cs with that in Listing 5-5.

Listing 5-5. Db2Connect.cs

```
using System;
    using System.Data;
using IBM.Data.DB2;
```

```csharp
namespace Db2Connect
{
   class Db2Connect
   {
      static void Main()
      {
         // Connection string
         string connString = @"
            database = sample;
         ";

         // Create connection
         DB2Connection conn = new DB2Connection(connString);

         try {
            // Open connection
            conn.Open();
            Console.WriteLine("Connection opened.");

            // Display connection properties
            Console.WriteLine("Connection Properties:");
            Console.WriteLine(
               "\tConnection String: {0}",
               conn.ConnectionString);
            Console.WriteLine(
               "\tDatabase: {0}",
               conn.Database);
            Console.WriteLine(
               "\tServerVersion: {0}",
               conn.ServerVersion);
            Console.WriteLine(
               "\tState: {0}",
               conn.State);
         }
         catch (DB2Exception e) {
            // Display error
            Console.WriteLine("Error: " + e);
         }
         finally {
            // Close connection
            conn.Close();
            Console.WriteLine("Connection closed.");
         }
      }
   }
}
```

3. Add a reference to the DB2 data provider assembly (IBM.Data.DB2.dll) to the project. Right-click the References item. Click Add Reference.... Navigate to IBM.Data.DB2.dll, and double-click it. Click OK.

Note With version 8.2, DB2 has a .NET Framework data provider, named IBM.Data.DB2—note the unconventional use of uppercase—in assembly file IBM.Data.DB2.dll. It's analogous to the SQL Server data provider, but uses *DB2* instead of *Sql* as the prefix for type names. Like every data provider, it has some connection string parameters and methods of its own, but otherwise it operates exactly as you'd expect. Since IBM.Data.DB2 isn't part of the .NET Framework Class Library, you need to explicitly add a reference for its assembly to your project.

---

4. Make this the startup project, and run it with Ctrl+F5. If the connection is successful, you'll see output like that shown in Figure 5-7.

Figure 5-7. *Connecting to DB2 with the* IBM.Data.DB2 *data provider*

How It Works

Except for the connection string and use of DB2 as the type name prefix, this code is just like the earlier examples.

Note that you omitted the WorkstationId property in the display. The IBM.Data.DB2 data provider doesn't support it.

Tip From the command line, you used the compiler option (note the quotes) -r:"c:\program files\ibm\sqllib\bin\netf11\ibm.data.db2.dll". Your path may differ depending on where DB2 was installed.

Connecting to MySQL with ByteFX.Data.MySqlClient

MySQL supplies a .NET Framework data provider for its RDBMS in the namespace
ByteFX.Data.MySqlClient.

Try It Out: Connecting to MySql with ByteFX.Data.MySqlClient

Follow these steps:

1. Add a C# console application named MySqlConnect, and rename the Class1.cs file to
   MySqlConnect.cs.

2. Replace the code in MySqlConnect.cs with that in Listing 5-6, changing the user id
   parameter value appropriately.

   Listing 5-6. MySqlConnect.cs

```
using System;
   using System.Data;
using ByteFX.Data.MySqlClient;

namespace MySqlConnect
{
   class MySqlConnect
   {
      static void Main()
      {
         // Connection string
         string connString = @"
            user id = jim;
         ";

         // Create connection
         MySqlConnection conn = new MySqlConnection(connString);

         try {
            // Open connection
            conn.Open();
            Console.WriteLine("Connection opened.");

            // Display connection properties
            Console.WriteLine("Connection Properties:");
            Console.WriteLine(
               "\tConnection String: {0}",
               conn.ConnectionString);
            Console.WriteLine(
               "\tDatabase: {0}",
               conn.Database);
```

```
            Console.WriteLine(
                    "\tServerVersion: {0}",
                    conn.ServerVersion);
                Console.WriteLine(
                    "\tState: {0}",
                    conn.State);
            }
            catch (MySqlException e) {
                // Display error
                Console.WriteLine("Error: " + e);
            }
            finally {
                // Close connection
                conn.Close();
                Console.WriteLine("Connection closed.");
            }
        }
    }
}
```

3. Add a reference to the MySQL data provider assembly (ByteFX.MySqlClient.dll) to the project. Right-click the References item. Click Add Reference.... Then click Browse..., navigate to ByteFX.MySqlClient.dll, and then double-click it. Click OK.

■Note The MySQL data provider is an open-source product developed by Reggie Burnett of ByteFX, Inc., under contract to MySQL AB. It's analogous to the SQL Server data provider but uses *MySql* instead of *Sql* as the prefix for type names. Like every data provider, it has some connection string parameters and methods of its own, but otherwise it operates as you'd expect. ByteFx.Data.MySqlClient isn't part of the .NET Framework Class Library, so you need to explicitly add a reference for its assembly to your project.

---

4. Make this the startup project, and run it with Ctrl+F5. If the connection is successful, you'll see output like that shown in Figure 5-8.

Figure 5-8. *Connecting to MySQL with the* ByteFX.Data.MySqlClient *data provider*

How It Works

Except for the connection string and use of `MySql` as the type name prefix, this code is just like the earlier examples.

Note that you omitted the `WorkstationId` property in the display. The `ByteFX.Data.MySqlClient` data provider doesn't support it.

Tip From the command line, you used the following compiler option (note the quotes and spaces): `-r:"c:\program files\bytefx\bytefx.data provider\bytefx.mysqlclient.dll"`. Your path may differ depending on where the data provider was installed.

Summary

In this chapter, you looked at connections using various data providers. You learned about connection strings and connection string parameters, and you saw how to open and close connections.

You examined different security options for SQL Server and other data sources and also saw how to display information about the connection after it's established, using the properties of a connection.

You saw how to handle exceptions generated by connection errors and learned to close the connection in the `finally` block of the exception handler to ensure that the connection is closed in all cases.

Finally, you looked at specific examples of connecting to different data sources, including the following:

- SQL Server

- Microsoft Access

- Oracle

- DB2

- MySQL

In the next chapter, you'll look at ADO.NET *commands* and see how to use them to access data.

Introducing Commands

Once you've established a connection to the database, you want to start interacting with it and getting it doing something useful for you. You may need to add, update, or delete some data, or perhaps modify the database in some other way. Whatever the task, it will inevitably involve a *command*.

In this chapter, we'll explain commands, which are objects that encapsulate the SQL for the action you want to perform and that provide methods for submitting it to the database. Each data provider has a command class that implements the System.Data.IDbCommand interface.

In this chapter, you'll learn how to do the following:

- Create commands

- Associate commands with connections

- Use connection methods that apply to commands

- Use command properties and methods

- Set command text

- Execute commands

- Process command results

- Use commands with different data providers

We'll use the SQL Server data provider (System.Data.SqlClient) in most of our examples. Its command is named SqlCommand. Then, at the end of the chapter, we'll touch on using commands with other data providers.

So then, let's get started by learning how to create a command.

Creating a Command

You can create a command either using the SqlCommand constructor or using methods that create the object for you. Let's look at the first of these alternatives.

Try It Out: Creating a Command with a Constructor

In this example you'll create a SqlConnection object but not yet do anything with it.

1. Open Visual Studio .NET, and create a new blank solution called Chapter6_Examples.

2. Within the new solution, create a new C# Console Application project named CommandExampleSql. Rename Class1.cs to CommandExampleSql.cs.

3. Replace the code in Class1.cs with that in Listing 6-1.

Listing 6-1. CommandExampleSql *(First Version)*

```csharp
using System;
using System.Data;
using System.Data.SqlClient;

namespace CommandExampleSql
{
    class CommandExampleSql
    {
        static void Main()
        {
            // create SqlConnection object
            SqlConnection thisConnection = new SqlConnection(
                @"Server=(local)\NetSDK;"    +
                "Integrated Security=SSPI;");

            // create SqlCommand
            SqlCommand thisCommand = new SqlCommand();
            Console.WriteLine("Command created.");

            try
            {
                // open connection
                thisConnection.Open();
            }
            catch (SqlException ex)
            {
                Console.WriteLine(ex.ToString());
            }
            finally
            {
                thisConnection.Close();
                Console.WriteLine("Connection Closed.");
            }
        }
    }
}
```

4. Run the program without debugging (Ctrl+F5). You should see the output in Figure 6-1.

Figure 6-1. CommandExampleSql *(first version)*

How It Works

You create a SqlCommand object using the default constructor, and print a message indicating you've created it.

```
// create SqlCommand
SqlCommand thisCommand = new SqlCommand();
Console.WriteLine("Command created.");
```

In this example, the command is empty. It isn't associated with a connection, and it doesn't have its text (in other words, SQL) set. You can't do much with it here, so let's move on and look at how you can associate it with your connection.

Associating a Command with a Connection

For your commands to be executed against the database of your choice, each command must be associated with a connection to that particular database. You do this by setting the Connection property of the command, and in order to save resources, multiple commands can use the same connection. You have a couple of ways to set this association up, so let's try them in the sample program.

Try It Out: Setting the Connection Property

To set the connection property, follow these steps:

1. Add the following bold code to the try block of Listing 6-1.

```
try
{
  // open connection
  thisConnection.Open();

  // connect command to connection
  thisCommand.Connection = thisConnection;
  Console.WriteLine("Created Command on this connection.");
}
```

2. Run it (Ctrl+F5). You should see the output in Figure 6-2.

Figure 6-2. `CommandExampleSql` *(second version)*

How It Works

As you saw in the previous example, you start the code by creating the connection and command.

```
// create SqlConnection object
SqlConnection thisConnection = new SqlConnection( ... );
// create SqlCommand
SqlCommand thisCommand = new SqlCommand();
```

At this point, both the connection and command exist, but they aren't associated with each other in any way. It's only when you assign the connection to the command's `Connection` property that they become associated.

```
// connect command to connection
thisCommand.Connection = thisConnection;
```

The actual assignment occurs after the call to `thisConnection.Open` in this particular example, but you could have done it before calling `Open`; the connection doesn't have to be open for the `Connection` property of the command to be set.

As mentioned earlier, you have a second option for associating a connection with a command; calling the connection's `CreateCommand` method will return a new command with the `Connection` property set to that connection.

```
// create SqlCommand
SqlCommand thisCommand = thisConnection.CreateCommand();
```

This block of code is equivalent to the previous one; in both cases you end up with a command associated with your connection. It's also just one line of code, because you don't have to assign the `Connection` property.

You still need one more thing in order to use the command, and that's the text of the command. Let's see how to set that next.

Assigning Text to a Command

Every command has a property, `CommandText`, that holds the SQL to execute. You can assign to this property directly or specify it when constructing the command. Let's look at these alternatives.

Try It Out: Setting the CommandText Property

To set the `CommandText` property, follow these steps:

1. Modify the `try` block with the following bold code:

```
try
{
  // open connection
  thisConnection.Open();

  // connect command to connection
  thisCommand.Connection = thisConnection;

  // associate SQL with command
  thisCommand.CommandText = "SELECT COUNT(*) FROM Employees";
  Console.WriteLine("Ready to execute SQL command: {0}",
      thisCommand.CommandText);
}
```

2. Run it (Ctrl+F5). You should see the output in Figure 6-3.

Figure 6-3. `CommandExampleSql` *(third version)*

How It Works

`CommandText` is just a string, so you can print it with `Console.WriteLine` just like any other string. The SQL, `"SELECT COUNT(*) FROM Employees"`, will return the number of employees in the `Northwind Employees` table when you're ready.

■**Note** You must set both the `Connection` and the `CommandText` properties of a command before the command can be executed.

You can set both of these properties when you create the command with yet another variation of its constructor, as shown here:

```
// create a command with both text and connection
SqlCommand thisCommand =
   new SqlCommand("SELECT COUNT(*) FROM Employees", thisConnection);
```

This is equivalent to the previous code that assigns each property explicitly. This is the most commonly used variation of the SqlCommand constructor, and you'll use this one for the rest of the chapter.

Executing Commands

Commands aren't much use unless you can execute them, so let's look at that now. Commands have several different methods for executing SQL. The differences between these methods depend on the results you expect from the SQL code. Queries return rows of data, but statements don't. You determine which method to use by considering what you expect to be returned (see Table 6-1).

Table 6-1. *Command Execution Methods*

If the Command Is Going to Return...	You Should Use...
Nothing. (It isn't a query.)	ExecuteNonQuery
A single value.	ExecuteScalar
Zero or more rows.	ExecuteReader
XML. (You'll learn more about this in Chapter 17.)	ExecuteXmlReader

The SQL code you just used in the example, "SELECT COUNT(*) FROM Employees", should return one value, the number of employees. Looking at Table 6-1. you can see that you should use the ExecuteScalar method of SqlCommand to return this one result. Let's try it.

Try It Out: Using the ExecuteScalar Method

To use the ExecuteScalar method, follow these steps:

1. Add a new C# Console Application project named CommandExampleScalar to your open solution, Chapter6_Examples. Rename Class1.cs to CommandExampleScalar.cs.

2. Replace the code in CommandExampleScalar.cs with the code in CommandExampleSql.cs.

3. Modify the code in CommandExampleScalar.cs as indicated by the bold lines in Listing 6-2.

    Listing 6-2. CommandExampleScalar

    ```
    using System;
    using System.Data;
    using System.Data.SqlClient;
    ```

```
namespace CommandExampleScalar
{
    class CommandExampleScalar
    {
        static void Main()
        {
            // create SqlConnection object
            SqlConnection thisConnection = new SqlConnection(
                @"Server=(local)\NetSDK;"    +
                "Integrated Security=true;" +
                "Database=Northwind;");

            // create SqlCommand
            SqlCommand thisCommand =
                new SqlCommand("SELECT COUNT(*) FROM Employees", thisConnection);

            try
            {
                // open connection
                thisConnection.Open();

                // execute query to return number of employees
                Console.WriteLine("Number of Employees is: {0}",
                    thisCommand.ExecuteScalar());
            }
            catch (SqlException ex)
            {
                Console.WriteLine(ex.ToString());
            }
            finally
            {
                thisConnection.Close();
                Console.WriteLine("Connection Closed.");
            }
        }
    }
}
```

4. Make it the startup project, and then run it (Ctrl+F5). You should see the output in Figure 6-4.

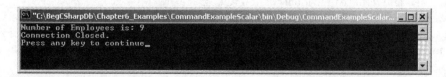

Figure 6-4. CommandExampleScalar

How It Works

ExecuteScalar takes the CommandText property and sends it to the database using the command's Connection property. It returns the result (9) as a single object, which you display with Console.WriteLine.

This is pretty simple to follow, but it's worth noting this really is simpler than you'll usually have it because Console.WriteLine takes any kind of object as its input. In fact, ExecuteScalar's return type is object, the superclass of all types in the .NET Framework, which makes perfect sense when you remember that a database can hold any type of data. So, if you want to assign the returned object to a variable of a specific type (int, for example), you must cast the object to the specific type. If the types aren't compatible, the system will generate a runtime error that indicates an invalid cast.

The following is an example that demonstrates this idea. In it, you store the result from ExecuteScalar in the variable count, casting it to the specific type int.

```
thisCommand.CommandText = "SELECT COUNT(*) FROM Employees";
int count = (int) thisCommand.ExecuteScalar();
Console.WriteLine("Number of Employees is: {0}", count);
```

If you're sure the type of the result will always be an int (a safe bet with COUNT(*)), then the previous code is safe. However, if you left the cast to int in place and changed the CommandText of the command to the following:

```
SELECT FirstName FROM Employees WHERE LastName='Davolio'
```

then ExecuteScalar would return the string Nancy instead of an integer, and you'd get this exception:

```
Unhandled Exception: System.InvalidCastException: Specified cast is not valid.
```

because you can't cast a string to an int.

Another problem may occur if a query actually returns multiple rows where you thought it would return only one; for example, what if there were multiple employees with the last name Davolio? In this case, ExecuteScalar just returns the first row of the result and ignores the rest. If you use ExecuteScalar, make sure you not only expect but actually get a single value returned.

Executing Commands with Multiple Results

For queries where you're expecting multiple rows and columns to be returned, use the command's ExecuteReader method.

ExecuteReader returns a data reader, an instance of the SqlDataReader class that you'll study in the next chapter. Data readers have methods that allow you to read successive rows in result sets and retrieve individual column values.

We'll leave the details of data readers for the next chapter, but for comparison's sake, we'll give a brief example here of using the ExecuteReader method to create a SqlDataReader from a command to display query results.

Try It Out: Using the ExecuteReader Method

To use the ExecuteReader method, follow these steps:

1. Add a new C# Console Application project named CommandExampleReader to your solution, Chapter6_Examples. Rename Class1.cs to CommandExampleReader.cs.

2. Replace the code in CommandExampleReader.cs with the code in Listing 6-3.

Listing 6-3. CommandExampleReader

```csharp
using System;
using System.Data;
using System.Data.SqlClient;
namespace CommandExampleReader
{
    class CommandExampleReader
    {
        static void Main()
        {
            // create SqlConnection object
            SqlConnection thisConnection =
                new SqlConnection(
                @"Server=(local)\NetSDK;"    +
                "Integrated Security=SSPI;" +
                "Database=Northwind;" );

            SqlCommand thisCommand =
                new SqlCommand("SELECT FirstName, LastName FROM Employees",
                    thisConnection);

            try
            {
                // open connection
                thisConnection.Open();

                SqlDataReader thisReader = thisCommand.ExecuteReader();

                while (thisReader.Read())
                {
                    Console.WriteLine("Employee name: {0} {1}",
                        thisReader.GetValue(0),
                        thisReader.GetValue(1));
                }
            }
            catch (SqlException ex)
            {
                Console.WriteLine(ex.ToString());
            }
```

```
                finally
                {
                    thisConnection.Close();
                    Console.WriteLine("Connection Closed.");
                }
            }
        }
    }
```

3. Make it the startup project, and then run it (Ctrl+F5). You should see the output in Figure 6-5, displaying the first and last names of all nine employees.

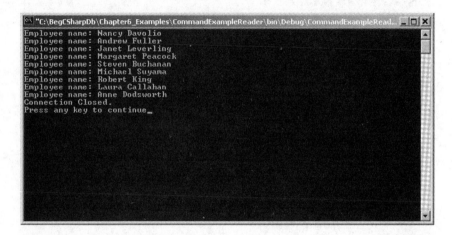

Figure 6-5. CommandExampleReader

How It Works

In this example you've used the ExecuteReader method to retrieve and then output the first and last names of all the employees in the Employees table. As with ExecuteScalar, ExecuteReader takes the CommandText property and sends it to the database using the connection from the Connection property.

When you used the ExecuteScalar method, you produced only a single scalar value. In contrast, using ExecuteReader returned a SqlDataReader object.

```
SqlDataReader thisReader = thisCommand.ExecuteReader();

while (thisReader.Read())
{
    Console.WriteLine("Employee name: {0} {1}",
        thisReader.GetValue(0),
        thisReader.GetValue(1));
}
```

The SqlDataReader object has a Read method that gets each row in turn and a GetValue method that gets the value of a column in the row. The particular column whose value it retrieves is given by the integer parameter indicating the index of the column. Note that GetValue uses a zero-based index, so the first column is column zero, the second column is column one, and so on. Since the query asked for two columns, FirstName and LastName, these are the columns numbered 0 and 1 in this query result.

Executing Statements

The ExecuteNonQuery method of the command executes SQL statements instead of queries. Let's try it.

Try It Out: Using the ExecuteNonQuery Method

To use the ExecuteNonQuery method, follow these steps:

1. Add a new C# Console Application project named CommandExampleNonQuery to your solution, Chapter6_Examples. Rename Class1.cs to CommandExampleNonQuery.cs.

2. Replace the code in CommandExampleNonQuery.cs with the code in Listing 6-4.

   Listing 6-4. CommandExampleNonQuery

```
using System;
using System.Data;
using System.Data.SqlClient;

namespace CommandExampleNonQuery
{
    class CommandExampleNonQuery
    {
        static void Main()
        {
            // create SqlConnection object
            SqlConnection thisConnection = new SqlConnection(
                @"Server=(local)\NetSDK;"   +
                "Integrated Security=SSPI;" +
                "Database=Northwind;");

            // create SqlCommands
            SqlCommand selectCommand =
                new SqlCommand("SELECT COUNT(*) FROM Employees", thisConnection);
            SqlCommand nonqueryCommand = thisConnection.CreateCommand();
```

```csharp
try
{
    // open connection
    thisConnection.Open();

    // execute query to return number of employees
    Console.WriteLine("Before INSERT: Number of Employees is: {0}",
        selectCommand.ExecuteScalar());
    nonqueryCommand.CommandText =
        "INSERT INTO Employees (Firstname, Lastname) " +
        "VALUES ('Zachariah', 'Zinn')";
    Console.WriteLine(nonqueryCommand.CommandText);
    Console.WriteLine("Number of Rows Affected is: {0}",
        nonqueryCommand.ExecuteNonQuery());
    Console.WriteLine("After INSERT: Number of Employees is: {0}",
        selectCommand.ExecuteScalar());
    nonqueryCommand.CommandText =
        "DELETE FROM Employees WHERE Firstname='Zachariah'" +
        "AND Lastname='Zinn'";
    Console.WriteLine(nonqueryCommand.CommandText);
    Console.WriteLine("Number of Rows Affected is: {0}",
        nonqueryCommand.ExecuteNonQuery());
    Console.WriteLine("After DELETE: Number of Employees is: {0}",
        selectCommand.ExecuteScalar());
}
catch (SqlException ex)
{
    Console.WriteLine(ex.ToString());
}
finally
{
    thisConnection.Close();
    Console.WriteLine("Connection Closed.");
}
    }
  }
}
```

3. Make it the startup project, and then run it (Ctrl+F5). You should see the output in Figure 6-6.

Figure 6-6. CommandExampleNonQuery

How It Works

In this program you actually create and use two commands. The first is selectCommand, which encapsulates a SELECT COUNT(*) query to count the rows in the Employees table, as you did in an earlier example. You'll use this command several times to monitor the number of rows as you insert and delete employees. The command text of selectCommand stays constant, so you initialize the command text using the variant of the SqlCommand constructor that sets its CommandText and Connection properties at the time you create selectCommand itself.

```
// create SqlCommands
SqlCommand selectCommand =
   new SqlCommand("SELECT COUNT(*) FROM Employees", thisConnection);
```

Next, you create another command named nonqueryCommand. This will be used for executing the INSERT and DELETE commands. Since the command text of this object won't remain constant (you'll change the text when you switch from INSERT to DELETE), you'll set the command text for these commands just before you execute the commands. The only property you'll initialize when constructing nonqueryCommand is the Connection property; the CreateCommand() method of the Connection object is an easy way to do this.

```
SqlCommand nonqueryCommand = thisConnection.CreateCommand();
```

The first operation performed after you open the connection is an INSERT to add a row to the table. First you need to open the connection, and then you use selectCommand to display the number of rows in the table before you modify anything.

```
// open connection
thisConnection.Open();

// execute query to return number of employees
Console.WriteLine("Before INSERT: Number of Employees is: {0}",
   selectCommand.ExecuteScalar());
```

Note that you called ExecuteScalar to execute the query, using the command text and connection as initialized when selectCommand was created. Next you create the command text for the insert and assign it to the CommandText property of nonqueryCommand. Then display the text on the console.

```
nonqueryCommand.CommandText =
    "INSERT INTO Employees (Firstname, Lastname) " +
    "VALUES ('Zachariah', 'Zinn')";
    Console.WriteLine(nonqueryCommand.CommandText);
```

Note that you haven't executed the command yet. You do this in the next line with a call to ExecuteNonQuery.

```
Console.WriteLine("Number of Rows Affected is: {0}",
    nonqueryCommand.ExecuteNonQuery());
```

ExecuteNonQuery returns an int indicating how many rows were affected by the command. Since you want to display the number of affected rows, you put the call to ExecuteNonQuery within the call to Console.WriteLine so you don't have to store the result in a temporary variable but instead use it directly. Again you use the scalar command to display the number of rows, this time after the INSERT operation.

```
Console.WriteLine("After INSERT: Number of Employees is: {0}",
    selectCommand.ExecuteScalar() );
```

Now you want to restore the table to its original state, so you need a DELETE statement to delete the employee you just inserted. You'll reuse nonqueryCommand and modify the CommandText property to hold a DELETE statement.

```
nonqueryCommand.CommandText =
    "DELETE FROM Employees WHERE Firstname='Zachariah'" +
    "AND Lastname='Zinn'";
Console.WriteLine(nonqueryCommand.CommandText);
```

Now you execute the DELETE statement with ExecuteNonQuery the same way you executed INSERT and again use selectCommand to display the results.

```
Console.WriteLine("Number of Rows Affected is: {0}",
    nonqueryCommand.ExecuteNonQuery());
Console.WriteLine("After DELETE: Number of Employees is: {0}",
    selectCommand.ExecuteScalar());
```

As we said, when INSERT, UPDATE, or DELETE execute, they affect some number of rows in the database; the return value from ExecuteNonQuery indicates how many rows were affected.

If this number comes back zero when you didn't expect it to do so, then maybe you specified the WHERE clause of the SQL statement incorrectly. For example, if you mistype the WHERE clause for the DELETE statement in the previous program, you may see the output shown in Figure 6-7.

Figure 6-7. *Misspelling* Zinn

We misspelled *Zinn* as *Xinn*, so it didn't find any rows to delete. The number of employees remaining after the DELETE is ten, not nine as expected. If you fix this error and rerun the program, you insert one more row but then delete two, as shown in Figure 6-8.

Figure 6-8. *Correcting* Zinn

This is because the second row was left behind when the previous DELETE failed to find it.

Creating Tables

Of course, adding data to and removing data from your tables aren't the only nonqueries you'll end up sending to your server. Often you'll need to create a table or other database object from your program, such as creating a temporary table to hold some data as part of your application processing on the server.

Such operations use the CREATE statement and are part of the Data Definition Language (DDL). This is distinguished from the Data Manipulation Language (DML), which includes INSERT, UPDATE, and DELETE.

You use ExecuteNonQuery to execute DDL as well as DML. Let's check it out.

Try It Out: Using ExecuteNonQuery for CREATE TABLE

The aim of this example is to create a table called MyTmpTable and insert some data into it by executing a CREATE TABLE statement on the tempdb database.

1. Add a new C# Console Application project called CommandExampleCreate to your solution, Chapter6_Examples. Rename Class1.cs to CommandExampleCreate.cs.

2. Replace the code in CommandExampleCreate.cs with the code in Listing 6-5.

Listing 6-5. CommandExampleCreate

```
using System;
using System.Data;
using System.Data.SqlClient;
namespace CommandExampleCreate
{
    class CommandExampleCreate
    {
        static void Main()
        {
            // create SqlConnection object
            SqlConnection thisConnection = new SqlConnection(
                @"Server=(local)\NetSDK;"      +
                "Integrated Security=SSPI;"    +
                "Database=tempdb;");

            // create SqlCommand object
            SqlCommand nonqueryCommand = thisConnection.CreateCommand();

            try
            {
                // open connection
                thisConnection.Open();

                // execute nonquery to create temporary table
                nonqueryCommand.CommandText =
                    "CREATE TABLE MyTmpTable (COL1 integer)";
                Console.WriteLine(nonqueryCommand.CommandText);
                Console.WriteLine("Number of Rows Affected is: {0}",
                    nonqueryCommand.ExecuteNonQuery());

                // execute nonquery to insert some data
                nonqueryCommand.CommandText = "INSERT INTO MyTmpTable VALUES (37)";
                Console.WriteLine(nonqueryCommand.CommandText);
                Console.WriteLine("Number of Rows Affected is: {0}",
                    nonqueryCommand.ExecuteNonQuery());
            }
            catch (SqlException ex)
            {
                Console.WriteLine(ex.ToString());
            }
            finally
            {
                thisConnection.Close();  // close connection
                Console.WriteLine("Connection Closed.");
```

```
        }
      }
    }
  }
```

3. Make it the startup project, and then run it (Ctrl+F5). You should see the output in Figure 6-9.

```
"C:\BegCSharpDb\Chapter6_Examples\CommandExampleCreate\bin\Debug\CommandExampleCreat...  _ □ ×
CREATE TABLE MyTmpTable (COL1 integer)
Number of Rows Affected is: -1
INSERT INTO MyTmpTable VALUES (37)
Number of Rows Affected is: 1
Connection Closed.
Press any key to continue_
```

Figure 6-9. `CommandExampleCreate`

How It Works

You repeat the style from the previous example, using `CreateCommand` to create a command named `nonqueryCommand` associated with the connection at create time.

```
SqlCommand nonqueryCommand = thisConnection.CreateCommand();
```

You have two tasks to do in this example—creating the table and then filling it with some data—so that's two commands you need to issue. As before, you'll need to change the `CommandText` property for each of these tasks before you execute the commands. First, you execute the `CREATE TABLE` statement.

```
// execute nonquery to create temporary table
nonqueryCommand.CommandText = "CREATE TABLE MyTmpTable (COL1 integer)";
Console.WriteLine(nonqueryCommand.CommandText);
Console.WriteLine("Number of Rows Affected is: {0}",
    nonqueryCommand.ExecuteNonQuery());
```

`ExecuteNonQuery` returns a negative one (-1) when executing DDL such as `CREATE TABLE`, since creating a new table doesn't affect any rows of existing tables. So you see the `CREATE TABLE` being executed, and the return value is -1.

Second, you execute the `INSERT` statement to put some data into the table.

```
// execute nonquery to insert some data
nonqueryCommand.CommandText = "INSERT INTO MyTmpTable VALUES (37)";
Console.WriteLine(nonqueryCommand.CommandText);
Console.WriteLine("Number of Rows Affected is: {0}",
    nonqueryCommand.ExecuteNonQuery());
```

The insert affects one row, so `ExecuteNonQuery` returns a positive one (1).

`ExecuteNonQuery` also returns -1 if you give it a query to execute. This is because you haven't changed any rows. However, don't use `ExecuteNonQuery` for queries; you'll want to look at the result set (or scalar value), and `ExecuteReader` or `ExecuteScalar` are the methods to use for this.

Note Note that because you created `MyTmpTable` in the `tempdb` temporary database, it will disappear the next time SQL Server is restarted. That's OK for this table; you were just using it as an example. However, don't use the `tempdb` database for any data you really want to be permanent.

Creating Databases

The previous example created a table in the `tempdb` database, which is always present in SQL Server for temporary tables. This is handy for incidental work, but it's often more convenient to create a whole database for your application rather than new tables in a database that already exists.

As it turns out, this is easy enough to program in ADO.NET; you just execute the Transact-SQL `CREATE DATABASE` statement. You have a chicken-and-egg problem, however, in that you can't connect to the database until the database exists. This is one reason why connections have a `ChangeDatabase` method. Let's see how it's used.

Try It Out: Creating a Database and Using It

To create a database and use it, follow these steps:

1. Add a new C# Console Application project named `CommandExampleCreateDb` to your solution, `Chapter6_Examples`. Rename `Class1.cs` to `CommandExampleCreateDb.cs`.

2. Replace the code in `CommandExampleCreateDb.cs` with the code in Listing 6-6, which is identical to Listing 6-5 except for the bold lines.

Listing 6-6. `CommandExampleCreateDb`

```
using System;
using System.Data;
using System.Data.SqlClient;
namespace CommandExampleCreateDb
{
    class CommandExampleCreateDb
    {
        static void Main()
        {
            // create SqlConnection object
            SqlConnection thisConnection = new SqlConnection(
                @"Server=(local)\NetSDK;"      +
                "Integrated Security=SSPI;"    +
                "Database=tempdb;");

            // create SqlCommands
            SqlCommand nonqueryCommand = thisConnection.CreateCommand();
```

```
            try
            {
                // open connection
                thisConnection.Open();

                // create new database called MyDatabase
                nonqueryCommand.CommandText = "CREATE DATABASE MyDb";
                Console.WriteLine(nonqueryCommand.CommandText);

                // always returns -1, no need to display return value
                nonqueryCommand.ExecuteNonQuery();
                Console.WriteLine("Database created, now switching");
                thisConnection.ChangeDatabase("MyDb");

                // execute nonquery to create temporary table
                nonqueryCommand.CommandText =
                    "CREATE TABLE MyTmpTable (COL1 integer)";
                Console.WriteLine(nonqueryCommand.CommandText);
                Console.WriteLine("Number of Rows Affected is: {0}",
                    nonqueryCommand.ExecuteNonQuery());

                // execute nonquery to insert some data
                nonqueryCommand.CommandText = "INSERT INTO MyTmpTable VALUES (37)";
                Console.WriteLine(nonqueryCommand.CommandText);
                Console.WriteLine("Number of Rows Affected is: {0}",
                    nonqueryCommand.ExecuteNonQuery());
            }
            catch (SqlException ex)
            {
                Console.WriteLine(ex.ToString());
            }
            finally
            {
                thisConnection.Close();  // close connection
                Console.WriteLine("Connection Closed.");
            }
        }
    }
}
```

3. Make it the startup project, and then run it (Ctrl+F5). You should see the output shown in Figure 6-10.

Figure 6-10. `CommandExampleCreateDb`

How It Works

This example works almost exactly the same as the previous one. The new addition is creating
the database and switching to the newly created database within C# without having to open
a new connection. When the database is created, the current database is the one specified when
you opened the connection (in this case `tempdb`, since you didn't change that part of the code).

```
SqlConnection thisConnection = new SqlConnection(
    @"Server=(local)\NetSDK;"     +
    "Integrated Security=SSPI;"    +
    "Database=tempdb;" );
```

If you don't specify the `Database` parameter in the connection string, then the default database, `master`, becomes the current database. However, the current database is irrelevant when
you issue the `CREATE DATABASE` command.

```
// create new database called MyDatabase
nonqueryCommand.CommandText = "CREATE DATABASE MyDatabase";
Console.WriteLine(nonqueryCommand.CommandText);
```

If you're creating this on your local machine, you can actually see the program pause and
hear your disk drive work as it creates the new file to contain the new database. Immediately
after creating the database, you switch to the new database.

```
Console.WriteLine("Database created, now switching");
thisConnection.ChangeDatabase("MyDatabase");
```

Now when the `CREATE TABLE` command is executed to create `MyTmpTable`, the table is created in `MyDatabase`, not `tempdb`.

```
// execute nonquery to create temporary table
nonqueryCommand.CommandText = "CREATE TABLE MyTmpTable (COL1 integer)";
Console.WriteLine(nonqueryCommand.CommandText);
nonqueryCommand.ExecuteNonQuery();
```

For temporary tables, just use the `tempdb` database. If you need to create permanent tables,
it's a good idea to put them in their own database. However, though it's possible to create databases in SQL Server this way, databases are usually not created in programs. Databases, even
small ones, aren't trivial matters.

Command Parameters

When the server executes SQL, all the information needed by the server must be contained within the string in the CommandText property. So if you want to insert some numbers into a column, you must specify the numbers as part of the string for the INSERT command, like so:

```
INSERT INTO MyTmpTable VALUES (1)
INSERT INTO MyTmpTable VALUES (2)
INSERT INTO MyTmpTable VALUES (3)
INSERT INTO MyTmpTable VALUES (4)
```

It'd get very tedious very quickly if you had to issue a separate INSERT for every value, so it'd be great if you could do it with a program. CommandText is a string, so you could build the string for the text by converting the variable containing the value you want to insert into the database into a string, like this:

```
try
{
    // open connection
    thisConnection.Open();
    int i;
    for (i=1; i<=4; i++)
    {
        nonqueryCommand.CommandText =
        "INSERT INTO MyTmpTable VALUES (" + i.ToString() + ")";

        Console.WriteLine(nonqueryCommand.CommandText);
        Console.WriteLine("Number of Rows Affected is: {0}",
            nonqueryCommand.ExecuteNonQuery());
    }
}
```

This approach to building the command text with normal string operations works just fine for simple INSERT statements and does the job with relatively few lines of code as well. However, it can get complicated to maintain, especially if you need to insert values into multiple columns, each of different types. Also, for data types (for example, byte arrays containing binary data) this method doesn't work correctly (ToString returns the name of the type rather than the data itself for many reference types).

A better way to handle these more complex cases is to use *command parameters*, which have the following advantages:

- The mapping between the variables in your code and the place where they're used in SQL is clearer and more readable.

- The conversion between C# types and SQL data types is cleaner and more correct with parameters. As you'll see, parameters let you use the type definitions that are specific to a particular ADO.NET data provider to ensure that your program variables are mapped to the correct SQL data types.

- Parameters let you use the `Prepare` method, which can make your code run faster. This is described in more detail in the "How It Works" section of the following example.

- Parameters are used extensively in more advanced programming techniques, such as when using stored procedures (see Chapter 14) and working with irregular data (see Chapter 21).

A parameter is a placeholder in the command text where a value will be substituted. In SQL Server, *named parameters* are used; these begin with @ followed by the parameter name with no intervening space. So then, in the following `INSERT` statement, `@MyName` and `@MyNumber` are both parameters:

```
INSERT INTO MyTable VALUES (@MyName, @MyNumber)
```

■**Note** Some data providers use the standard SQL *parameter marker*, a question mark (?), instead of named parameters. You'll look at this when you look at other data providers' commands in the "Using Commands with Other Data Providers" section.

Try It Out: Using Command Parameters and the Prepare Method

Follow these steps:

1. Add a new C# Console Application project named `CommandExampleParameters` to your solution, `Chapter6_Examples`. Rename `Class1.cs` to `CommandExampleParameters.cs`.

2. Replace the code in `CommandExampleParameters.cs` by copying the code from the previous example, `CommandExampleCreateDB.cs`. Change the namespace and class to `CommandExampleParameters`, and edit the `try` block with the bold code in Listing 6-7.

Listing 6-7. *Modifications for* `CommandExampleParameters`

```
try
{
    // open connection
    thisConnection.Open();

    // execute nonquery to create temporary table
    nonqueryCommand.CommandText =
      "CREATE TABLE MyTable (MyName VARCHAR (30), MyNumber integer)";
    Console.WriteLine(nonqueryCommand.CommandText);
      nonqueryCommand.ExecuteNonQuery();

    // create INSERT statement with named parameters
    nonqueryCommand.CommandText =
      "INSERT INTO MyTable VALUES (@MyName, @MyNumber)";
```

```
    // add parameters to command Parameters collection
    nonqueryCommand.Parameters.Add("@MyName", SqlDbType.VarChar, 30);
    nonqueryCommand.Parameters.Add("@MyNumber", SqlDbType.Int);

    // prepare command for repeated execution
    nonqueryCommand.Prepare();

    // data to be inserted
    string[] names = { "Enrico", "Franco", "Gloria", "Horace" } ;
    int i;
    for (i=1; i<=4; i++)
    {
        nonqueryCommand.Parameters["@MyName"].Value = names[i-1];
        nonqueryCommand.Parameters["@MyNumber"].Value = i;
        Console.WriteLine(nonqueryCommand.CommandText);
        Console.WriteLine("Number of Rows Affected is: {0}",
        nonqueryCommand.ExecuteNonQuery());
    }
}
```

3. Make it the startup project, and then run it (Ctrl+F5). You should see the output in
   Figure 6-11.

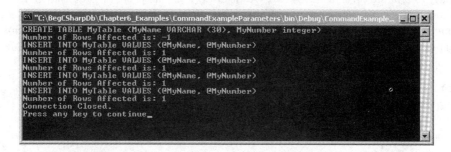

Figure 6-11. `CommandExampleParameters`

How It Works

The general outline of this example is similar to the first example that created a table in `tempdb`
and inserted a row into the table. Other than that, you created a table with two columns instead
of one and changed class names, all the code up to setting the text for the first `INSERT` is the same
as in previous examples. Here's where you first specify the parameters `@MyName` and `@MyNumber`
inside the text of the `INSERT` statement:

```
// create INSERT statement with named parameters
nonqueryCommand.CommandText =
    "INSERT INTO MyTable VALUES (@MyName, @MyNumber)";
```

Next you need to add these parameters to the command's `Parameters` collection. `Parameters` is a property that's a collection of `SqlParameter` objects. You use the collection's `Add` method to add new members to the collection.

```
// add parameters to command Parameters collection
thisCommand.Parameters.Add("@MyName", SqlDbType.VarChar, 30);
thisCommand.Parameters.Add("@MyNumber", SqlDbType.Int);
```

Each `SqlParameter` object has a name that must match a name used in the command text and a type that's specified by the `System.Data.SqlDbType` enumeration. `SqlDbType` lets you specify a SQL Server–specific data type for columns. This helps ensure correct type conversion when variables from your C# program are substituted for the parameters. Next you call the command's `Prepare` method. `Prepare` lets the database server know that a command with parameters is going to be repeated several times, so it can precompile the command at the server, resulting in faster execution and less memory usage.

```
// prepare command for repeated execution
nonqueryCommand.Prepare();
```

The `Prepare` method isn't a requirement for using parameters, but it's a good idea if you're going to execute the same command multiple times with the only change to the command being different values for the parameter variables. Be aware that not every database and data provider supports the preparing SQL for execution, but SQL Server and the `SqlClient` data provider do.

With the parameters set up, it's just a matter of inserting the various data values as required. You have four names in an array, so `names[0]` is Enrico, `names[1]` is Franco, and so on. You use a `for` loop and set the `@MyName` parameter to a name from the `names[]` array and the `@MyNumber` parameter to an integer from the loop index for each iteration through the loop. By assigning the `Value` property of the parameter, you tell the system to convert the value from the variable in the program to the appropriate text to substitute into the `INSERT` statement.

```
// data to be inserted
string[] names = { "Enrico", "Franco", "Gloria", "Horace" } ;
int i;
for (i=1; i<=4; i++)
{
    nonqueryCommand.Parameters["@MyName"].Value = names[i-1];
    nonqueryCommand.Parameters["@MyNumber"].Value = i;
```

Next you display the command text.

```
Console.WriteLine(nonqueryCommand.CommandText);
```

Notice that it prints the parameter name rather than the actual substituted value. For each iteration of the loop, you get this:

```
INSERT INTO MyTable VALUES (@MyName, @MyNumber)
```

This is because the parameter substitution doesn't actually change the command text string; instead, parameters are substituted at the time the command is executed at the server, which is the next step.

```
Console.WriteLine("Number of Rows Affected is: {0}",
    nonqueryCommand.ExecuteNonQuery() );
}
```

When the command is actually executed, the server substitutes Enrico for @MyName and 0 for @MyNumber on the first iteration, Frances for @MyName and 1 for @MyNumber on the next iteration, and so on. Each of the four times the command is executed, one row is affected. The result is the same as if you had executed the literal commands.

```
INSERT INTO MyTable VALUES ('Enrico', 0)
INSERT INTO MyTable VALUES ('Frances', 1)
INSERT INTO MyTable VALUES ('Gloria', 2)
INSERT INTO MyTable VALUES ('Horace', 3)
```

After you finish inserting the data, you close the connection. This example finishes your look at how commands are used with the SQL Server data provider. The SqlCommand class has a few more methods and properties, but they're beyond the scope of this book. You'll finish this chapter with a look at how the commands are used with other data providers.

Using Commands with Other Data Providers

The OLE DB and ODBC data providers have commands, OleDbCommand and OdbcCommand, and both act very much the same as SqlCommand. Let's look at a couple of examples.

Try It Out: Using OleDbCommand

This example accesses a Northwind database, but this time it accesses the one that comes with Microsoft Access (Northwind.mdb).

1. Add a new C# Console Application project named CommandOleDbQuery to your solution, Chapter6_Examples. Rename Class1.cs to CommandOleDbQuery.cs.

2. Replace the code in CommandOleDbQuery.cs with the code in Listing 6-8.

Listing 6-8. CommandOleDbQuery

```
using System;
using System.Data;
using System.Data.OleDb;
namespace CommandOleDbQuery
{
    class CommandOleDbQuery
    {
        static void Main()
```

```csharp
        {
            OleDbConnection thisConnection = new OleDbConnection(
                @"Provider=Microsoft.Jet.OLEDB.4.0;" +
                @"Data Source=" +
                @"C:\Program Files\Microsoft Office\Office10\Samples\" +
                @"northwind.mdb");

            OleDbCommand thisCommand =
                new OleDbCommand("SELECT ProductID, ProductName FROM Products",
                    thisConnection);

            try
            {
                // open connection
                thisConnection.Open();
                OleDbDataReader thisReader = thisCommand.ExecuteReader();

                while (thisReader.Read())
                {
                    Console.WriteLine("Product ID and Name: {0} {1}",
                        thisReader.GetValue(0),
                        thisReader.GetValue(1));
                }
            }
            catch (OleDbException ex)
            {
                Console.WriteLine(ex.ToString());
            }
            finally
            {
                thisConnection.Close();
                Console.WriteLine("Connection Closed.");
            }
        }
    }
}
```

3. Make it the startup project, and then run it (Ctrl+F5). You should see the output in Figure 6-12.

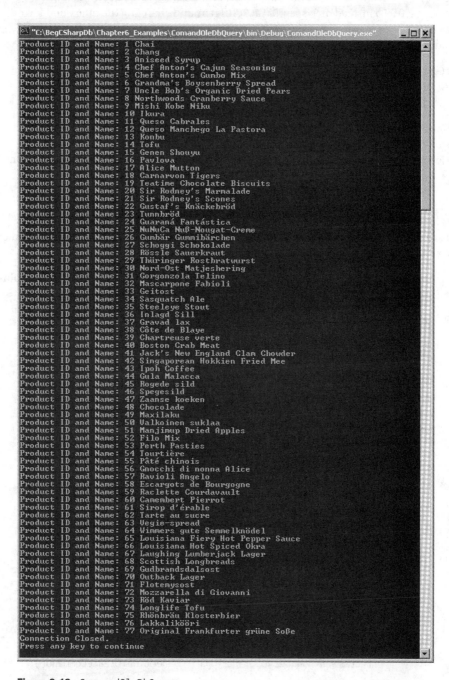

Figure 6-12. CommandOleDbQuery

How It Works

The code in this example is similar to the CommandExampleReader example (Listing 6-3), using System.Data.OleDb instead of System.Data.SqlClient and changing the query and formatting for the new database. You construct OleDbCommand in the same way as SqlCommand, specifying the command text and connection.

```
OleDbCommand thisCommand =
    new OleDbCommand("SELECT ProductID, ProductName FROM Products",
        thisConnection);
```

The SQL accepted by the Microsoft Access (Jet) engine has some differences from Transact-SQL, but for basic operations they're the same.

Now let's try an example with the ODBC data provider. You'll discover once again that only a few differences between it and the SQL Server data provider exist.

Try It Out: Using OdbcCommand

For this example, you'll base the code on the command parameters example you created earlier (CommandExampleParameters.cs).

1. Add a new C# Console Application project named CommandOdbcExample to your solution, Chapter6_Examples. Rename Class1.cs to CommandOdbcExample.cs.

2. Replace the code in CommandOdbcExample.cs with the code in Listing 6-9.

Listing 6-9. CommandOdbcExample

```
using System;
using System.Data;
using System.Data.Odbc;
namespace CommandOdbcExample
{
    class CommandOdbcExample
    {
        static void Main()
        {
            // create OdbcConnection object
            OdbcConnection thisConnection = new OdbcConnection(
                "DRIVER={MySQL ODBC 3.51 Driver};" +
                "SERVER=localhost;" +
                "DATABASE=test;" +
                "UID=root;" +
                "PASSWORD=;");

            // create OdbcCommands
            OdbcCommand nonqueryCommand = thisConnection.CreateCommand();
```

```
try
{
    // open connection
    thisConnection.Open();

    // execute nonquery to create temporary table
    nonqueryCommand.CommandText =
    "CREATE TABLE MyTable (MyName VARCHAR (30), MyNumber integer)";
    Console.WriteLine(nonqueryCommand.CommandText);
    nonqueryCommand.ExecuteNonQuery();

    // create INSERT command with ? unnamed parameters
    nonqueryCommand.CommandText =
        "INSERT INTO MyTable VALUES (?, ?)";

    // add parameters to command Parameters collection
    nonqueryCommand.Parameters.Add("@MyName", OdbcType.VarChar, 30);
    nonqueryCommand.Parameters.Add("@MyNumber", OdbcType.Int);

    // prepare not supported by current version of myODBC and mySQL
    // nonqueryCommand.Prepare();

    // data to be inserted
    string[] names = { "Enrico", "Franco", "Gloria", "Horace" } ;
    int i;
    for (i=1; i<=4; i++)
    {
        nonqueryCommand.Parameters["@MyName"].Value = names[i-1];
        nonqueryCommand.Parameters["@MyNumber"].Value = i;
        Console.WriteLine(nonqueryCommand.CommandText);
        Console.WriteLine("Number of Rows Affected is: {0}",
            nonqueryCommand.ExecuteNonQuery());
    }

    // check to see the data we inserted
    nonqueryCommand.CommandText =
        "SELECT MyName, MyNumber FROM MyTable";
    OdbcDataReader thisReader = nonqueryCommand.ExecuteReader();

    while (thisReader.Read())
    {
        Console.WriteLine("Name and Number: {0} {1}",
        thisReader.GetValue(0),
        thisReader.GetValue(1));
    }
    // close the reader so we can execute another command
    thisReader.Close();
```

```
                // drop temporary table
                nonqueryCommand.CommandText = "DROP TABLE MyTable";
                nonqueryCommand.ExecuteNonQuery();
              }
            catch (OdbcException ex)
            {
                Console.WriteLine(ex.ToString());
            }
            finally
            {
                thisConnection.Close();  // close connection
                Console.WriteLine("Connection Closed.");
            }
          }
        }
      }
```

3. Make it the startup project, and then run it (Ctrl+F5). You should see the output in Figure 6-13.

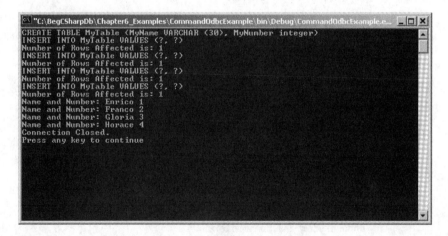

Figure 6-13. CommandOdbcExample

How It Works

Again you see the differences in the names of the data provider objects `OdbcConnection` and `OdbcCommand` as well as in the connection string.

Command parameters are an area where several differences exist among the data providers. The ODBC provider doesn't support named parameters; instead it uses unnamed parameters indicated in the text of the command by the standard SQL question mark.

```
// create INSERT command with ? unnamed parameters
nonqueryCommand.CommandText =
    "INSERT INTO MyTable VALUES (?, ?)";
```

Unnamed parameters are position dependent; the first parameter added will be associated with the first question mark, and so on, in order. Here you do the Add operation; note the names are used here, but they're ignored when substituting into the command text:

```
// add parameters to command Parameters collection
nonqueryCommand.Parameters.Add("@MyName", OdbcType.VarChar, 30);
nonqueryCommand.Parameters.Add("@MyNumber", OdbcType.Int);
```

Note you use the OdbcType enumeration that lists the ODBC data provider types; the SqlDbType used in the previous example is specific to SQL Server, even though the same basic types are supported.

```
// prepare not supported by current version of myODBC and MySQL
      // nonqueryCommand.Prepare();
```

MySQL doesn't support the Prepare method, so you don't call it here; as stated earlier, it's optional. This is an optimization issue; it doesn't affect the program except potentially in performance.

The insertion loop is the same as in the earlier example.

```
// data to be inserted
string[] names = { "Enrico", "Franco", "Gloria", "Horace" } ;
int i;
for (i=1; i<=4; i++)
{
   thisCommand.Parameters["@MyName"].Value = names[i-1];
   thisCommand.Parameters["@MyNumber"].Value = i;
   Console.WriteLine(thisCommand.CommandText);
   Console.WriteLine("Number of Rows Affected is: {0}",
      thisCommand.ExecuteNonQuery());
}
```

You added a data reader to check on the data you inserted; note that it's an OdbcDataReader.

```
// check to see the data we inserted
nonqueryCommand.CommandText = "SELECT MyName, MyNumber FROM MyTable";
OdbcDataReader thisReader = nonqueryCommand.ExecuteReader();
```

You also added a DROP TABLE statement to get rid of the table, since it's supposed to be temporary. Note that you have to close the data reader first.

```
// close the reader so we can execute another command
thisReader.Close();

// drop temporary table
nonqueryCommand.CommandText = "DROP TABLE MyTable";
nonqueryCommand.ExecuteNonQuery();
```

That finishes the ODBC example and the chapter as well. Let's summarize.

Summary

In this chapter, you learned the following:

- What an ADO.NET command is and does

- How to create a command

- How to associate a command with a connection

- How to set command text

- When to use the different command execution methods

- How to use `ExecuteScalar` for queries that return single values

- How to use `ExecuteReader` to process result sets

- How to use `ExecuteNonQuery` for DML and DDL

- How to create databases and tables using `ExecuteNonQuery()`

- What command parameters are and how to use them

- How to use commands, specifically `OleDbCommand` and `OdbcCommand`, with other data providers

In the next chapter, you'll look at data readers.

CHAPTER 7

■ ■ ■

Introducing Data Readers

In previous chapters you occasionally used data readers, which you can use to retrieve data from a result set in a connected manner. In this chapter, you'll look at data readers in more detail. As you progress, you'll gradually learn how they're used, and you'll learn their importance in ADO.NET programming.

In particular, you'll see how to use data readers to do the following:

- Retrieve query results

- Get information with ordinal and column name indexers

- Get result set information

- Get schema information

- Process multiple result sets

Understanding Data Readers in General

The third component of a data provider, in addition to connections and commands, is the *data reader*. Once you've connected to a database and queried it, you need some way to read the result set. This is where the data reader comes in.

If you're from an ADO background, an ADO.NET data reader is like an ADO forward-only/read-only client-side recordset, but it's not a COM object.

Data readers are objects that implement the System.Data.IDataReader interface. A data reader is a fast, unbuffered, forward-only, read-only connected stream of data that retrieves data on a per-row basis. Alternatively, you could say that it reads one row at a time as it loops through a result set.

You can't directly instantiate a data reader; instead, you create one with the ExecuteReader method of a command. For example, the following line of code shows a call made to ExecuteReader on an OLE DB command (cmd):

```
OleDbDataReader OleDbReader = cmd.ExecuteReader();
```

When you need to query a database—for instance, if you queried the Northwind Employees table with the OLE DB data provider—the ExecuteReader method would be called to create an OleDbDataReader instance for the query. Once at your disposal, you can use this data reader to access the result set.

■**Tip** One point that we'll discuss further in the next chapter is choosing a data reader vs. a dataset. The general rule is to always use a data reader for simply retrieving data. If all you need to do is display data, all you need to use in most cases is a data reader.

We'll now demonstrate basic data reader usage with a few examples. The first example is the most basic; it simply uses a data reader to loop through a result set.

Let's say you've successfully established a connection with the database, a query has been executed for results, and everything seems to be going fine—what now? The next sensible thing to do would be to retrieve the records and then possibly display them. You know that the ExecuteReader method returns a data reader instance for you to use. So now, you start reading.

The following console application illustrates how to use a SqlDataReader and shows you how to loop through a result set to retrieve rows.

Try It Out: Looping Through a Result Set

To loop through a result set, follow these steps:

1. In Visual Studio, create a new blank solution named Chapter7_Examples.

2. Add a C# console application named DataLooper, and rename the Class1.cs file to DataLooper.cs.

3. Replace the code in DataLooper.cs with that in Listing 7-1.

   Listing 7-1. DataLooper.cs

```csharp
using System;
using System.Data;
using System.Data.SqlClient;

namespace DataLooper
{
    class DataLooper
    {
        static void Main(string[] args)
        {
            // Connection string
            string connString = @"
                server = (local)\netsdk;
                integrated security = sspi;
                database = northwind
            ";
```

```csharp
        // Query
        string sql = @"
           select
               contactname
           from
               customers
        ";

        // Pass connection string to connection
        SqlConnection conn = new SqlConnection(connString);

        try
        {
           // Open connection
           conn.Open();

           // Pass query string and connection to command
           SqlCommand cmd = new SqlCommand(sql, conn);

           // Get data reader
           SqlDataReader reader = cmd.ExecuteReader();

           // Loop through reesult set
           while(reader.Read())
           {
              // Print one row at a time
              Console.WriteLine("{0}", reader[0]);
           }

           // Close data reader
           reader.Close();
        }
        catch(Exception e)
        {
           Console.WriteLine("Error Occurred: " + e);
        }
        finally
        {
           //Close connection
           conn.Close();
        }
     }
  }
}
```

4. Run it with Ctrl+F5. You should see the output in Figure 7-1.

Figure 7-1. DataLooper

How It Works

Let's walk through the code and see what you've created. You began your program with the usual set of instructions, including importing commonly used namespaces, setting up the connection details, and creating a query for your database, as shown in the following code:

```csharp
using System;
using System.Data;
using System.Data.SqlClient;

namespace DataLooper
{
    class DataLooper
    {
        static void Main(string[] args)
        {
            // Connection string
            string connString = @"
                server = (local)\netsdk;
                integrated security = sspi;
                database = northwind
            ";
```

```
// Query
string sql = @"
    select
        contactname
    from
        customers
";

// Pass connection string to connection
SqlConnection conn = new SqlConnection(connString);

try
{
    // Open connection
    conn.Open();

    // Pass query string and connection to command
    SqlCommand cmd = new SqlCommand(sql, conn);
```

In the past few chapters, we've gone over connections and the commands quite extensively. Since you're already familiar with the two objects and their usage, let's get straight down to the intricacies of using a data reader.

Recall from previous chapters that an SqlDataReader class is an abstract class and can't be instantiated explicitly. For this reason, you obtain an instance of a SqlDataReader by executing the ExecuteReader method of SqlCommand. You do this with the following line of code:

```
SqlDataReader reader = cmd.ExecuteReader();
```

Once you have a reader attached to the active connection, you can loop through each row of the returned dataset, provided that the dataset isn't empty, and retrieve values column by column. To do this, you need to make a call to the Read method of SqlDataReader, which returns true if a "next" row is available and advances the cursor or returns false if another row isn't available. Since Read advances the cursor to the next available record, you have to call it each time manually. So for this purpose, you use the following while loop in the example to do the job:

```
while(reader.Read())
```

Once you call the Read method, the next row is returned as a collection and stored in the SqlDataReader object itself. To access data from a specific column, you can use a number of methods (we'll cover these in the next section), but for this application you used the ordinal indexer lookup method, giving the column number to the reader to retrieve values (just as you'd give an index to an array of integers perhaps). Since in this case you chose a single column from the Customers table while querying the database, only the "zeroth" indexer is accessible, so you use the following line of code to display each record one by one:

```
Console.WriteLine("{0}", reader[0]);
```

To be able to use the connection for another purpose or to run another query on the database, it's important you call the Close method of SqlDataReader to close the reader explicitly. This is because, once the reader is attached to an active connection, the connection remains

busy fetching data for the reader and remains unusable for another purpose until the reader
has been detached from it. The following line shows this being done after you've looped
through the dataset and you're done using the data reader:

```
reader.Close();
```

Once the connection has been used, it's closed explicitly in the finally clause. If for
some reason you don't close the connection, the garbage collector will. However, remember,
sometimes you may have pending queries or transactions lined up in a queue, and closing
the connection explicitly makes sure they're all processed and executed before the application ends. The garbage collector won't do this; it'll just collect unreferenced objects, and you
may end up losing some of the changes you made to the data since the queue wouldn't be
processed. It's advisable that you close the connection explicitly with the Close method.

```
finally
{
   //Close connection
   conn.Close();
}
```

Using Ordinal Indexers

In the previous example, we mentioned using ordinal indexers when retrieving column data
from the database. You'll look at the same code snippet again and learn more about it. However, to avoid any kind of confusion, you'll consider only the piece of code where the actual
index has been referenced.

```
sqlReader[0]
```

Does this look familiar? If you've ever used arrays, this line shouldn't be foreign to you.
This is one of the ways you can request that a data reader fetch data, and this method of fetching data is called the *ordinal indexer method*. The indexer you pass to the data reader object is
actually an item property, and the return value is an object.

Compared to column name indexing, which you'll learn about in the next section, this
method is faster simply because the reader doesn't have to find the column from the row but
jumps right to it with the index provided, saving time, energy, and resources. The following
example demonstrates this more clearly.

Try It Out: Using Ordinal Indexers

Let's compare ordinal indexing to a real-world example; say you're standing in a street of 50
houses and you have to find someone named John Hook. All you're aware of is his name, and
you don't know which house is his. To find him, you'll have to individually check each house.
Wouldn't it be a lot easier if you knew his address instead and stepped right to it? Sure it would!
That's just what ordinal indexing is.

Let's consider a small console application that uses the ordinal indexer lookup method
and later compare the results with that of the field name indexing method, which we'll cover
in the next section.

To be able to start and execute your program, perform the following steps:

1. Add a C# console application named OrdinalIndexer, and rename the Class1.cs file to OrdinalIndexer.cs.

2. Replace the code in OrdinalIndexer.cs with that in Listing 7-2.

Listing 7-2. OrdinalIndexer

```
using System;
using System.Data;
using System.Data.SqlClient;

namespace OrdinalIndexer
{
    class OrdinalIndexer
    {
        static void Main(string[] args)
        {
            // Connection string
            string connString = @"
                server = (local)\netsdk;
                integrated security = sspi;
                database = northwind
            ";

            // Query
            string sql = @"
                select
                    companyname,
                    contactname
                from
                    customers
                where
                    contactname like 'M%'
            ";

            // Pass connection string to connection
            SqlConnection conn = new SqlConnection(connString);

            try
            {
                // Open connection
                conn.Open();

                // Pass query string and connection command
                SqlCommand cmd = new SqlCommand(sql, conn);

                // Get data reader
                SqlDataReader reader = cmd.ExecuteReader();
```

```
        // Print titles
        Console.WriteLine("\t{0}    {1}",
            "Company Name".PadRight(25),
            "Contact Name".PadRight(20));

        Console.WriteLine("\t{0}    {1}",
            "============".PadRight(25),
            "============".PadRight(20));

        // Loop through result set
        while(reader.Read())
        {
            Console.WriteLine(" {0} | {1}",
                reader[0].ToString().PadLeft(25),
                reader[1].ToString().PadLeft(20));
        }

        // Close reader
        reader.Close();
    }
    catch(Exception e)
    {
        Console.WriteLine("Error Occurred: " + e);
    }
    finally
    {
        // Close connection
        conn.Close();
    }
}
}
}
```

3. Make this the startup project, and run it with Ctrl+F5. You should see the output in Figure 7-2.

Figure 7-2. OrdinalIndexer

How It Works

Since you've looked at the connection details for examples such as this in earlier chapters, we won't dwell on that here. Let's move onto the data reader–specific code.

For this example, you queried the Customers table for the columns CompanyName and ContactName, where contact names begin with the letter *M*.

```
// Query
string sql = @"
   select
       companyname,
       contactname
   from
       customers
   where
       contactname like 'M%'
";
```

Since two columns were selected by your query, the returned data would also comprise a collection of rows from only these two columns, thus allowing access to only two possible data reader indexers, 0 and 1.

You call on the ordinal indexers in a while loop, fetching values of the two columns for you, as the cursor advances to a new row in the dataset every time a call to the Read method is made. Since the returned value is an object, you need to explicitly convert the value into a string so that you can use the PadLeft function for displaying the output in an organized manner.

```
while(reader.Read())
{
   Console.WriteLine(" {0} | {1}",
       reader[0].ToString().PadLeft(25),
       reader[1].ToString().PadLeft(20));
}
```

After retrieving column values, you explicitly close the reader to free or unbind your connection or any other resource and close the connection in the finally block.

```
// Close reader
reader.Close();
...
// Close connection
conn.Close();
```

Using Column Name Indexers

It's true that most of the time we don't really keep track of column numbers and prefer retrieving values by their respective column names, simply because it's much easier to remember them by their names, which also makes the code more self-documenting.

You perform column name indexing by passing a column name to the data reader, as opposed to the ordinal indexer method. This has many advantages. For instance, it could happen, for whatever reason, that a table is changed by the addition or deletion of one or more columns, thereby upsetting column ordering and rising exceptions in older code that used the ordinal indexer lookup method. Using column name indexers could take care of most of these issues, but it's preferred that you use the ordinal lookup method for faster results, especially when it comes to accessing hundreds of records from a number of columns and tables.

The following code snippet retrieves the same columns (CompanyName and ContactName) that the last example did, using the column name indexer method:

```
Console.WriteLine("{0} | {1}",
    reader["CompanyName"].ToString().PadLeft(25),
    reader["ContactName"].ToString().PadLeft(20));
```

You can use this code snippet with the example you saw for the ordinal indexer method by performing the following steps:

1. Open the code for the previous example, and search for the following lines of code:

```
Console.WriteLine(" {0} | {1}",
    reader[0].ToString().PadLeft(25),
    reader[1].ToString().PadLeft(20));
```

2. Replace these lines with the following ones:

```
Console.WriteLine(" {0} | {1}",
    reader["CompanyName"].ToString().PadLeft(25),
    reader["ContactName"].ToString().PadLeft(20));
```

3. Save the project, and execute it. This will produce the same result that you saw for the ordinal indexer method.

The next section may prove to be a much better approach for most cases.

Using Typed Accessor Methods

You've probably noticed how simple it is to retrieve data from any OLE DB–specific data source using the OLE DB data provider, or even from a SQL Server back end using the SQL Server data provider, but has it occurred to you that the string or the integer values you retrieve would probably not be represented the same way in the database? It could simply be a varchar, a text, an nvarchar, or a numeric value stored in the database that you conveniently retrieve and use without knowing what's really going on behind the scenes. It's true that SQL supports retrieving column data in various data formats by simply requesting it in that type.

When a data reader returns a value from a data source, the resulting value is retrieved and stored locally in a .NET Framework type rather than the original data source type. This in-place type conversion feature is a trade-off between consistency and speed, so to give some control over the data being retrieved, the data reader exposes typed accessor methods that you can use if you know the specific type of the value being returned.

Typed accessor methods all begin with a Get, take an ordinal for data retrieval, and are type safe; C# won't allow you to get away with unsafe casts. These methods turn out to be faster than both the ordinal and the column name indexer methods. Being faster than column name indexing seems only logical as the typed accessor methods take ordinals for referencing; however, we need to explain how it's faster than ordinal indexing. This is because even though both techniques take in a column number, the conventional ordinal indexing method needs to look up the data type of the result and then eventually go through a type conversion. On the contrary, the overhead of looking up the schema is disregarded in the case of typed accessor calls.

For almost all data types supported by SQL Server or by OLE DB–specific databases (since some databases support data types such as Oracle's VARCHAR2, in contrast to varchar in SQL Server), respective .NET Framework types and typed accessor methods are available.

Table 7-1 should give you a brief idea of when to use typed accessors and with what data type. You'll first consider SQL Server data types, their corresponding .NET Framework types, typed accessors, and special SQL Server–specific typed accessor methods designed particularly for returning objects of type System.Data.SqlTypes.

Table 7-1. *SQL Server Accessor Types*

SQL Server Data Types	.NET Framework Type	.NET Framework Typed Accessor	SqlType Typed Accessor
bigint	Int64	GetInt64	GetSqlInt64
binary	Byte[]	GetBytes	GetSqlBinary
bit	Boolean	GetBoolean	GetSqlBit
char	String or Char[]	GetString or GetChars	GetSqlString
datetime	DateTime	GetDateTime	GetSqlDateTime
decimal	Decimal	GetDecimal	GetSqlDecimal
float	Double	GetDouble	GetSqlDouble
image or long varbinary	Byte[]	GetBytes	GetSqlBinary
int	Int32	GetInt32	GetSqlInt32
money	Decimal	GetDecimal	GetSqlMoney
nchar	String or Char[]	GetString or GetChars	GetSqlString
ntext	String or Char[]	GetString or GetChars	GetSqlString
numeric	Decimal	GetDecimal	GetSqlDecimal
nvarchar	String or Char[]	GetString or GetChars	GetSqlString
real	Single	GetFloat	GetSqlSingle
smalldatetime	DateTime	GetDateTime	GetSqlDateTime
smallint	Int16	GetInt16	GetSqlInt16
smallmoney	Decimal	GetDecimal	GetSqlDecimal
sql_variant	Object	GetValue	GetSqlValue
long varchar	String or Char[]	GetString or GetChars	GetSqlString
timestamp	Byte[]	GetBytes	GetSqlBinary
tinyint	Byte	GetByte	GetSqlByte
uniqueidentifier	Guid	GetGuid	GetSqlGuid
varbinary	Byte[]	GetBytes	GetSqlBinary
varchar	String or Char[]	GetString or GetChars	GetSqlString

And now you'll look at some available OLE DB data types, their corresponding .NET Framework data types, and their typed accessor methods (see Table 7-2).

Table 7-2. *OLE DB Accessor Types*

OLE DB Type	.NET Framework Type	.NET Framework Typed Accessor
DBTYPE_I8	Int64	GetInt64
DBTYPE_BYTES	Byte[]	GetBytes
DBTYPE_BOOL	Boolean	GetBoolean
DBTYPE_BSTR	String	GetString
DBTYPE_STR	String	GetString
DBTYPE_CY	Decimal	GetDecimal
DBTYPE_DATE	DateTime	GetDateTime
DBTYPE_DBDATE	DateTime	GetDateTime
DBTYPE_DBTIME	DateTime	GetDateTime
DBTYPE_DBTIMESTAMP	DateTime	GetDateTime
DBTYPE_DECIMAL	Decimal	GetDecimal
DBTYPE_R8	Double	GetDouble
DBTYPE_ERROR	ExternalException	GetValue
DBTYPE_FILETIME	DateTime	GetDateTime
DBTYPE_GUID	Guid	GetGuid
DBTYPE_I4	Int32	GetInt32
DBTYPE_LONGVARCHAR	String	GetString
DBTYPE_NUMERIC	Decimal	GetDecimal
DBTYPE_R4	Single	GetFloat
DBTYPE_I2	Int16	GetInt16
DBTYPE_I1	Byte	GetByte
DBTYPE_UI8	UInt64	GetValue
DBTYPE_UI4	UInt32	GetValue
DBTYPE_UI2	UInt16	GetValue
DBTYPE_VARCHAR	String	GetString
DBTYPE_VARIANT	Object	GetValue
DBTYPE_WVARCHAR	String	GetString
DBTYPE_WSRT	String	GetString

To see typed accessor methods in action, let's now look at a console application that uses them. For this example, you'll use the Products table from the Northwind database.

Table 7-3 shows the data design of the table. Note that the data types given in the table will be looked up for their corresponding typed methods from Tables 7-1 and 7-2 so you can use them correctly in your application.

Table 7-3. Northwind Products *Table Data Types*

Column Name	Data Type	Length	Allow Nulls?
ProductID (unique)	int	4	No
ProductName	nvarchar	40	No
SupplierID	int	4	Yes
CategoryID	int	4	Yes
QuantityPerUnit	nvarchar	20	Yes
UnitPrice	money	8	Yes
UnitsInStock	smallint	2	Yes
UnitsOnOrder	smallint	2	Yes
ReorderLevel	smallint	2	Yes
Discontinued	bit	1	No

Try It Out: Using Typed Accessor Methods

To use typed accessor methods, follow these steps:

1. Add a C# console application named TypedMethods, and rename the Class1.cs file to TypedMethods.cs.

2. Replace the code in TypedMethods.cs with that in Listing 7-3.

Listing 7-3. TypedMethods

```
using System;
using System.Data;
using System.Data.SqlClient;

namespace TypedMethods
{
    class TypedMethods
    {
        static void Main(string[] args)
        {
            // Connection string
            string connString = @"
                server = (local)\netsdk;
                integrated security = sspi;
                database = northwind
            ";
```

```csharp
// Query
string sql = @"
   select
       productname,
       unitprice,
       unitsinstock,
       discontinued
   from
       products
";


// Pass connection string to connection
SqlConnection conn = new SqlConnection(connString);

try
{
   // Open connection
   conn.Open();

   // Create command
   SqlCommand cmd = new SqlCommand(sql, conn);

   // Get data reader
   SqlDataReader reader = cmd.ExecuteReader();

   // Fetch data
   while(reader.Read())
   {
      Console.WriteLine(
          "{0}\t {1}\t\t {2}\t {3}",
          // nvarchar
          reader.GetString(0).PadRight(30),
          // money
          reader.GetDecimal(1),
          // smallint
          reader.GetInt16(2),
          // bit
          reader.GetBoolean(3));
   }

   // Close data reader
   reader.Close();
}
catch(Exception e)
{
   Console.WriteLine("Error Occurred: " + e);
}
```

```
            finally
            {
                // Close connection
                conn.Close();
            }
        }
    }
}
```

3. Make this the startup project, and run it with Ctrl+F5. You should see the output in Figure 7-3.

Figure 7-3. TypedMethods

How It Works

After establishing a connection, you query the Products table for ProductName, UnitPrice, UnitsInStock, and Discontinued.

```
// Query
string sql = @"
    select
        productname,
        unitprice,
        unitsinstock,
        discontinued
    from
        products
";
```

The reason for our choice of columns was to deal with different kinds of data types and show how you could use relevant typed methods to obtain the correct results.

After obtaining a data reader (and executing the query) with ExecuteReader, you come to the part where you used the typed accessor methods.

```
// Fetch data
while(reader.Read())
{
    Console.WriteLine(
        "{0}\t {1}\t\t {2}\t {3}",
        // nvarchar
        reader.GetString(0).PadRight(30),
        // money
        reader.GetDecimal(1),
        // smallint
        reader.GetInt16(2),
        // bit
        reader.GetBoolean(3));
}
```

Tallying with the tables, given earlier, for native data types, you can see that you can access a nvarchar, a money, a smallint, and a bit data type in SQL Server by using the GetString, GetDecimal, GetInt16, and the GetBoolean accessor methods, respectively.

This technique is fast and completely type safe. By this we mean that the implicit conversions from native data types to the .NET Framework types are completely safe and handled, thus leveraging speed and performance. Also, if a typed method is used incorrectly—for example, with a noncompatible data type—an exception is thrown for invalid casts. For instance, if you try using the GetString method on a bit data type instead of using the GetBoolean method, a "Specified cast is not valid" exception will be thrown.

Talking about speed and performance, remember how much we've stressed using the right provider for a specific database? If you're using SQL Server 7.0 or newer, the .NET Framework has much more to offer. Along with these relatively general typed methods (you can use these typed methods with any version of SQL Server), the Framework offers optimized typed methods specifically designed for SQL Server 7 and newer. You can spot these typed methods by the addition of the phrase *Sql* in the middle. For instance, the GetString method's SQL Server 7 (and newer) counterpart is GetSqlString.

You can use these methods just like other typed methods, but it's worth mentioning that they return types in the System.Data.SqlTypes namespace. For instance, the GetSqlString method returns an object of type System.Data.SqlTypes.SqlString and not of type System.String, which the GetString method returns.

Getting Data About Data

So far all you've learned to do is retrieve data from the data source. Once you have a populated data reader in your hands, you can do a lot more. You're exposed to a number of useful methods that you can use for retrieving schema information or retrieving information directly related to the returned data. Table 7-4 describes the functions and properties of the data reader.

Table 7-4. *Data Reader Metadata Properties and Methods*

Method or Property Name	Description
Depth	A property that gets the depth of nesting for the current row
FieldCount	A property that holds the number of columns in a result set
GetDataTypeName	A method that accepts an index and returns a string containing the name of the column data type
GetFieldType	A method that accepts an index and returns the .NET Framework type of the object
GetName	A method that accepts an index and returns the name of the specified column
GetOrdinal	A method that accepts a column name and returns the column index

Let's look at a sample application that utilizes some of these methods and properties.

Try It Out: Getting Information About a Result Set with a Data Reader

To get information about a result set with a data reader, follow these steps:

1. Add a C# console application named ResultSetInfo, and rename the Class1.cs file to ResultSetInfo.cs.

2. Replace the code in ResultSetInfo.cs with that in Listing 7-4.

Listing 7-4. ResultSetInfo

```csharp
using System;
using System.Data;
using System.Data.SqlClient;

namespace ResultSetInfo
{
    class ResultSetInfo
    {
        static void Main(string[] args)
        {
            // Connection string
            string connString = @"
                server = (local)\netsdk;
                integrated security = sspi;
                database = northwind
            ";
```

```csharp
// Query
string sql = @"
   select
      contactname,
      contacttitle
   from
      customers
   where
      contactname like 'M%'
";

// Pass connection string to connection
SqlConnection conn = new SqlConnection(connString);

try
{
   conn.Open();

   SqlCommand cmd = new SqlCommand(sql, conn);

   SqlDataReader reader = cmd.ExecuteReader();

   // Get column names
   Console.WriteLine(
      "Column Name:\t{0} {1}",
      reader.GetName(0).PadRight(25),
      reader.GetName(1));

   // Get column data types
   Console.WriteLine(
      "Data Type:\t{0} {1}",
      reader.GetDataTypeName(0).PadRight(25),
      reader.GetDataTypeName(1));

   Console.WriteLine();

   while(reader.Read())
   {
      // Get column values for all rows
      Console.WriteLine(
         "\t\t{0} {1}",
         reader.GetString(0).ToString().PadRight(25),
         reader.GetString(1));
   }

   // Get number of columns
   Console.WriteLine();
   Console.WriteLine(
      "Number of columns in a row: {0}",
      reader.FieldCount);
```

```
            // Get info about each column
            Console.WriteLine(
                "'{0}' is at index {1} " +
                "and its type is: {2}",
                reader.GetName(0),
                reader.GetOrdinal("contactname"),
                reader.GetFieldType(0));

            Console.WriteLine(
                "'{0}' is at index {1} " +
                "and its type is: {2}",
                reader.GetName(1),
                reader.GetOrdinal("contacttitle"),
                reader.GetFieldType(1));

            reader.Close();
        }
        catch(Exception e)
        {
            Console.WriteLine("Error Occurred: " + e);
        }
        finally
        {
            conn.Close();
        }
    }
  }
}
```

3. Make this the startup project, and run it with Ctrl+F5. You should see the output in Figure 7-4.

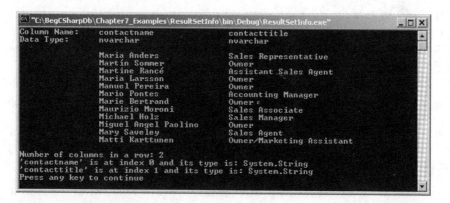

Figure 7-4. ResultSetInfo

How It Works

The GetName method gets a column name by its index. This method returns information *about* the result set, so it can be called before the first call to Read.

```
// Get column names
Console.WriteLine(
    "Column Name:\t{0} {1}",
    reader.GetName(0).PadRight(25),
    reader.GetName(1));
```

The GetDataTypeName method returns the database data type of a column. It too can be called before the first call to Read.

```
// Get column data types
Console.WriteLine(
    "Data Type:\t{0} {1}",
    reader.GetDataTypeName(0).PadRight(25),
    reader.GetDataTypeName(1));
```

The FieldCount property of the data reader contains the number of columns in the result set. This is useful for looping through columns without knowing their names or other attributes.

```
// Get number of columns
Console.WriteLine();
Console.WriteLine(
    "Number of columns in a row: {0}",
    reader.FieldCount);
```

Finally, we demonstrate how the GetOrdinal and GetFieldType methods are used. The former returns a column index based on its name; the latter returns the C# type. These are the converses of GetName and GetDataTypeName, respectively.

```
// Get info about each column
Console.WriteLine(
    "'{0}' is at index {1} " +
    "and its type is: {2}",
    reader.GetName(0),
    reader.GetOrdinal("contactname"),
    reader.GetFieldType(0));
```

So much for obtaining information about result sets. You'll now learn how to get information about schemas.

Getting Data About Tables

The term *schema* has several meanings in relational databases. Here, we use it to refer to the design of a data structure, particularly a database table. A table consists of rows and columns, and each column can have a different data type. The columns and their attributes (data type, length, and so on) make up the table's schema.

To retrieve schema information easily, you can call the GetSchemaTable method on a data reader. As the name suggests, this method returns a System.Data.DataTable object, which is a representation (schema) of the table queried and contains a collection of rows and columns in the form of DataRow and DataColumn objects. These rows and columns are returned as collection objects by the properties Rows and Columns of the DataTable class.

However, here's where a slight confusion usually occurs. Data columns aren't column values but are column definitions (also called *column schemas*) that represent and control the behavior of individual columns. The object can be looped through by using a column name indexer and can tell you a lot about the dataset. Let's begin with a practical demonstration of the GetSchemaTable method.

Try It Out: Getting Schema Information

To get schema information, follow these steps:

1. Add a C# console application named SchemaTable, and rename the Class1.cs file to SchemaTable.cs.

2. Replace the code in SchemaTable.cs with that in Listing 7-5.

Listing 7-5. SchemaTable

```
using System;
using System.Data;
using System.Data.SqlClient;

namespace SchemaTable
{
    class SchemaTable
    {
        static void Main(string[] args)
        {
            // Connection string
            string connString = @"
                server = (local)\netsdk;
                integrated security = sspi;
                database = northwind
            ";

            // Query
            string sql = @"
                select
                    *
                from
                    employees
            ";

            // Pass connection string to connection
            SqlConnection conn = new SqlConnection(connString);
```

```
        try
        {
            conn.Open();

            SqlCommand cmd = new SqlCommand(sql, conn);
            SqlDataReader reader = cmd.ExecuteReader();

            // Store the Employees schema in a data table
            DataTable schema = reader.GetSchemaTable();

            // Display info from each row in the data table.
            // Each row describes a column in the database table.
            foreach (DataRow row in schema.Rows)
            {
                foreach (DataColumn col in schema.Columns)
                    Console.WriteLine(col.ColumnName + " = " + row[col]);
                Console.WriteLine("----------------");
            }

            reader.Close();
        }
        catch(Exception e)
        {
            Console.WriteLine("Error Occurred: " + e);
        }
        finally
        {
            conn.Close();
        }
    }
  }
}
```

3. Make this the startup project, and run it with Ctrl+F5. You should see the output in Figure 7-5.

Figure 7-5. SchemaTable

How It Works

Other than connection similarities, the code is quite different from the code you saw earlier. When the call to the GetSchemaTable method is made (as follows), a populated instance of a data table is returned. You can use a data table to represent a complete table in a database, either in the form of a table that represents its schema or in the form of a table that holds all its original data for offline use.

```
// Store the Employees schema in a data table
DataTable schema = reader.GetSchemaTable();
```

In this example, once you grab hold of a schema table, you retrieve a collection of rows through the Rows property of DataTable and a collection of columns through the Columns property of the DataTable. (You can use the Rows property to add a new row into the table altogether

or remove one, and you can use the `Columns` property for adding or deleting an existing column—
we'll cover this in Chapter 8.) Each row returned by the table describes one column in the
original table, so for each of these rows, you traverse through the column's schema information
one by one, using a nested `foreach` loop.

```
// Display info from each row in the data table.
// Each row describes a column in the database table.
foreach (DataRow row in schema.Rows)
{
    foreach (DataColumn col in schema.Columns)
        Console.WriteLine(col.ColumnName + " = " + row[col]);
    Console.WriteLine("----------------");
}
```

Notice how you used the `ColumnName` property of the `DataColumn` object to retrieve the current schema name in the loop, and then you retrieved the value related to that schema by using
the familiar indexer-style method that uses the `DataRow` object. The `DataRow` accepts a number of
overloaded indexers, and this is only one of the few ways of doing it. You can also access the column schema separately if you give a schema name to the `DataRow` object, for example, like this:

```
Console.WriteLine("Null value allowed: " + col.AllowDBNull);
```

The previous line displays whether the column supports null values (in other words,
whether the `AllowDBNull` property of the data column is `true` [allowed] or `false`).

Using Multiple Result Sets with a Data Reader

Sometimes you may really want to get a job done quickly and also want to query the database
with two or more queries at the same time. As well as this, you wouldn't want the overall application performance to suffer in any way either by instantiating more than one command or
data reader or by exhaustively using the same objects over and over again, adding to the code
as you go.

So, is there a way you can get a single data reader to loop through multiple result sets?
Yes, data readers have a method, `NextResult`, that advances the reader to the next result set.
Let's try it.

Try It Out: Handling Multiple Result Sets

To handle multiple result sets, follow these steps:

1. Add a C# console application named `MultipleResults`, and rename the `Class1.cs` file
   to `MultipleResults.cs`.

2. Replace the code in `MultipleResults.cs` with that in Listing 7-6.

   Listing 7-6. `MultipleResults`

   ```
   using System;
   using System.Data;
   using System.Data.SqlClient;
   ```

```csharp
namespace MultipleResults
{
    class MultipleResults
    {
        static void Main(string[] args)
        {
            // Connection string
            string connString = @"
                server = (local)\netsdk;
                integrated security = sspi;
                database = northwind
            ";

            // Query 1
            string sql1 = @"
                select
                    companyname,
                    contactname
                from
                    customers
                where
                    companyname like 'A%'
            ";

            // Query 2
            string sql2 = @"
                select
                    firstname,
                    lastname
                from
                    employees
            ";

            // Combine queries
            string sql = sql1 + sql2;

            // Pass connection string to connection
            SqlConnection conn = new SqlConnection(connString);

            try
            {
                // Open connection
                conn.Open();

                // Get command
                SqlCommand cmd = new SqlCommand(sql, conn);
```

```csharp
            // Get data reader
            SqlDataReader reader = cmd.ExecuteReader();

            // Loop through result sets
            do
            {
               while(reader.Read())
               {
                  // Print one row at a time
                  Console.WriteLine("{0} : {1}", reader[0], reader[1]);
               }
               Console.WriteLine("".PadLeft(60, '='));
            }
            while(reader.NextResult());

            // Close data reader
            reader.Close();
         }
         catch(Exception e)
         {
            Console.WriteLine("Error Occurred: " + e);
         }
         finally
         {
            // Close connection
            conn.Close();
         }
      }
   }
}
```

3. Make this the startup project, and run it with Ctrl+F5. You should see the output in Figure 7-6.

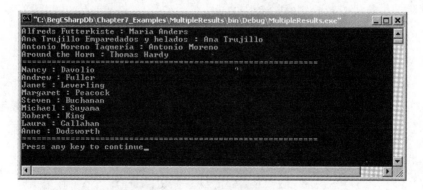

Figure 7-6. MultipleResults

How It Works

This program is essentially the same as the first, `DataLooper` (Listing 7-1). Here, you define two separate queries and then combine them.

```
// Combine queries
string sql = sql1 + sql2;
```

■**Caution** Some RDBMSs require an explicit character as a separator between multiple queries, but SQL Server requires only whitespace before subsequent SELECT keywords, which you have because of the verbatim strings.

This only other change is how you loop through the result sets. You nest the loop inside one that retrieves rows inside one that moves through result sets.

```
// Loop through result sets
do
{
   while(reader.Read())
   {
      // Print one row at a time
      Console.WriteLine("{0} : {1}", reader[0], reader[1]);
   }
   Console.WriteLine("".PadLeft(60, '='));
}
while(reader.NextResult());
```

We chose only two-character string columns per query to simplify things. Extending this to handle result tables with different numbers of columns and column types is straightforward.

Summary

In this chapter you learned how to use data readers to perform a variety of common tasks, from simply looping through single result sets to handling multiple result sets. You learned how to retrieve values for columns by column name and index and learned about the methods available for handling values of different data types. You also learned how to get information about result sets and get schema information.

CHAPTER 8

■ ■ ■

Introducing Datasets and Data Adapters

In the previous chapter you saw how to use data readers to access database data in a connected, forward-only, read-only fashion. Often, this is all you want to do, and a data reader suits your purposes perfectly.

In this chapter, you'll look at a new object for accessing data, the *dataset*. Unlike data readers, which are objects of data provider-specific classes that implement the System.Data.IDataReader interface, datasets are objects of the class System.Data.DataSet, a distinct ADO.NET component used by all data providers. Datasets are completely independent of and disconnected from data sources. Their fundamental purpose is to provide a relational view of data stored in an in-memory cache.

Note In yet another somewhat confusing bit of terminology, the class is named DataSet, but the generic term is spelled *dataset* (when one expects *data set*). Why Microsoft does this is unclear, especially since *data set* is the more common usage outside ADO.NET. Nonetheless, we'll follow the .NET convention and call DataSet objects *datasets*.

So, if a dataset isn't connected in any way to a database, then how do you populate it with data and save its data back to the database? This is where *data adapters* come in. Think of data adapters as bridges between datasets and data sources. Without a data adapter, a dataset can't access any kind of data source. The data adapter takes care of all connection details for the dataset, populates it with data, and updates the data source.

In this chapter, we'll cover the following:

- Datasets and data adapters

- How data is stored in a dataset with data tables, data rows, and data columns

- How to get different views of the data in a dataset

- How to manipulate data in a dataset

- How to persist changes in the dataset back to the original data source

- Working with datasets and XML

- Typed and untyped datasets

Understanding the Object Model

We'll start this chapter with a quick presentation of all the new objects you'll need to understand in order to work with datasets and data adapters. You'll start by looking at the difference between datasets and data readers and then move on to look in more detail at how data is structured within a dataset and how a dataset works in collaboration with a data adapter.

Datasets vs. Data Readers

If you simply want to read and display data, then you need to use only a data reader, as you saw in the previous chapter, particularly if you're working with large quantities of data. In situations where you need to loop through thousands or millions of rows, you want a fast sequential reader (reading a single row from the result set at one time), and the data reader does this job in an efficient way.

If you need to manipulate the data in any way and then update the database, then you need to use a dataset. A data adapter fills a dataset by using a data reader, and with a dataset, additional resources are needed to save data for disconnected use. You need to think about whether you really need a dataset; otherwise, you'll just be wasting resources. Unless you need to update the data source or use other dataset features such as reading and writing to XML files, exporting database schemas, and creating XML views of a database, you should use a data reader.

A Brief Introduction to Datasets

The notion of a dataset in ADO.NET is a big step in the world of multitiered database application development. When retrieving or modifying large amounts of data, maintaining an open connection to a data source while waiting for users to make requests is an enormous waste of precious resources.

Datasets help tremendously here, because they enable you to store and modify large amounts of data in a local cache, view the data as tables, and process the data in an *offline* mode (in other words, disconnected from the database).

Let's look at an example. Imagine you're trying to connect to a remote database server over the Internet for detailed information about some business transactions. You search on a particular date for all available transactions, and the results are displayed. Behind the scenes, your application creates a connection with the data source, joins a couple of tables, and retrieves the results. Suppose you now want to edit this information and add or remove details. Whatever the reason, your application will go through the same cycle over and over again: creating a new connection, joining tables, and retrieving data. Not only is there overhead in creating a new connection each time, but you may be doing a lot of other redundant work, especially if you're dealing with the same data. Wouldn't it be better if you could connect to the data source once, store the data locally in a structure that resembles a relational database, close the connection, modify the local data, and then propagate the changes to the data source when the time is right?

This is exactly what the dataset is designed to do. A dataset stores relational data as collections of *data tables*. You met data tables briefly in the previous chapter when a `System.Data.DataTable` object was to hold schema information. In that instance, however, the data table contained only schema information, but in a dataset, the data tables contain both metadata describing the structure of the data and the data itself.

Figure 8-1 shows the dataset architecture.

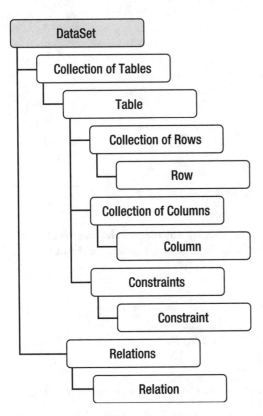

Figure 8-1. *Dataset architecture*

The architecture mirrors the logical design of a relational database. You'll see how to use data tables, data rows, and data columns in this chapter, but we'll leave relationships and constraints until Chapter 12.

A Brief Introduction to Data Adapters

When you first instantiate a dataset, it contains no data. You obtain a populated dataset by passing it to a data adapter, which takes care of connection details and is a component of a data provider. A dataset isn't part of a data provider. It's like a bucket, ready to be filled with water, but it needs an external pipe to let the water in. In other words, the dataset needs a data adapter to populate it with data and to support access to the data source.

Each data provider has its own data adapter in the same way that it has its own connection, command, and data reader. Figure 8-2 depicts the interactions between the dataset, data adapter, and data source.

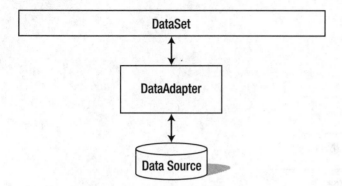

Figure 8-2. *Interactions between dataset, data adapter, and data source*

The data adapter constructor is overloaded. You can use any of the following to get a new data adapter. We're using the SQL Server data provider, but the constructors for the other data providers are analogous.

```
SqlDataAdapter da = new SqlDataAdapter();
SqlDataAdapter da = new SqlDataAdapter(cmd);
SqlDataAdapter da = new SqlDataAdapter(sql, conn);
SqlDataAdapter da = new SqlDataAdapter(sql, connString);
```

So, you can create a data adapter in four ways:

- You can use its parameterless constructor (assigning SQL and the connection later).

- You can pass its constructor a command (here, cmd is a SqlCommand object).

- You can pass a SQL string and a connection.

- You can pass a SQL string and a connection string.

You'll see all this working in action shortly. For now, we'll move on and show how you use data tables, data columns, and data rows. You'll use these in upcoming sections.

A Brief Introduction to Data Tables, Data Columns, and Data Rows

A data table is an instance of the class `System.Data.DataTable`. It's conceptually analogous to a relational table. As shown in Figure 8-1, a data table has collections of data rows and data columns. You can access these nested collections via the `Rows` and `Columns` properties of the data table.

A data table can represent a stand-alone independent table, either inside a dataset—as you'll see in this chapter—or as an object created by another method, as you saw in the previous chapter when a data table was returned by calling the method `GetSchemaTable` on a data reader.

A data column represents the schema of a column within a data table and can then be used to set or get column properties. For example, you could use it to set the default value of a column by assigning a value to the `DefaultValue` property of the data column.

You obtain the collection of data columns using the data table's `Columns` property, whose indexer accepts either a column name or a zero-based index; see the following example (where `dt` is a data table):

```
DataColumn col = dt.Columns["ContactName"];
DataColumn col = dt.Columns[2];
```

A data row represents the data in a row. You can programmatically add, update, or delete rows in a data table. To access rows in data table, you use `Rows` property, whose indexer accepts a zero-based index (for example, where `dt` is a data table).

```
DataRow row = dt.Rows[2];
```

That's enough theory for now. It's time to do some coding and see how these objects work together in practice!

Working with Datasets and Data Adapters

The dataset constructor is overloaded.

```
DataSet ds = new DataSet();
DataSet ds = new DataSet("MyDataSet");
```

If you use the parameterless constructor, the dataset name defaults to `NewDataSet`. If you need more than one dataset, it's good practice to use the other constructor and name it explicitly. However, you can always change the dataset name by setting its `DataSetName` property.

You can populate a dataset in one of two ways.

- Using a data adapter

- Reading from an XML document

In this chapter, you'll use data adapters. However, in the "Using Datasets and XML" section, you'll take a quick peek at the converse of the second method, when you write from a dataset to an XML document.

Try It Out: Populating a Dataset with a Data Adapter

In this example, you'll create a dataset, populate it with a data adapter, and then display its contents.

1. Create a new blank solution named Chapter8_Examples.

2. Add a C# console application named PopDataset, and rename the Class1.cs file to PopDataset.cs.

3. Replace the code in PopDataset.cs with that in Listing 8-1.

Listing 8-1. PopDataset

```
using System;
using System.Data;
using System.Data.SqlClient;

namespace PopDataset
{
    class PopDataset
    {
        static void Main()
        {
            // Connection string
            string connString = @"
                server = (local)\netsdk;
                integrated security = sspi;
                database = northwind
            ";

            // Query
            string sql = @"
                select
                    productname,
                    unitprice
                from
                    products
                where
                    unitprice < 20
            ";

            // Create connection
            SqlConnection conn = new SqlConnection(connString);
```

```csharp
        try
        {
            // Open connection
            conn.Open();

            // Create data adapter
            SqlDataAdapter da = new SqlDataAdapter(sql, conn);

            // Create and fill dataset
            DataSet ds = new DataSet();
            da.Fill(ds, "products");

            // Get data table
            DataTable dt = ds.Tables["products"];

            // Display data
            foreach (DataRow row in dt.Rows)
            {
                foreach (DataColumn col in dt.Columns)
                    Console.WriteLine(row[col]);
                Console.WriteLine("".PadLeft(20, '='));
            }
        }
        catch(Exception e)
        {
            Console.WriteLine("Error: " + e);
        }
        finally
        {
            // Close connection
            conn.Close();
        }
    }
  }
}
```

4. Run it with Ctrl+F5. You should see the output in Figure 8-3.

Figure 8-3. PopDataset

How It Works

After defining a query and opening a connection, you create and initialize a data adapter.

```
// Create data adapter
SqlDataAdapter da = new SqlDataAdapter(sql, conn);
```

You then create the dataset.

```
// Create and fill dataset
DataSet ds = new DataSet();
```

At this stage, all you have is an empty dataset. The key line is where you use the Fill method on the data adapter to execute the query, retrieve the data, and populate the dataset.

```
da.Fill(ds, "products");
```

The Fill method uses a data reader internally to access the table schema and data and then uses them to populate the dataset.

Note that this method isn't just used for filling datasets. It has a number of overloads and can also be used for filling an individual data table without a dataset, if needed.

If you don't provide a name for the table to Fill method, it will automatically be named Table*n*, where *n* starts as an empty string (the first table name is simply Table) and increments every time a new table is inserted into the dataset. It's better practice to explicitly name data tables, but here it doesn't really matter.

If the same query is run more than once, on the dataset that already contains data, then Fill updates the data, skipping the process of redefining the table based on the schema.

It's worth mentioning here that the following code would have produced the same result. Instead of passing the SQL and connection to the data adapter's constructor, you could have set its SelectCommand property with a command that you created with the appropriate SQL and connection.

```
// Create data adapter
SqlDataAdapter da = new SqlDataAdapter();
da.SelectCommand = new SqlCommand(sql, conn);
```

With a populated dataset at your disposal, you can now access the data in individual data tables. (The dataset contains only one data table.)

```
// Get data table
DataTable dt = ds.Tables["products"];
```

Finally, you use nested foreach loops to access the columns in each row and output their data values to the screen.

```
// Display data
foreach (DataRow row in dt.Rows)
{
    foreach (DataColumn col in dt.Columns)
        Console.WriteLine(row[col]);
    Console.WriteLine("".PadLeft(20, '='));
}
```

Filtering and Sorting in a DataSet

In the previous example, you saw how to extract data from a dataset. However, if you're working with datasets, then the chances are that you're going to want to do more with the data than merely displaying it. Often, you'll want to dynamically filter or sort the data. In the following example, you'll see how you can use data rows to do this.

Try It Out: Dynamically Filtering and Sorting Data in a Dataset

Follow these steps:

1. Add a C# console application named FilterSort, and rename the Class1.cs file to FilterSort.cs.

2. Replace the code in FilterSort.cs with that in Listing 8-2.

   Listing 8-2. FilterSort

   ```
   using System;
   using System.Data;
   using System.Data.SqlClient;
   ```

```
namespace FilterSort
{
    class FilterSort
    {
        static void Main(string[] args)
        {
            // Connection string
            string connString = @"
                server = (local)\netsdk;
                integrated security = sspi;
                database = northwind
            ";

            // Query 1
            string sql1 = @"
                select
                    *
                from
                    customers
            ";

            // Query 2
            string sql2 = @"
                select
                    *
                from
                    products
                where
                    unitprice < 10
            ";

            // Combine queries
            string sql = sql1 + sql2;

            // Create connection
            SqlConnection conn = new SqlConnection(connString);

            try
            {
                //Create data adapter
                SqlDataAdapter da = new SqlDataAdapter();
                da.SelectCommand = new SqlCommand(sql, conn);

                //Create and fill data set
                DataSet ds = new DataSet();
                da.Fill(ds, "customers");

                // Get the data tables collection
                DataTableCollection dtc = ds.Tables;
```

```csharp
            // Display data from first data table
            //
            // 1. Display output header
            Console.WriteLine("Results from Customers table:");
            Console.WriteLine(
                "CompanyName".PadRight(20) +
                "ContactName".PadLeft(23) + "\n");
            // 2. Set display filter
            string fl = "country = 'Germany'";
            // 3. Set sort
            string srt = "companyname asc";
            // 4. Display filtered and sorted data
            foreach (DataRow row in dtc["customers"].Select(fl, srt))
            {
              Console.WriteLine(
                "{0}\t{1}",
                row["CompanyName"].ToString().PadRight(25),
                row["ContactName"]);
            }

            // Display data from second data table
            //
            // 1. Display output header
            Console.WriteLine("\n----------------------------");
            Console.WriteLine("Results from Products table:");
            Console.WriteLine(
                "ProductName".PadRight(20) +
                "UnitPrice".PadLeft(21) + "\n");
            // 2. Display data
            foreach (DataRow row in dtc[1].Rows)
            {
                Console.WriteLine("{0}\t{1}",
                    row["productname"].ToString().PadRight(25),
                    row["unitprice"]);
            }
        }
        catch(Exception e)
        {
            Console.WriteLine("Error: " + e);
        }
        finally
        {
            // Close connection
            conn.Close();
        }
      }
    }
}
```

3. Make this the startup project, and run it with Ctrl+F5. You should see the output in Figure 8-4.

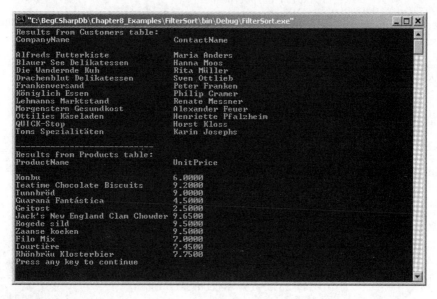

Figure 8-4. FilterSort

How It Works

You code and combine two queries and then create a connection.

```
// Query 1
string sql1 = @"
   select
      *
   from
      customers
";

// Query 2
string sql2 = @"
   select
      *
   from
      products
   where
      unitprice < 10
";

// Combine queries
string sql = sql1 + sql2;
```

```
// Create connection
SqlConnection conn = new SqlConnection(connString);
```

You create a dataset and a data adapter assigning the SelectCommand property of the data adapter a command that encapsulates the query and connection (for internal use by its Fill method).

```
//Create data set
DataSet ds = new DataSet();

//Create data adapter
SqlDataAdapter da = new SqlDataAdapter();
da.SelectCommand = new SqlCommand(sql, conn);
```

You then fill the dataset. Each query returns a separate result set, and each result set is stored in a separate data table (in the order in which the queries were specified). The first table is explicitly named customers; the second will be given the default name customers1.

```
//Fill data set
da.Fill(ds, "customers");
```

You get the data table collection from the dataset Tables property for ease of reference later.

```
// Get the data tables collection
DataTableCollection dtc = ds.Tables;
```

As part of displaying the first data table, you declare two strings.

```
// 2. Set display filter
string fl = "country = 'Germany'";
// 3. Set sort
string srt = "companyname asc";
```

The first string is a *filter expression* that specifies row selection criteria. It's syntactically the same as a SQL WHERE clause predicate. You want only rows where the Country column equals "Germany". The second string specifies your sort criteria and is syntactically the same as a SQL ORDER BY specifier, giving a data column name and sort sequence.

You use a foreach loop to display the rows selected from the data table, passing the filter and sort strings to the Select method of the data table. This particular data table is the one named customers in the data table collection.

```
// 4. Display filtered and sorted data
foreach (DataRow row in dtc["customers"].Select(fl, srt))
{
  Console.WriteLine(
      "{0}\t{1}",
      row["CompanyName"].ToString().PadRight(25),
      row["ContactName"]);
}
```

Here you obtain a reference to a single data table from the collection (the dtc object) using the table name that you specified when creating the dataset. The overloaded Select method does an internal search on the data table, filters out rows not satisfying the selection criterion, sorts the result as prescribed, and finally returns an array of data rows. You access each column in the row, using the column name in the indexer.

It's important to note that you could have achieved the same result—much more efficiently— had you simply used a different query for the Customer data.

```
select
    *
from
    customers
where
    country = 'Germany'
order by
    companyname
```

This would be ideal in terms of performance, but it'd be feasible only if the data you needed were limited to these specific rows in this particular sequence. However, if you were building a more elaborate system, it may be better to pull all the data once from the database (as you do here) and then filter and sort it in different ways. ADO.NET's rich suite of methods for manipulating datasets and their components gives you a broad range of techniques for meeting specific needs in an optimal way.

■**Tip** In general, try to exploit SQL, rather than code C# procedures, to get the data you need from the database. Database servers are optimized to perform selections and sorts, as well as other things. Queries can be far more sophisticated and powerful than the ones you've been playing with in this chapter. By carefully (and creatively) coding queries to return *exactly* what you need, you not only minimize resource demands (on memory, network bandwidth, and so on) but also reduce the code you must write to manipulate and format result set data.

The loop through the second data table is interesting mainly for its first line

```
foreach (DataRow row in dtc[1].Rows)
```

which uses an ordinal index. Since you didn't rename the second data table (you could have done so with its TableName property), it was better to use the index rather than the name (customers1), since a change to the name in the Fill call would require you to change it here, an unlikely thing to remember to do, if the case ever arose.

Comparing FilterSort to PopDataset

In the first example, PopDataset (Listing 8-1), you saw how simple it is to get data into a dataset. The second example, FilterSort (Listing 8-2), was just a variation, demonstrating how multiple result sets are handled and how to filter and sort data tables. However, the two programs have one major difference. Did you notice it?

FilterSort doesn't explicitly open a connection! In fact, it's the first (but won't be the last) program you've written that doesn't. Why doesn't it?

The answer is simple but *very* important. The Fill method *automatically* opens a connection if it's not open when Fill is called. It then closes the connection after filling the dataset. However, if a connection is open when Fill is called, it uses that connection and *doesn't* close it afterward.

So, although datasets are completely independent of databases (and connections), just because you're using a dataset doesn't mean you're running disconnected from a database. If you want to run disconnected, use datasets, but don't open connections before filling them (or, if a connection is open, close it first). Datasets in themselves don't imply either connected or disconnected operations.

You left the standard connection closed in the finally block. Since it can be called without error on a closed connection, it presents no problems if called unnecessarily but definitely guarantees that the connection will be closed, whatever may happen in the try block.

■**Note** If you want to prove this for yourself, simply open the connection in FilterSort before calling Fill and then display the value of the connection's State property. It will be Open. Comment out the Open call, and run it again. State will be closed.

Using Data Views

In the previous example, you saw how to dynamically filter and sort data contained by a data table using the Select method. However, ADO.NET has another approach for doing much the same thing and more, *data views*. A data view (an instance of class System.Data.DataView) enables you to create dynamic views of the data stored in an underlying data table, reflecting all the changes made to its content and the ordering. This differs from the Select method, which returns an array of data rows whose contents reflect the changes to data values but not the data ordering.

■**Note** A *data view* is a dynamic representation of the contents of a data table. Like a SQL view, it doesn't actually hold data.

Try It Out: Refining Data with a Data View

We won't cover all aspects of data views here, as they're beyond the scope of this book. However, to show how it can be used, we'll present a short example that uses a data view to dynamically sort and filter an underlying data table.

1. Add a C# console application named DataViewExample, and rename the Class1.cs file to DataViewExample.cs.

2. Replace the code in DataViewExample.cs with that in Listing 8-3.

Listing 8-3. DataViewExample

```
using System;
using System.Data;
using System.Data.SqlClient;

namespace DataViewExample
{
    class DataViewExample
    {
        static void Main()
        {
            // Connection string
            string connString = @"
                server = (local)\netsdk;
                integrated security = sspi;
                database = northwind
            ";

            // Query
            string sql = @"
                select
                    contactname,
                    country
                from
                    customers
            ";

            // Create connection
            SqlConnection conn = new SqlConnection(connString);

            try
            {
                //Create data adapter
                SqlDataAdapter da = new SqlDataAdapter();
                da.SelectCommand = new SqlCommand(sql, conn);

                //Create and fill dataset
                DataSet ds = new DataSet();
                da.Fill(ds, "customers");

                //Get data table reference
                DataTable dt = ds.Tables["customers"];
```

```
        // Create data view
        DataView dv = new DataView(
            dt,
            "country = 'Germany'",
            "country",
            DataViewRowState.CurrentRows);

        // Display data from data view
        foreach (DataRowView drv in dv)
        {
            for (int i = 0; i < dv.Table.Columns.Count; i++)
                Console.Write(drv[i] + "\t");
                Console.WriteLine();
        }
    }
    catch(Exception e)
    {
        Console.WriteLine("Error: " + e);
    }
    finally
    {
        // Close connection
        conn.Close();
    }
}
}
}
```

3. Make this the startup project, and run it with Ctrl+F5. You should see the output in Figure 8-5.

Figure 8-5. DataViewExample

How It Works

This program is basically the same as the other examples, so we'll focus on its use of a data view. You create a new data view and initialize it by passing four parameters to its constructor.

```
// Create data view
DataView dv = new DataView(
    dt,
    "country = 'Germany'",
    "country",
    DataViewRowState.CurrentRows);
```

The first parameter is a data table, the second is a filter for the contents of the data table, the third is the sort column, and the fourth specifies the types of rows to include in the data view.

System.Data.DataViewRowState is an enumeration of states that rows can have in a data view's underlying data table. Table 8-1 summarizes the states.

Table 8-1. *Data View Row States*

DataViewRowState **Members**	Description
Added	A new row
CurrentRows	Current rows including unchanged, new, and modified ones
Deleted	A deleted row
ModifiedCurrent	The current version of a modified row
ModifiedOriginal	The original version of a modified row
None	None of the rows
OriginalRows	Original rows, including unchanged and deleted
Unchanged	A row that hasn't been modified

Every time a row is added, modified, or deleted, its row state changes to the appropriate one in Table 8-1. This is useful if you're interested in retrieving, sorting, or filtering specific rows based on their state (for example, all new rows in the data table or all rows that have been modified).

You then loop through the rows in the data view.

```
// Display data from data view
foreach (DataRowView drv in dv)
{
    for (int i = 0; i < dv.Table.Columns.Count; i++)
        Console.Write(drv[i] + "\t");
        Console.WriteLine();
}
```

Just as a data row represents a single row in a data table, a *data row view* (perhaps it would have been better to call it a *data view row*) represents a single row in a data view. You retrieve the filtered and the sorted column data for each data row view and output it to the console.

As this simple example suggests, data views offer a powerful and flexible means of dynamically changing what data one works with in a data table.

Modifying Data in a Dataset

In the following sections, you'll work through a practical example showing a number of ways to update data in data tables programmatically. Note that here you'll just modify the data in the dataset but not update the data in the database. You'll see in the "Propagating Changes to a Data Source" section how to persist changes to a dataset in the original data source.

■**Note** Changes you make to a dataset aren't automatically propagated to a database. To save the changes in a database, you need to connect to the database again and explicitly perform the necessary updates.

Try It Out: Modifying a Data Table in a Dataset

Follow these steps:

1. Add a C# console application named ModifyDataTable, and rename the Class1.cs file to ModifyDataTable.cs.

2. Replace the code in ModifyDataTable.cs with that in Listing 8-4.

   Listing 8-4. ModifyDataTable

```
using System;
using System.Data;
using System.Data.SqlClient;

namespace ModifyDataTable
{
    class ModifyDataTable
    {
        static void Main()
        {
            // Connection string
            string connString = @"
                server = (local)\netsdk;
                integrated security = sspi;
                database = northwind
            ";

            // Query
            string sql = @"
                select
                    *
                from
                    employees
                where
                    country = 'UK'
            ";
```

```csharp
// Create connection
SqlConnection conn = new SqlConnection(connString);

try
{
    //Create data adapter
    SqlDataAdapter da = new SqlDataAdapter();
    da.SelectCommand = new SqlCommand(sql, conn);

    // Create and fill dataset
    DataSet ds = new DataSet();
    da.Fill(ds, "employees");

    // Get data table reference
    DataTable dt = ds.Tables["employees"];

    // FirstName column should be nullable
    dt.Columns["firstname"].AllowDBNull = true;

    // Modify City in first row
    dt.Rows[0]["city"] = "Wilmington";

    // Add a row
    DataRow newRow = dt.NewRow();
    newRow["firstname"] = "Roy";
    newRow["lastname"] = "Beatty";
    newRow["titleofcourtesy"] = "Sir";
    newRow["city"] = "Birmingham";
    newRow["country"] = "UK";
    dt.Rows.Add(newRow);

    // Display Rows
    foreach (DataRow row in dt.Rows)
    {
        Console.WriteLine(
            "{0} {1} {2}",
            row["firstname"].ToString().PadRight(15),
            row["lastname"].ToString().PadLeft(25),
            row["city"]);
    }

    //
    // Code for updating the database would come here
    //
}
catch(Exception e)
```

```
            {
                Console.WriteLine("Error: " + e);
            }
            finally
            {
                // Close connection
                conn.Close();
            }
        }
    }
}
```

3. Make this the startup project, and run it with Ctrl+F5. You should see the output in Figure 8-6.

Figure 8-6. ModifyDataTable

How It Works

As before, you use a single data table from the dataset.

```
// Get data table reference
DataTable dt = ds.Tables["employees"];
```

Next, you can see an example of how you can change the schema information. You select the FirstName column, whose AllowNull property is set to false in the database, and you change it—just for the purposes of demonstration—to true.

```
// FirstName column should be nullable
dt.Columns["firstname"].AllowDBNull = true;
```

Note that you could have used an ordinal index (for example, dt.Columns[1]) if you knew what the index for the column was, but using * to select all columns makes this less reliable since the position of a column may change if the database table schema changed.

You can modify a record using the same technique. You simply select the appropriate row and set its columns to whatever values you want, consistent with the column data types, of course. The following line shows the City column of the first row of the dataset being changed to *Wilmington*:

```
// Modify City in first row
dt.Rows[0]["city"] = "Wilmington";
```

Next you add a new row to the data table, like so:

```
// Add a row
DataRow newRow = dt.NewRow();
newRow["firstname"] = "Roy";
newRow["lastname"] = "Beatty";
newRow["titleofcourtesy"] = "Sir";
newRow["city"] = "Birmingham";
newRow["country"] = "UK";
dt.Rows.Add(newRow);
```

The NewRow method creates a data row (a System.Data.DataRow instance). You use the data row's indexer to assign values to its columns. Finally, you add the new row to the data table, calling the Add method on the data table's Rows property, which references the rows collection.

Note that you don't provide a value for EmployeeID since it's an IDENTITY column. If you persisted the changes to the database, then SQL Server would automatically provide a value for it.

Updating data sources requires learning more about data adapter methods and properties. Let's take a look at these now.

Propagating Changes to a Data Source

You've seen how a data adapter populates a dataset's data tables. What you haven't looked at yet is how a data adapter updates and synchronizes a data source with data from a dataset. It has three properties that support this (analogous to its SelectCommand property that supports queries).

- UpdateCommand

- InsertCommand

- DeleteCommand

We'll describe each of these properties briefly and then put them to work.

UpdateCommand Property

The UpdateCommand property of the data adapter holds the command used to update the data source when the data adapter's Update method is called.

For example, to update the City column in the Employees table with the data from a data table, one approach is to write code such as the following (where da is the data adapter, dt is the data table, conn is the connection, and ds is the dataset):

```
// Create command to update Employees City column
da.UpdateCommand = new SqlCommand(
    "update employees "
  + "set "
  + "   city = "
  +         "'" + dt.Rows[0]["city"] + "' "
  + "where employeeid = "
  +         "'" + dt.Rows[0]["employeeid"] + "' "
  , conn);
```

```
// Update Employees table
da.Update(ds, "employees");
```

This isn't very pretty—or useful. Basically, you coded an UPDATE statement and embedded two data column values for the first row in a data table in it. It's valid SQL, but that's its only virtue and it's not much of one, since it updates only one database row, the row in Employees corresponding to the first data row in the employees data table.

Another approach works for any number of rows. Recall from the CommandExampleParameters program in Chapter 6 how you used command parameters for INSERT statements. You can use them in any query or data manipulation statement. Let's recode the previous with command parameters.

```
// SQL to update Employees
string sql = @"
   update employees
   set
      city = @city
   where
      employeeid = @employeeid
";

// Update employees
//
// 1. Create command
SqlCommand cmd = new SqlCommand(sql, conn);
//
// 2. Map parameters
//
// 2.1. City
cmd.Parameters.Add(
   "@city",
   SqlDbType.NVarChar,
   15,
   "city");
//
// 2.2. Employee ID
SqlParameter parm =
   cmd.Parameters.Add(
      "@employeeid",
      SqlDbType.Int,
      4,
      "employeeid");
parm.SourceVersion = DataRowVersion.Original;

// Update Employees
da.UpdateCommand = cmd;
da.Update(ds, "employees");
```

Try It Out: Propagating Dataset Changes to a Data Source

Follow these steps:

1. Add a C# console application named PropagateChanges, and rename the Class1.cs file to PropagateChanges.cs.

2. Replace the code in PropagateChanges.cs with that in Listing 8-5. This is a variation on ModifyDataTable in Listing 8-4, with the nullability and insertion logic removed since they're irrelevant here.

Listing 8-5. PropagateChanges

```csharp
using System;
using System.Data;
using System.Data.SqlClient;

namespace PropagateChanges
{
    class PropagateChanges
    {
        static void Main()
        {
            // Connection string
            string connString = @"
                server = (local)\netsdk;
                integrated security = sspi;
                database = northwind
            ";

            // Query
            string qry = @"
                select
                    *
                from
                    employees
                where
                    country = 'UK'
            ";

            // SQL to update employees
            string upd = @"
                update employees
                set
                    city = @city
                where
                    employeeid = @employeeid
            ";
```

```csharp
// Create connection
SqlConnection conn = new SqlConnection(connString);

try
{
    //Create data adapter
    SqlDataAdapter da = new SqlDataAdapter();
    da.SelectCommand = new SqlCommand(qry, conn);

    // Create and fill dataset
    DataSet ds = new DataSet();
    da.Fill(ds, "employees");

    // Get data table reference
    DataTable dt = ds.Tables["employees"];

    // Modify City in first row
    dt.Rows[0]["city"] = "Wilmington";

    // Display Rows
    foreach (DataRow row in dt.Rows)
    {
        Console.WriteLine(
            "{0} {1} {2}",
            row["firstname"].ToString().PadRight(15),
            row["lastname"].ToString().PadLeft(25),
            row["city"]);
    }

    // Update employees
    //
    // 1. Create command
    SqlCommand cmd = new SqlCommand(upd, conn);
    //
    // 2. Map parameters
    //
    // 2.1. City
    cmd.Parameters.Add(
        "@city",
        SqlDbType.NVarChar,
        15,
        "city");
    //
    // 2.2. Employee ID
    SqlParameter parm =
        cmd.Parameters.Add(
            "@employeeid",
```

```
                    SqlDbType.Int,
                    4,
                    "employeeid");
                parm.SourceVersion = DataRowVersion.Original;
                //
                // 3. Update employees
                da.UpdateCommand = cmd;
                da.Update(ds, "employees");
            }
            catch(Exception e)
            {
                Console.WriteLine("Error: " + e);
            }
            finally
            {
                // Close connection
                conn.Close();
            }
        }
    }
}
```

3. Make this the startup project, and run it with Ctrl+F5. You should see the output in Figure 8-7.

Figure 8-7. PropagateChanges

How It Works

You added an UPDATE statement (and changed the name of the original query string variable from sql to qry in order to clearly distinguish it from this statement).

```
// SQL to update employees
string upd = @"
    update employees
    set
      firstname = @firstname
    where
      employeeid = @employeeid
";
```

You replaced the update comment in the try block with quite a bit of code. Let's look at it piece by piece. Creating a command is nothing new, but notice that you use the update SQL variable (upd), not the query one (sql).

```
// Update employees
//
// 1. Create command
SqlCommand cmd = new SqlCommand(upd, conn);
```

Then you configure the command parameters. The @firstname parameter is mapped to a data column named firstname. Note that you don't specify the data table, but you must be sure the type and length are compatible with this column in whatever data table you eventually use.

```
// 2.1. First name
cmd.Parameters.Add(
    "@firstname",
    SqlDbType.NVarChar,
    10,
    "firstname");
```

Next, you configure the @employeeid parameter, mapping it to a data column named employeeid. Unlike @firstname, which by default takes values from the current version of the data table, you want to make sure that @employeeid gets values from the version *before* any changes. Although it doesn't really matter here, since you didn't change any employee IDs, it's a good habit to specify the original version for primary keys, so if they do change, the correct rows are accessed in the database table. Note also that you save the reference returned by the Add method so you can set its SourceVersion property. Since you didn't need to do anything else with @firstname, you didn't have to save a reference to it.

```
// 2.2. Employee ID
SqlParameter parm =
    cmd.Parameters.Add(
        "@employeeid",
        SqlDbType.Int,
        4,
        "employeeid");
parm.SourceVersion = DataRowVersion.Original;
```

Finally, you set the data adapter's UpdateCommand property with the command to update the Employees table so it will be the SQL the data adapter executes when you call its Update method. You then call Update on the data adapter to propagate the change to the database. Here you had only one change, but since the SQL is parameterized, the data adapter will look for all changed rows in the employees data table and submit updates for all of them to the database.

```
// 3. Update employees
da.UpdateCommand = cmd;
da.Update(ds, "employees");
```

If you check with Server Explorer or the SQL Tool application, you'll see the update has been propagated to the database. The city for employee Steven Buchanan is now Wilmington, not London.

InsertCommand Property

The data adapter uses the InsertCommand property for inserting rows into a table. Upon calling the Update method, all rows added to the data table would be searched for and propagated to the database.

Let's again modify ModifyDataTable (Listing 8-4) to propagate its new row to the database.

Try It Out: Propagating New Dataset Rows to a Data Source

Follow these steps:

1. Add a C# console application named PropagateAdds, and rename the Class1.cs file to PropagateAdds.cs.

2. Replace the code in PropagateAdds.cs with that in Listing 8-6. This is a variation on ModifyDataTable in Listing 8-4, with the nullability and update logic removed since they're irrelevant here.

Listing 8-6. PropagateAdds

```
using System;
using System.Data;
using System.Data.SqlClient;

namespace PropagateAdds
{
    class PropagateAdds
    {
        static void Main()
        {
            // Connection string
            string connString = @"
                server = (local)\netsdk;
                integrated security = sspi;
                database = northwind
            ";

            // Query
            string qry = @"
                select
                    *
                from
                    employees
                where
                    country = 'UK'
            ";
```

```
// SQL to insert employees
string ins = @"
    insert into employees
    (
        firstname,
        lastname,
        titleofcourtesy,
        city,
        country
    )
    values
    (
        @firstname,
        @lastname,
        @titleofcourtesy,
        @city,
        @country
    )
";

// Create connection
SqlConnection conn = new SqlConnection(connString);

try
{
    //Create data adapter
    SqlDataAdapter da = new SqlDataAdapter();
    da.SelectCommand = new SqlCommand(qry, conn);

    // Create and fill dataset
    DataSet ds = new DataSet();
    da.Fill(ds, "employees");

    // Get data table reference
    DataTable dt = ds.Tables["employees"];

    // Add a row
    DataRow newRow = dt.NewRow();
    newRow["firstname"] = "Roy";
    newRow["lastname"] = "Beatty";
    newRow["titleofcourtesy"] = "Sir";
    newRow["city"] = "Birmingham";
    newRow["country"] = "UK";
    dt.Rows.Add(newRow);
```

```
                    // Display Rows
                    foreach (DataRow row in dt.Rows)
                    {
                        Console.WriteLine(
                            "{0} {1} {2}",
                            row["firstname"].ToString().PadRight(15),
                            row["lastname"].ToString().PadLeft(25),
                            row["city"]);
                    }

                    // Insert employees
                    //
                    // 1. Create command
                    SqlCommand cmd = new SqlCommand(ins, conn);
                    //
                    // 2. Map parameters
                    cmd.Parameters.Add(
                        "@firstname",
                        SqlDbType.NVarChar,
                        10,
                        "firstname");
                    cmd.Parameters.Add(
                        "@lastname",
                        SqlDbType.NVarChar,
                        20,
                        "lastname");
                    cmd.Parameters.Add(
                        "@titleofcourtesy",
                        SqlDbType.NVarChar,
                        25,
                        "titleofcourtesy");
                    cmd.Parameters.Add(
                        "@city",
                        SqlDbType.NVarChar,
                        15,
                        "city");
                    cmd.Parameters.Add(
                        "@country",
                        SqlDbType.NVarChar,
                        15,
                        "country");
                    //
                    // 3. Insert employees
                    da.InsertCommand = cmd;
                    da.Update(ds, "employees");
                }
                catch(Exception e)
```

```
        {
            Console.WriteLine("Error: " + e);
        }
        finally
        {
            // Close connection
            conn.Close();
        }
    }
}
}
```

3. Make this the startup project, and run it with Ctrl+F5. You should see the output in Figure 8-8.

Figure 8-8. PropagateAdds

How It Works

You added an INSERT statement (and changed the name of the original query string variable from sql to qry in order to clearly distinguish it from this statement).

```
// SQL to insert employees
string ins = @"
    insert into employees
    (
        firstname,
        lastname,
        titleofcourtesy,
        city,
        country
    )
    values
    (
        @firstname,
        @lastname,
        @titleofcourtesy,
        @city,
        @country
    )
";
```

You replaced the update comment in the try block with quite a bit of code. Let's look at it piece by piece. Creating a command is nothing new, but notice that you use the update SQL variable (upd), not the query one (sql).

```
// Insert employees
//
// 1. Create command
SqlCommand cmd = new SqlCommand(upd, conn);
```

Then you configure the command parameters. The five columns for which you'll provide values are each mapped to a named command parameter. You don't supply the primary key value since it's generated by SQL Server, and the other columns are nullable, so you don't have to provide values for them. Note that all the values are current values, so you don't have to specify the SourceVersion property.

```
// 2. Map parameters
cmd.Parameters.Add(
    "@firstname",
    SqlDbType.NVarChar,
    10,
    "firstname");
cmd.Parameters.Add(
    "@lastname",
    SqlDbType.NVarChar,
    20,
    "lastname");
cmd.Parameters.Add(
    "@titleofcourtesy",
    SqlDbType.NVarChar,
    25,
    "titleofcourtesy");
cmd.Parameters.Add(
    "@city",
    SqlDbType.NVarChar,
    15,
    "city");
cmd.Parameters.Add(
    "@country",
    SqlDbType.NVarChar,
    15,
    "country");
```

Finally, you set the data adapter's InsertCommand property with the command to insert into the Employees table so it will be the SQL the data adapter executes when you call its Update method. You then call Update on the data adapter to propagate the change to the database. Here you added only one row, but since the SQL is parameterized, the data adapter will look for all new rows in the employees data table and submit inserts for all of them to the database.

```
// 3. Insert employees
da.InsertCommand = cmd;
da.Update(ds, "employees");
```

If you check with Server Explorer or the SQL Tool application, you'll see the new row has been propagated to the database. Sir Roy Beatty is now in the Employees table.

DeleteCommand Property

You use the DeleteCommand property to execute SQL DELETE statements.

Let's again modify ModifyDataTable (Listing 8-4) to propagate its new row to the database.

Try It Out: Propagating New Dataset Rows to a Data Source

Follow these steps:

1. Add a C# console application named PropagateDeletes, and rename the Class1.cs file to PropagateDeletes.cs.

2. Replace the code in PropagateDeletes.cs with that in Listing 8-7. This is a variation on ModifyDataTable in Listing 8-4, with irrelevant logic removed.

Listing 8-7. PropagateDeletes

```
using System;
using System.Data;
using System.Data.SqlClient;

namespace PropagateDeletes
{
    class PropagateDeletes
    {
        static void Main()
        {
            // Connection string
            string connString = @"
                server = (local)\netsdk;
                integrated security = sspi;
                database = northwind
            ";

            // Query
            string qry = @"
                select
                    *
                from
                    employees
                where
                    country = 'UK'
            ";
```

```csharp
// SQL to delete employees
string del = @"
   delete from employees
   where
      employeeid = @employeeid
";

// Create connection
SqlConnection conn = new SqlConnection(connString);

try
{
   //Create data adapter
   SqlDataAdapter da = new SqlDataAdapter();
   da.SelectCommand = new SqlCommand(qry, conn);

   // Create and fill dataset
   DataSet ds = new DataSet();
   da.Fill(ds, "employees");

   // Get data table reference
   DataTable dt = ds.Tables["employees"];

   // Delete employees
   //
   // 1. Create command
   SqlCommand cmd = new SqlCommand(del, conn);
   //
   // 2. Map parameters
   cmd.Parameters.Add(
      "@employeeid",
      SqlDbType.Int,
      4,
      "employeeid");
   //
   // 3. Select employees
   string filt = @"
         firstname = 'Roy'
         and
         lastname = 'Beatty'
   ";
   //
   // 4. Delete employees
   foreach (DataRow row in dt.Select(filt))
   {
      row.Delete();
   }
   da.DeleteCommand = cmd;
   da.Update(ds, "employees");
```

```
            // Display Rows
            foreach (DataRow row in dt.Rows)
            {
                Console.WriteLine(
                    "{0} {1} {2}",
                    row["firstname"].ToString().PadRight(15),
                    row["lastname"].ToString().PadLeft(25),
                    row["city"]);
            }
        }
        catch(Exception e)
        {
            Console.WriteLine("Error: " + e);
        }
        finally
        {
            // Close connection
            conn.Close();
        }
    }
  }
}
```

3. Make this the startup project, and run it with Ctrl+F5. You should see the output in Figure 8-9.

Figure 8-9. PropagateDeletes

How It Works

You added a DELETE statement (and changed the name of the original query string variable from sql to qry in order to clearly distinguish it from this statement).

```
// SQL to delete employees
string del = @"
   delete from employees
   where
      employeeid = @employeeid
";
```

You inserted the delete code ahead of the display. After creating a command and mapping a parameter, like so:

```
// Delete employees
//
// 1. Create command
SqlCommand cmd = new SqlCommand(del, conn);
//
// 2. Map parameters
cmd.Parameters.Add(
    "@employeeid",
    SqlDbType.Int,
    4,
    "employeeid");
```

you select the row to delete and delete it. Actually, you select all rows for employees named Roy Beatty, since you don't know (or care about) their employee IDs. Although you expect only one row to be selected, you use a loop to delete all the rows. (If you ran the PropagateInserts program multiple times, you'd have more than one row that matches this selection criteria.)

```
// 3. Select employees
string filt = @"
        firstname = 'Roy'
        and
        lastname = 'Beatty'
";
//
// 4. Delete employees
foreach (DataRow row in dt.Select(filt))
{
    row.Delete();
}
da.DeleteCommand = cmd;
da.Update(ds, "employees");
```

Finally, you set the data adapter's DeleteCommand property with the command to delete from the Employees table so it will be the SQL the data adapter executes when you call its Update method. You then call Update on the data adapter to propagate the changes to the database. Whether you delete one row or several, your SQL is parameterized, and the data adapter will look for all deleted rows in the employees data table and submit deletes for all of them to the database.

If you check with Server Explorer or the SQL Tool application, you'll see the row has been removed from the database. Sir Roy Beatty is no longer in the Employees table.

Command Builders

Although straightforward, it's a bit of a hassle to code SQL statements for the UpdateCommand, InsertCommand, or DeleteCommand properties, so each data provider has its own *command builder*. If a data table corresponds to a single database table, then you can use a command builder to automatically generate the appropriate UpdateCommand, InsertCommand, and DeleteCommand properties for a data adapter. This is all done transparently when a call is made to the data adapter's Update method.

To be able to dynamically generate INSERT, DELETE, and UPDATE statements, the command builder uses the data adapter's SelectCommand property to extract metadata for the database table. If any changes are made to the SelectCommand property after invoking the Update method, you should call the RefreshSchema method on the command builder to refresh the metadata accordingly.

To create a command builder, you create an instance of the data provider's command builder class, passing a data adapter to its constructor. For example, the following code creates a SQL Server command builder:

```
SqlDataAdapter da = new SqlDataAdapter();
SqlCommandBuilder cb = new SqlCommandBuilder(da);
```

■**Note** For a command builder to work, the SelectCommand data adapter property must contain a query that returns either a primary key or a unique key for the database table. If none is present, an InvalidOperation exception is generated, and the commands aren't generated.

Let's convert the PropagateAdds application in Listing 8-6 to use a command builder.

Try It Out: Using SqlCommandBuilder

Follow these steps:

1. Add a C# console application named PropagateAddsBuilder, and rename the Class1.cs file to PropagateAddsBuilder.cs.

2. Replace the code in PropagateAddsBuilder.cs with that in Listing 8-8. This is a variation on PropagateAdds in Listing 8-6.

   Listing 8-8. PropagateAddsBuilder

   ```
   using System;
   using System.Data;
   using System.Data.SqlClient;

   namespace PropagateAddsBuilder
   {
       class PropagateAddsBuilder
       {
           static void Main()
           {
               // Connection string
               string connString = @"
   ```

```
        server = (local)\netsdk;
        integrated security = sspi;
        database = northwind
";

// Query
string qry = @"
    select
        *
    from
        employees
    where
        country = 'UK'
";

// Create connection
SqlConnection conn = new SqlConnection(connString);

try
{
    //Create data adapter
    SqlDataAdapter da = new SqlDataAdapter();
    da.SelectCommand = new SqlCommand(qry, conn);

    //Create command builder
    SqlCommandBuilder cb = new SqlCommandBuilder(da);

    // Create and fill dataset
    DataSet ds = new DataSet();
    da.Fill(ds, "employees");

    // Get data table reference
    DataTable dt = ds.Tables["employees"];

    // Add a row
    DataRow newRow = dt.NewRow();
    newRow["firstname"] = "Roy";
    newRow["lastname"] = "Beatty";
    newRow["titleofcourtesy"] = "Sir";
    newRow["city"] = "Birmingham";
    newRow["country"] = "UK";
    dt.Rows.Add(newRow);

    // Display Rows
    foreach (DataRow row in dt.Rows)
```

```
                {
                    Console.WriteLine(
                        "{0} {1} {2}",
                        row["firstname"].ToString().PadRight(15),
                        row["lastname"].ToString().PadLeft(25),
                        row["city"]);
                }

                // Insert employees
                da.Update(ds, "employees");
            }
            catch(Exception e)
            {
                Console.WriteLine("Error: " + e);
            }
            finally
            {
                // Close connection
                conn.Close();
            }
        }
    }
}
```

3. Make this the startup project, and run it with Ctrl+F5. You should see the output in Figure 8-10.

Figure 8-10. `PropagateAddsBuilder`

How It Works

The most interesting things to note aren't the line (yes, just one plus a comment) you added as much as what you replaced. The single statement

```
//Create command builder
SqlCommandBuilder cb = new SqlCommandBuilder(da);
```

made all the following code unnecessary:

```
// SQL to insert employees
string ins = @"
    insert into employees
    (
        firstname,
```

```
            lastname,
            titleofcourtesy,
            city,
            country
        )
        values
        (
            @firstname,
            @lastname,
            @titleofcourtesy,
            @city,
            @country
        )
    ";

        // 1. Create command
        SqlCommand cmd = new SqlCommand(ins, conn);
        //
        // 2. Map parameters
        cmd.Parameters.Add(
            "@firstname",
            SqlDbType.NVarChar,
            10,
            "firstname");
        cmd.Parameters.Add(
            "@lastname",
            SqlDbType.NVarChar,
            20,
            "lastname");
        cmd.Parameters.Add(
            "@titleofcourtesy",
            SqlDbType.NVarChar,
            25,
            "titleofcourtesy");
        cmd.Parameters.Add(
            "@city",
            SqlDbType.NVarChar,
            15,
            "city");
        cmd.Parameters.Add(
            "@country",
            SqlDbType.NVarChar,
            15,
            "country");
        //
        // 3. Insert employees
        da.InsertCommand = cmd;
```

Obviously, using command builders is preferable to manually coding SQL; however, remember that they work only on single tables and that the underlying database table must have a primary or unique key. Also, the data adapter SelectCommand property must have a query that includes the key columns.

■Note Though all five of the data providers in the .NET Framework Class Library have command builder classes, no class or interface exists in the System.Data namespace that defines them. So, if you want to learn more about command builders, the best place to start is the description for the builder in which you're interested. The System.Data.DataSet class and the System.Data.IDataAdapter interface define the underlying components that command builders interact with, and their documentation provides the informal specification for the constraints on command builders.

Concurrency

You've seen that updating a database with datasets and data adapters is relatively straightforward. However, we've oversimplified things; you've been assuming that no other changes have been made to the database while you've been working with disconnected datasets.

Imagine two separate users trying to make conflicting changes to the same row in a dataset and then trying to propagate these changes to the database. What happens? How does the database resolve the conflicts? Which row gets updated first, or second, or at all? The answer is unclear. As with so many real-world database issues, it all depends on a variety of factors. However, ADO.NET provides a fundamental level of concurrency control that's designed to prevent update anomalies. The details are beyond the scope of this book, but the following is a good conceptual start.

Basically, a dataset marks all added, modified, and deleted rows. If a row is propagated to the database but has been modified by someone else since the dataset was filled, the data manipulation operation for the row is ignored. This technique is known as *optimistic concurrency* and is essentially the job of the data adapter. When the Update method is called, the data adapter attempts to reconcile all changes. This works well in an environment where users seldom contend for the same data.

This type of concurrency is different from what's known as *pessimistic concurrency*, which *locks* rows upon modification (or sometimes even on retrieval) to avoid conflicts. Most database managers use some form of locking to guarantee data integrity.

Disconnected processing with optimistic concurrency is essential to successful multitier systems. How to employ it most effectively given the pessimistic concurrency of RDBMs is a thorny problem. Don't worry about it, but keep in mind that many issues exist, and the more complex your application, the more likely you'll have to become an expert in concurrency.

Using Datasets and XML

XML is the fundamental medium for data transfer in the .NET environment. In fact, XML technologies are a major foundation for ADO.NET. Datasets organize data internally in XML format and have a variety of methods for reading and writing in XML. For example:

- You can import and export the structure of a dataset as an XML schema using `System.Data.DataSet`'s `ReadXmlSchema` and `WriteXmlSchema` methods.

- You can read the data (and, optionally, the schema) of a dataset from and write it to an XML file with `ReadXml` and `WriteXml`. This can be useful when exchanging data with another application or making a local copy of a dataset.

- You can bind a dataset to an XML document (an instance of `System.Xml.XmlDataDocument`). The dataset and data document are *synchronized*, so either ADO.NET or XML operations can be used to modify it.

Let's look at one of these in action, copying a dataset to an XML file.

Note If you're unfamiliar with XML, don't worry. ADO.NET doesn't require any detailed knowledge of it. Of course, the more you know, the better you can understand what's happening transparently, so we've provided a short primer on XML in Appendix B.

Try It Out: Extracting a Dataset to an XML File

You can preserve the contents and schema of a dataset in one XML file using the dataset's `WriteXml` method or in separate files using `WriteXml` and `WriteXmlSchema`. `WriteXml` is overloaded, and in this example we'll show a version that extracts both data and schema.

1. Add a C# console application named `WriteXML`, and rename the `Class1.cs` file to `WriteXML.cs`.

2. Replace the code in `WriteXML.cs` with that in Listing 8-9.

   Listing 8-9. WriteXML

   ```
   using System;
   using System.Data;
   using System.Data.SqlClient;

   namespace WriteXML
   {
       class WriteXML
       {
           static void Main()
           {
               // Connection string
               string connString = @"
                   server = (local)\netsdk;
                   integrated security = sspi;
                   database = northwind
               ";
   ```

```csharp
            // Query
            string qry = @"
               select
                  productname,
                  unitprice
               from
                  products
            ";

            // Create connection
            SqlConnection conn = new SqlConnection(connString);

            try
            {
               //Create data adapter
               SqlDataAdapter da = new SqlDataAdapter();
               da.SelectCommand = new SqlCommand(qry, conn);

               //Open connection
               conn.Open();

               // Create and fill dataset
               DataSet ds = new DataSet();
               da.Fill(ds, "products");

               // Extract dataset to XML file
               ds.WriteXml(
                  @"c:\begcsharpdb\chapter8_examples\productstable.xml");
            }
            catch(Exception e)
            {
               Console.WriteLine("Error: " + e);
            }
            finally
            {
               // Close connection
               conn.Close();
            }
         }
      }
   }
```

3. Make this the startup project, and run it with Ctrl+F5. You should see the output in Figure 8-11.

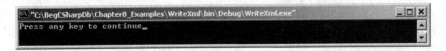

Figure 8-11. `WriteXML`

4. Not much seems to have happened, but that's because you wrote to a file rather than to the screen. Right-click the solution, select Add ➤ Add Existing Item..., and double-click `productstable.xml` in the list that appears. You should see the display in Figure 8-12.

■ **Tip** XML files are plain text. If you compiled from a command prompt, simply open the `productstable.xml` file in any editor, or use the `type` or `more` commands, to view it.

```
Start Page  WriteXml.cs  productstable.xml
  1  <?xml version="1.0" standalone="yes"?>
  2  <NewDataSet>
  3    <products>
  4      <productname>Chai</productname>
  5      <unitprice>18.0000</unitprice>
  6    </products>
  7    <products>
  8      <productname>Chang</productname>
  9      <unitprice>19.0000</unitprice>
 10    </products>
 11    <products>
 12      <productname>Aniseed Syrup</productname>
 13      <unitprice>10.0000</unitprice>
 14    </products>
 15    <products>
 16      <productname>Chef Anton's Cajun Seasoning</productname>
 17      <unitprice>22.0000</unitprice>
 18    </products>
 19    <products>
 20      <productname>Chef Anton's Gumbo Mix</productname>
 21      <unitprice>21.3500</unitprice>
```

Figure 8-12. `products.xml` *file displayed in Visual Studio*

How It Works

This program is just like the others. The only change was replacing the usual console display loop with the method call to write the XML file.

```
// Extract dataset to XML file
ds.WriteXml(
    @"c:\begcsharpdb\chapter8_examples\productstable.xml");
```

You gave the full path for the XML file to place it in the solution directory. Had you given only the filename, it would have been placed in the `bin\Debug` subdirectory under the `WriteXml` project directory.

Note that the XML has simply mapped the dataset as a hierarchy. The first XML element `<NewDataSet>` is the dataset name (defaulted since you didn't specify one to the dataset constructor). The next element, `<products>`, uses the data table name (you have only one data table since you used only one query to populate the dataset), and it's nested inside the dataset element. The data column elements, `<productname>` and `<unitprice>`, are nested inside this element.

The data for each column appears (as plain text) between the *start tag* (for example, `<productname>`) and the *end tag* (for example, `</productname>`) for each column element. Note that the elements named for the data table actually represent individual rows, not the whole table. So, each pair of column elements are contained within the start tag `<products>` and end tag `</products>` for each row.

If you scroll to the bottom of the XML file, you'll find the end tag `</NewDataSet>` for the dataset.

XML is fundamental to ADO.NET. You'll see more of it in Chapter 17.

Understanding Typed and Untyped Datasets

Datasets can be typed or untyped. The datasets you've used have all been untyped. They were instances of `System.Data.DataSet`. An untyped dataset has no built-in schema. The schema is only implicit. It grows as you add tables and columns to the dataset, but these objects are exposed as collections rather than as XML schema elements. However, as you learned in the previous section, you can explicitly export a schema for an untyped dataset with `WriteXmlSchema` (or `WriteXml`).

A typed dataset is one that's derived from `System.Data.DataSet` and uses an XML Schema (typically in an `.xsd` file) in declaring the dataset class. Information from the schema (tables, columns, and so on) is extracted, generated as C# code, and compiled, so the new dataset class is an actual .NET type with appropriate objects and properties.

Either untyped or typed datasets are equally valid, but typed datasets have many advantages; in particular, Visual Studio offers extensive support for them, and they make programming easier and less prone to error.

For example, using an untyped dataset, you'd need to write this:

```
Console.WriteLine(ds.Tables[0].Rows[0]["CompanyName"]);
```

to get the value for the `CompanyName` data column (of the `Customers` table), assuming that the data table was the first in the dataset.

With a typed dataset, you can access its data tables and data columns as class members. You could replace the previous code with this:

```
Console.WriteLine(ds.Customers[0].CompanyName);
```

This makes the code easier to write and more intuitive. In addition, Visual Studio has IntelliSense support for typed datasets.

Technically speaking, typed datasets are faster and more efficient than untyped datasets, because typed datasets have a defined schema, and when they're populated with data, runtime type identification and conversion isn't necessary, since this has been taken care of at compile time. Untyped datasets do a lot more work to do every time a result set is loaded.

However, typed datasets aren't always the best choice. If you're dealing with data that isn't basically well defined, whose definition dynamically changes, or is only of temporary interest, the flexibility of untyped datasets outweighs the many benefits of typed ones.

The intricacies of creating typed datasets are beyond the scope of this book, primarily because creating them is best done with Visual Studio facilities that aren't the most user-friendly and because creating an .xsd file requires more knowledge of XML than we presume. Visual Studio offers both the Component Designer and XML Schema Designer, which support creating typed dataset classes and XML schema files, respectively, and are well worth trying. They're accessible by selecting the Component Class or XML Schema templates when adding a new item to a project. But, to use them, be prepared to spend quite a bit of time studying their dynamic help information.

Summary

In this chapter, you learned the basics of datasets and data adapters. A dataset is a relational representation of data that has a collection data tables, with each data table having collections of data rows and data columns. A data adapter is an object that controls how data is loaded into a dataset and how changes to the dataset data are propagated back to the data source.

You studied techniques to fill and access datasets, how to filter and sort data tables, and noted that though datasets are database-independent objects, disconnected operation isn't the default mode. You learned how to propagate data modifications back to databases with parameterized SQL and the data adapter's `UpdateCommand`, `InsertCommand`, and `DeleteCommand` properties, and you saw how command builders simplify this for single-table updates.

We briefly discussed the important issue of concurrency and then introduced XML, the fundamental technology behind ADO.NET.

Finally, we discussed typed and untyped datasets.

CHAPTER 9

■ ■ ■

Building Windows Forms Applications

Recall the simple Windows Forms database application that you developed in Chapter 2? Since then, you've looked at using data access techniques, getting used to terms such as *connection strings*, *data readers*, and *datasets*, and using these items in console applications. You'll now return to the visual side of database applications and visit the world of Windows Forms applications.

Applications can deliver data to users in numerous ways, but it's important to consider the most effective mode of delivery. Windows Forms offer many benefits; they're easy to use, simple to implement, and can transparently iterate through database data. They're also better looking and more user friendly than dull console windows.

This chapter will introduce Windows Forms database applications. You'll see how Window Forms controls can bind to data and support interaction with a database. Specifically, you'll look at the following:

- Simple data binding

- Complex data binding

- How data binding works

- Different types of data structures, including arrays, data tables, datasets, and data views

- How a data grid works and how to use this powerful control in applications

We'll demonstrate data binding with various controls, including Label, TextBox, ListBox, and DataGrid.

Let's start by looking at data binding.

What's Data Binding?

The term *data binding* has a literal meaning when it comes to Windows Forms applications. It refers to the technique of interfacing elements of a data source with a graphical interface, such as using a TextBox control to bind to a single value from a column.

ADO.NET provides a neat data binding infrastructure for graphical controls to seamlessly bind themselves to almost any structure that contains data. This means that the data source can be anything from an array of values to a set of rows; in fact, it can be anything (such as class System.Data.DataView) that implements the System.Collections.IEnumerable interface.

Using data binding in applications essentially reduces the amount of code you have to write for retrieving data from databases. It's true that using data objects in code provides greater control over data, but data binding can achieve the same results if used properly.

You can bind Windows Forms controls to data in the following two ways:

- Simple data binding

- Complex data binding

Performing Simple Data Binding

This type of data binding is a one-to-one association between an individual control property and a single element of a data source. You can use it for controls that show only one value at a time. For example, you can bind the Text property of a TextBox control to a DataTable column. If the underlying data source is modified, the control's Refresh method updates the bound value, reflecting any changes.

To get comfortable with the idea, let's code a small Windows Forms application that uses simple data binding to bind two TextBox controls to two different columns of the Northwind database's Employees table.

Try It Out: Coding the First Simple Data Binding Application

In this application, you'll bind two values to two text boxes to display the first and last names of an employee.

1. In Visual Studio, create a new solution named Chapter9_Examples.

2. Add a C# Windows application named DataBinding.

3. You should now be in Design view. In the Toolbox, either double-click the TextBox control twice to produce two text boxes that you can position on the form or drag two TextBox controls onto the form. Make your form look similar to the one in Figure 9-1.

Figure 9-1. DataBinding *text boxes*

4. Press F7 to go to Code view. Add the following using directive:

   ```
   using System.Data.SqlClient;
   ```

5. Go back to Design view by clicking the Design tab, and double-click the form (but outside the text boxes) to go to the underlying code. Your cursor should now be positioned

in the Form1_Load method, which was added when you double-clicked the form. Add the following code, and run the program with F5:

```
string connString = @"
    server = (local)\netsdk;
    integrated security = sspi;
    database = northwind
";

string sql = @"
  select
     *
  from
     employees
";

SqlConnection conn = new SqlConnection(connString);
SqlDataAdapter da = new SqlDataAdapter(sql, conn);
DataSet ds = new DataSet();
da.Fill(ds, "employees");

// Bind to FirstName column of the Employees table
textBox1.DataBindings.Add("text", ds, "employees.firstname");
// Bind to LastName column of the Employees table
textBox2.DataBindings.Add("text", ds, "employees.lastname");
```

6. Run the code with Ctrl+F5, and after the program compiles, you should see the form in Figure 9-2.

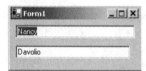

Figure 9-2. DataBinding *text boxes bound to data columns*

How It Works

When the application is first created, Visual Studio .NET automatically generates a lot of code for you, which exists for the most part to handle all the initialization for you. You're mainly concerned with the Form1_Load method that you created when you double-clicked the form in Design view, since that's the method called when the form is first displayed.

Your first task is to establish a connection with the database and fill a newly created dataset with the result set. Once you have all the data fetched, you perform the actual bindings with the following lines of code:

```
textBox1.DataBindings.Add("text", ds, "employees.firstname");
textBox2.DataBindings.Add("text", ds, "employees.lastname");
```

Each data-bound control in a Windows Forms application maintains a list of bindings for all its data-bound properties. The bindings are in a property named DataBindings, which holds a collection of type ControlBindingsCollection (more on this later in the "Understanding Data Binding: Behind the Scenes" section). This collection can contain a number of individual control property bindings, with each binding added using the Add method.

Since a text box is capable of displaying only one value at a time, you bind its Text property to the FirstName column of the Employees table using the Add method. The Add method has the following parameters:

- The name of the control property to bind to

- The data source

- A string identifying the data source member to bind to

Since you're using a dataset as the data source, the data member is a data column in a data table. In the example, the last parameter is used to bind the Text property to the firstname and the lastname data columns of the employees data table.

Performing Complex Data Binding

Unlike simple data binding, complex data binding is an association between the control and one or more data elements of the data source. You can perform this type of binding with controls that allow more than one value to be displayed at one time, such as a data grid or a data list.

The next example is a Windows Forms application, using a data grid, which displays all columns of the Northwind database's Customers table.

Try It Out: Coding the First Complex Data Binding Application

Follow these steps:

1. Add a C# Windows application named ComplexBinding.

2. Add a DataGrid control from the Toolbox. Your form should look similar to the one shown in Figure 9-3.

Figure 9-3. ComplexBinding *data grid*

3. Press F7 to go to Code view. Add the following using directive:

```
using System.Data.SqlClient;
```

4. Double-click the form to go to the underlying code. Your cursor should now be positioned in the Form1_Load method. Add the following code, and run the program with F5:

```
string connString = @"
    server = (local)\netsdk;
    integrated security = sspi;
    database = northwind
";

string sql = @"
    select
        *
    from
        customers
";

SqlConnection conn = new SqlConnection(connString);
SqlDataAdapter da = new SqlDataAdapter(sql, conn);
DataSet ds = new DataSet();
da.Fill(ds, "customers");

// Bind the data table to the data grid
dataGrid1.SetDataBinding(ds, "customers");
```

5. Make this the startup project, and run the code with Ctrl+F5. You should see the form in Figure 9-4.

Figure 9-4. ComplexBinding *data grid bound to data table*

How It Works

Just like the previous example, this example goes through a similar progression, with Visual Studio automatically generating code for you and doing the main initialization for the DataGrid control. Your interest, again, lies with the Form1_Load method where you insert code to render data from a table, using the data grid.

Once you've established a connection with the data source, you populate a dataset from the Customers table using a data adapter. Next, you need to bind the DataGrid control to the newly populated dataset. You do so by using the following line of code:

```
dataGrid1.SetDataBinding(ds, "customers");
```

The SetDataBinding method of the DataGrid control accepts two parameters: the data source object and a string literal that describes a data member in the data source. Here, a data source can be any object that's capable of holding data, such as an array or a data table. The data member describes what element to bind to the control. In the case, you used a dataset as the data source, and the customers data table contained in the dataset as a data member.

A call to the SetDataBinding method binds all columns of the customers data table to the DataGrid control at runtime, which renders the data in the style of a spreadsheet.

You previously used the DataBindings collection property to add bindings to the control. You could use this method in the code if you were to bind the DataSource property of the control to the customers data table. The following line of code is an alternative to using the SetDataBinding method:

```
dataGrid1.DataBindings.Add("datasource", ds, "customers");
```

This syntax is particularly useful if you need to add more bindings for other individual properties of the control.

You'll learn more about the DataGrid control and the advantages of using a SetDataBinding method later in the "Using Data Grids" section.

Understanding Data Binding: Behind the Scenes

In the previous few sections you saw running examples of Windows Forms applications using data-bound controls. But how does all this work? How do controls *really* bind themselves? To answer these questions, we'll give you some insight into the data binding mechanism and show how it works.

The Windows data-bound controls (such as a Label, a Button, or a TextBox) are able to bind to data because of the functionality made available by the Binding class (System.Windows.Forms.Binding), which is provided by the .NET Framework. This class is responsible for creating a simple binding between a single control property and a data element in a data source. Have a look at the following code:

```
textBox1.DataBindings.Add("text", ds, "employees.firstname");
```

This line was taken from the first example in the chapter. Recall that we mentioned that the DataBindings property of a control (any class that derives from the System.Windows.Forms.Control class) returns a ControlBindingsCollection object, which is a collection of Binding objects, each of which can be added by using the Add method. This means that a data-bound control can have a collection of bindings, each associated with a different property of the control; for example, you could bind the Text property of a Label control to a single column in a table and, at the same time, bind its ForeColor property to an array of different color values, completely unrelated to the table.

The Add method has two overloads: one that takes a single Binding object and another that implicitly creates an instance of a Binding object by calling the Binding class constructor (the one you used in the previous examples).

The Binding class constructor takes three parameters. The first parameter can be the name of a property of a control, such as the Text property of a TextBox control or the DataSource property of a DataGrid control.

The second parameter of the Binding class constructor can be an instance of the DataSet, DataTable, DataView, or DataViewManager class or any class that implements the System.Collections.IList interface. You'll look at a number of examples using different data sources later in the "Understanding Types of Data Sources" section.

The third parameter describes a data member from a data source. It's a string literal that must resolve into a scalar value, such as a data column in a data table.

If you'd rather declare a Binding object explicitly, the following code is an example of what your code would look like if you were to bind the Text property of a TextBox control to a data element in a table:

```
Binding newBind = new Binding("text", ds, "employees.firstname");
textBox1.DataBindings.Add(newBind);
```

This approach could be useful in situations where you'd like to bind two or more controls to the same data element. For example, if you have a Label control and a TextBox control in a Windows Forms application and you'd like to bind both of these controls to the same column in a table, for whatever reason, you could create one Binding object and add that to the ControlBindingsCollection of each of the controls by calling the Add method.

The following code describes one such scenario of binding the Text property of the two controls to the same column in the Employees table, assuming you already have a Label control and a TextBox control on your Windows Forms application:

```
Binding newBind = new Binding("text", ds, "employees.firstname");
textBox1.DataBindings.Add(newBind);
Label1.DataBindings.Add(newBind);
```

Note that when you use a dataset as a data source for binding your control, you actually are binding to a data view invisibly, behind the scenes. Recall from the discussion in the previous chapter that data views are specifically designed for providing different views of the data stored in an underlying data table, so they're useful when it comes to data binding Windows Forms controls.

A data view can allow two or more controls to be bound to the same data source, thus allowing each bound control to have a different view of data altogether. For instance, one control could display all available rows in a table (using as a DataGrid control), and another could display selected data.

Similarly, a bound DataRow object is actually a DataRowView object that provides a customizable view.

Synchronizing Controls with a Data Source

Data binding is a powerful feature, allowing your application to make the most of rendering data dynamically and making it simple to synchronize bound controls with the underlying data source.

Suppose you build a Windows Forms–based application that uses a couple of TextBox controls to bind to the same data source, each control bound to a different column in a table. Realistically, the data source will probably have more than one row, such as how the Employees table in the Northwind database holds a number of rows. In the first example of simple data binding, you bound a couple of text boxes to the data source and displayed only one row (the first row from the result set, to be precise). Most likely, you'd want to allow the user to navigate back and forth through the available rows using Next and Back buttons. For this to happen, your controls will need to be synchronized so that they display the correct data from the current row, as they're currently bound to two different columns.

The System.Windows.Forms namespace includes an abstract class for this purpose. A *binding manager* is an instance of a class that derives from the abstract BindingManagerBase class.

The binding manager enables greater control over the data being displayed by bound controls, which are bound to the same data source, by maintaining the current position of the row pointer. This means that whenever a data source evaluates a list of data elements, the binding manager supervises and keeps track of the ordinal position of the current row in the data source. Also, the binding manager fires events to notify the application if the current position in the data source has changed.

The two fundamental properties of a binding manager are Position and Current. Position is a zero-based integer value that describes an ordinal position of the rows being read in the data source. With the Position property, you can programmatically advance the row pointer to move onto the next row and vice versa. The Current property returns the data object at the current position in the data source.

The two concrete binding managers are CurrencyManager and PropertyManager. CurrencyManager is specifically designed for data sources that implement IList (or the interfaces, such as IListSource and IBindingList, that are based on it), such as Array, DataSet, and DataTable. The PropertyManager, on the other hand, is returned for a data source that's neither a list nor a collection but is a single property of another object or is a single value. Note that you can use it only for maintaining the Current property of the object. Trying to use the Position property will have no effect, since the data source isn't a list but a single value.

You can't create an instance to the BindingManagerBase class directly because it's an abstract base class, but you can obtain instances to its derived classes by calling the BindingContext property of a Windows form, which returns an instance of an appropriate binding manager type, depending on the type of data source being used.

Every Windows form groups all bindings defined by its child controls into a collection called BindingContext. This collection returns an appropriate binding manager for the specified data source and data member.

Let's now look at a simple example that illustrates how to use a binding manager. The application will extend beyond the use of a couple of TextBox controls by introducing two buttons, Next and Back, that you'll use for navigating through the data source.

Try It Out: Creating a Simple Application Using a Binding Manager

Follow these steps:

1. Add a C# Windows application named BindingManagerEx.

2. In Design view, drag two TextBox controls and two Button controls from the Toolbox onto the form. Change the Text property of one button to << Back. Change the text of other button to Next >>. Your form should look similar to Figure 9-5.

Figure 9-5. BindingManagerEx *buttons*

3. Change the (Name) property of one button to buttonBack and the other button to buttonNext.

4. In the Toolbox, click the Data tab and drag a DataSet control onto the form. You should see the window in Figure 9-6.

Figure 9-6. BindingManagerEx: *Adding a dataset*

5. Choose Untyped Dataset, and click OK. This will create a dataset in the component tray.

6. Press F7 to go to Code view. Add the following using directive:

```
using System.Data.SqlClient;
```

7. Add the following field to the Form1 class declaration.

```
// Declare a binding manager field
private BindingManagerBase bMgr;
```

8. In Design mode, double-click the form, and you'll be taken to the underlying code for the Form1_Load method. Add the following code to the method:

```
string connString = @"
    server = (local)\netsdk;
    integrated security = sspi;
    database = northwind
";

string sql = @"
    select
        *
    from
        employees
";

SqlConnection conn = new SqlConnection(connString);
SqlDataAdapter da = new SqlDataAdapter(sql, conn);
da.Fill(dataSet1, "employees");
```

```
// Bind text boxes to data columns
textBox1.DataBindings.Add("text", dataSet1, "employees.firstname");
textBox2.DataBindings.Add("text", dataSet1, "employees.lastname");

// Create the binding manager (CurrencyManager)
bMgr = this.BindingContext[dataSet1, "employees"];
```

9. Return to Design view, and double-click the Next button. Place the following code in the buttonNext_Click method:

```
// Point to the next row and refresh the contents of the text box
bMgr.Position += 1;
```

10. Return to Design view, and double-click the Back button. Place the following code in the buttonBack_Click method:

```
// Point to the previous row and refresh contents of the text box
bMgr.Position -= 1;
```

11. Make this the startup project, and run the code with Ctrl+F5. You should see the form in Figure 9-7.

Figure 9-7. BindingManagerEx *running*

How It Works

This code is similar to the first example you saw in this chapter, with the exception of the binding manager used to navigate through the data source. Since this example is a mere upgrade of the one you saw earlier, we can safely skip details regarding simple data binding techniques and move onto the part where you've actually used the binding manager to do the job.

After declaring a BindingManagerBase field, the next thing you do is get a suitable binding manager from the BindingContext property of the form. This happens in the following line of code:

```
bMgr = this.BindingContext[dataSet1, "employees"];
```

In this case, BindingContext returns an instance of a CurrencyManager since a DataSet implements the IListSource interface. With a binding manager at hand, you can now manage all data bindings in the Windows Forms application that various controls set on the specified data source.

The next step is to implement the navigational buttons. The buttonNext_Click method is called every time the Next button is clicked. The body of the method includes a single line of code, as follows, that basically increments the position of the current row in the data source by incrementing the value returned by the Position property of the binding manager:

```
bMgr.Position += 1;
```

Similarly, the buttonBack_Click method is called every time the Back button is clicked. This method uses a single line of code, as follows, to decrement the position of the current row in the data source by decrementing the value returned by the Position property of the binding manager:

```
bMgr.Position -= 1;
```

Understanding Types of Data Sources

Earlier in the chapter you learned that a set of interfaces exists that can be derived from, and any class that implements any one of these interfaces is eligible for use with bound controls, as a valid data source.

Coming back to the same list of interfaces, you'll spend the following sections studying some available classes that implement these interfaces and see how they can be used with data that's bound to controls.

Binding to Arrays

In most cases, an Array is best suited to storing and retrieving consistent data. Arrays have runtime support for manipulating data and are easy to work with in the code via the ICollection interface.

At times you may want to display the contents of an array in a TextBox control. For example, you may have details of cars stored in an array and would like to display the data to a potential customer in a text box. Let's take a look at a quick example.

Try It Out: Building a Simple Application That Binds to an Array

Follow these steps:

1. Add a C# Windows application named Arrays.

2. In Design view, drag a TextBox control from the Toolbox onto the form. Double-click the form, and enter the following code in the Form1_Load method. Your form should look similar to Figure 9-8.

    ```
    String[] carDetails = new String[] {
        "Mercedes", "Black", "E320", "1999", "$1 million"
    };
    textBox1.DataBindings.Add("text", carDetails, null);
    ```

3. Make this the startup project, and run the code with Ctrl+F5. You should see the form in Figure 9-8.

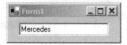

Figure 9-8. Arrays: *Binding a text box to an array*

How It Works

The code shows an array of strings bound to the Text property of the TextBox control. You pass null to the Add method since the array doesn't have data members or a navigation path that could be further resolved into a single scalar value. Ideally, this parameter should be used for a DataSet or a DataTable since they can be navigated through a set of tables or columns.

To be able to iterate through the array, you can use the Position property of the binding manager for the purpose. However, you'll have to pass null as the data member of the BindingContext property since it's an array and has no member objects. You could do this with the following code:

```
BindingManagerBase bMgr = this.BindingContext[carDetails, null];
```

Binding to Data Tables

The DataTable class implements the IListSource interface. As you may recall, a DataTable either can be accessed from within a DataSet or can exist as an independent object, consisting of rows and columns. You'll consider the latter case for the time being.

A DataTable is another good example of a data source, and it's a typical one, since it can be used for both simple and complex binding examples. To bind a DataTable to a control, you have two options. You can bind the whole table to a control that supports complex binding (a control that can display more than one row at one time), or you can bind a single column to a control that supports simple binding.

Let's look at an example of an application that implements both simple and complex bound controls.

Try It Out: Building a Simple Application That Binds to a Data Table

Follow these steps:

1. Add a C# Windows application named DataTableBinding.

2. In Design view, add two TextBox controls and a ListBox control to the form. Your form should look similar to Figure 9-9.

Figure 9-9. `DataTableBinding`: *Form layout*

3. Click the Data tab in the Toolbox, and drag a `DataSet` control onto the form. In the window that appears, select Untyped Dataset, and click OK.

4. Press F7 to go to Code view. Add the following using directive:

```
using System.Data.SqlClient;
```

5. In Design view, double-click the form, and add the following code to the `Form1_Load` method:

```
string connString = @"
    server = (local)\netsdk;
    integrated security = sspi;
    database = northwind
";

string sql = @"
    select
        firstname,
        lastname
    from
        employees
";

SqlConnection conn = new SqlConnection(connString);
SqlDataAdapter da = new SqlDataAdapter(sql, conn);
da.Fill(dataSet1, "employees");
DataTable dt = dataSet1.Tables["employees"];

// Complex-bind a ListBox control at design time to
// display values from the firstname data column
listBox1.DataSource = dt;
listBox1.DisplayMember = "firstname";
// Bind the Text property to the firstname data column
textBox1.DataBindings.Add("text", dt, "firstname");
// Bind the Text property to the firstname data column
textBox2.DataBindings.Add("text", dt, "lastname");
```

6. Make this the startup project, and run the code with Ctrl+F5. You should see the form in Figure 9-10.

Figure 9-10. DataTableBinding *running*

How It Works

In this example you have a ListBox control bound to a DataTable object extracted from a populated DataSet, as shown in the following code:

```
DataTable dt = dataSet1.Tables["employees"];

// Complex-bind a ListBox control at design time to
// display values from the firstname data column
listBox1.DataSource = dt;
listBox1.DisplayMember = "firstname";
```

You bound the ListBox control at design time by setting its DataSource and DisplayMember properties. The DataSource property takes a collection object as a data source, such as a DataTable or a DataSet. The DisplayMember property takes a data member from within the data source for filling the ListBox with data. In the example, since you have a DataTable object as a data source, the DisplayMember property takes a column name for binding to the control.

Similarly, the text boxes are bound to the DataTable by adding bindings to the DataBindings collection and providing the column names from the DataTable as data members.

```
// Bind the Text property to the firstname data column
textBox1.DataBindings.Add("text", dt, "firstname");
// Bind the Text property to the firstname data column
textBox2.DataBindings.Add("text", dt, "lastname");
```

■**Caution** You used a select list to retrieve specific columns from the Employees table not only because it's best practice (asking only for what you need) but also because the DisplayMember property is case sensitive. Had you used a * instead of the column names, the column names would have been FirstName and LastName, and you would have had to provide the display member as FirstName. Further, had you spelled it in the select list as firstName instead of firstname, the DisplayMember argument would have had to be firstName! In general, select only the columns you need and keep in mind that although SQL isn't case sensitive, some ADO.NET features (unfortunately) are. Whatever case you use for table and column names, use the same case when the names are contained in strings.

Binding to Datasets

The most flexible data source in the toolkit is the dataset. System.Data.DataSet implements the System.ComponentModel.IListSource interface.

Throughout the rest of this chapter, you'll be looking at code that uses datasets to navigate through tables and rows, not only because it's easier to handle but also because data binding is quick and straightforward. When we discussed datasets in detail in the previous chapter, you discovered that they could be used to store relational data disconnected from a data source. This makes them great candidates for being sources for data-bound controls.

Try It Out: Building a Simple Application That Binds to a Dataset

Follow these steps:

1. Add a C# Windows application named DataSetBind.

2. Replace the code in Form1.cs with that in Listing 9-1.

   Listing 9-1. DataSetBind.cs

```
using System;
using System.Drawing;
using System.Collections;
using System.ComponentModel;
using System.Windows.Forms;
using System.Data;
using System.Data.SqlClient;

namespace DataSetBind
{
    public class Form1 : System.Windows.Forms.Form
    {
            private System.Windows.Forms.Label label1;
            private System.Windows.Forms.Label label2;
            private System.Data.DataSet dataSet1;

        private System.ComponentModel.Container components = null;
```

```csharp
        public Form1()
        {

            InitializeComponent();
                  }

        protected override void Dispose( bool disposing )
        {
            if (disposing)
            {
                if  (components != null)
                {
                    components.Dispose();
                }
                }
            base.Dispose(disposing);
        }

        private void InitializeComponent()
        {
this.label1 = new System.Windows.Forms.Label();
this.label2 = new System.Windows.Forms.Label();
this.dataSet1 = new System.Data.DataSet();
((System.ComponentModel.ISupportInitialize)(this.dataSet1)).BeginInit();
this.SuspendLayout();

this.label1.Location = new System.Drawing.Point(16, 8);
this.label1.Name = "label1";
this.label1.Size = new System.Drawing.Size(72, 16);
this.label1.TabIndex = 0;
this.label1.Text = "label1";

this.label2.Location = new System.Drawing.Point(16, 40);
this.label2.Name = "label2";
this.label2.Size = new System.Drawing.Size(72, 16);
this.label2.TabIndex = 1;
this.label2.Text = "label2";

this.dataSet1.DataSetName = "NewDataSet";
this.dataSet1.Locale = new System.Globalization.CultureInfo("en-GB");

this.AutoScaleBaseSize = new System.Drawing.Size(5, 13);
this.ClientSize = new System.Drawing.Size(128, 69);
this.Controls.AddRange(new System.Windows.Forms.Control[] {
                                                this.label2,
                                                this.label1});

this.Name = "Form1";
this.Text = "Form1";
this.Load += new System.EventHandler(this.Form1_Load);
```

```
            ((System.ComponentModel.ISupportInitialize)(this.dataSet1)).EndInit();
            this.ResumeLayout(false);

        }

            [STAThread]
            static void Main()
            {
                                    Application.Run(new Form1());
            }

        private void Form1_Load(object sender, System.EventArgs e)
        {
            string ConStr = @"server=(local)\NetSDK;" +
                "Integrated Security=SSPI;" +
                "database=Northwind";

            // Get Data from Employees table
            string SQL = @"
                select
                    *
                from
                    products
            ";

            SqlConnection Conn = new SqlConnection(ConStr);
            SqlDataAdapter da = new SqlDataAdapter(SQL, Conn);

            // Fill DataSet with data
            da.Fill(dataSet1, "Products");

            // Bind the Label's Text property to the ProductID of the Products table
            label1.DataBindings.Add("Text", dataSet1, "Products.ProductName");
            // Bind the second label's Text property to the UnitPrice column
            label2.DataBindings.Add("Text", dataSet1, "Products.UnitPrice");
        }
    }
}
```

3. Make this the startup project, and run the code with Ctrl+F5. You should see the output in Figure 9-11.

Figure 9-11. DataSetBind *running*

How It Works

First, you populate a dataset with data from the Products table of the Northwind database.

```
// Fill DataSet with data
da.Fill(dataSet1, "Products");
```

Second, you bind specific fields to the two Label controls.

```
// Bind the Label's Text property to the ProductID of the Products table
label1.DataBindings.Add("Text", dataSet1, "Products.ProductName");
// Bind the second label's Text property to the UnitPrice column
label2.DataBindings.Add("Text", dataSet1, "Products.UnitPrice");
```

As with the first example, you have no facility to page forward or backward through the data, but you could add this functionality using code similar to that used in the BindingManagerEx example.

Binding to Data Views

The DataView class implements the System.ComponentModel.ITypedList interface and presents a customizable view of a data table. Binding to a DataView object is as simple as binding to a DataTable object since a DataView provides a dynamic view of the contents of a data table. In fact, using a data view can provide further control over the data you display by implementing custom sorts and filters.

Try It Out: Building a Simple Application That Binds to a Data View

Follow these steps:

1. Add a C# Windows application named DataViewBind.

2. Replace the code in Form1.cs with that in Listing 9-2.

   Listing 9-2. DataViewBind.cs

   ```
   using System;
   using System.Drawing;
   using System.Collections;
   using System.ComponentModel;
   using System.Windows.Forms;
   using System.Data;
   using System.Data.SqlClient;

   namespace DataViewBind
   {
       public class Form1 : System.Windows.Forms.Form
       {
           private System.Windows.Forms.TextBox textBox1;
           private System.Windows.Forms.TextBox textBox2;
           private System.Data.DataSet dataSet1;
   ```

```
          private System.ComponentModel.Container components = null;

          public Form1()
          {

              InitializeComponent();

          }

          protected override void Dispose( bool disposing )
          {
              if ( disposing )
              {
                  if (components != null)
                  {
                      components.Dispose();
                  }
              }
              base.Dispose( disposing );
          }

          private void InitializeComponent()
          {
              this.textBox1 = new System.Windows.Forms.TextBox();
              this.textBox2 = new System.Windows.Forms.TextBox();
              this.dataSet1 = new System.Data.DataSet();
              ((System.ComponentModel.ISupportInitialize)(this.dataSet1)).BeginInit();
              this.SuspendLayout();

              this.textBox1.Location = new System.Drawing.Point(16, 0);
              this.textBox1.Name = "textBox1";
              this.textBox1.TabIndex = 0;
              this.textBox1.Text = "textBox1";

              this.textBox2.Location = new System.Drawing.Point(16, 24);
              this.textBox2.Name = "textBox2";
              this.textBox2.TabIndex = 1;
              this.textBox2.Text = "textBox2";

              this.dataSet1.DataSetName = "NewDataSet";
              this.dataSet1.Locale = new System.Globalization.CultureInfo("en-GB");

              this.AutoScaleBaseSize = new System.Drawing.Size(5, 13);
              this.ClientSize = new System.Drawing.Size(128, 45);
              this.Controls.AddRange(new System.Windows.Forms.Control[] {
                                                              this.textBox2,
                                                              this.textBox1});
```

```csharp
        this.Name = "Form1";
        this.Text = "Form1";
        this.Load += new System.EventHandler(this.Form1_Load);
        ((System.ComponentModel.ISupportInitialize)(this.dataSet1)).EndInit();
        this.ResumeLayout(false);

    }

    [STAThread]
    static void Main()
    {
        Application.Run(new Form1());
    }

    private void Form1_Load(object sender, System.EventArgs e)
    {
        string ConStr = @"server=(local)\NetSDK;" +
            "Integrated Security=SSPI;" +
            "database=Northwind";

        // Get Data from Employees table
        string SQL = @"
          select
              *
          from
            employees
        ";

        SqlConnection Conn = new SqlConnection(ConStr);
        SqlDataAdapter da = new SqlDataAdapter(SQL, Conn);

        // Fill DataSet with data
        da.Fill(dataSet1, "Employees");

        DataTable myTable = dataSet1.Tables["Employees"];
        // Create a DataView, set a Filter and a Sort order
        DataView dv = new DataView(myTable, "Country='UK'",
            "FirstName", DataViewRowState.CurrentRows);

        // Bind the Text property to the FirstName
        // column of the Employees table
        textBox1.DataBindings.Add("Text", dv, "FirstName");
        // Bind the Text property to the LastName
        // column of the Employees table
        textBox2.DataBindings.Add("Text", dv, "LastName");
    }
  }
}
```

3. Make this the startup project, and run the code with Ctrl+F5. You should see the output in Figure 9-12.

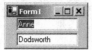

Figure 9-12. `DataViewBind` *running*

How It Works

You use a `DataView` object to simply filter and sort the contents of a data table, and then you display them in the controls.

```
// Fill DataSet with data
da.Fill(dataSet1, "Employees");


DataTable myTable = dataSet1.Tables["Employees"];
// Create a DataView, set a Filter and a Sort order
DataView dv = new DataView(myTable, "Country='UK'",
    "FirstName", DataViewRowState.CurrentRows);
```

As with the previous examples, you first fill a dataset with data. The next step is to create a data table to represent the table in which you're interested. You then refine the data using the data view to select the first name column of all employees based in the United Kingdom from the table in the data table.

The next step is to bind to the text boxes.

```
// Bind the Text property to the FirstName
// column of the Employees table
textBox1.DataBindings.Add("Text", dv, "FirstName");
// Bind the Text property to the LastName
// column of the Employees table
textBox2.DataBindings.Add("Text", dv, "LastName");
```

Using Data Grids

The `DataGrid` control is one of the most powerful Windows Forms controls (and indeed it also exists as a Web Forms control, too, as you'll see in the next chapter). A `DataGrid` control resembles a spreadsheet in its appearance. Like the name suggests, it provides you with a scrollable grid of rows and columns, completely customizable for displaying data in a number of ways and accessing data just the way you want.

To add to the flavor, you can use it with almost any data source, such as an `Array` or a `DataSet`, as long as it implements either the `IList` interface or the `IListSource` interface. You can provide a modifiable, formatted user interface of a `DataSet` from the most humble appearance, such as displaying a single table at one time, to the most superior, displaying related tables in a parent-child fashion. (You'll find out a lot more about parent-child tables and relationships in Chapter 12.)

You can bind the DataGrid to a data source using the DataSource and the DataMember properties at design time, or you can use the SetDataBinding method at runtime. The difference between runtime and design-time binding is that with design-time binding, you can't reset the DataSource and the DataMember properties once they've been set. On the other hand, using the SetDataBinding method, you can set a data source at runtime, switching between sources when desired. Also, in most cases, the object to which you want to bind doesn't exist until runtime. This is true for structures such as an Array, which typically needs to be instantiated and populated at runtime. For this reason, it's a good idea to bind objects programmatically at runtime, rather than binding them at design time.

Previously, you used a DataGrid for data binding. You'll now look at a simple application that binds a data grid to a dataset and displays data in a parent-child fashion, showing related data in two tables.

Try It Out: Binding a Data Grid to Show Data in a Parent-Child Relationship

Follow these steps:

1. Add a C# Windows application named MultiTableDataGrid.

2. In Design view, add a DataGrid control to the form. Your form should look similar to Figure 9-13.

Figure 9-13. MultiTableDataGrid *layout*

3. In the Toolbox, click the Data tab and drag a DataSet control onto the form, and again choose Untyped Dataset in the window that appears.

4. Press F7 to go to Code view. Add the following using directive:

   ```
   using System.Data.SqlClient;
   ```

5. In Design mode, double-click the form, and add the following code to the Form1_Load method:

```
string connString = @"
   server = (local)\netsdk;
   integrated security = sspi;
   database = northwind
";

string qry1 = @"
   select
      *
   from
      employees
";

string qry2 = @"
   select
      *
   from
      orders
";

string sql = qry1 + qry2;

SqlConnection conn = new SqlConnection(connString);
SqlDataAdapter da = new SqlDataAdapter(sql, conn);

// Map default table names to employees and Orders
da.TableMappings.Add("Table", "employees");
da.TableMappings.Add("Table1", "orders");
da.Fill(dataSet1);

// Create a relation between the two tables
DataRelation dr = new DataRelation(
   "employeeorders",
   dataSet1.Tables[0].Columns["employeeid"],
   dataSet1.Tables[1].Columns["employeeid"]
);
dataSet1.Relations.Add(dr);

// Bind the data grid at run time
dataGrid1.SetDataBinding(dataSet1, "employees");
```

6. Make this the startup project, and run the code with Ctrl+F5. You should see the form in Figure 9-14 after clicking the plus sign next to the second employee.

Figure 9-14. `MultiTableDataGrid`: *Employee list*

7. Click the *EmployeeOrders* link, and you should see the form in Figure 9-15, displaying the orders for the selected employee.

Figure 9-15. `MultiTableDataGrid`: *Related orders*

How It Works

The `DataGrid` can present data from the two tables in a very organized manner. What's good about a `DataGrid` is that it allows you to navigate through related tables with ease. After clicking the plus sign on the side of a row that contains related data in a distinct table, a hyperlink appears, leading you to yet another table (the related table) for displaying all available related rows. Let's see how the code managed to do so.

In the `Form1_Load` method, you submitted two queries.

```
string qry1 = @"
    select
        *
    from
        employees
";
```

```
string qry2 = @"
    select
        *
    from
        orders
";
```

```
string sql = qry1 + qry2;
```

Next, you filled the DataSet with the data from two result sets returned, but before calling the Fill method, you mapped custom table names to the default table names (Table and Table1) provided by the data adapter and added these mapped names to the data adapter's table mappings collection. This ensures that the data table named (by default) Table in the dataset can be referenced as employees; the one named Table1 can be referenced as orders. Note that this is just for your convenience and isn't mandatory.

```
// Map default table names to employees and orders
da.TableMappings.Add("Table", "employees");
da.TableMappings.Add("Table1", "orders");
da.Fill(dataSet1);
```

The next two statements illustrate a DataRelation object being used for relating two distinct tables inside a DataSet.

```
// Create a relation between the two tables
DataRelation dr = new DataRelation(
    "employeeorders",
    dataSet1.Tables[0].Columns["employeeid"],
    dataSet1.Tables[1].Columns["employeeid"]
);
dataSet1.Relations.Add(dr);
```

In ADO.NET, you use a DataRelation object to create a relation between two data tables in a dataset. This so-called relation (it is actually a *relationship* and has nothing to do with the relational database concept of a relation) is established between common columns (corresponding columns must have the same data type but can have different names) belonging to two distinct tables, which logically relate the tables. We'll cover relationships between tables in Chapter 12.

After a relationship has been defined programmatically, it's added to the Relations collection of the dataset. The next thing you do is bind the employees data table to the DataGrid control.

```
// Bind the data grid at run time
dataGrid1.SetDataBinding(dataSet1, "employees");
```

Once the data grid is bound, it automatically searches for all tables related to the bound data table and presents the data in a scrollable grid form.

A data grid is a great way of quickly prototyping your applications, because it does a lot of work for you. It's also simple to update the data source using a bound DataGrid control, and that's just what you'll explore next.

Updating a Data Source Using a Data Grid

Until now, all you've learned to do is display data using data-bound controls. It's time you see how modified data in a bound control can be propagated to the data source using very little code.

In the previous chapters you discovered how to use DataCommand, DataAdapter, and CommandBuilder objects to update data in the data source, and we've discussed when to use which object. Based on that knowledge, you'll use a SqlDataAdapter and a SqlCommandBuilder in a simple application that binds a DataSet object to a DataGrid control. The example illustrates how easy it is to apply the techniques of updating the data source that you used in a console application in a Windows Forms application.

Try It Out: Updating a Data Source with a Bound Data Grid

Follow these steps:

1. Add a C# Windows application named DataGridUpdate.

2. Add a DataGrid control and a Button control to the form. Change the Text property of your button to Update and the name of the button to buttonUpdate. Your form should look similar to the one shown in Figure 9-16.

Figure 9-16. DataGridUpdate *layout*

3. Add a DataSet control to the form, selecting Untyped Dataset when prompted.

4. Now choose a SqlCommand control from the Toolbox, and drag it onto the form. This will create a SqlCommand object reference in your application named sqlCommand1.

5. Press F7 to go to the Code view. Add the following using directive:

   ```
   using System.Data.SqlClient;
   ```

6. Add the following fields to the Form1 class declaration:

   ```
   private SqlCommandBuilder cb;
   private SqlDataAdapter da;
   ```

7. Add the following to the Form1_Load method:

```
string connString = @"
    server = (local)\netsdk;
    integrated security = sspi;
    database = northwind
";

string sql = @"
    select
        *
    from
        employees
";

SqlConnection conn = new SqlConnection(connString);

// Create a command
sqlCommand1 = new SqlCommand(sql, conn);

// Create a data adapter
da = new SqlDataAdapter();
da.SelectCommand = sqlCommand1;

// Create a SqlCommandBuilder object
cb = new SqlCommandBuilder(da);

// Fill dataset
da.Fill(dataSet1, "employees");

// Bind the data grid at run time
dataGrid1.SetDataBinding(dataSet1, "employees");
```

8. Double-click the Update button. Add the following code to the buttonUpdate_Click method:

```
da.Update(dataSet1, "employees");
```

9. Make this the startup project, and run the code with Ctrl+F5. You should see the form in Figure 9-17.

Figure 9-17. DataGridUpdate *running*

How It Works

To be able to use a SqlCommandBuilder object, you create a SqlCommand object and pass it to the SqlDataAdapter object (recall that you learned how to use a SqlCommandBuilder in the previous chapter). The following code shows a SqlCommand object being created and passed to the SqlDataAdapter you created for filling the DataSet:

```
// Create a command
sqlCommand1 = new SqlCommand(sql, conn);

// Create a data adapter
da = new SqlDataAdapter();
da.SelectCommand = sqlCommand1;
```

You then created a SqlCommandBuilder object. You used a SqlCommandBuilder so that you don't have to explicitly code update, insert, or delete statements, since the command builder will generate SQL for you.

```
// Create a SqlCommandBuilder object
cb = new SqlCommandBuilder(da);
```

Next, you filled the DataSet with data and bound it to your DataGrid control.

```
// Fill dataset
da.Fill(dataSet1, "employees");

// Bind the data grid at run time
dataGrid1.SetDataBinding(dataSet1, "employees");
```

Clicking the Update button updates the data source. The `buttonUpdate_Click` method has only one line of code, which does all the work for you.

```
da.Update(dataSet1, "employees");
```

This line calls the `Update` method of the data adapter, which in turn uses the command builder to generate suitable SQL from the metadata it collects.

Using a data grid for modifying tabular data is extremely simple. It has built-in functionality for notifying different events that are launched every time data in the grid changes.

Summary

In this chapter, we discussed various ways to fetch data automatically from an external data source, be it an array, a database, a dataset, or any data structure capable of storing and retrieving data. You also saw how Windows Forms controls offer built-in support for binding to data sources and retrieving and modifying them. The main topics covered in this chapter were as follows:

- Understanding what data binding is

- Understanding the types of data-bound controls (simple and complex binding)

- Synchronizing controls with a data source

- Understanding the types of bindable data sources

- Using a data grid for data binding

- Updating data sources with bound controls

In the next chapter, you'll meet the Web equivalents to a lot of these controls, as you look into ASP.NET and the world of Web Forms.

CHAPTER 10

■ ■ ■

Using ASP.NET

ASP.NET is the featured Microsoft technology for building Web applications. You can deploy these applications on a Web server, for the entire Internet to reach, or perhaps on an intranet, for just the workers in your department. With the .NET Compact Framework you even get support for cell phones and other mobile devices. ASP.NET is so rich in functionality that it can't be covered in a single book, let alone a single chapter. Bearing this in mind, this chapter will focus on an important topic for database development: data binding with the `DataGrid` Web Forms control. By the end of the chapter you should have a solid understanding of the following data grid features:

- Performing basic data binding

- Paging rows

- Selecting a row to detail

- Customizing the column display

- Editing rows

- Deleting rows

- Sorting rows

Along the way you'll build a simple ASP.NET Web application and learn a few of the differences between Windows Forms and Web Forms development.

Understanding the Basics

You first need to understand some of the basic ground rules for the technology you'll be using.

Visual Studio .NET provides a similar environment for developing Web Forms applications as it does for Windows Forms applications. You can drag-and-drop controls onto Web Forms applications, double-click to handle events, and right-click controls to set properties. Most of the techniques you've learned for Windows Forms applications are also applicable to Web Forms applications developed with ASP.NET. Web Forms applications work in a slightly different manner under the covers, however, so being aware of these differences can help you build better Web applications.

A Web browser will request a Web form using the Hypertext Transfer Protocol (HTTP) network protocol. HTTP is a stateless protocol, meaning each request has no knowledge of any of the previous requests or information pertinent to the user's session on the Web site. Instead, the Web application has the burden of managing the user's session state; for example, it must remember the items in a customer's shopping cart as they move from Web form to Web form. Managing state yourself makes building Web applications a little more complicated than a traditional form application, but fortunately ASP.NET provides a feature-rich infrastructure to ease the burden.

Web Forms also pander their output format to the software and hardware on which they will be displayed. Windows Forms render themselves graphically using the native controls and user interface elements of the operating system. Web Forms, on the other hand, render themselves using Hypertext Markup Language (HTML), Wireless Markup Language (WML), XML, and script: all text formats. Although a text format may sound limiting, you can actually reach a larger variety of clients using Web Forms. Web browsers on Linux, Solaris, and cell phones can translate the textual representation of a Web form into a graphical display for the host platform.

Understanding Web Forms

Throughout the chapter you'll uncover more nuances in Web Forms programming, but you already have enough information now to begin your first simple application.

Try It Out: Creating Your First Web Forms Project

You'll use Visual Studio 2003 to create a new ASP.NET Web application. If you're using Visual C# or a different version of Visual Studio .NET, you may see a few minor details that differ from our figures, but you'll be able to follow the examples without a problem.

You'll be adding functionality to this project through a series of examples in this chapter that will show you more about how ASP.NET can work with data. Let's start by creating the project.

1. Open Visual Studio .NET, and create a new blank solution called Chapter10_Examples.

2. Add a new C# ASP.NET project to the solution by selecting File ➤ Add Project ➤ New Project.... Select Visual C# Projects, click the ASP.NET Web Application icon, specify Location as http://localhost/WebDataGrid, and click OK, as in Figure 10-1.

Figure 10-1. *Creating the* WebDataGrid *project*

3. As shown in Figure 10-1, the project creation dialog box takes on a slightly different look when selecting a Web application instead of a Windows application. Instead of finding a drive location for the new project, you need to enter an HTTP location. Internet Information Services (IIS), Microsoft's Web server, will process and serve your ASP.NET Web Forms application, so the form must be located in a directory managed by IIS. Visual Studio .NET will set up the application's IIS environment for you. All you need to do is give it a name—and make sure that IIS is already running. In this example you simply create the project on the local machine, and Visual Studio .NET configures IIS to accept the new project named WebDataGrid.

■**Tip** You control IIS with the Internet Services Manager. IIS should have been installed as part of your Windows environment. If it is, you can get to its documentation by going to http://localhost/iisHelp in any browser.

---

4. Once you click OK, your hard drive will get busy spinning, and eventually you'll have the basic building blocks of a Web application ready to go.

How It Works

Let's take a look at what Visual Studio .NET has created for you. When Visual Studio .NET displays your new project, you may notice some file types you don't recognize in Solution Explorer. Click the Show All Files icon, and expand the WebForm1.aspx item. Solution Explorer will appear as in Figure 10-2.

Figure 10-2. WebDataGrid *items expanded*

The following are important items specific to Web applications:

- Global.asax contains the code for responding to application-level events (for example, the Application_Start and Application_End events that fire when a Web application begins and ends).

- Web.config is an XML configuration file for the application. This file contains security, debugging, and other configuration information.

- WebForm1.aspx contains the *visual elements* of your Web Forms page, such as the controls and text to be rendered in HTML, XML, and so on.

- WebForm1.aspx.cs is the *code-behind* file for the Web form. The code-behind file contains the application logic to drive the .aspx.

Technically, you can place both code and controls inside the same .aspx file, but the separation makes the ongoing development and maintenance of the forms that much easier. For example, it allows a Web page designer to adjust the look and feel of a Web page independently of the programmer who is writing the code to implement the page's functionality. The .aspx file contains the control tags, HTML, and script sent to the Web browser, and the code-behind file contains C# code in a class.

Later in the chapter we'll discuss how the ASP.NET runtime binds these two pieces together when a client requests the form using a Web browser. For now, let's add some functionality to the application.

Try It Out: Designing the Web Form

Once Visual Studio .NET has finished creating all the files in the project, it automatically opens the Web form .aspx page and displays it in Design view, which, by default, starts off in Grid Layout mode. This mode allows the precise placement of the visual elements on your Web form using X and Y coordinates in much the same way controls are arranged in Windows form development.

An alternate layout mode is Flow Layout mode in which controls are arranged top to bottom as you add them to the form. Instead of having precise control over the placement of controls, flow layout lets the client's Web browser arrange the controls to match the user's environment as best it can; this is a good choice if you're trying to reach as many different types of clients as possible.

1. You'll work in Flow Layout mode, so the first thing to do is switch over from Grid Layout mode. Right-click the form, and select Properties from the context menu. In the Property Pages dialog box (Figure 10-3), change the Page Layout option to FlowLayout and click OK.

Figure 10-3. *Changing page layout*

2. When you're working with Web Forms in Design view, Visual Studio .NET adds two sections to the Toolbox window, called Web Forms and HTML, that contain the ASP.NET and HTML controls you can place on your Web form.

   You'll be using the DataGrid control from the Web Forms Toolbox. Make sure the Web Forms horizontal divider is selected, and within that pop-up group, double-click the DataGrid control. You'll see a data grid appear on the previously empty form (see Figure 10-4).

Figure 10-4. *Web Forms Toolbox*

3. Let's add some styling to the control. Right-click the data grid and select Auto Format... from the context menu to pick from a predesigned list of color schemes. Choose the Simple3 format, and click OK (see Figure 10-5).

Figure 10-5. *Selecting an Auto Format style*

4. The only other control you'll put on the form for the time being is a SqlConnection. You'll find it under the Data tab of the Toolbox. Double-click it to add it to the form,

and you'll notice it appears in the component tray. This is because the SqlConnection won't be visible to users who access your application.

5. Click the SqlConnection, and find the ConnectionString property. Select the blank box next to it, and a drop-down list will appear containing a list of all the database connections you have defined in Server Explorer and an option will appear to create a new connection. Back in Chapter 1, you created a connection to the Northwind database, and it's this that you'll select from the list. If it doesn't appear, choose the New Connection option and follow the steps in Chapter 1 to create it.

6. So far the Web form looks like the one in Figure 10-6. This is the Design view of the form. From here you can continue to tweak the design by setting properties and viewing the results in the What You See Is What You Get (WYSIWYG) editor. To get to the underlying source for the .aspx page, click the HTML button on the bottom of the Design window.

Figure 10-6. WebForm1 *layout*

How It Works

Let's walk through what you've created and examine some of the code that's generated automatically for you by Visual Studio .NET.

■Tip You may recall back in step 2 you learned that you can add both HTML controls and Web Forms controls to your Web form—let's take a quick look at what we meant by that. *HTML controls* are simple static controls, each control mapping to an equivalent HTML element. These controls are useful when you want to place, for example, a label on the page and not modify the contents when the page executes. By adding a `Runat="Server"` clause in the HTML of the page, though, you can interact with the controls on the server. This comes in handy when migrating a Web application already in place to ASP.NET, replacing old HTML directly with the equivalent control.

On the other hand, Web Forms controls, also known as *server controls*, are accessible by default from the code-behind C# code, meaning you can change a server control's appearance and populate the control with data specific to each incoming request. These controls reside in the `System.Web.UI.WebControls` namespace.

You've added two controls to the page, a `DataGrid` and a `SqlConnection`. However, the `SqlConnection` won't be displayed on the screen and so is dealt with only in the code-behind for the page and not the HTML determining how it looks on the screen. To see that this is so, you can click the HTML tab at the bottom of the Design window and look at the underlying `.aspx` source code (see Figure 10-7).

Figure 10-7. `WebForm1` *HTML view*

Let's walk through this code.

```
<%@ Page
    language="c#"
    Codebehind="WebForm1.aspx.cs"
    AutoEventWireup="false"
    Inherits="WebDataGrid.WebForm1" %>
```

The beginning of the file contains the @ Page directive. This gives the ASP.NET engine processing instructions for the .aspx, including the following:

- The source language for the file

- Where to find the corresponding code-behind file

- Whether you'll manually assign event handlers for the page in your own code (AutoEventWireup).

- The name of the C# class (declared in the code-behind file) with the logic for this page (Inherits)

Following the page directive, the head of the HTML page contains meta tags declaring the server- and client-side languages being used and the application generating the code.

```
<HEAD>
    <title>WebForm1</title>
    <meta name="GENERATOR" Content="Microsoft Visual Studio .NET 7.1">
    <meta name="CODE_LANGUAGE" Content="C#">
    <meta name="vs_defaultClientScript" content="JavaScript">
    <meta name="vs_targetSchema"
        content="http://schemas.microsoft.com/intellisense/ie5">
</HEAD>
```

The body of the HTML page contains the code for the DataGrid control you've pulled onto the form (see Listing 10-1).

Listing 10-1. *Body of* WebDataGrid *HTML Page*

```
<body>
    <form id="Form1" method="post" runat="server">
        <asp:DataGrid
            id="DataGrid1"
            runat="server"
            BorderColor="#336666"
            BorderStyle="Double"
            BorderWidth="3px"
            BackColor="White"
            CellPadding="4"
            GridLines="Horizontal">
            <SelectedItemStyle
```

```
                  Font-Bold="True"
                  ForeColor="White"
                  BackColor="#339966">
            </SelectedItemStyle>
            <ItemStyle
                  ForeColor="#333333"
                  BackColor="White">
            </ItemStyle>
            <HeaderStyle
                  Font-Bold="True"
                  ForeColor="White"
                  BackColor="#336666">
            </HeaderStyle>
            <FooterStyle
                  ForeColor="#333333"
                  BackColor="White">
            </FooterStyle>
            <PagerStyle
                  HorizontalAlign="Center"
                  ForeColor="White"
                  BackColor="#336666"
                  Mode="NumericPages">
            </PagerStyle>
        </asp:DataGrid>
    </form>
</body>
```

Server control tags (such as `<asp:DataGrid>`) contain all the color and style attributes for the control. The `Simple3` template you used to autoformat the grid set all these properties for you. Notice also that the nested properties will control the appearance of the column header, footer, and selected item.

The most important attributes in the server control tag are the `runat` and `id` attributes. Setting `runat="server"` tells ASP.NET to execute the control on the server, before the page goes to the client, allowing you to manipulate the control in C#, and `id` allows you to give the control a name with which you can access it from within your code. Let's look at the code itself now.

Viewing the Code-Behind File

The easiest way to view the code behind the form is to right-click the form (in Design view or in the Solution Explorer window) and select View Code from the context menu. Visual Studio .NET has generated all the code in this file, but you'll be adding your own code throughout the rest of the chapter. At the top, you'll find a set of `using` directives that allow you to access the types inside the other namespaces common in Web applications.

```
using System;
using System.Collections;
using System.ComponentModel;
using System.Data;
using System.Drawing;
using System.Web;
using System.Web.SessionState;
using System.Web.UI;
using System.Web.UI.WebControls;
using System.Web.UI.HtmlControls;
```

Of particular note in the next section of code are the two fields: sqlConnection1 and DataGrid1. These represent the components you dropped onto the form earlier. The ASP.NET runtime will initialize these variables to reference the form components when the user requests the page; you'll learn more about this subject in the "Understanding the ASP.NET Page Life Cycle" section. The class here is derived from the System.Web.UI.Page class. The Page class represents the .aspx form and provides a number of methods, properties, and events you'll use in the course of writing the data grid application.

```
namespace WebDataGrid
{
    /// <summary>
    /// Summary description for WebForm1.
    /// </summary>
    public class WebForm1 : System.Web.UI.Page
    {
        protected System.Web.UI.WebControls.DataGrid DataGrid1;
        protected System.Data.SqlClient.SqlConnection sqlConnection1;
```

The next method, Page_Load, is an event handler that the runtime will call after the page is initialized and the member variables reference the controls. In later examples you'll use this method to perform the data binding.

```
private void Page_Load(object sender, System.EventArgs e)
{
    // Put user code to initialize the page here
}
```

The rest of the file, between the #region markers, is managed by the designer. The two methods here are responsible for the initialization of variables and event handlers. You can see here the connection string you created back in step 5 is given to the sqlConnection1 member. You won't be changing any of the code in this section.

```
#region Web Form Designer generated code
override protected void OnInit(EventArgs e)
{
    //
    // CODEGEN: This call is required by the ASP.NET Web Form Designer.
    //
```

```
            InitializeComponent();
                            base.OnInit(e);
        }

        /// <summary>
        /// Required method for Designer support - do not modify
        /// the contents of this method with the code editor.
        /// </summary>
        private void InitializeComponent()
        {
            this.sqlConnection1 = new System.Data.SqlClient.SqlConnection();
            this.Load += new System.EventHandler(this.Page_Load);
        }
        #endregion
    }
}
```

Binding Data to a Data Grid

The first task is to bind some data that you'll pull from the Northwind database to the DataGrid control that you've added to our form. As you want to have the data display on the screen when the page is loaded, you'll tie this data binding into the Page_Load event, but it's perfectly possible to leave it until a user has clicked a button on the page first.

Try It Out: Binding Data

If you look back to the InitializeComponent method generated by Visual Studio .NET, you'll see that it automatically sets up an event handler to call the Page_Load method as the page is loaded. It's this method that lets you set up objects before the page generates any HTML output, and it's this method in which you'll do the data binding.

You don't need to add any more controls to the form itself, so all you need do is add to the code-behind in WebForm1.aspx.cs.

1. Add a using directive for the System.Data.SqlClient namespace at the top of the file. This will give you access to the SQL Server .NET data provider methods you'll need.

2. The way to bind data to a data grid is straightforward, but it's good practice to write it as a method that you can call more than once. Indeed, you'll see later in the chapter how this provides you with some flexibility when adding additional functionality. With the method written, all we need do then is call it from Page_Load.

```
private void Page_Load(object sender, System.EventArgs e)
{
    BindDataGrid();
}

private void BindDataGrid()
```

```
{
    SqlCommand sqlCommand = new SqlCommand();
    sqlCommand.CommandText = @"
        select
            firstname,
            lastname,
            title,
            extension
        from
            employees
    ";
    sqlConnection1.Open();
    sqlCommand.Connection = sqlConnection1;
    SqlDataReader sqlDataReader = sqlCommand.ExecuteReader();
    DataGrid1.DataSource = sqlDataReader;
    DataGrid1.DataBind();
    sqlConnection1.Close();
}
```

3. Build, and run with Ctrl+F5. Visual Studio will compile the code-behind file, launch Internet Explorer, and navigate the browser to the .aspx page, giving you the display in Figure 10-8.

Figure 10-8. WebDataGrid *running*

How It Works

If you look at `BindDataGrid` again, you'll find that all but the penultimate two lines of the method look decidedly familiar. All they're doing is creating a `DataReader` object that contains the data returned from the query you sent to `Northwind`. It's the following two calls to the data grid that actually do all the hard work:

```
DataGrid1.DataSource = sqlDataReader;
DataGrid1.DataBind();
```

The first call sets the `DataSource` property of the data grid to the data reader.

Tip Note that a data grid's data source could be a data view, an array, or indeed any object that implements the `System.Collections.IEnumerable` interface.

The actual binding takes place when you invoke the `DataBind` method of the data grid. Just like a Windows Forms data grid, the Web Forms data grid can display all the query results using the column names as headers.

The first data grid example is easy to get running, but it doesn't have much functionality. Throughout the rest of the chapter you'll add the ability to edit, delete, and sort rows in the data grid, as well as look at some of the additional differences in Web programming. The first feature you'll add is the ability to page the results.

Paging in a Data Grid

If you've ever used a Web-based search engine, then you've probably come across the scenario where your query has returned several million results, but rather than display all those results on one page, the page shows them in groups of 10, 50, or 100 at a time. Chances are you'll find what you're looking for in the first two or three pages anyway.

This act of breaking up a large set of results into groups that are easier to handle and adding controls for the user to navigate through these groups is known as *paging*.

Paging is important in Web applications for two reasons. First, it's nice to present your users with manageable chunks of information. If the `Employees` table of `Northwind` contained 5,000 rows, throwing all 5,000 items into the Web browser would create a long page of information. Second, the time needed to download the entire data for 5,000 rows could be quite a while. Even as broadband usage continues to pick up, keeping your pages small increases the perceived performance of the application. Showing only 50 rows at once is faster for the client than waiting for all 5,000 rows to appear.

Try It Out: Data Grid Paging

You can enable paging in a data grid in several ways, but they all amount to setting the data grid's `AllowPaging` property to `true`.

1. Right-click the data grid, and select Properties to open the Properties window and set `AllowPaging`.

2. Add the attribute to the @ Page server control tag in the `.aspx` (`AllowPaging="True"`).

3. If paging depends on some user preference setting (some users may want paged results, others may not), you could conditionally set the property in the Page_Load method using this:

```
DataGrid1.AllowPaging = FindThisUsersPagingPreference();
```

4. Set the property using the data grid's Property Builder.

In this example, you'll use the Property Builder. This tool categorizes the wide selection of properties for a data grid into functional tabs, and it's handy to know how to use it. You'll use it a few more times in this chapter before you finish.

1. Switch to Design view, and right-click the data grid. Select Property Builder... from the context menu. When the dialog box appears, click Paging in the left column (see Figure 10-9).

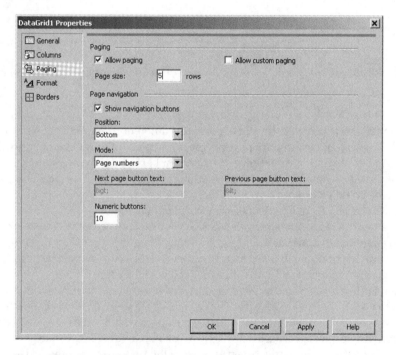

Figure 10-9. *Data grid Properties dialog box*

2. As shown in Figure 10-9, set the AllowPaging property to true by selecting the Allow Paging check box. Set the Page Size option (the number of rows to display per page) to 5. You can leave the location and the type of page navigation controls (next and previous hyperlinks vs. page-numbered hyperlinks) for the data grid at their defaults. However, if you wanted to provide your own custom navigation bar for moving among the pages, you'd clear the Show Navigation Buttons check box. Click OK.

3. With the data now separated into pages, you have to teach the data grid what to do when someone chooses to change the page. You do this by creating an event handler for the PageIndexChanged event.

   To assign an event handler, select the data grid in Design view and click the lightning bolt at the top of the Properties pane to switch to the event view for the data grid where you'll find an empty entry for the PageIndexChanged event.

4. Double-click the PageIndexChanged item, and the integrated development environment (IDE) opens the code-behind file and inserts an empty event handler for it. All you need to do is add these lines:

```
DataGrid1.CurrentPageIndex = e.NewPageIndex;
BindDataGrid();
```

5. Replace the code in the Page_Load method with the following:

```
if (!Page.IsPostBack)
{
    BindDataGrid();
}
```

6. Don't build and run this example yet. You won't see what you expect.

How It Works

So what will happen when you click the grid to move to a different page? Well, the Web form performs what's known as a *postback*. It's possibly the nicest piece of infrastructure provided by ASP.NET. A postback carries information from the client back to the Web server and allows you to handle events inside the Web form class—something that wouldn't happen automatically over the stateless HTTP protocol.

The PageIndexChanged event handler takes an argument of type DataGridPageChangedEventArgs containing the new page number to use in the NewPageIndex property. If you simply assign this value to the grid's CurrentPageIndex property and rebind the data, the data grid is smart enough to extract and display the rows for the new page. The grid then packages the rows as HTML and sends them back to the client.

You may remember you also had a call to BindDataGrid in the Page_Load method. Now you don't want to execute it again in Page_Load when a postback event occurs because the event handler will handle binding if needed. You need to check whether the page has been loaded as a result of a postback, because if it was, you'd end up binding to the data grid twice.

Fortunately, you inherit a property, IsPostBack, from the System.Web.UI.Page class to tell you if you're in a postback. That's why you modified the Page_Load method.

Combining a Data Grid and Dataset

Although the SqlDataReader class is the best choice for performance, it now has a limitation. If you compile and execute the code you have so far, you'll get the error shown in Figure 10-10.

Figure 10-10. WebDataGrid *error*

Although the DataSource property of the data grid accepts any object implementing IEnumerable, paging requires the data source object to implement ICollection, which SqlDataReader doesn't. Both ICollection and IEnumerable interfaces allow the grid to loop through each row in the result set, but ICollection provides a count of the total number if items in the result set, and IEnumerable doesn't.

The grid uses this count to determine the total number of pages required. You could perform some custom paging calculations to replace the pieces of ICollection that would do this automatically, but you'll take an alternate route and replace the data reader with a data view.

Try It Out: Binding to a Data View

All of the changes you need to switch from a data reader to a data view are in the BindDataGrid method.

1. Replace the existing version of BindDataGrid with the following code. Notice you're using the same query as before, but you now populate a dataset with the result set instead of retrieving it with a data reader. Note also that you used mixed case for the column names as a convenient way to display capitalized column headings. This isn't necessarily the most professional way to do things, but it's a simple expedient for the example's purposes.

```
private void BindDataGrid()
{
    string sql = @"
        select
            FirstName,
            LastName,
            Title,
```

```
              Extension
        from
            employees
    ";

    sqlConnection1.Open();
    SqlDataAdapter sqlDataAdapter =
        new SqlDataAdapter(sql, sqlConnection1);
    DataSet ds = new DataSet();
    sqlDataAdapter.Fill(ds, "employees");
    DataGrid1.DataSource = ds.Tables["employees"].DefaultView;
    DataGrid1.DataBind();
    sqlConnection1.Close();
}
```

How It Works

The reworked BindDataGrid pulls the data from the Northwind database into a data table in a dataset. The data grid's DataSource property is then set to the DefaultView of that data table. Note that it's the DefaultView property (a data view) of the data table rather than the data table itself that implements ICollection and allows the data grid to perform paging calculations for you.

Using a dataset will turn out to have several other advantages for you, as you'll see later, but right now, let's make sure it actually works. You should now be able to build and execute the form without errors. As shown in Figure 10-11, the form will display five rows with hyperlink page numbers to click and see the rest.

Figure 10-11. *Revised* WebDataGrid *running*

The next step in the application is to build in a small caching feature, but before you do that it'll help a lot if you take a step back and look at how the ASP.NET runtime processes the page. This background information will allow you to make some more improvements to the application in addition to caching.

Understanding the ASP.NET Page Life Cycle

The first time a request arrives for an `.aspx` page, the ASP.NET runtime combines the `.aspx` page with the class in the code-behind file and creates a new class. The runtime dynamically compiles this new class and caches the result to service future requests. Figure 10-12 depicts the life cycle.

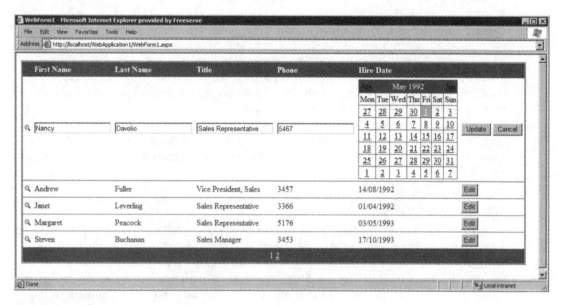

Figure 10-12. *ASP.NET page life cycle*

For each request, the runtime will instantiate a new instance of this class. This means when a user requests the paged data grid you built and then clicks a new page number, a new instance of the dynamically generated class services the request—you don't have the same instance of the class you used for the initial request. This is a primary difference between Web Forms and Windows Forms. In Windows Forms, the same class can continue to handle events for a user during the entire life of the application.

To help cover these seams, the ASP.NET runtime will repopulate the form's controls on post-back with all the properties just as they appeared on the client. So, for instance, a check box control marked *checked* on the client and then posted to the Web server will have its Checked property set to true, instead of the default value of false. ASP.NET refers to this process as restoring the *view state*.

After restoring the view state, the runtime fires the Load event, and the code can perform any initialization you need. Once this step is complete, any postback events are fired, such as the OnPageIndexChanged event you handle in the paged data grid. Finally, the page will render itself, and the result is a combination of HTML and script sent back over the network to the client. After rendering, the class is disposed of, freeing up resources to handle other incoming requests. Remember, in Web applications, thousands of users may be requesting Web Forms at the same time.

Building for Scalability

Scalable software has the ability to perform well as the number of concurrent users increases. The ASP.NET runtime engine provides everything you need to write robust and scalable Web applications, as long as you follow a few guidelines. Let's go through a few basic tips for scalability in database Web applications.

First, you need to be conservative with server resources such as memory and database connections. In the sample code for this chapter, you'll close the database connection explicitly when you're finished with the queries. This immediately frees up a connection to use elsewhere. You could wait for the runtime to dispose of the page and let the garbage collection close the database connection, but doing so only holds a resource for longer than you need and may prevent other requests from executing immediately.

Second, avoid trips to the database when possible. For example, we avoid binding the data grid during the Page_Load method during a postback. We know the postback event will rebind the data if necessary. Try to avoid unnecessary queries, and retrieve only the data you need for processing.

Understanding Caching

Like any programming guidelines, however, one must often be traded off against the other, and it's left to you to determine the balance for your own application. The balance between the two recommendations we've given, for example, applies when you start to think about caching data you've pulled from the database. Caching a query result in memory on the server uses more memory resources; on the other hand, it also saves a trip to the database. Evaluating these types of trade-offs correctly can help the performance of your application.

For example, once you query the Employees table and send the results to the client in a paged data grid, you can assume the client is probably going to examine more rows. If you simply reload the dataset from memory instead of from the database, you can save a trip to the database. Caching the dataset sounds like a good idea, particularly since you have a small number of rows in the table. If the Employees table contained thousands of rows, you may use too much memory for caching and actually hurt server performance. Evaluating these trade-offs usually requires you to factor in the number of users you support, the hardware your application runs on, and even how users navigate through the application.

Many techniques for caching are available in ASP.NET. In this example you'll use the Session object. The Session object allows you to store data specific to each client. ASP.NET creates a new session when a client first navigates to your site. After a specified amount of inactivity (20 minutes is the default), ASP.NET will clear a user's session contents to conserve resources.

You can configure ASP.NET to store session contents in memory (the default option and also the fastest option) or even in a SQL Server database. Although storing the results of a database query in a database may sound strange, if the original query is particularly compli-cated, you still may see a performance gain. Also, remember you could store multiple queries in the same dataset.

Try It Out: Using a Session

Follow these steps:

1. First, update the BindDataGrid method with the code in Listing 10-2. We've highlighted new and changed code in bold. Notice the method takes a bool parameter to force a refresh of the dataset from the database instead of the session cache.

Listing 10-2. *Revised* BindDataGrid

```
private void BindDataGrid(bool refresh)
{
    DataSet ds = null;
    if (refresh == true >> Session["employees"] == null)
    {
        string sql = @"
            select
                FirstName,
                LastName,
                Title,
                Extension
            from
                employees
        ";

        sqlConnection1.Open();
        SqlDataAdapter sqlDataAdapter =
            new SqlDataAdapter(sql, sqlConnection1);
        ds = new DataSet();
        sqlDataAdapter.Fill(ds, "employees");
        Session["employees"] = ds;
        sqlConnection1.Close();
    }
    else
    {
        ds = (DataSet)Session["employees"];
    }

    DataGrid1.DataSource = ds.Tables["employees"].DefaultView;
    DataGrid1.DataBind();
    sqlConnection1.Close();
}
```

2. Add a second version of BindDataGrid (see Listing 10-3). This parameterless version forwards the call to the boolean BindDataGrid without requesting a refresh of the dataset from the database. This will allow you to bind a data grid without always specifying a refresh parameter.

Listing 10-3. *Parameterless* BindDataGrid

```
private void BindDataGrid()
{
    BindDataGrid(false);
}
```

3. In the Page_Load method, add a true argument to the call to BindDataGrid. This ensures the most recent data is retrieved when the page is first loaded. DataGrid1_PageIndexChanged can remain the same and pull data from the Session cache.

```
private void Page_Load(object sender, System.EventArgs e)
{
    if (!Page.IsPostBack)
    {
        BindDataGrid(true);
    }
}
```

How It Works

You've now overloaded the BindDataGrid method, creating two versions with different signatures. The first now has a boolean parameter (or *flag*) to force a refresh of the session contents, because one other big danger in caching data is showing your user out-of-date results when someone else has changed the underlying data. The best data to cache is static data; trying to cache rapidly changing information may show incorrect results.

Notice that you first test the Session collection (an instance of the HttpSessionState class) to see if an item named employees exists. If this returns null, or if the refresh flag is set, you need to query the database and populate a new dataset to store in the session. During Page_Load, you force a refresh to ensure the user sees the most current data, but during processing of the OnPageIndexChanged event, you allow the page to use a cached copy of the data and save yourself a trip to the database.

Selecting a Row

So far, so good—the data grid has done everything you've asked of it so far, but it's not the be-all and end-all of simple data retrieval. Indeed, it's just not suited to displaying some types of data, be it for practical or aesthetic reasons. Take, for instance, the Notes field in Northwind's Employees table, which contains some additional facts and background information about staff stored as free-form text.

Rather than displaying this text directly in the data grid, which would clutter up the screen quite a bit, you'll implement a more elegant solution and allow users to select the row containing the employee they want to know more about. When they do select a row, the Notes about that employee will appear in a separate area of the Web form.

Adding a select capability to the data grid is similar to the steps you just used in adding paging. First, you'll adjust the data grid properties and then add an event handler. You'll also need to add some more user interface elements to display the employee's notes.

Try It Out: Adding a Detail Display

Follow these steps:

1. Return to the property builder once more by right-clicking the DataGrid control in Design view and selecting Property Builder....

2. Select Columns. Under the list of available columns, expand the Button Column node and move a Select node into the list of Selected columns. Change the Button type to PushButton, and leave the defaults for all other settings. This will give you a column of buttons for the user to push when selecting a row.

3. Check the Create Columns Automatically at Run Time check box. If you fail to do this, the grid will display only your columns of check boxes. The Property Builder should look like Figure 10-13. Click OK.

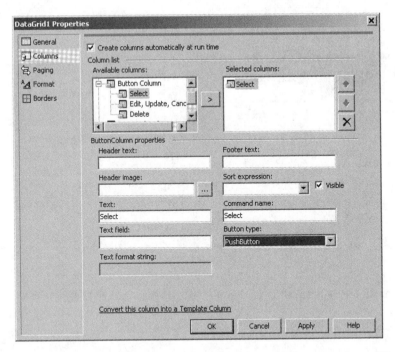

Figure 10-13. *Adding a button column to a data grid with Property Builder*

4. Drag a Panel Web control from the Toolbox onto the form. A panel is a container for other controls, which will come in handy when you want to show and hide the detail

information display. Set the panel's Visible property to False. Instead of hiding and displaying all the controls individually, you'll just hide and display the panel control (and therefore all its contents as well) instead.

5. Widen the panel on the form to 250 × 50 pixels. Add a Table to it. It should have one column and two rows.

6. Drag a Label control from the Web Forms section of the Toolbox to the second row of the table. You'll use it to display the notes. In keeping with the color scheme, you'll adjust the layout and color properties of the two new controls so the Design view of the updated form looks like Figure 10-14.

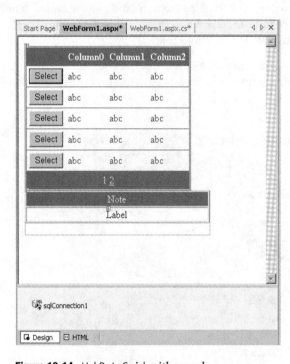

Figure 10-14. WebDataGrid *with panel*

The .aspx for this section of the page should contain the code in Listing 10-4.

Listing 10-4. WebDataGrid *Panel* .aspx *Code*

```
<asp:Panel
    id="Panel1"
    runat="server"
    HorizontalAlign="Center"
    Width="260px"
    Height="50px"
    Visible="False">
```

```
<TABLE
    id="Table1"
    cellSpacing="1"
    cellPadding="1"
    width="300"
    border="1">
    <TR>
        <TD
            style="COLOR: white"
            align="middle"
            bgColor="#336666"
            colSpan="1"
            rowSpan="1">
            Note
        </TD>
    </TR>
    <TR>
        <TD align="middle">
            <asp:Label
                id="Label1"
                runat="server">
                Label
            </asp:Label>
        </TD>
    </TR>
</TABLE>
</asp:Panel>
```

7. The event you want to catch when a user has selected a row is the SelectedIndexChanged
   event, so you need to create a handler for it. Right-click the grid, select Properties from
   the context menu, and click the Events icon (the lightning bolt) in the Properties pane.
   Double-click the SelectedIndexChange event to switch to the code-behind file with the
   focus on an empty event handler. Add the following code to the empty method:

```
string key = DataGrid1.DataKeys[DataGrid1.SelectedIndex].ToString();
string sql = @"
    select
        Notes
    from
        Employees
    where
        EmployeeID = @EmployeeID
";
sqlConnection1.Open();
SqlCommand sqlCommand = new SqlCommand(sql, sqlConnection1);
sqlCommand.Parameters.Add("@EmployeeID", key);
SqlDataReader sqlDataReader = sqlCommand.ExecuteReader();
```

```
        if(sqlDataReader.Read())
        {
          Label1.Text = sqlDataReader["Notes"].ToString();
          Panel1.Visible = true;
        }
        sqlDataReader.Close();
        sqlConnection1.Close();
```

How It Works

The first step in the event handler is finding the EmployeeID of the employee to detail. You haven't needed to access this in this example yet, so you'll have to add EmployeeID to the query in BindDataGrid.

```
string sql = @"
   select
      EmployeeID,
      FirstName,
      LastName,
      Title,
      Extension
   from
      employees
         ";
```

The EmployeeID field will now be bound to the grid with the other information, but how do you retrieve the ID of the selected employee from the grid? You actually have several ways to achieve this, but one of the safest approaches is to use the DataKeys collection of the data grid. This property is specifically designed to hold the primary key values for each row as they appear in the grid. All you need to do is to give the data grid the name of the field containing the key values, in this case EmployeeID. You add the following code to the BindDataGrid method, just after assigning the DataSource property.

```
DataGrid1.DataSource = dataSet.Tables["Employees"].DefaultView;
DataGrid1.DataKeyField = "EmployeeID";
```

You can retrieve the correct ID to use from DataKeys by using the SelectedIndex property of the data grid. Once you've retrieved the results of the query, you simply need to set the Label control's Text property to display the notes and then unhide the Panel control. The grid will automatically highlight the selected row for you using the SelectedItem style property. The resulting display should look like Figure 10-15.

Note that EmployeeID is now also shown in the grid, even though it's of no real use to the user. In the "Using Bound Columns" section, you'll look at keeping EmployeeID from being displayed in the data grid and use the column only to populate the DataKeys collection.

Figure 10-15. *Displaying* Notes *for a selected employee*

Tweaking the View State

If you build and run the page now, you'll see that everything seems to be working fine. However, a problem exists that's easy to re-create. Select a row on the first page (say, row two) and then move to page two. Without some additional code, you'll see that the data grid will still think the second row on this new page is the one that has been selected, which it isn't. If you had selected the fifth row, this would have been even more awkward because page two doesn't have a fifth row to display.

The problem lies in that when ASP.NET rebuilds the data grid as a form is posted back, it simply re-creates the whole of a server control's view state unless told otherwise. Consider that when a row is selected, you don't call BindDataGrid in the respective event handler, because nothing in the data grid has changed. The data grid can continue to use the same information you sent during the initial page request. The data grid saved the initial information in the view state, and the runtime restored this information during the initialization step of the postback request. During rendering, the data grid simply rewrote the HTML, with some slight adjustments to the formatting for the selected row.

What you need to do is reset the SelectedIndex property of the data grid to –1, meaning no row is selected, and then rehide the detail panel. The updated code for the DataGrid1_PageIndexChanged event handler for the paging event is as follows:

```
DataGrid1.CurrentPageIndex = e.NewPageIndex;
DataGrid1.SelectedIndex = -1;
Panel1.Visible = false;
BindDataGrid();
```

You're starting to see a fairly functional database application emerge. However, you have still some cosmetic problems. For instance, the column names use the name of the database field instead of a friendly name. In the next section, you'll look at how to customize the columns of the data grid.

Using Bound Columns

Bound columns give you more control over the look of the columns in a data grid. Instead of letting the data grid create, name, and format columns automatically, you can explicitly specify the columns for the grid to use.

Try It Out: Adding Bound Columns

Follow these steps:

1. You begin again with the Property Builder dialog box for the grid by right-clicking the data grid, selecting PropertyBuilder..., and selecting Columns. Uncheck the Create Columns Automatically at Run Time check box.

2. From the Available columns list, move a Bound Column node into the Selected columns list for each column you need to display. For each column you set the Header text to the text you prefer (for instance, *First Name*) and the Data Field to the database column to bind to (*FirstName*). Move a Bound Column node over for First Name, Last Name, Title, and Phone.

3. You'll now add the staff's hire dates to the grid to demonstrate how you can format a column automatically. Add `HireDate` to the query in the `BindDataGrid` method.

```
string sql = @"
    select
        EmployeeID,
        FirstName,
        LastName,
        Title,
        Extension,
        HireDate
    from
        employees
";
```

4. Back in the Property Builder, add another bound column for the Hire Date and set the Data Formatting Expression option to {0:d}. This is the same format specifier as used in the Format method of the String class. It indicates a short date format and will exclude the time of day in the output. Check the Read Only check box as well (see Figure 10-16). You'll see why in the "Editing a Data Grid" section.

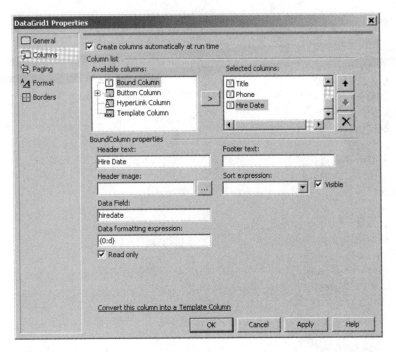

Figure 10-16. *Adding a read-only column*

5. Last but not least, you'll alter the button column in the grid to use your own image rather than a button. Select the Select column in the Selected Columns list box and change Button Type to LinkButton and Text to `<img border=0 src=magnify.gif>`. (You'll find this image in the code download in the Chapter 10 solution.)

Behind the scenes, the Property Builder has been turning your bound instructions into their corresponding code within the `<asp:datagrid>` controls tags.

```
<asp:datagrid
  id="DataGrid1"
  runat="server"
  BorderColor="#336666"
    BorderStyle="Double"
    BorderWidth="3px"
  BackColor="White"
  CellPadding="4"
  GridLines="Horizontal"
  PageSize="5"
  AllowPaging="True">
  <SelectedItemStyle
    Font-Bold="True"
    ForeColor="White"
    BackColor="#339966">
  </SelectedItemStyle>
  <ItemStyle
```

```
            ForeColor="#333333"
            BackColor="White">
        </ItemStyle>
        <HeaderStyle
            Font-Bold="True"
            ForeColor="White"
            BackColor="#336666">
        </HeaderStyle>
        <FooterStyle
            ForeColor="#333333"
            BackColor="White">
        </FooterStyle>
        <Columns>
            <asp:ButtonColumn
                Text="&lt;img border=0 src=magnify.gif&gt;"
                CommandName="Select">
            </asp:ButtonColumn>
            <asp:BoundColumn
                DataField="firstname"
                HeaderText="First Name">
            </asp:BoundColumn>
            <asp:BoundColumn
                DataField="lastname"
                HeaderText="Last Name">
            </asp:BoundColumn>
            <asp:BoundColumn
                DataField="title"
                HeaderText="Title">
            </asp:BoundColumn>
            <asp:BoundColumn
                DataField="extension" HeaderText="Phone">
            </asp:BoundColumn>
            <asp:BoundColumn
                DataField="hiredate"
                ReadOnly="True"
                HeaderText="Hire Date"
                DataFormatString="{0:d}">
            </asp:BoundColumn>
        </Columns>
        <PagerStyle
            HorizontalAlign="Center"
            ForeColor="White"
            BackColor="#336666"
            Mode="NumericPages">
        </PagerStyle>
    </asp:datagrid>
```

6. Rebuild, and run the new version of WebDataGrid. It should now look like Figure 10-17.

Figure 10-17. *Revised* WebDataGrid

How It Works

This example has two interesting items to note. First, you didn't specify a column for the EmployeeID field, but it's still a part of the query. You need EmployeeID when a user clicks to see more details about an employee, so you still include this field in the query and assign EmployeeID to the DataKeyField property of the data grid. However, since you now have control over which columns from the dataset appear, and since an internal identifier may not be of much value to the user, you simply don't provide a column to display EmployeeID.

Second, you slightly changed the ButtonColumn. Instead of displaying a push button for selecting a row, you now display a link button. In addition, you changed the Text property of the column to write an HTML image tag. This gives our grid a slightly fancier look with a custom icon (a magnifying glass).

Editing a Data Grid

So far, you've worked with the DataGrid control purely as a means to view the data already stored in a database, but you can use it to edit and update data as well.

Try It Out: Adding Editing Capability

To trigger the data grid's inline editing facilities, you'll add another button to the right of each row so users can indicate which row they want to alter.

1. Open the Property Builder dialog box for the data grid once again. In the dialog box, go to the Available Columns area and expand the Button Column node. Then move an Edit, Update, Cancel button into the list of selected columns. You'll place this new

column at the end of the list so the buttons appear on the far right. Change the Button type to PushButton. The new column will give you three new events to handle.
Click OK.

This new button column means you now have to cater for the three possibilities
you've given the user: edit a row, update the database, and cancel editing and return to
read-only mode. The next job, then, is to write the handlers for these three events.

2. First, you'll deal with a click of the Edit button. In Design view, select the data grid and
switch to the Events view (click the lightning bolt) in the Properties pane. Double-click
EditCommand. Add the following code to the newly generated handler:

```
DataGrid1.EditItemIndex = e.Item.ItemIndex;
BindDataGrid();
```

3. Double-click CancelCommand in the event list, and add the following code to handle the
Cancel button:

```
DataGrid1.EditItemIndex = -1;
BindDataGrid();
```

4. You need to code an UPDATE statement for the data grid, using the values from the text
box controls in the edited row. Double-click UpdateCommand, and add the following code:

```
string key = DataGrid1.DataKeys[DataGrid1.EditItemIndex].ToString();
string sql =   @"
    update employees
    set
        firstname = @firstname,
        lastname = @lastname,
        title = @title,
        extension = @extension
    where
        employeeid = @employeeid
";

sqlConnection1.Open();
SqlCommand sqlCommand = new SqlCommand(sql, sqlConnection1);
sqlCommand.Parameters.Add("@employeeid", key);
sqlCommand.Parameters.Add("@firstname",
                    ((TextBox)(e.Item.Cells[1].Controls[0])).Text);
sqlCommand.Parameters.Add("@lastname",
                    ((TextBox)(e.Item.Cells[2].Controls[0])).Text);
sqlCommand.Parameters.Add("@title",
                    ((TextBox)(e.Item.Cells[3].Controls[0])).Text);
sqlCommand.Parameters.Add("@extension",
                    ((TextBox)(e.Item.Cells[4].Controls[0])).Text);

sqlCommand.ExecuteNonQuery();
sqlConnection1.Close();
```

```
DataGrid1.EditItemIndex = -1;
BindDataGrid(true);
```

5. Build and run the Web form with Ctrl+F5. Click the Edit button in the fourth row to see Figure 10-18.

Figure 10-18. WebDataGrid *with editing buttons*

How It Works

When you click the Edit button, the DataGrid1_EditCommand method is invoked, and you can find out which row is selected from the DataGridCommandEventArgs parameter. Making the row into a set of editable text boxes is then a matter of updating the data grid's EditItemIndex property and rebinding the data to update the new edit controls. The data grid will then provide an edit box for each column in the row, with the exception of Hire Date, because you marked this column as read-only.

Once a row is in edit mode, the user can change the values in each text box and click either Cancel or Update. These are the other two events you handle. For a cancel event, you just need to reset the data grid's EditItemIndex property to –1, indicating no row is being edited, and then rebind the data to ensure the data grid reflects this.

To handle the update event, the first step is retrieving the EmployeeID to update from the DataKeys collection.

```
string key = DataGrid1.DataKeys[DataGrid1.EditItemIndex].ToString();
```

Then, to get the updated field values, you use the DataGridCommandEventArgs parameter. As you saw earlier, this parameter contains an Item property representing the currently selected row in the data grid. Item is a reference to a DataGridItem object. Previously you used the ItemIndex property of DataGridItem to simply see which row the user clicked, but this time you need to dig a little deeper.

The DataGridItem contains a Cells collection, and one cell exists for each column in the grid. The first cell (Cell[0]) is the select column with the magnifying glass. The second cell

(Cell[1]) is the first name column—and so on for each column. You must visit each cell containing a value you need and extract the contents of the edited text box.

Each cell contains a property named Controls. This collection contains all the child controls in the cell. For bound columns in a data grid, the text box is always the only control in the collection; thus you use Controls[0] to retrieve a reference to the text box. You cast the object returned from the Controls collection to a TextBox and then extract the Text property.

```
sqlCommand.Parameters.Add("@firstname",
                     ((TextBox)(e.Item.Cells[1].Controls[0])).Text);
sqlCommand.Parameters.Add("@lastname",
                     ((TextBox)(e.Item.Cells[2].Controls[0])).Text);
sqlCommand.Parameters.Add("@title",
                     ((TextBox)(e.Item.Cells[3].Controls[0])).Text);
sqlCommand.Parameters.Add("@extension",
                     ((TextBox)(e.Item.Cells[4].Controls[0])).Text);
```

Before you leave the DataGrid1_UpdateCommand method you have to reset the EditItemIndex property to force the grid out of edit mode. Then you have to bind the data source again, forcing a refresh by passing true to BindDataGrid so the refresh will pick up the new values from the database and reset the cached dataset in the Session.

Finally, you need to modify the DataGrid1_PageIndexChanged event handler one more time. You need to ensure that edit mode is canceled if the user changes pages in the middle of an edit. This will prevent the same problem discussed earlier when a row is selected and the page is changed. The following code shows the updated method. Add the bold line to the method.

```
public void DataGrid1_PageIndexChanged(object source,
             DataGridPageChangedEventArgs e)
{
    DataGrid1.CurrentPageIndex = e.NewPageIndex;
    DataGrid1.SelectedIndex = -1;
    DataGrid1.EditItemIndex = -1;
    Panel1.Visible = false;
    BindDataGrid();
}
```

In the next section you'll allow the user to also edit the hire date but with a new type of column: a *template* column.

Using Template Columns

A template column affords you the highest level of control over a data grid column's appearance. It's completely up to you as the developer to determine when and how to display data from the data source using a *data binding expression*. You could, for example, combine the first name and last name columns into a single column using a template column. To demonstrate, you'll use a template column to display the hire date.

Try It Out: Using a Template Column

Follow these steps:

1. Open the Property Builder for the data grid again, and select the Hire Date column in the list of Selected Columns. Click the Convert This Column into a Template Column link. Click OK.

2. You'll modify the Template Column directly in HTML view. Visual Studio .NET has already coded for the static view of the date, but you'll add the template for editing the date. Add the bold code to the asp:TemplateColumn element.

```
<asp:TemplateColumn HeaderText="Hire Date">
  <ItemTemplate>
    <asp:Label
      runat="server"
      Text=
      '<%# DataBinder.Eval(Container,"DataItem.HireDate","{0:d}")%>'>
    </asp:Label>
  </ItemTemplate>
  <EditItemTemplate>
    <asp:Calendar
      ID="Calendar1" Runat="server" BorderColor="#336666"
      ShowGridLines="True" NextPrevFormat="ShortMonth"
      VisibleDate='<%# DataBinder.Eval(Container, "DataItem.HireDate") %>'
      SelectedDate='<%# DataBinder.Eval(Container, "DataItem.HireDate") %>'>
      <TitleStyle ForeColor="White" BackColor="#336666"></TitleStyle>
    </asp:Calendar>
  </EditItemTemplate>
</asp:TemplateColumn>
```

3. The grid is now set up to edit HireDate, but you need to adjust the event handler for the Update button so that it will update the HireDate column as well. Modify the UpdateCommand handler with the following bold code:

```
private void DataGrid1_UpdateCommand(object source,
  System.Web.UI.WebControls.DataGridCommandEventArgs e)
{
  string key = DataGrid1.DataKeys[DataGrid1.EditItemIndex].ToString();
    string sql = @"
      update employees
      set
        firstname = @firstname,
        lastname = @lastname,
        title = @title,
        extension = @extension,
        hiredate = @hiredate
      where
        employeeid = @employeeid
    ";
```

```
sqlConnection1.Open();
SqlCommand sqlCommand = new SqlCommand(sql, sqlConnection1);
sqlCommand.Parameters.Add("@employeeid", key);
sqlCommand.Parameters.Add("@firstname",
    ((TextBox)(e.Item.Cells[1].Controls[0])).Text);
sqlCommand.Parameters.Add("@lastname",
    ((TextBox)(e.Item.Cells[2].Controls[0])).Text);
sqlCommand.Parameters.Add("@title",
    ((TextBox)(e.Item.Cells[3].Controls[0])).Text);
sqlCommand.Parameters.Add("@extension",
    ((TextBox)(e.Item.Cells[4].Controls[0])).Text);
sqlCommand.Parameters.Add("@hiredate",
    ((Calendar)
     (e.Item.Cells[5].FindControl("Calendar1"))).
        SelectedDate.ToString());

    sqlCommand.ExecuteNonQuery();
    sqlConnection1.Close();

    DataGrid1.EditItemIndex = -1;
    BindDataGrid(true);
    }
```

4. Run with Ctrl+F5. When you try to edit a column, a `Calendar` control will appear in place of the date for you to choose another one (see Figure 10-19).

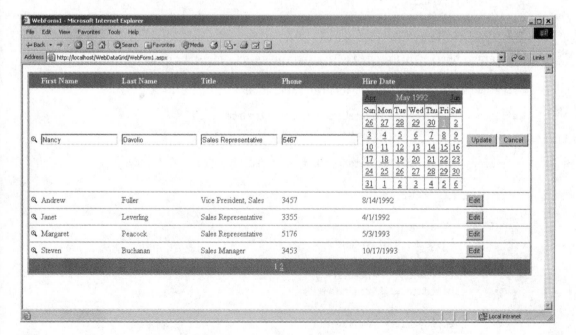

Figure 10-19. Calendar *control provided for editing*

How It Works

Every template column is composed of one or more item templates. In this example, you use an ItemTemplate and an EditItemTemplate, but HeaderTemplates and FooterTemplates exist as well. The ItemTemplate controls the appearance of the data during normal viewing, and the EditItemTemplate controls the view when the item is in edit mode.

For the item template, you've used a simple Label control, and for the edit template, you've used a Calendar control. While the regular display for the hire date will look the same as when the column was a bound column, the edit display will look entirely different, albeit somewhat ungainly. (As an exercise you may like to try to improve the aesthetics.)

It's possible to insert any amount of text, HTML, and server-side controls into a template to achieve the desired result. When you're ready to display data from the data source, you'll need to use a data binding expression.

As you can see from the previous .aspx code snippet, data bindings use a special expression format. You always place the expression between the delimiters: <%# and %>.

```
<asp:Label
  runat="server"
  Text=
  '<%# DataBinder.Eval(Container,"DataItem.HireDate","{0:d}")%>'>
</asp:Label>
```

Inside these delimiters you use the static Eval method of the DataBinder class; this method was designed for just this purpose. Eval has two required parameters: first the container and then the expression to evaluate against the container. For a data grid, the container is always the Container. The expression is the field name to use, in this case DataItem.HireDate.

In the previous example you set the Label control's Text property to the result of a data binding expression. For the calendar control, you need to set both the SelectedDate and VisibleDate properties to make sure the hire date is both highlighted and visible in the monthly calendar.

Updating the employee hire date value uses the same basic logic to extract the date value from the Calendar control but with one slight difference—you can't be exactly sure where the Calendar control actually appears in the cell's Control collection. To get a reference to the calendar then, you use the cell's FindControl method and pass it the ID of the calendar control, as shown in the following expression:

```
sqlCommand.Parameters.Add("@hiredate",
    ((Calendar)
    (e.Item.Cells[5].FindControl("Calendar1"))).
        SelectedDate.ToString());
```

Deleting Rows

With what you've learned in this chapter, you should find adding the ability to delete a row an almost familiar task, and indeed it is. Again, the data grid provides you with a lot of help to achieve this.

Try It Out: Deleting Rows

Follow these steps:

1. In Design view, right-click the data grid and open the Property Builder again. Click Columns, expand the Button Column node, and move a Delete button into the list of Selected Columns. Click OK.

2. Now open the Properties pane for the data grid and switch to Events view. Double-click the DeleteCommand entry in the event list, and add the following code to the new event handler:

```
DataGrid1.SelectedIndex = -1;
Panel1.Visible = false;
DataGrid1.EditItemIndex = -1;

string key = DataGrid1.DataKeys[e.Item.ItemIndex].ToString();
string sql = @"
    delete from employees
    where
        employeeid = @employeeid
";

sqlConnection1.Open();

SqlCommand sqlCommand = new SqlCommand(sql, sqlConnection1);
sqlCommand.Parameters.Add("@employeeid", key);
sqlCommand.ExecuteNonQuery();

sqlConnection1.Close();

BindDataGrid(true);
```

3. Run with Ctrl+F5. You'll be able to delete from the Employees table any employee who has taken no orders. If they have, however, deleting them without first deleting their orders would violate referential integrity, and you'll get an error.

How It Works

The event handler for the Delete button is quite straightforward. First you set the data grid back to its original state by resetting SelectedIndex and EditItemIndex and making the Notes panel invisible again.

```
DataGrid1.SelectedIndex = -1;
Panel1.Visible = false;
DataGrid1.EditItemIndex = -1;
```

Second, you grab the EmployeeID of the row to be deleted from the DataKeys collection, as you've done before, and build a DELETE statement.

```
string key = DataGrid1.DataKeys[e.Item.ItemIndex].ToString();
string sql = @"
    delete from employees
    where
        employeeid = @employeeid
";
```

Finally, you execute the query and force a refresh while rebinding the data grid.

```
sqlConnection1.Open();

SqlCommand sqlCommand = new SqlCommand(sql, sqlConnection1);
sqlCommand.Parameters.Add("@employeeid", key);
sqlCommand.ExecuteNonQuery();

sqlConnection1.Close();

BindDataGrid(true);
```

Sorting a Data Grid

The final feature to add to the data grid is the ability to sort the rows by any column.

Try It Out: Adding Sorting to a Data Grid

Follow these steps;

1. Adding the ability to sort begins with, as you may have guessed by now, the Property Builder dialog box. In the General section of the dialog box, check the Allow Sorting check box. Doing this will change the column headings into hyperlinks that will raise the OnSortCommand when they're clicked.

2. For each bound column, specify a Sort Expression matching the Data Field. For example, set the Sort Expression for the First Name column to firstname, the Last Name column to lastname, and so on. When you've finished, click OK.

3. Now open the Properties pane for the data grid, and switch to Events view. Double-click the SortCommand entry in the event list, and add the following code to the new event handler. Notice that you modify the data binding code to accept a sort expression and simply forward the sort expression to this method for processing.

   ```
   DataGrid1.SelectedIndex = -1;
   Panel1.Visible = false;
   DataGrid1.EditItemIndex = -1;
   BindDataGrid(e.SortExpression);
   ```

4. BindDataGrid won't accept a sort expression until you update it. You'll overload it with two new versions. A caller will now be able to pass no parameters, just a refresh flag, just a sort expression, or both a refresh flag and a sort expression. Replace the two BindDataGrid methods with the following code:

```
private void BindDataGrid()
{
    BindDataGrid(false, null);
}

private void BindDataGrid(bool refresh)
{
    BindDataGrid(refresh, null);
}

private void BindDataGrid(string sortExpression)
{
    BindDataGrid(false, sortExpression);
}

private void BindDataGrid(bool refresh, string sortExpression)
{
    DataSet dataSet = null;
    if(refresh == true || Session["Employees"] == null)
    {
        string sql = @"
            select
                employeeid,
                firstname,
                lastname,
                title,
                extension,
                hiredate
            from
                employees
        ";

        sqlConnection1.Open();
        SqlDataAdapter sqlDataAdapter =
                        new SqlDataAdapter(sql, sqlConnection1);
        dataSet = new DataSet();
        sqlDataAdapter.Fill(dataSet, "employees");
```

```
        Session["employees"] = dataSet;
        sqlConnection1.Close();
    }
    else
    {
        dataSet = (DataSet)Session["employees"];
    }

    DataView dataView = dataSet.Tables["employees"].DefaultView;
    if (sortExpression != null)
    {
        dataView.Sort = sortExpression;
    }
    DataGrid1.DataSource = dataView;
    DataGrid1.DataKeyField = "employeeid";
    DataGrid1.DataBind();
}
```

5. Run with Ctrl+F5. Click any column heading to sort that column in ascending order. Figure 10-20 shows a sort by last name.

Figure 10-20. *Sorting by columns*

How It Works

When you click a column heading and raise a SortCommand event, its handler takes two parameters. One is the source, and the other is of type DataGridSortCommandEventArgs. One of the properties of this parameter is a string, SortExpression. You can specify a sort expression for each bound column and template column in the data grid. The sort expression passed in the event handler parameter is the sort expression given to the column. For example, you gave the

Last Name column the sort expression `lastname`. When a user clicks on the Last Name header, this is the sort expression used by the event handler.

If you don't specify a sort expression for a bound column, the column doesn't display with a hyperlink and isn't sortable. You can specify any string for the sort expression; however, to make programming easier, you used a sort expression compatible with the `DataView`'s `Sort` property. This property accepts a column name followed by `ASC` for an ascending sort or `DESC` for a descending sort. If the sort order isn't specified, ascending is the default.

Summary

In this chapter we demonstrated how powerful ASP.NET, and in particular the Web Forms `DataGrid` control, are for online database applications. Using just a small amount of code, you wrote an application that lets you select, edit, delete, update, and sort rows in a data grid. You also saw how to control rendering of data using bound columns and how to use data binding expressions inside template columns.

Along the way you learned some of the differences between Web Forms and Windows Forms programming. You'll build on what you learned in this chapter when you study validation controls and ASP.NET data input next.

■ ■ ■

Validating Web User Input

Data validation is important in any application. Making sure data conforms to required constraints is vital to data integrity. Before inserting data into a database, you need to make sure the user has entered all the necessary information, that all dates are valid, that all numbers are within valid ranges, and that all other checks take place to guarantee the data conforms to both the database definition and the business rules.

In Web applications, data validation is as important as in Windows applications, but it has a different twist. Over the Internet, a user will enter information into a Web form and then post that to a server, which provides the opportunity to validate the data twice: once on the client side and once on the server side. This allows you to quickly respond to errors detected on the client and still preserve a high level of security on the server.

ASP.NET provides a number of validation controls that facilitate validation on both sides of the network. These controls are the main focus of this chapter, which will cover the following topics:

- Using the ASP.NET validation controls: `RequiredFieldValidator`, `RangeValidator`, `CompareValidator`, and `RegularExpressionValidator`

- Creating custom client- and server-side validations with the `CustomValidator`

- Displaying validation error messages in detail and in summary

You'll build a Web Forms page to validate and insert new employees into the `Northwind` database. You'll also learn some additional tips for server-control data binding. Before getting into validation control details, however, let's build a simple application to demonstrate how the controls work.

Try It Out: Creating a Validation Example

For the first example you'll create an ASP.NET Web application named `WebDataValidation`.

1. Open Visual Studio .NET, and create a new blank solution called `Chapter11_Examples`.

2. Add a new ASP.NET project called `WebDataValidation` to the solution by selecting File ➤ Add Project ➤ New Project.... (see Figure 11-1). As you saw in the previous chapter, Visual Studio .NET will take care of configuring IIS to support the new application.

Figure 11-1. *Creating* WebDataValidation

3. Once the new application is set up, switch the layout mode of WebForm1.aspx from Grid Layout to Flow Layout by right-clicking the empty form, selecting Properties from the context menu, and changing the PageLayout property.

4. You'll begin by placing four controls from the Web Forms section of the Toolbox onto the form. First, place a TextBox control and give it an (ID) of FirstNameTextBox, one RequiredFieldValidator (FirstNameRequiredFieldValidator), and two Button controls (SubmitButton and CancelButton).

5. For the CancelButton, find the CausesValidation property in the Properties window for the button and set it to false.

6. This RequiredFieldValidator forces the user to enter text into the control associated with the validator. In this case, it's the text box. To link the validator with text box then, select the validator, find the ControlToValidate property, and select FirstNameTextBox from the drop-down list. First Name is now a required field in the form. Set the valida- tor's ErrorMessage property to First name is required. as well.

7. In Design view, drag the controls around so the form looks similar to Figure 11-2. Notice how you can see the RequiredFieldValidator error message displayed on the form. This is the exact position the error message will appear if validation fails.

Figure 11-2. WebDataValidation *layout*

8. For this first example, you don't need to place much code into the code-behind file. Double-click the SubmitButton control, and add the following code to the event handler given by the IDE:

```
if (Page.IsValid)
{
    //process input here
}
```

9. Switch back to Design view of the form, and double-click the Cancel button. Add the following code to the new event handler for the click event:

```
FirstNameTextBox.Text = "";
```

10. Build and run the Web page. Type in a name, and press Submit. Nothing will happen. Pressing Cancel meanwhile will remove the name from the text box. Now press Submit again. This time the validator will pop up an error message telling you to type a first name in the box.

How It Works

So far, the page isn't doing very much, but you've already laid the foundations for a useful page. Switch to HTML view, and you'll see in the <body> of the page the new button validation property and validator control.

```
<body>
    <form id="Form1" method="post" runat="server">
        <asp:RequiredFieldValidator id="FirstNameRequiredFieldValidator1"
            style="Z-INDEX: 101; LEFT: 200px;
            POSITION: absolute; TOP: 64px"
            runat="server" ErrorMessage="First name is required."
            ControlToValidate="FirstNameTextBox">
        </asp:RequiredFieldValidator>
        <asp:Label id="Label1" style="Z-INDEX: 105; LEFT: 40px;
            POSITION: absolute; TOP: 24px"
            runat="server">First Name</asp:Label>
        <asp:Button id="SubmitButton" style="Z-INDEX: 102; LEFT: 40px;
            POSITION: absolute; TOP: 128px"
            runat="server" Text="Submit"></asp:Button>
        <asp:Button id="CancelButton" style="Z-INDEX: 103; LEFT: 112px;
            POSITION: absolute; TOP: 128px"
            runat="server" Text="Cancel"
            CausesValidation="False"></asp:Button>
        <asp:TextBox id="FirstNameTextBox" style="Z-INDEX: 104; LEFT: 32px;
            POSITION: absolute; TOP: 64px"
            runat="server"></asp:TextBox>
    </form>
</body>
```

By default, whenever a button is clicked on a Web form, it's validated, but by setting the Cancel button's CausesValidation property to false, you can override this. On this page, pressing Cancel will clear all the fields on the form, so you don't have to validate any of the fields when the user click this button. The only field on the form is the text box at the moment, so when a user clicks the Cancel button you simply clear the control and allow the user to start anew.

Although the event handler for the Submit button currently performs no activity in the database, clicking Submit will cause the form to validate its contents against whatever validation checks are in place. In this case, it's just the RequiredFieldValidator, so the text box is checked for content. If something has been typed in, it will pass the page as valid; if not, it will raise the error given by its ErrorMessage property.

Before the end of the chapter, you'll be inserting the information from the form into Northwind in the SubmitButton_Click handler, but for now, notice that you check the IsValid property of the base class performing any action. If IsValid returns a value of true, you can be certain all of the validation checks were successful. Notice that this also means the form validation takes place before the code in the event handler.

Technically, the RequiredFieldValidator fails when the value in the associated control matches the value of the InitialValue property of the RequiredFieldValidator. If you want to make sure the user changes some default value placed into the control, set the control's Text value and the InitialValue property of the RequiredFieldValidator to the same value. In other words, the ControlToValidate doesn't need to be empty to fail a validation, it simply needs to contain the same value as the InitialValue of the RequiredFieldValidator, which in this example is empty.

As another example, suppose you wanted to make sure the First Name text box first appeared on the form with the text *No Name* appearing inside. You could set the InitialValue property of the `RequiredFieldValidator` control and the `Text` property of the `TextBox` control to the string `No Name`. This will allow the string to appear on the form but force the user to change the value in the text box before the form will pass its validation checks.

Performing Web Validation

With the first example of using an ASP.NET validation control under your belt, we'll take a minute to discuss how to validate data on both the client and server sides, how ASP.NET controls work in both situations, and how to apply that knowledge to your Web Forms applications.

Enabling Client-Side Validation

If a user's browser (or other Web client) is capable and configured to execute client-side script—for example, JavaScript—validation will occur on the client before the browser posts the data to the server. Internet Explorer 4.0 and newer can perform client-side validation if scripting is enabled.

Client-side validation provides the user with quick feedback since the validation code is executed on the client machine. By default, whenever the user clicks a button on the form, the script executes the validation checks for each validation control on the form. If *any* of the validation controls on a form fails, the script cancels the postback to the server and displays error messages on the form. This behavior creates a quick turnaround time for users since they don't wait on a server round-trip to discover errors. It also helps save resources on the server since you won't waste time processing a request with invalid information. For these two reasons, client-side validations are a good feature to offer in a Web application.

Disabling Client-Side Validation

Every good rule of thumb deserves an exception though, and there are times when you'll want to avoid client-side validation checks. We have seen one such example in our first form. By setting the `CausesValidation` property of a `Button` to `false` you can disable all validation checks when a user presses that particular button. This is useful when you have a button control that does not require validation checks, such as a cancel button or a refresh button. Likewise, if a client-side check is likely to be unacceptably slow—for example, because the form requires checking against a long list on the server.

If you want to disable client-side validation for a specific validation control, you can set the control's `EnableClientScript` property to `false`.

Server-Side Validation

When a button is clicked by a user and a button-click event is fired, a postback is initiated. All data requiring validation is then validated by ASP.NET on the server side. It's possible, however, to completely disable a validation control by setting its `Enabled` property to `false`.

Of course, you should always perform validation checks on the server, even if the client supports validation. Not executing server-side checks leaves your application code vulnerable to malicious users who may circumvent client-side validations in an effort to break into or damage your servers. For situations where you are verifying passwords or product activation codes, it's vital that you validate these items on the server. Simply put, you can never trust the data in an incoming request and must always validate on the server.

Understanding Validation in the Page Life Cycle

The previous chapter talked about the typical ASP.NET page life cycle. After a request arrives, the server instantiates an object built from the code-behind logic and the ASPX file. The ASP.NET runtime then initializes this object, restores the view state of the server controls, and fires the Load event, which you typically handle with the Page_Load method. Once these steps are complete, the runtime will execute all the enabled server validation controls. It's possible to force validation again programmatically later, but we'll leave this topic for the time being. If any of the controls fail, the IsValid Page property will test false. Finally, the engine fires the postback event (such as a button-click event), and then it renders and disposes of the page. Validation is already complete by the time you reach a click event in your code-behind file.

■**Note** When validation fails, the normal flow of execution continues. You need to check the IsValid property to know if a validation check failed.

One of the great features of the built-in validation controls is how they will keep your server-side and client-side validation checks synchronized. When modifying an existing application, it's sometimes easy to update half of the validation code and not the other. The server validation controls keep this logic packaged into a single component.

So then, the validation controls take care of validation on both the server and the client unless you tell them otherwise. Except for a few situations, this validation is recommended. In the next section, you'll learn about the rest of the ASP.NET validation controls.

With a better understanding of the theory and mechanics behind validation controls, let's move on to an overview of the controls provided by the .NET Framework.

Using the ASP.NET Validation Controls

ASP.NET provides six validation-related controls (in namespace System.Web.UI.WebControls), and although they each check something different, they all work in much the same way as the RequiredFieldValidator control you saw earlier (see Table 11-1).

Table 11-1. *ASP.NET Validation Controls*

Control Name	Description
RequiredFieldValidator	Shown earlier. Makes the input control a required field.
CompareValidator	Compares the value in a control against a constant value or the value in another input control.
RangeValidator	Checks that the value in a control is within a range of values.
RegularExpressionValidator	Matches the value in an input control against a pattern.
CustomValidator	Performs user-defined validation on an input control.
ValidationSummary	Summarizes error messages for a form in a Web page, message box, or both.

All these validation controls, with the exception of the ValidationSummary class, derive from the BaseValidator class, giving them common methods and properties. Indeed, you're already familiar with two key points concerning them that you must not forget.

- Validation controls execute when the user clicks a Button control, be it an HTML button server control or an <ASP:.. button server control such as the LinkButton or ImageButton.

- Validation controls must have the ControlToValidate property set before rendering the page, or the control throws a System.Web.HttpException. The one exception to this rule is the CustomValidator component, which doesn't need to be tied to a specific control to validate.

The standard controls you can associate a validator with are TextBox, ListBox, DropDownList, and RadioButtonList. You can also validate some HTML controls, including HtmlInputText, HtmlInputFile, HtmlSelect, and HtmlTextArea.

You saw the RequiredFieldValidator control in the first sample program, so let's move on to examine the rest of the controls.

Using the RangeValidator Control

The next control you'll use, the RangeValidator control, ensures the value inside a control stays within a specified range. For example, you may need to restrict the value of an input box between 0 and 100 to represent a percentage. Alternately, in this example you'll restrict input in a text box to a range of dates. The date must be within one week (plus or minus) of the current date.

Try It Out: Using the RangeValidator Control

Follow these steps:

1. Continuing to build on the first example Web form, add an additional TextBox control, and set the (ID) property to HireDateTextBox.

2. Drag a RangeValidator control onto the form beside the HireDateTextBox control. Set the (ID) property to HireDateValidator. Set the ControlToValidate property to HireDateTextBox, and set the Type property to Date. Set the ErrorMessage to The hire date must be within one week of today's date. The form should now look like Figure 11-3.

Figure 11-3. *Revised* WebDataValidation *layout*

3. Change the Display property of the RangeValidator from Static to Dynamic.

4. Drag a RequiredFieldValidator control beside the RangeValidator. Set its (ID) property to HireDateRequiredFieldValidator, and set the ControlToValidate to the HireDateTextBox. The error message for this control is Hire Date is required.

5. Right-click the form, select View Code, and add the following code to the form's Page_Load function:

```
if (!Page.IsPostBack)
{
    DateTime nextWeek = DateTime.Today + TimeSpan.FromDays(7);
    DateTime lastWeek = DateTime.Today - TimeSpan.FromDays(7);
    HireDateValidator.MaximumValue = nextWeek.ToShortDateString();
    HireDateValidator.MinimumValue = lastWeek.ToShortDateString();
}
```

6. You also need to add a line of code to clear the HireDateTextBox control when the Cancel button is clicked.

```
private void CancelButton_Click(object sender, System.EventArgs e)
{
  FirstNameTextBox.Text="";
  HireDateTextBox.Text="";
}
```

7. Build and run the page. Try to raise the two possible errors for HireDateTextBox on your own. Remember that validation will fail for a given input control if the value of the control doesn't convert into the Type property of the RangeValidator. For instance, an invalid (unconvertible) string will generate a validation error, as shown in Figure 11-4.

Figure 11-4. WebDataValidation *range error*

How It Works

In the previous example you created a text box in which you require a date be added that's neither seven days more nor less than today's date. To enforce this, you tied two validation controls to the form and tied them to the HireDateTextBox. Behind the scenes, the HTML looks like this:

```
<asp:TextBox
    id="HireDateTextBox"
    style="Z-INDEX: 107;
LEFT: 32px;
POSITION: absolute;
TOP: 176px"
    runat="server">
</asp:TextBox>
<asp:RangeValidator
    id="HireDateValidator"
    style="Z-INDEX: 108;
LEFT: 200px;
POSITION: absolute;
TOP: 176px"
    runat="server"
    ErrorMessage="The hire date must be within a week of today's date."
    ControlToValidate="HireDateTextBox"
    Type="Date"
    Display="Dynamic">
```

```
</asp:RangeValidator>
<asp:RequiredFieldValidator
    id="HireDateRequiredFieldValidator"
    style="Z-INDEX: 109;
    LEFT: 536px;
    POSITION: absolute;
    TOP: 176px"
    runat="server"
    ErrorMessage="Hire date is required."
    ControlToValidate="HireDateTextBox">
</asp:RequiredFieldValidator>
```

Without the RequiredFieldValidator, users don't have to type a value into the HireDateTextBox control, but if they do, it must be in a proper date format and in the specified range. The RangeValidator will make this range check for you. Why not just use the RangeValidator by itself? You shouldn't do this simply because this control will not validate the contents of an input control if the control is empty, and thus you need the RequiredFieldValidator.

When multiple validation controls reference an input, all the validation checks must pass for the field to be valid. On the other hand, you need to be careful if you do use multiple Validator controls that they don't contradict each other. For example, two RangeValidators referencing a text box with one specifying a range of 0 to 50 and the other a range of 100 to 150 will always fail that text box, and IsValid will return false for the page. By definition, the value in the text box will always be outside the given range of at least one of the checks.

Remember also that the RangeValidator has a Type property. This property can take one of the following values: String, Integer, Double, Date, or Currency. If the value the RangeValidator is examining isn't of the type expected, it will first try to convert the value into the correct type. If it can't do this, the validation will fail automatically.

Your requirement was to force a user to enter a date within one week of the current system time. Obviously, you can't enter a MinimumValue and MaximumValue at design time, so you need to set these properties when the page is executed and thus alter the Page_Load handler. Fortunately, validation controls, like all the Web Forms server controls, are available as member variables in the code-behind page, so you can set the range limits programmatically.

```
private void Page_Load(object sender, System.EventArgs e)
{
    // Put user code to initialize the page here
    if(!Page.IsPostBack)
    {
        DateTime nextWeek = DateTime.Today + TimeSpan.FromDays(7);
        DateTime lastWeek = DateTime.Today - TimeSpan.FromDays(7);

        HireDateValidator.MaximumValue = nextWeek.ToShortDateString();
        HireDateValidator.MinimumValue = lastWeek.ToShortDateString();
    }
}
```

Using the CompareValidator Control

The third control you'll use is the CompareValidator control, which compares the value of an input control to either a constant value (possibly from a database) or the value in another input control. If the former, you can specify the constant in the ValueToCompare property. If the latter, you specify the ID of the control containing the value you want for comparison in the ControlToCompare property.

■**Note** You don't want to set both the ControlToCompare property and the ValueToCompare property. If this happens, however, the ControlToCompare property takes precedence, and the only validation will happen against the value in the second control.

Like the RangeValidator, the CompareValidator has a Type property you can set to String, Integer, Double, Date, or Currency. The value in or pointed at by the ControlToValidate property must convert to this type for validation to succeed.

Try It Out: Using the CompareValidator Control

To demonstrate the CompareValidator, you'll use the scenario of setting a password. When the user types a password into the box, the letters will display as asterisks. Since it's difficult for users to know if they made a typing mistake, users are generally given two input controls: one to enter the password and another to confirm the password. These input values have to match for a valid password.

1. Drag two Web Forms TextBox controls onto the form. Set the (ID) properties to PasswordTextBox1 and PasswordTextBox2, and set the TextMode properties on both controls to Password.

2. Drag a CompareValidator onto the form. Set the (ID) property to PasswordCompareValidator. Set the ErrorMessage property to the string Passwords do not match. Set the ControlToValidate to PasswordTextBox2, and set the ControlToCompare to PasswordTextBox1. The form should now look like Figure 11-5.

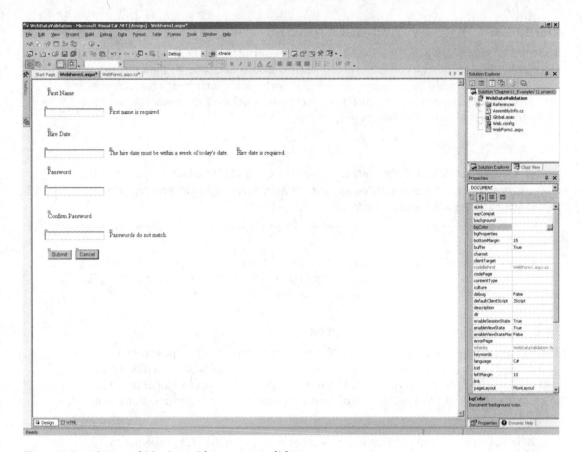

Figure 11-5. WebDataValidation *with compare validator*

3. Build and run the page. Experiment with different strings to see what passes as valid.

How It Works

If you enter text into both of the password TextBox controls, the CompareValidator will perform a validation check. The validator will first try to convert the contents of the TextBox to the Type specified by the Type property of the validator. In this example, you left the Type as the default of String, but you can also select Integer, Double, Date, and Currency.

The CompareValidator control also has an Operator property to describe the type of comparison to perform. You've left this property at the default setting of Equal, but you can also perform greater-than and less-than comparisons.

Notice you haven't placed a RequiredFieldValidator on either of the password input controls. This will allow the user to complete the form with an empty password. However, it also exposes the problem that CompareValidator will compare an empty string with a nonempty string and not raise an error.

Using the RegularExpressionValidator Control

The previous validator control for which ASP.NET predetermines the functionality is the RegularExpressionValidator control. This powerful control allows you to make sure the input of a certain control matches a certain pattern such as a phone number or e-mail address in the correct format. It also follows the same rules you've seen for the previous controls. For instance, it won't fail validation on an empty input control, and you specify the control to validate using the ControlToValidate property.

You must give the pattern to check the input against in the ValidationExpression property as a *regular expression*, which, while powerful, uses a flexible but somewhat cryptic syntax. For example, the regular expression *.cs will match the strings webform1.cs and myform.cs but not the string myform.csx. You may recognize this as one of the specifiers from a File Open or File Save dialog box. You probably use regular expressions quite a few times a day without realizing it.

■**Tip** You won't work through the regular expression (RE) syntax here, as it'd take quite some time, but needless to say, if you want to go deeply into it, the .NET documentation has a large section devoted to REs.

You can't do justice to the full capabilities of regular expressions in this chapter, so instead of covering how to design your own regular expressions, you'll work with some of the expressions built into the RegularExpressionValidator.

Try It Out: Using the RegularExpressionValidator Control

For this example, you'll add a control to the Web form for a user to enter a Web address and use a RegularExpressionValidator to ensure the string entered by the user is a proper HTTP URL.

1. Drag a new TextBox control onto the form. Give it an (ID) of PhotoUrlTextBox.

2. Drag a RegularExpressionValidator onto the form. Give it an (ID) of PhotoUrlRegularExpressionValidator and the ErrorMessage This is not a valid URL. Your form should now look like Figure 11-6.

Figure 11-6. WebDataValidation *with regular expression validator*

3. You now need to set a control to validate and an expression with which to validate it. Right-click the new validator, and open the Properties dialog box. Choose PhotoUrlTextBox from the drop-down for ControlToValidate. Find the ValidationExpression property, and click the ellipsis to enter the Regular Expression Editor (see Figure 11-7). The dialog box contains a variety of predefined regular expressions to validate phone numbers, postal codes, and more. You can also enter a custom regular expression or build on one of the predefined items. Select Internet URL, and click OK.

Figure 11-7. *Regular Expression Editor*

4. Build the page, and run it. Try to enter some values into the new text box, and see what's valid. The predefined regular expression will force you to enter a URL of the form *http://computer.domain*.

Using the CustomValidator Control

If none of the validation controls we've covered so far provides the check you need on your page, it's time to write your own validation logic in a `CustomValidator` control. A custom validator is useful in a number of circumstances, including the following:

- The validation requires a database query.

- The validation requires a mathematical expression beyond a simple comparison.

- The validation requires the inspection of multiple input controls.

`CustomValidator` objects obey most of the rules that govern the other validation controls, with the exception that the need to set the `ControlToValidate` property is optional. You have free reign in the validation code to gather and analyze any information required to declare the page valid.

Try It Out: Using the CustomValidator Control

As an example, let's assume that the image URL you introduced in the previous example points to a JPG format file. Although this validation is also possible to achieve with a custom regular expression, you can demonstrate a straightforward `CustomValidator` for the same result.

1. Drag a `CustomValidator` from the Toolbox onto the form next to the `RegularExpressionValidator` and set its (ID) to `PhotoUrlCustomValidator`. Set the `ControlToValidate` property to `PhotoUrlTextBox`, and the `ErrorMessage` property to the string `Unsupported file format.`

2. Now set the `ClientValidationFunction` to `validate_photoformat`. This is the name of the function you'll write in the next step.

3. Switch to HTML view, and place the following JavaScript block at the top of the page's HTML `<body>`. This is the client-side validation routine for the `CustomValidator` control.

```
<body>
<script language="javascript">
  function validate_photoformat(oSrc, args)
  {
    args.IsValid = false;
    if(args.Value)
    {
      var length = args.Value.length;
      var endsWidth = args.Value.substr(length - 3, 3);
      if(endsWidth == "jpg")
      {
        args.IsValid = true;
      }
    }
  }
</script>
<form id="Form1" method="post" runat="server">
```

4. Switching back to Design view, select the CustomValidation control, and click the lightning bolt in the Properties window to open the Event view. Double-click the ServerValidate event, and add the following code to the empty event handler that's generated for you:

```
args.IsValid = false;
if (args.Value != null)
{
    int length = args.Value.Length;
    string endsWidth = args.Value.Substring(length - 3);
    if (endsWidth == "jpg")
    {
        args.IsValid = true;
    }
}
```

5. Build and run the page. You'll find that the URLs in PhotoUrlTextBox must now end with jpg. It's not perfect, however; for example, http://www.apress.com/images/myjpg will be considered valid by this code.

How It Works

When you use a CustomValidator, you must supply code for both client- and server-side validation. The client-side code takes the shape of a JavaScript function placed directly into the .aspx page between <script> and </script> tags and sent directly to a client's Web browser for execution as needed. The server-side code is housed inside the validator's ServerValidate event handler and is written in C#.

First, let's review the ClientValidationFunction property. This property is specific to the CustomValidator and allows you to give the name of a function existing in client-side script to act as your client-side validation routine.

```
<asp:CustomValidator
   id="PhotoUrlCustomValidator"
 style="Z-INDEX: 118;
 LEFT: 360px;
 POSITION: absolute;
 TOP: 496px"
 runat="server"
 ErrorMessage="Unsupported file format."
 ControlToValidate="PhotoUrlTextBox"
 ClientValidationFunction="validate_photoformat">
</asp:CustomValidator>
```

If this property isn't set, you can still perform a server-side validation. You implemented this function in client-side script by adding code to the ASPX file inside a `script` tag.

The name of the function must match the value of the `ClientValidationFunction` property, and it must take two arguments.

```
function validate_photoformat(oSrc, args)
```

The second variable passed to the function (`args`) is the primary variable here. It's a collection with two members.

- The `IsValid` member (which you have to set) indicates if the validation has passed or failed.

- The `Value` member contains the text from the control you need to validate. If no control was specified with the `ControlToValidate` property of the `CustomValidator`, the `Value` property contains an empty string.

The code here is quite simple to follow. You start by assuming that the control isn't valid until you prove otherwise.

```
args.IsValid = false;
```

If no `Value` exists to check against, it remains invalid, and you leave the function. If it does have a value, you just extract the last three characters and see if they're `jpg`. If so, you say the value in the control is valid. If not, then it isn't.

```
if (args.Value != null)
{
   int length = args.Value.Length;
   string endsWidth = args.Value.Substring(length - 3);
   if (endsWidth == "jpg")
   {
      args.IsValid = true;
   }
}
```

The code in the server-side validation isn't very different from the JavaScript version. The method accepts two arguments, with the second of type `ServerValidateEventArgs` containing the important `IsValid` and `Value` properties.

Note that if you want to write your own client-side routines, you need to write them in JavaScript, PerlScript, or some other scripting language that can be placed inside <script> tags.

Using the ValidationSummary Control

The last control to cover in this chapter doesn't actually do any validation itself but does interact with all the validation controls you've covered. The ValidationSummary control, then, lets you display all the validation errors in a single location of the Web form in a number of different formats.

It takes only a few simple steps to achieve this behavior.

1. Add a ValidationSummary control to the form.

2. Choose how to display the errors by setting the DisplayMode property of the control to List, BulletList, or SingleParagraph. You probably want to try each of these settings to see which looks best with your form layout.

3. Set the Display property for each control to None if you don't want the validation controls themselves to display errors on the form. This will force the ErrorMessage to display only inside the ValidationSummary control.

Try It Out: Creating the Validation Example in Full

In this final example, we've prepared a new .aspx page for you to use. You'll find it in the code download in SummaryForm.aspx. You'll see that like the previous examples, it contains several TextBox controls and validators that check each of them.

Unlike the previous examples, however, each of the validator controls has had its Display property set to None, as indicated by their error messages being enclosed in braces ([ ]) on the form. You'll also see that we've placed a ValidationSummary control on the right side of the form with the DisplayMode property set to List (see Figure 11-8).

```
<TD rowSpan="3">
    <asp:validationsummary
        id="EmployeeValidationSummary"
        runat="server"
        DisplayMode="List">
    </asp:validationsummary>
</TD>
```

Figure 11-8. SummaryForm *layout*

Figure 11-9. SummaryForm *running*

That's actually all the code you need to use the ValidationSummary control (the runtime will automatically place error messages inside the control for you), but before you can run the page, you'll need to make sure that sqlConnection1 is pointing at your copy of the Northwind database. Alter its ConnectionString property accordingly.

Now build and run the page. If you launch the form and click Submit without entering any values, you should see the Web page in Figure 11-9. Notice that all the validation errors appear in the validation summary, but unfortunately you see no indication of which fields have produced the errors. This will place the burden on the user to find the input controls with the invalid values. In the next section you'll try to improve the error feedback.

How It Works

The majority of SummaryForm.aspx is simply the previous example rearranged a bit so that the effect of the ValidationSummary control is a bit more obvious than it would be otherwise. Besides this control on the right of the form, you'll notice that you now have a drop-down control for the user to select the employee's manager in the bottom-left corner of the form. To populate this, you'll call a method to create a list of employees from the Employees table in the Northwind database and copy those names into the control. You need this to occur before the page is rendered, so you call this method from within the Page_Load event handler.

```
private void Page_Load(object sender, System.EventArgs e)
{
    // Put user code to initialize the page here
    if (!Page.IsPostBack)
    {
        BindReportToDropDown();
```

While this behavior seems unrelated to validation, it's a good example of the data binding capability of Web Forms controls, and it offers an example of how you can help the user avoid validation errors by forcing a selection from a list of good values. By not allowing the user to make a mistake, you've improved the quality of the user experience with your application.

The method to bind the data to the drop-down list is as follows:

```
private void BindReportToDropDown()
{
    SqlCommand sqlCommand = new SqlCommand();
    sqlCommand.CommandText = @"
        select
            employeeid,
            firstname + ' ' + lastname as name
        from
            employees
    ";

    sqlConnection1.Open();
    sqlCommand.Connection = sqlConnection1;
    SqlDataReader sqlDataReader = sqlCommand.ExecuteReader();

    ReportsToDropDownList.DataSource = sqlDataReader;
    ReportsToDropDownList.DataTextField = "Name";
    ReportsToDropDownList.DataValueField = "EmployeeId";
    ReportsToDropDownList.DataBind();

    sqlDataReader.Close();
    sqlConnection1.Close();
}
```

Note that you've retrieved both the name and employee ID from the database. The list of names will be displayed in the DropDownList (as given by setting DataTextField), and the corresponding IDs will be the value returned by the list when a name is selected (as given by setting DataValueField). This distinction between display and value comes in handy when you examine the new code to insert an employee record into the database. The ReportsTo field in the Employees table holds the ID, rather than the name, of the new hire's boss, so the code will need to extract the EmployeeId of the selected manager to generate the correct INSERT statement for you. Thanks to this little trick, you can easily pull the EmployeeId using the value field of the selected item in the DropDownList.

The following code shows the updated event handler invoked when the user clicks the Submit button on the form:

```
private void SubmitButton_Click(object sender, System.EventArgs e)
{
  if (Page.IsValid)
    {
       SqlCommand sqlCommand  = new SqlCommand();
       sqlCommand.CommandText = @"
          insert into employees
             (
             firstname,
             lastname,
             hiredate,
             birthdate,
             reportsto,
             photopath
             )
          values
             (
             firstname,
             lastname,
             hiredate,
             birthdate,
             reportsto,
             photourl
             )
       ";

       sqlCommand.Parameters.Add(
          "@firstname",
          FirstNameTextBox.Text
       );
       sqlCommand.Parameters.Add(
          "@lastname",
          LastNameTextBox.Text
       );
       sqlCommand.Parameters.Add(
```

```
        "@hiredate",
        HireDateTextBox.Text
    );
    sqlCommand.Parameters.Add(
        "@birthdate",
        BirthDateTextBox.Text
    );
    sqlCommand.Parameters.Add(
        "@reportsto",
        ReportsToDropDownList.SelectedItem.Value
    );
    sqlCommand.Parameters.Add(
        "@photourl",
        PhotoURLTextBox.Text
    );

    sqlConnection1.Open();
    sqlCommand.Connection = sqlConnection1;
    sqlCommand.ExecuteNonQuery();
    sqlConnection1.Close();

    ClearFields();
  }
}
```

The last line of the handler makes a call to the helper method ClearFields. This short method simply clears each of the text boxes and the drop-down list in the form. It is also called when the Cancel button is clicked.

```
private void ClearButton_Click(object sender, System.EventArgs e)
{
  ClearFields();
}

private void ClearFields()
{
  FirstNameTextBox.Text = "";
  LastNameTextBox.Text = "";
  HireDateTextBox.Text = "";
  BirthDateTextBox.Text = "";
  PhotoURLTextBox.Text = "";
  ReportsToDropDownList.SelectedIndex = 0;
}
```

Using Inline and Summary Errors

You may or may not have noticed during the chapter that all the validation controls have an additional property named Text. When no ValidationSummary control is present on a Form, the runtime will use the Text property (if present) to display an error message on the form instead of the ErrorMessage property. However, when a ValidationSummary control is present on the form, the ErrorMessage text displays in the ValidationSummary area, but the Text property still displays inline where the validation control exists on the form. You used this behavior to indicate the input controls failing validation.

Note that for each validation control you set the Display property to Static and the Text to an asterisk. The effect was indicated by the asterisks in Figure 11-8.

When you execute the form and validation errors occur, you get the display shown in Figure 11-10. Each input control with an error is marked with an asterisk, which helps the user locate the problem data. In this figure, the Submit button has been clicked without entering any data.

Figure 11-10. SummaryForm *with errors*

As you can see, the ValidationSummary control is useful for collecting validation errors into a single location on the WebForm control. Remember to use the ErrorMessage and Text properties of your validation control to control the placement of your error messages while letting the user know where to correct the errors.

Performing Programmatic Validation

If the need arises, you can force validation checks to occur in addition to those that run automatically. For example, you may want to populate a form with information during initialization and need to check that it will validate. In the Page_Load handler, you may want to check the IsValid property of the page to see if the initialized data validates. Without adding an additional step, however, a call to IsValid produces the error shown in Figure 11-11.

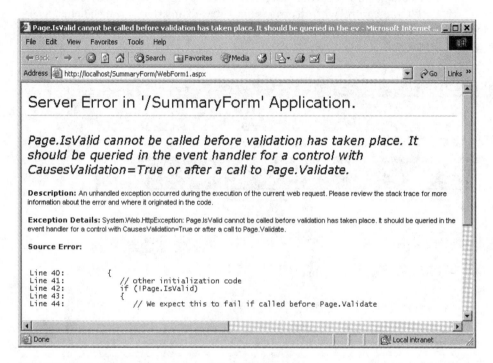

Figure 11-11. SummaryForm *premature* IsValid *error*

Calling the Validate method of the Page before checking the IsValid property will fix the exception shown in Figure 11-11. This is the same method used by the ASP.NET runtime when a user clicks a Button control with the CausesValidation property set to true. If you place this call in the Page_Load method as follows, any validation errors will appear on the first page view for the user:

```
private void Page_Load(object sender, System.EventArgs e)
{
    // Put user code to initialize the page here
    if (!Page.IsPostBack)
    {
        // other initialization code
        Page.Validate();
        if (!Page.IsValid)
```

```
        {
            // We expect this to fail if called before Page.Validate
        }
    }
}
```

Summary

Providing quality feedback to users on data entry errors is an important feature for any type of application. You learned how Web applications are special cases, because you can perform validation logic on both the client and the server. The validation controls covered is this chapter will give you the capability to perform these validations inside a neatly designed framework where you can customize the validation logic if need be. During this chapter you saw how to perform the following:

- Use the `RequiredFieldValidator` to require a user to enter data into a field.

- Use the `RangeValidator` to restrict data to a range of valid values.

- Use the `CompareValidator` to compare the values of two input controls.

- Use the `RegularExpressionValidator` to match input to a pattern.

- Implement custom server-side and client-side validation logic in a `CustomValidator`.

- Place error messages into a single location using the `ValidationSummary` control.

The features covered in this chapter are extremely useful for ASP.NET database applications. In Chapter 15, you'll see how to use database constraints as another mechanism to ensure only valid data enters a database.

■ ■ ■

Working with Tables and Relationships

In Chapter 1 you briefly learned about the structure of a database, and you know that a relational database uses tables to store and manage data in an organized way. In this chapter you'll learn how to design tables and define relationships between tables. Specifically, we'll cover the following:

- Creating and deleting tables

- Using primary and foreign keys

- Understanding referential integrity

- Understanding normalization and denormalization

Working with Tables

As you know, *tables* are the fundamental structure in a relational database. In fact, both data and relationships are stored simply as data in tables.

Tables, called *tuples* (rhymes with *couples*) in the relational model, are composed of *rows* and *columns*. Each column (called an *attribute* in the relational model) represents a piece of information. For example, the LastName column in the Northwind database's Employees table represents the last name for each employee. A table must have one or more columns. In the Employees table, each row is an instance of an employee. A table can have zero or more rows.

Each column in a table is strongly typed, just like every field in C#, but a difference exists (called by many *impedance*) between SQL data types and C# types. Recall from Chapters 3 and 7 that SQL data types are mapped to .NET types to handle this difference.

Let's start by creating a table with a few columns. You'll do it using Server Explorer, and then you'll see the equivalent SQL.

Creating a Table

You can create a table in two ways.

- Using a visual tool that generates and executes a CREATE TABLE statement

- Manually coding a CREATE TABLE statement

In the following example, you'll use Server Explorer to create a table named `test_Employees` in the `Northwind` database. Note that this table name is prefixed with `test_` to distinguish it from the `Employees` table.

Try it Out: Creating a Table Using Server Explorer

Follow these steps:

1. Open Server Explorer, expand the `Northwind` connection, right-click the Tables node, and click New Table.

2. In the window that opens, enter the information shown in Figure 12-1. We've specified three columns: `EmployeeId` of type `int`, `LastName` of type `varchar(30)`, and `BirthDate` of type `datetime`. You can choose the data type by clicking a Data Type cell and picking it from the drop-down list. Note that the BirthDate column has Allow Nulls checked. This means that rows can be inserted without birth date values (in other words, you may not know the birth date).

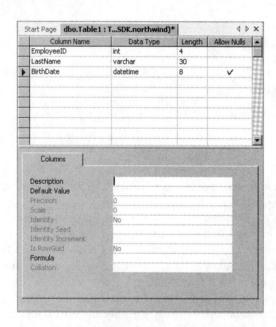

Figure 12-1. *Defining a table in Server Explorer*

3. Click the Save icon on the toolbar. When prompted for a name for the table, enter `test_Employees` and then click OK (see Figure 12-2).

Figure 12-2. *Naming a table in Server Explorer*

How It Works

If all has gone well, Visual Studio .NET has created a new database with one table. Now, to verify that the table was saved, expand the Tables node in Server Explorer. It should appear as in Figure 12-3, with the column names you specified.

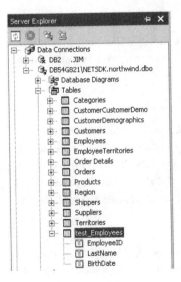

Figure 12-3. `test_Employees` *columns in Server Explorer*

That should have refreshed your memory on how to create tables in a database using Server Explorer. Now let's see how you do it using SQL.

Try It Out: Creating a Table Using SQL

Tables are created with SQL using the `CREATE TABLE` statement. The simplest form of this statement is as follows:

```
CREATE TABLE tablename
    (
    column1 datatype1 nullspec1,
    column2 datatype2 nullspec2,
    ...,
    columnn datatypen nullspecn
    )
```

where `tablename` is the name of the table you want to create, `column1` is the name of the column, `datatype1` is the data type of `column1`, and `nullspec1` specifies whether the column should allow null values.

To create a table similar to the one you saw in the previous section using the `CREATE TABLE` statement, use the following SQL to create a `test_Employees` table:

```
create table test_Employees
    (
    EmployeeID int not null,
    LastName varchar(30) not null,
    BirthDate datetime null
    )
```

While most parts of this syntax are intuitive, notice that the null specifications for columns are either `NULL` or `NOT NULL`. Also note that a database can have only one table with the same name, which is why you renamed the table in this example.

Note Actually, table names in SQL Server are composed of three parts, and it's the combination that must be unique within a database. For simplicity you've avoided the issue by using a unique table name. Further, though you can use mixed case for table and column names, and SQL Server accepts this as the spelling for these database objects, SQL references to database objects aren't case sensitive. For example, you can refer to table `test_Employees` as `test_employees` (or even `Test_employeeS`); this also applies to column names.

When a table is created using Server Explorer, behind the scenes a `CREATE TABLE` statement is issued against the database. You can also explicitly issue the `CREATE TABLE` statement in the following ways:

- A stored procedure (which we'll cover in Chapter 14)

- The SQL tool built into Visual Studio .NET (as you saw in Chapter 3)

- An application, such as the one you'll build later in the chapter

- Query Analyzer, if you have SQL Server and not just MSDE

- The `osql` command-line tool (which you also saw in Chapter 3)

Adding Rows to a Table

After creating a table, you can add rows to it in several ways. You'll explore two of these ways in this chapter.

- Server Explorer

- A C# application

Let's add rows using Server Explorer.

Try It Out: Adding Rows to a Table with Server Explorer

To add rows to a table with Server Explorer, do this:

1. In Server Explorer, right-click the test_Employees table and select Retrieve Data from Table. This presents you with a data grid where you can add rows. Add the row for Gregory, as shown in Figure 12-4.

Figure 12-4. *Adding a row to* test_Employees *with Server Explorer*

How It Works

When you enter values for a new row, the row isn't actually added until all data has been entered and you move to another row. Then Server Explorer creates an INSERT statement in the background and runs that statement against the table. If all the data entered is consistent with the column data types, the row is inserted into the table.

To add another row to test_Employees using SQL, you could code the following:

```
insert into test_employees
  (
  employeeid,
  lastname,
  birthdate
  )
values (2, 'Boyce', '12/28/1969')
```

or you could use this:

```
insert into test_employees
values (2, 'Boyce', '12/28/1969')
```

since when you provide all values, the column list is optional—but always the best practice.

Dropping a Table

Dropping a table from the database will completely remove it from the database and will lose all the data and dependency relationships. You can drop a table with Server Explorer by right-clicking the table and selecting Delete. You can also drop a table with the following SQL:

```
DROP TABLE tablename
```

where tablename is the name of the table to drop from the database.

Now that you can create and drop tables with relative ease, create the columns, and choose the data types you want to use, you'll move on to the really exciting and powerful features of relational databases.

Specifying Table Relationships

In the first part of this chapter you learned how to create a single table. So far in this book, the information you've worked with in a table has been about a single entity and attribute—for example, an employee's last name, first name, phone number, and so on. But information is never isolated in our thoughts. You can easily move from one thought to another because they're all related. In a previous example in Chapter 7, you saw two tables that contained related information—the employees in one table took the orders stored in the other table. Any table can be related to another if a relationship exists between the two sets of information you want to track.

You can have many tables in a relational database, all containing related data. If you relate loosely to the Northwind scenario, one sales rep in a company may have generated many orders, which have been placed by quite a few companies. These companies may, however, have placed many different orders. The parts on the orders may have come from different suppliers, but chances are that each supplier can supply more than one part to the Northwind Traders company. Already you can probably see some groups of entities—employees, customers, orders, and suppliers. In the Northwind example, many more tables exist that help to relate the data, using different types of relationships.

The following three types of relationship exist:

- One-to-one

- Many-to-one

- One-to-many

If you have two tables related in a database, then it's intuitive to think that you need rules in order to ensure that changes to the first table won't make data in the second table inconsistent. This is where keys and constraints play a big role. In the next section of the chapter, you'll look at keys and constraints and the benefits they bring to relational databases.

Understanding Keys and Constraints

Two main types of keys are used in a database: *primary keys* and *foreign keys*.

Constraints are important for validating data. For example, if you were storing ages in a table, then someone who accidentally hit the minus sign before typing in an age could create all sorts of problems. A constraint that checked for positive ages would avoid this sort of error.

Primary Keys

Let's take a closer look at the original Employee table in the Northwind database. The first column is EmployeeID. The IDs range from 1–9, and each employee has a unique EmployeeID assigned to him or her. A column or a combination of columns that uniquely identifies each row in a table is called the *primary key*. Additionally, no part of a primary key can have a null value. EmployeeID uniquely identifies each employee and is the primary key of the Employees table. On the other hand, the LastName column can't be specified as the primary key since more than one employee could have the same last name.

To specify the primary key for a table using Visual Studio .NET, follow these steps:

1. In Server Explorer, right-click the test_Employee table in the Northwind database and select Design Table.

2. Right-click the column you want to be the primary key and select Set Primary Key, or select the column and click the Set Primary Key icon (the key icon) in the table's toolbar.

Whichever method you choose, the column that now holds the primary key is marked with a key symbol, as shown in Figure 12-5.

Figure 12-5. *Specifying a primary key*

When using SQL, you can add a primary key at design time with the following by simply adding the keywords PRIMARY KEY to the column definition:

```
create table test_Employees
    (
    EmployeeID int not null primary key,
    LastName varchar(30) not null,
    BirthDate datetime null
    )
```

Foreign Keys

A *foreign key* is a column or a combination of columns that matches the primary key (or, in most RDBMSs including SQL Server, any unique key) of another table. To better understand what this means, let's examine the Orders, Order Details, Employees, and Products tables. Figure 12-6 shows the tables with their columns.

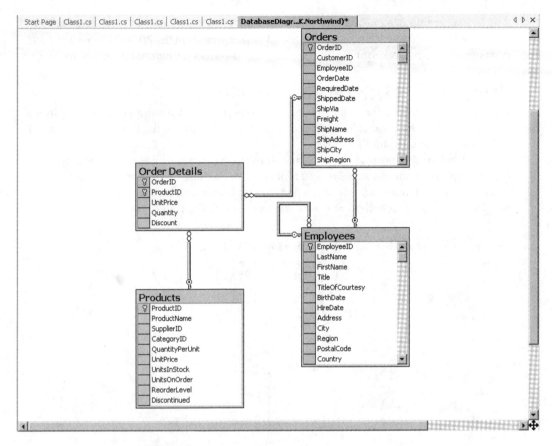

Figure 12-6. *Some* Northwind *table relationships*

Say you want to determine which employee generated an order for tofu. Here are the steps you follow:

1. First you find the ProductID for tofu in the Products table, which is 14.

2. You look at the Order Details table and find that the OrderID corresponding to the ProductID of 14 is 10249.

3. Then you scan the Orders table and find that the EmployeeID corresponding to the OrderID of 10249 is 6.

4. Finally, you look at the Employees table and find that the EmployeeID of 6 belongs to Michael Suyama.

We've intuitively explained the concept of the foreign key in the preceding example. The ProductID column in the Order Details table references the ProductID primary key of the Products table. This guarantees that each ProductID in the Order Details table has a matching ProductID in the Products table. If you can't find a matching ProductID in the Products table, you can't figure out what the product is. You can eliminate situations such as these by constraining the ProductID column in the Order Details table with the foreign key. If an attempt is made to insert a bogus row for which no corresponding ProductID exists in the Products table, then the database will produce an error. Foreign keys are also known as *referential integrity constraints*.

Understanding Types of Relationships

Relationships specify that one table relates to another table. Relationships ensure integrity and reduce the data redundancy. You enforce relationships by matching the foreign key of one table with the primary key of another table.

As mentioned, three main types of relationship exist: one-to-one, one-to-many, and many-to-many. To understand the differences between these types, consider another MSDE sample database named pubs, which has tables such as employee, publishers, pub_info, titles, titleauthor, and authors, as shown in Figure 12-7.

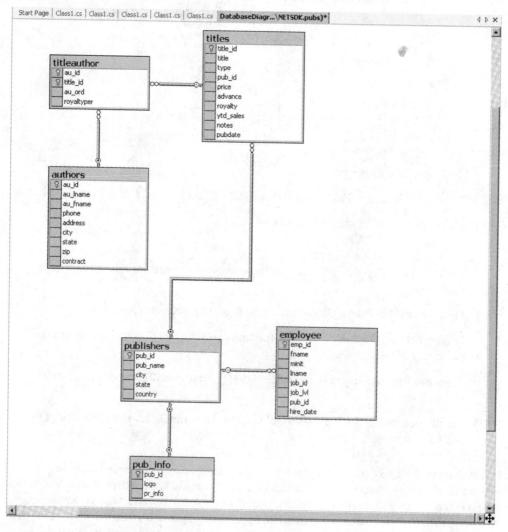

Figure 12-7. *Some* pubs *table relationships*

From Figure 12-7, you can see that the following is true:

- `employee` contains employee information, including the ID of the publisher for which the employees work.

- `publishers` contains publisher information.

- `pub_info` contains the publisher's logo.

- `titles` contains book information, including the ID of the publisher.

- `authors` contains author information, including the ID of the publisher for which the employees work.

- `titleauthor` contains both the author and title IDs.

The tables in Figure 12-7 all have varying types of relationships to each other. The following list explains the different types more clearly:

One-to-one relationships: In a one-to-one relationship, a row in table A has exactly one matching row in table B, and vice versa. The relationship between the `publishers` and `pub_info` tables is a one-to-one relationship—each publisher in the `publishers` table has only one logo, so only one related row is in the `pub_info` table. In Figure 12-7, the one-to-one relationship is shown with a key on both sides of the relationship.

One-to-many relationships: In a one-to-many relationship, one row in table A can have many matching rows in table B. But any one row in table B can have only one matching row in table A. The relationship between the `publishers` and `employee` tables is a one-to-many relationship. One publisher can have many employees.

Many-to-many relationships: In a many-to-many relationship, a row in table A can have many matching rows in table B, and vice versa. The relationship between the `titles` and `authors` tables is a many-to-many relationship. Several authors can write one title, and one author can write several titles. A many-to-many relationship is created by a third table (here, `titleauthor`), sometimes called a *junction table*.

The primary key of a junction table consists of the foreign keys to both table A and table B. The many-to-many relationship here is actually defined by two one-to-many relationships, from `titles` and `authors` to `titleauthor`.

Now that you have an understanding of relationships and the different types of keys, let's look at what they mean in terms of relational databases in this example.

Understanding Referential Integrity

Once you define a relationship between tables, you need to enforce *referential integrity* (RI) between the tables. RI exists when all foreign key values in the child table match primary key values in the parent table.

Enforcing RI is essential to prevent inconsistent data from being entered into a database. Let's look at an example to demonstrate the point.

Try It Out: Enforcing Referential Integrity

You can verify the RI violation by opening the Order Details table in the Northwind database and inserting a row with OrderID of 20000 and ProductID of 77. You'll get the error message in Figure 12-8.

Figure 12-8. *Violating RI*

How It Works

When you attempted to add a row with OrderID of 20000 and ProductID of 77 to Order Details, SQL Server enforced the foreign key constraint between Orders and Order Details. Since an Order with OrderID of 20000 doesn't exist, an error was raised.

Understanding Database Diagrams

Database diagrams show tables and their relationships. Relationships among tables can easily be specified and conceptualized in database diagrams. A large database with many tables can have several diagrams; for example, a Sales diagram and an Invoicing diagram can show only the tables and the relationships relevant to Sales and Invoicing, respectively. Database diagrams are objects in a SQL Server database just like tables and stored procedures are.

■**Note** Database diagrams aren't part of either the relational model or standard SQL. SQL Server provides them as database objects, but other RDBMSs don't. Check your RDBMS to see if it offers a similar database design facility.

Let's try defining relationships using a database diagram.

Try It Out: Defining Relationships Using a Database Diagram

Let's create a database diagram to show the Orders, Order Details, and Products tables in the Northwind database and the relationships between them.

■**Tip** This feature isn't available in Visual C# Standard Edition, but Microsoft Access offers it, and the procedure in Access is similar to that for Visual Studio .NET.

Follow these steps:

1. In Server Explorer, right-click Database Diagrams and select New Diagram.

2. The screen that pops up will list all the tables in the database. Select Order Details, Orders, and Products, as shown in Figure 12-9, and click Add.

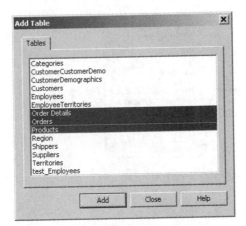

Figure 12-9. *Adding tables to a database diagram*

3. The tables and relationships among them will be added to the diagram. You'll now remove a relationship line and learn how to define the relationship. To remove a relationship, right-click a relationship, and select Delete Relationship from Database (see Figure 12-10). Delete the relationship between Orders and Order Details.

Figure 12-10. *Deleting a relationship*

4. Now let's redefine the relationship between Orders and Order Details. Note that the OrderID column is the primary key of the Orders table and a foreign key in the Order Details table. Drag the OrderID column from the Order Details table to the Orders table. The Create Relationship dialog box pops up immediately, as shown in Figure 12-11.

Figure 12-11. *Create Relationship window*

■Note The Orders table is listed as the primary key table, and Order Details is listed as the foreign key table. The primary key (OrderID) of the parent table is listed in the left pane, and the foreign key (again, OrderID) in the child table is listed in the right pane. A relationship will be created between the tables based on these keys. The name of this relationship is [FK_Order Details_Orders]. The relationship requires that every OrderID value in the Order Details table must also exist in the Orders table.

---

5. Check both the cascade-related boxes, and then click OK to create the relationship.

6. Click the Save icon in the toolbar to save the relationship. You'll be asked to specify a name for the diagram. Name the diagram Sales. Click OK.

7. When the Save window appears, click Yes.

You can access a saved diagram from Server Explorer by double-clicking the diagram node after expanding the Database Diagrams node.

How It Works

In this exercise, you defined a relationship by linking the primary key and foreign keys. When a relation is set, RI is enforced. You can change the relationships between the tables in the diagram and add more tables to it if you want.

The Order Details table has a *composite* primary key, which is the combination of the OrderID and ProductID columns. So, you can associate a given order with a given ProductID only once, but you can associate it with any or all (or no) products.

If you think about it, this makes sense, because in a single order you wouldn't list a product a thousand times over; you'd list it once and specify the quantity ordered.

Constraints

A primary key is one kind of *constraint* on a table. So is a foreign key. Other constraints can be specified for a table and its columns. Constraints are typically used for validation and for ensuring data integrity; in Chapter 15 you'll look at constraints in detail. The following is a brief list of them:

- **NOT NULL**: When a column is specified to be NOT NULL, null values can't be assigned to that column. This means that either the column must have a default value or the user will be forced to enter a value for it before the row is inserted into the table.

- **UNIQUE**: A unique constraint on a table requires that values for a column or set of columns are unique. It can be specified in addition to the primary key, which by definition is unique.

- **DEFAULT**: When a default constraint is specified on a column, a default value is generated if no value is supplied for that column.

- **CHECK**: The check constraint checks if the value of the column satisfies a certain criterion.

Normalization

Normalization is a technique for minimizing redundant data in a logical database design. Normalized designs are less subject to update anomalies because they (ideally) keep each data item in only one place. Normalized database designs usually reduce data storage demands, typically enhancing the performance data manipulation operations while making query processing more complicated. These trade-offs must be carefully evaluated in terms of the required performance profile of a database. Often, a database design needs to be *denormalized* to adequately satisfy operational needs.

Normalizing a logical database design involves a set of formal processes to separate the data into multiple, related tables. The result of each process is referred to as a *normal form*. Five normal forms have been identified in theory, but most of the time third normal form (3NF) is as far as one needs to go in practice. Since to be in 3NF a *relation* (the formal term and more precise concept for what SQL calls a table) must already be in second normal form (2NF), and 2NF requires a relation to be in first normal form (1NF). Let's look briefly at what these normal forms mean.

First normal form (1NF) means that all column values are *scalar*; in other words, they have a single value that can't be further decomposed in terms of the data model. For example, although individual characters of a string can be accessed through a procedure that decomposes the string, the characters aren't accessible *by name* in SQL, so, as far as the data model is concerned, they aren't part of the model. Likewise, in a table with a manager column and a column containing a list of employees who work for a given manager, the manager and the list would be accessible by name but the individual employees wouldn't be. All relations—and SQL tables—are by definition in 1NF since the lowest level of accessibility by name (known as the table's *granularity*) is the column level, and, as you've just seen, column values are scalars in SQL.

Second normal form (2NF) requires that *attributes* (the formal term for SQL columns) that aren't parts of keys be *functionally dependent* on a key that uniquely identifies them. Functional dependence basically means that for a given key value only one value exists in a table for a column or set of columns. For example, if a table contained employees and their titles, and more than one employee could have the same title (very likely), a key that uniquely identified employees wouldn't uniquely identify titles, so the titles wouldn't be functionally dependent on a key of the table. To put the table into 2NF, you'd create a separate table for titles—with its own unique key—and replace the title in the original table with the key from the new table. Note how this reduces data redundancy. The titles themselves now appear only once in the database. Only their keys appear in other tables, and key data isn't considered redundant (though, of course, it requires columns in other tables and data storage).

Third normal form (3NF) extends the concept of functional dependence to *full functional dependence*. Essentially, this means that all nonkey columns in a table are uniquely identified by the whole primary key, not just part of the primary key. For example, if you revised the 1NF `managers-employees` table to have three columns (`managername`, `employeeid`, and `employeename`) instead of two, and you defined the composite primary key as `managername` + `employeeid`, the table would be in 2NF (since `employeename`, the nonkey column, is dependent on the primary key), but it wouldn't be in 3NF since `employeename` is uniquely identified by part of the primary key (`employeeid`). Creating a separate table for employees and removing `employeename` from `managers-employees` would put the table into 3NF. Note that even though this table is now normalized to 3NF, the database design is still not as normalized as it should be. Creating another table for managers, using an ID shorter than the manager's name, though not required for normalization here, is definitely the better approach and would be needed for a real-world database.

Database design (even of small databases) is an art more than a science, and applying normalization wisely is always important. On the other hand, normalization inherently increases the number of tables and therefore the number of joins required to retrieve data. *Denormalizing* one or more tables, by intentionally providing redundant data to reduce the complexity of joins and get quicker query response times, may be necessary. With either normalization or denormalization, the goal is to control redundancy so that the database design adequately (and ideally, optimally) supports the actual use of the database.

Working with SQL in C#

Up until now you've seen how to access databases using Server Explorer. You'll now submit SQL from a C# application against the `Northwind` database.

Try It Out: Creating a SQL Statement Processor

Follow these steps:

1. Create a solution named `Chapter12_Examples`. Then, add a C# Windows application named `StatementProcessor` to the solution.

2. Change the name of the form to `StatementProcessor.cs`.

3. Add a text box named txtSql and a button named cmdExecute.

4. Add another text box named txtResult to see the result of the execution.

5. Set the MultiLine property of the text boxes to True.

6. Add two labels with the text shown Figure 12-12.

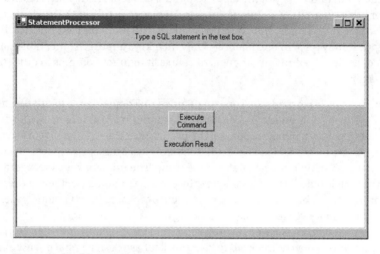

Figure 12-12. StatementProcessor *layout*

7. Add the following directive to the StatementProcessor.cs file:

```
using System.Data.SqlClient;
```

8. Double-click the Execute Command button, and add the following code to the cmdExecute_Click method:

```
try
{
    //Create connection
    SqlConnection conn = new SqlConnection(@"
        Data Source=(local)\NETSDK;
        Integrated Security=SSPI;
        database=Northwind
    ");

    //Open connection
    conn.Open();
    //Get the SQL from the text box
    string strSQL=txtSql.Text;
    // Create command
    SqlCommand cmd= new SqlCommand(strSQL, conn);
```

```
    //Execute command
    cmd.ExecuteNonQuery();
    // Close connection.
    conn.Close();
    // Display result message.
    txtResult.Text = "SQL executed successfully.";
}
catch (System.Data.SqlClient.SqlException ex)
{
    // Display error message.
    txtResult.Text =
        "There was an error in executing the SQL. " +
        "Error Message:" + ex.Message;
}
```

9. Before running the application, delete (in Server Explorer) the test_Employees table that you created earlier, as you'll be re-creating it.

10. Run the application with Ctrl+F5. In the upper text box, enter the CREATE TABLE statement as shown in Figure 12-13, and then click the Execute Command button. After a pause you should see the text *SQL executed successfully* in the lower text box.

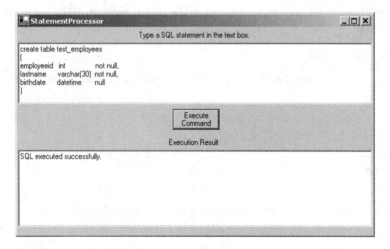

Figure 12-13. StatementProcessor *running*

11. Verify whether the table exists in the Northwind database by right-clicking the Tables node in Server Explorer and selecting Refresh. You'll see that the test_Employees table has been created with three columns, as shown in Figure 12-14.

Figure 12-14. *Table* test_employees *in Server Explorer*

How It Works

You begin by adding the following directive to the queries.cs file, since you'll be using the SqlClient namespace.

```
using System.Data.SqlClient;
```

In the cmdExecute_Click event handler, you create a connection to the database, like so:

```
//Create connection
SqlConnection conn = new SqlConnection(@"
    Data Source=(local)\NETSDK;
    Integrated Security=SSPI;
     database=Northwind
");
```

Now that the connection has been created, you open it using the Open method.

```
//Open connection
conn.Open();
```

Next, you get the SQL that was entered into a string variable strSQL.

```
//Get the SQL from the text box
string strSQL=txtSql.Text;
```

Then you create a command object. As you've seen, you use command objects to execute SQL statements against the database. The command object needs two parameters, the SQL statement itself, which is stored in strSQL, and the connection to the database, which is the object named cn created earlier.

```
// Create command
SqlCommand cmd= new SqlCommand(strSQL, conn);
```

Following this you can execute the ExecuteNonQuery method of the command. SQL statements such as CREATE TABLE, INSERT, UPDATE, and so on, don't return data. The ExecuteNonQuery method executes SQL statements. It returns an integer representing the number of rows affected by an INSERT, UPDATE, or DELETE operation. In this case, you choose not to catch the return value since you're creating a table and not inserting, updating, or deleting rows.

```
//Execute command
cmd.ExecuteNonQuery();
```

Now that the command has been executed, you close the connection using the Close method.

```
// Close connection.
conn.Close();
```

Then you display a success message in the resulting text box.

```
// Display result message.
txtResult.Text = "SQL executed successfully.";
```

If during the execution of the SQL statement any error is encountered, this is trapped and shown in the resulting text box.

```
catch (System.Data.SqlClient.SqlException ex)
{
   // Display error message.
   txtResult.Text =
      "There was an error in executing the SQL. " +
      "Error Message:" + ex.Message;
}
```

That's it! You've created a useful little tool for executing SQL statements. Now let's see how you can add rows to your table using the application you've just built.

Try It Out: Adding Rows to a Table

Recall that initially you used Server Explorer to insert rows, but this time you'll use your application to submit your SQL. All you have to do is execute an INSERT statement against the test_employees table. To do this, follow these steps:

1. Enter the statement to insert a row for the employee Boyce, as shown in Figure 12-15.

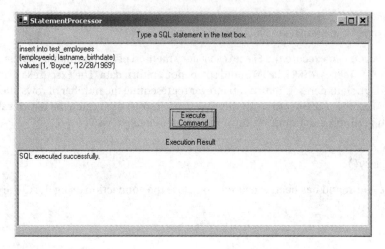

Figure 12-15. *Inserting a row into* test_employees

2. You can verify that the row was added with Server Explorer.

3. Now let's try to add another row with the same employeeid. While it doesn't make sense for two different employees to have the same ID, the test_employees table will at this time allow it, as shown in Figure 12-16. You can verify that the row was added with Server Explorer.

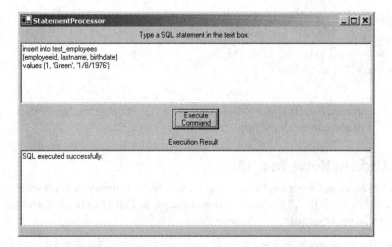

Figure 12-16. *Inserting a duplicate row into* test_employees

How It Works

At the moment, no constraint on test_employees enforces uniqueness, so you're allowed to create multiple rows with the same employeeid. To prevent two rows from having the same employeeid, you must specify employeeid as the primary key of test_employees. If you try to apply this to the table in its current state, you'll get an error, because there are duplicate employeeids in the table and because a primary key must be unique.

Let's look at how you can test primary and foreign key constraints, as well as how to drop tables using SQL.

Try It Out: Testing the Primary Key Constraint

Follow these steps:

1. In StatementProcessor, delete all the rows in test_employees with the following SQL statement (that you first met in Chapter 3):

   ```
   truncate table test_Employees
   ```

2. In Server Explorer, right-click test_employees, and select Design Table. In the design grid that appears, right-click the employeeid row and select Set Primary Key.

3. Click the Save icon to save the change to the table design, and then close the design window.

4. In StatementProcessor, add an employee to the table for employeeid 1 using the following statement. (Note that you can omit the column list since you're providing values for all columns in the order in which the columns are defined in the table.)

   ```
   insert into test_Employees
   values (1,'Boyce', '12/28/1969')
   ```

5. Add another employee with a different last name and birth date but the same employeeid.

   ```
   insert into test_Employees
   values (1,'Green', '1/8/1976')
   ```

If the constraint is being enforced, then you won't be able to enter duplicate data into the table, and you'll get the error message in Figure 12-17.

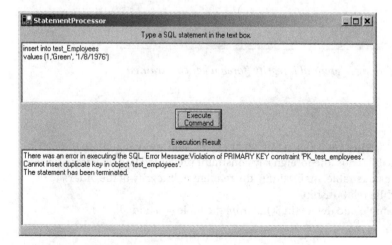

Figure 12-17. *Preventing a duplicate row in* test_employees

How It Works

As you expected, an error message was given. The error message indicates that the primary key constraint has been violated by attempting to insert a second employee with an employeeid of 1.

Now let's see an example where a foreign key constraint is violated.

Try It Out: Testing the Foreign Key Constraint (Referential Integrity)

Notice from the earlier example involving the Order Details table in the Northwind database that it's a child of the Orders table. This relationship requires that for every order in the Order Details table, that order must also exist in the parent Orders table. Let's try to violate this relationship and see what kind of error you encounter.

1. In StatementProcessor, enter the INSERT statement as shown in Figure 12-18 and notice the resulting error message. (Note that you enclose the table name in double quotes because it contains an embedded blank. This is standard SQL. Transact-SQL also accepts square brackets in place of double quotes.)

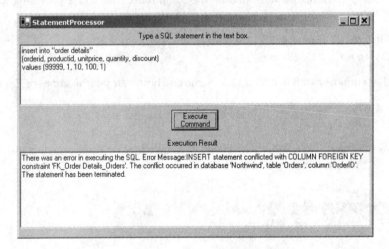

Figure 12-18. *Enforcing referential integrity (foreign key constraints)*

How It Works

As you can see, the message indicates that a foreign key constraint was violated, so the INSERT statement wasn't successful. Thus, the foreign key constraint prevented bad data from finding its way into the Order Details table, maintaining the referential integrity of the Orders to Order Details parent-child relationship.

Let's do one last example and delete (in SQL, *drop*) the table you added.

Try It Out: Dropping a Table

Let's try to drop the `test_Employees` table, regardless of how many rows it may have.

   1. In `StatementProcessor`, enter the `INSERT` statement as shown in Figure 12-19.

Figure 12-19. *Dropping a table*

How It Works

You can verify that the table has been deleted from the `Northwind` database with Server Explorer. Note that you didn't receive a single warning message telling you that you were about to make a significant change to your database. The statement was simply executed. Remember that care must be exercised when issuing the `DROP TABLE` statement as it completely removes both the table definition and its data. If you accidentally drop a table, the only way to restore it is from a backup of the database.

Summary

In this chapter you took some significant steps in furthering your understanding of relational databases. The ability to establish relationships between tables gives you a lot of flexibility and power. As you worked through the chapter, you did the following:

   • You learned how to create and drop tables.

   • You learned what primary keys and foreign keys are and how they're used to define relationships among tables. You also learned about the different types of relationships and how to define them using database diagrams.

- You learned how to normalize tables during database design and why normalization and denormalization are important.

- You learned how to add rows to a table using Server Explorer and use a C# application.

- You learned about error messages that are generated when primary key and foreign key constraints are violated.

In the next chapter you'll move from SQL statements to revisit SQL queries and experiment with more advanced query facilities.

Learning More About Queries

In Chapter 3, you learned about queries and the INSERT, UPDATE, and DELETE statements. In Chapter 12 you learned how to create tables and relationships between them. Now you'll look at more SQL for specifying queries. SQL has a wide variety of functions and constructs for querying, so it's impossible to cover all permutations of them in one chapter. You'll look at the more frequently used ones.

Specifically, you'll learn about the following SQL features:

- DISTINCT keyword

- Subqueries

- GROUP BY clause

- Aggregate functions

- CASE expressions

- Date functions

- Joins

Before diving in, you'll first modify the C# application from the previous chapter to run queries and display their results. Then you'll practice coding various types of queries against the Northwind database.

Building the Northwind Query Application, Part II

The revised application is similar to the one in Chapter 12, but it differs in how it handles result sets returned from queries. In Chapter 12, you used DDL statements such as CREATE TABLE and DML statements such as INSERT that don't return rows. You used the ExecuteNonQuery method on a command. With queries, though, you may get zero, one, or many rows, containing one or more columns of data. Let's see how to revise the application to handle any number of rows and columns.

Try It Out: Extending the Northwind SQL Application

Follow these steps:

1. Create a solution named Chapter13_Examples.

2. Add a C# Windows application, named QueryProcessor, to it.

3. Rename Form1.cs to QueryProcessor.cs. Change its Text property to QueryProcessor, and then add a label, a multiline text box, a button, and a list view so that the form looks like Figure 13-1.

Figure 13-1. QueryProcessor *layout*

4. Name the text box txtSql, the Execute button cmdExecute, and the list view lvwResult.

5. Set the View property of the list view to Details so that the results will be displayed with column headers. Set the GridLines property to True.

6. Add the following directive to the QueryProcessor.cs file since you'll be using the SqlClient namespace:

   using System.Data.SqlClient;

7. Return to Design view, and double-click the Execute button. Add the following code to the cmdExecute_Click method:

```
//Create connection
SqlConnection conn = new SqlConnection(@"
    data source = (local)\netsdk;
    integrated security = sspi;
    database = northwind
");

try
{
    //Clear list view column header and items
    lvwResult.Columns.Clear() ;
    lvwResult.Items.Clear();

    //Open connection
    conn.Open();

    //Create command with SQL entered by user
    SqlCommand cmd = conn.CreateCommand();
    cmd.CommandText = txtSql.Text;

    //Create data reader
    SqlDataReader dr = cmd.ExecuteReader();

    //Get colummn names from data reader and show in list view
    for (int i = 0; i< dr.FieldCount; i++)
    {
        ColumnHeader ch = new ColumnHeader();
        ch.Text=dr.GetName(i);
        lvwResult.Columns.Add(ch);
    }

    //Get values of each row in data reader and show in list view
    ListViewItem itmX;
    while (dr.Read())
    {
        //create list view item
        itmX=new ListViewItem();

        //Specify text and subitems of list view
        itmX.Text= dr.GetValue(0).ToString();
        for (int i=1 ; i< dr.FieldCount; i++)
        {
            itmX.SubItems.Add(dr.GetValue(i).ToString());
        }

        //Add item to list view Items collection
        lvwResult.Items.Add(itmX);
    }
```

```
    //close reader
    dr.Close();
}
catch ( System.Data.SqlClient.SqlException  ex)
{
    // Display error Message.
    MessageBox.Show ("There was an error in executing the SQL." +
                     "\nError Message:" + ex.Message, "SQL");
}
finally
{
    // Close connection
    conn.Close();
}
```

8. Run it with Ctrl+F5. If you enter the query in Figure 13-2, you should see the result shown in the figure.

Figure 13-2. QueryProcessor: *Executing a query*

How It Works

Most of the exercises should be familiar to you now, but we'll still run through the code for practice. You begin by creating a connection. (Note that you do it outside the try block so you can use it in the finally block.) Within a try block you clear the column captions and the rows in the list view. These statements are needed because you'll be using the application to execute diverse SQL queries and statements, and each will return different results. You therefore clear the list view completely before repopulating it with a new result.

```
//Create connection
SqlConnection conn = new SqlConnection(@"
    data source = (local)\netsdk;
    integrated security = sspi;
    database = northwind
");

try
{
    //Clear list view column header and items
    lvwResult.Columns.Clear() ;
    lvwResult.Items.Clear();
```

Note Remember that a list view has both a Columns and an Items collection. The Columns collection contains ColumnHeader objects that represent the header of a list view, and the Items collection contains ListViewItem objects that represent data.

Then you open a connection to the Northwind database.

```
//Open connection
conn.Open();
```

Now that you have a connection to the database, you need a command that can be configured to execute the SQL against the database. You do this by creating a SqlCommand object and assigning the text in the text box to its CommandText property.

```
//Create command with SQL entered by user
SqlCommand cmd = conn.CreateCommand();
cmd.CommandText = txtSql.Text;
```

Now you call the ExecuteReader method on the command. This will execute a SQL query and return a DataReader object.

```
//Create data reader
SqlDataReader dr = cmd.ExecuteReader();
```

The next few lines of code read the column names of the data reader and display them as headers in the list view. To do this, you iterate through the columns of the data reader until you reach FieldCount, the number of columns in the data reader.

Then, a ColumnHeader object represents each column of the list view. For each column in the data reader, a corresponding column header is created in the list view. The data reader's

GetName method returns the name of the column at a specified index. This name is used as the name of the list view's column. Finally, the column header is added to the Columns collection of the list view, as follows, so that the list view will have a corresponding column for each column in the data reader.

```
//Get colummn names from data reader and show in list view
for (int i=0; i< dr.FieldCount; i++)
{
    ColumnHeader ch = new ColumnHeader();
    ch.Text=dr.GetName(i);
    lvwResult.Columns.Add(ch);
}
```

Following this, you declare a ListViewItem object to represent each row that will be added to the list view. You call this item itmX.

```
//Get values of each row in data reader and show in list view
ListViewItem itmX;
```

Next you iterate through the rows of the data reader.

```
while (dr.Read())
{
```

Then you create a ListViewItem item and set its text value to the value of the first column of the data reader.

```
//create list view item
itmX=new ListViewItem();

//Specify text and subitems of list view
itmX.Text= dr.GetValue(0).ToString();
for (int i = 1 ; i< dr.FieldCount; i++)
{
    itmX.SubItems.Add(dr.GetValue(i).ToString());
}
```

The first column of the ListView has an index of zero. The second column of a ListView is called the first SubItem, the third column is the second SubItem, and so on. You now iterate from the second column of the ListView (index=1) and get the value of the row corresponding to the second column and add it to the SubItems collection of the item.

Then you add the item to the Items collection of the list view.

```
//Add item to list view Items collection
lvwResult.Items.Add(itmX);
}
```

After looping through all the rows, you close the data reader.

```
//close reader
dr.Close();
}
```

The exception handler simply shows the error message if one occurs.

```
catch ( System.Data.SqlClient.SqlException  ex)
{
    // Display error Message.
    MessageBox.Show ("There was an error in executing the SQL." +
                        "\nError Message:" + ex.Message, "SQL");
}
```

You then close the connection.

```
finally
{
    // Close connection
    conn.Close();
}
```

Now that you've created an application that will execute and display results conveniently, you'll learn more about writing queries.

Writing More SQL Query Syntax

It's highly important for any serious database programmer to master SQL, and with this in mind you'll expand your knowledge of SQL query syntax. For the rest of this chapter, you'll query the Northwind database in a variety of ways using the QueryProcessor application.

DISTINCT

The DISTINCT keyword is used in a query to exclude duplicate values from the result set. It can be used only once in the select list of a query. If multiple columns are selected, DISTINCT eliminates rows where the combination of all the column values are identical.

Say you want to find the ProductIDs against which orders have been placed. DISTINCT certainly helps you with this type of query.

Try It Out: Querying Using DISTINCT

To query using DISTINCT, follow these steps:

1. Enter the following query into the QueryProcessor application, and click Execute:

```
select
    productid
from
    [order details]
```

2. All the product IDs that have an order placed against them are returned (see Figure 13-3).

Figure 13-3. *Querying product IDs without the* `DISTINCT` *keyword*

Now change the query to include `DISTINCT`.

```
select distinct
    productid
from
    [order details]
```

3. You should see the result in Figure 13-4. The product IDs are returned but without duplicates.

Figure 13-4. *Using the* DISTINCT *keyword*

How It Works

You know that Order Details contains ProductIDs for various orders and that Products has a list of products available for sale. Obviously, different orders can contain the same ProductID, so you use DISTINCT to eliminate duplicates and get a simple list of product IDs.

Subqueries

Subqueries are queries embedded in other queries that use the result of the subquery as part of their own retrieval logic. You can use subqueries in many contexts to create sophisticated queries. If you keep in mind that all queries are simply operations on tables that produce a single table (a result set, called a *derived table* in standard SQL), understanding subqueries will not be difficult. Let's look at some of their typical uses.

IN

The IN operator (the IN predicate in standard SQL) determines if the value of a specific column matches a list of values. The list must be of a data type compatible with the column to be matched and may be composed of either literals separated by commas or the result set from a subquery, but not both. The following is some example syntax:

```
SELECT
    column1, column2, ..., columnN
FROM
    table1
WHERE
    columnX IN (1, 10, 14)
```

Here, the list contains three integer literals. The matching column (columnX, which is some column in the table but not necessarily one in the select list) must be of a numeric data type for this list to be compatible. Only the rows in table1 whose columnX value is 1, 10, or 14 will be selected.

```
SELECT
    column1, column2, ..., columnN
FROM
    table1
WHERE
    columnX IN
      (
        SELECT
            column1
        FROM
            table2
      )
```

This query accomplishes much the same result as the first, but instead of a list of literals it uses the values from a column in another table to populate the list. If column1 of table2 had only the values 1, 10, and 14, this would have the same effect as the first query. Of course, if other values occurred in table2, they would also occur in the list, and the outer query probably wouldn't produce the same result set as the first query. (A subquery is often referred to as an *inner query*, and the query that contains it is referred to as an *outer query*.)

You have many, many variations on how you can code subqueries. Since they *are* queries, all the clauses and other keywords available for queries can be used in them. Our goal here is to simply show the straightforward pattern they follow and, in this case, to demonstrate how they can be used to replace a list of literals.

Now let's look more closely at the IN predicate itself. For example, you may want to get a list of all orders entered by employees with IDs of 1 and 6.

Try It Out: Using the IN Predicate

To use the IN predicate, do this:

1. Enter the following query into the QueryProcessor application, and execute it. You should see the results shown in Figure 13-5. (Scroll down, and you'll see that only rows where EmployeeID equals 1 or 6 are selected.)

```
select
    *
from
    orders
where
    employeeid in (1, 6)
order by
    employeeid
```

■Tip Recall that SELECT * is actually bad practice in real-world programming. Best practice is to specify explicitly the columns to select. We'll use SELECT * for simplicity, but you should use a select list in serious applications.

Figure 13-5. *Using the* IN *predicate*

How It Works

Here, you use a list of literal values with the IN operator. The following WHERE clause specifies that only rows where EmployeeID equals either 1 or 6 should be retrieved:

```
where
    employeeid in (1, 6)
```

The keyword NOT, used in conjunction with IN, selects rows that don't match any value in a list. Let's say you need to get a list of all orders that have been entered by employees other than the ones with IDs of 1 or 6.

Try It Out: Using the NOT IN Predicate

To use the NOT IN predicate, do this:

1. Enter the following query into the QueryProcessor application, and execute it. You should see the results shown in Figure 13-6.

```
select
    *
from
    orders
where
    employeeid not in (1, 6)
order by
    employeeid
```

Figure 13-6. *Using the* NOT IN *predicate*

How It Works

Here, you use the same list of literal values with the IN operator. The following WHERE clause specifies that only rows where EmployeeID doesn't equal either 1 or 6 should be retrieved:

```
where
    employeeid not in (1, 6)
```

You can use functions along with the IN operator. For example, the SUBSTRING function returns a portion of a string. You could use this instead of the LIKE predicate if you needed to find all the employees whose last name begins with a *D* or an *S*.

Try It Out: Using a Function with the IN Predicate

To use a function with the IN predicate, do this:

1. Enter the following query into the QueryProcessor application, and execute it. You should see the results shown in Figure 13-7.

```
select
    *
from
    employees
where
    substring(lastname, 1, 1) in ('D', 'S')
```

Figure 13-7. *Using a function with the* IN *predicate*

How It Works

Here, you use a list of literal values with the IN operator, but instead of matching a column against them, you match the result of a function applied against a column value. The following WHERE clause specifies that only rows where the first character of the employee's last name is either *D* or *S* should be retrieved:

```
where
    substring(lastname, 1, 1) in ('D', 'S')
```

In the SUBSTRING function, the first argument specifies the character data type column (or other string expression) from which you want to extract a substring. The second argument specifies the position where you want to begin extracting the substring. In this case, by specifying 1, you start the extract at the first character. The third argument specifies the number of characters you want to extract. In this case, by specifying 1, you extract one character.

The net effect of this function is that, for each row in the table, the first character of the LastName column is extracted by the function. Then the substring is compared to the list. If it matches an entry in the list, the row is selected.

GROUP BY

The GROUP BY clause groups rows sharing common values for the purpose of calculating an aggregate. Often you'll want to generate reports from the database with summary figures for a particular column or set of columns. For example, you may want to find out the total quantity for each order from the Order Details table.

Try It Out: Using the GROUP BY Clause

The Order Details table contains the list of products for each order and the quantity of each product ordered. You need to total the quantity of all products in each order.

1. Enter the following query into the QueryProcessor application, and execute it. You should see the results shown in Figure 13-8.

```
select
    orderid        'Order ID',
    sum(quantity) 'Total Quantity Ordered'
from
    [order details]
group by
    orderid
```

■**Tip** The literals Order ID and Total Quantity Ordered provide *aliases* for the columns. (In SQL Server you could use square brackets instead of the standard SQL single quotes.) Neither alias is required, but when using functions it's typical to specify an alias. Otherwise the column heading would have been blank (or sum(quantity), depending on your RDBMS). We added the alias for OrderID to demonstrate how you can specify explicit column names in SQL. This is better practice than relying on whatever spelling may automatically be used based on the column name in the database or the query.

Figure 13-8. *Using the* GROUP BY *clause*

How It Works

You use the SUM function to total the Quantity column of the Order Details table by OrderID. The alias provides a custom column header for the total.

```
    sum(quantity) 'Total Quantity Ordered'
from
    [order details]
group by
    orderid
```

Other Aggregates

SQL has several built-in functions that aggregate the values of a column. Aggregate functions return a single value. For example, you can use the aggregate functions to calculate the total number or average value of orders placed. You can find the order with the least value or the most expensive order. Aggregate functions, as their name indicates, work on a set of records and then calculate the appropriate aggregated value. SUM, MIN, MAX, AVG, and COUNT are the frequently used aggregate functions.

Let's assume you want to find the minimum, maximum, and average number of items of each product from the Order Details table.

Try It Out: Using the MIN, MAX, and AVG Functions

To use these functions, do this:

1. Enter the following query into the QueryProcessor application, and execute it. You should see the results shown in Figure 13-9.

```
select
    productid      'Product ID',
    min(quantity) 'Minimum',
    max(quantity) 'Maximum',
    avg(quantity) 'Average'
from
    [order details]
group by
    productid
order by
    productid
```

Figure 13-9. *Using the* MIN, MAX, *and* AVG *functions*

How It Works

You used the MIN and MAX functions to find the minimum and maximum values and the AVG function to calculate the average value.

```
    min(quantity) 'Minimum',
    max(quantity) 'Maximum',
    avg(quantity) 'Average'
from
    [order details]
group by
    productid
```

Since you wanted the results listed by product, you used the GROUP BY clause. From the result set you see that product 1 had a minimum order quantity of 2, a maximum order quantity of 80, and an average order quantity of 21.

■Note You used an ORDER BY clause to assure the results were in product ID sequence. Some RDBMSs would have inferred this sequence from the GROUP BY clause, but SQL Server doesn't. In general, unless you explicitly use ORDER BY, the sequence of the rows in a result set can't be predicted.

Datetime Functions

Although the SQL standard defines a DATETIME data type and its components YEAR, MONTH, DAY, HOUR, MINUTE, and SECOND, it doesn't dictate how an RDBMS makes this data available. Each RDBMS offers a suite of functions that extract parts of DATETIMEs. Let's look at some examples of Transact-SQL datetime functions.

Try It Out: Using Transact-SQL Date and Time Functions

To use Transact-SQL data and time functions, do this:

1. Enter the following query into the QueryProcessor application, and execute it. Widen the first two columns, and you should see the results shown in Figure 13-10.

```
select
    current_timestamp        [standard datetime],
    getdate()                [Transact-SQL datetime],
    datepart(year, getdate()) [datepart year],
    year(getdate())          [year function],
    datepart(hour, getdate()) [hour]
```

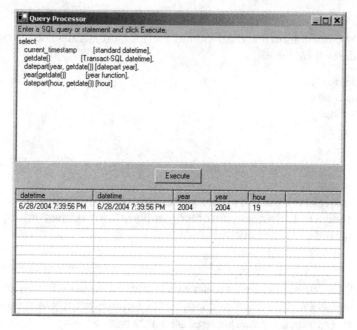

Figure 13-10. *Handling dates and times in Transact-SQL*

How It Works

You used a nonstandard version of a query, omitting the FROM clause, to display the current date and time and individual parts of them. The first two columns in the select list give the complete date and time.

```
current_timestamp        [standard datetime],
getdate()                [Transact-SQL datetime],
```

The first line uses the CURRENT_TIMESTAMP value function of standard SQL; the second uses the GETDATE function of Transact-SQL. They're equivalent in effect, both returning the complete current date and time. (Note that the output format is specific to your RDBMS.)

The next two lines each provide the current year. The first uses the Transact-SQL DATEPART function; the second uses the Transact-SQL YEAR function. Both take a datetime argument and return the integer year. The DATEPART function's first argument specifies what part of a datetime to extract. Note that Transact-SQL doesn't provide a date specifier for extracting a complete date, and it doesn't have a separate DATE function.

```
datepart(year, getdate()) [datepart year],
year(getdate())           [year function],
```

The final line gets the current hour. The Transact-SQL DATEPART function must be used here since no HOUR function is analogous to the YEAR function. Note that Transact-SQL doesn't provide a time specifier for extracting a complete time, and it doesn't have a separate TIME function.

```
datepart(hour, getdate()) [hour]
```

You can format dates and times and alternative functions for extracting and converting them in various ways. Dates and times can also be added and subtracted and incremented and decremented. How this is done is RDBMS-specific, though all RDBMSs comply to a reasonable extent with the SQL standard in how they do it. Whatever RDBMS you use, you'll find that dates and times are the most complicated data types to use. But, in all cases you'll find that functions (typically a richer set of them than in Transact-SQL) are the basic tools for working with dates and times.

Tip When providing date and time input, character string values are typically expected; for example, 6/28/2004 would be the appropriate way to specify the value for a column holding the current date from the example. However, RDBMSs store datetimes in system-specific encodings. When you use date and time data, read the SQL manual for your database carefully to see how to best handle it.

CASE Expressions

The CASE expression allows an alternative value to be displayed depending on the value of a column. For example, a CASE expression can provide *Texas* in a result set for rows that have the value *TX* in the state column. Let's take a look at the syntax of the CASE expression. It has two different forms: the simple CASE and the searched CASE.

This is the simple CASE syntax, where the ELSE part is optional:

```
CASE <case operand>
    WHEN <when operand> THEN
        <when result>
    ELSE
        <else result>
END
```

The CASE keyword is followed by a column name or expression that's to be tested against the operand (a scalar value) following the WHEN keyword. If <case operand> has the same value as <when operand>, <when result> is used; otherwise, <else result> is used as the selection list value.

Try It Out: Using a Simple CASE Expression

To use a simple CASE expression, do this:

1. Enter the following query into the QueryProcessor application, and execute it. You should see the results as in Figure 13-11.

```
select distinct
    year(orderdate) NumYear,
    case year(orderdate)
        when 1998 then
            'Last year'
        else
            'Prior year'
    end LabYear
from
    orders
```

Figure 13-11. *Using a simple* CASE *expression*

How It Works

You're simply labeling years as either *Last year* or *Prior year* depending on whether they were 1998 (the last year for orders in this version of the Northwind database) or earlier (in this database none are later than 1998). The first two lines get a list of the distinct years (in the Orders table).

```
select distinct
    year(orderdate) NumYear,
```

Note that you specify an alias NumYear, but since it doesn't include blanks, you don't have to enclose it in single quotes (or brackets).

The next item in the select list (note that a CASE expression is used just like a column name or function call) is a simple CASE expression where you provide the result of the YEAR function applied to the order date as the <case operand>, the numeric literal 1998 as the <when operand>, and two strings to label the last year and the prior years, depending on whether the year is 1998 (in other words, whether it matches the <when operand>).

```
case year(orderdate)
   when 1998 then
       'Last year'
   else
       'Prior year'
end LabYear
```

Note that since a CASE expression is merely another member of a select list, you can (and do) give it an alias, LabYear.

Let's modify the CASE expression to get an idea of how flexible it can be.

Try It Out: Using a More Complex Simple CASE Expression

To use a more complex simple CASE expression, do this:

1. Enter the following query into the QueryProcessor application, and execute it. You should see the results as in Figure 13-12.

```
select distinct
    year(orderdate) NumYear,
    case year(orderdate)
        when 1998 then
            str(year(orderdate))
        else
            case year(orderdate)
                when 1997 then
                    'Prior'
                else
                    'Earlier'
            end
    end LabYear
from
    orders
```

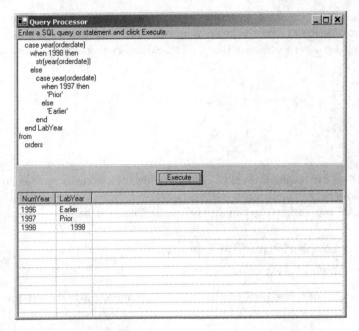

Figure 13-12. *Using a more complex simple* CASE *expression*

How It Works

You do a couple interesting things here. First, you change the label for the last year to the year itself rather than a string, showing that the <when operand> can be a data value (here, in fact, the result of a function applied to a column).

```
when 1998 then
    str(year(orderdate))
```

Note that you use the STR function to convert the integer returned by YEAR to a string, since you're planning to use strings for the alternative labels, and a CASE expression must return values of a single data type.

You then nest a CASE expression inside the original ELSE (they can also be nested in the WHEN part) to support labeling the other years separately. You label 1997 as *Prior* and all others as *Earlier.*

```
else
    case year(orderdate)
        when 1997 then
            'Prior'
        else
            'Earlier'
    end
```

Many other variations are possible. The simple CASE expression can be quite complex. Exploit it to achieve query results that would otherwise require a lot more work—for both you and the database! Now, let's examine the searched CASE.

The following is the searched CASE syntax, where the ELSE part is optional:

```
CASE
    WHEN <search condition> THEN
        <when result>
    ELSE
        <else result>
END
```

Note the differences between the searched and simple CASEs. The searched CASE has no <case operand>, and <when operand> is replaced by <search condition>. These seemingly minor changes add an enormous amount of power. Let's modify the simple CASE example to demonstrate.

Try It Out: Using a Searched CASE Expression

To use a searched CASE expression, do this:

1. Enter the following query into the QueryProcessor application, and execute it. You should see the results as in Figure 13-13.

```
select distinct
    year(orderdate) NumYear,
    case
        when
            year(orderdate) =
                (
                select
                    max(year(orderdate))
                from
                    orders
                )
        then
            'Last year'
        else
            'Prior year'
    end LabYear
from
    orders
```

Figure 13-13. *Using a searched* CASE *expression*

How It Works

The original query, though it worked, was severely limited in that it works correctly only if
1998 is really the last year for orders. You corrected this flaw with a searched CASE. Now the
query will do the right thing whatever years are in the Orders table! You replace the numeric
literal, <when operand>, like so:

```
when 1998 then
```

with a predicate (which can be just as complex as any predicate in a WHERE clause), like so:

```
year(orderdate) =
  (
  select
      max(year(orderdate))
  from
      orders
  )
```

This predicate includes a subquery. Remember, subqueries are simply queries embedded
in other queries. Here, one is embedded in a CASE expression rather than in an IN predicate
(as demonstrated earlier in the chapter). The value returned by the subquery is the maximum
year in the Orders table, so whenever you run the query, you'll get the correct last year—
without ever having to know what it is.

> ■**Note** Complex queries are a normal part of database applications. The more you learn about SQL, the better you'll be able to exploit its considerable power. All major RDBMSs have *very* intelligent query optimizers that can find efficient access paths for even complex queries. You should code whatever complexity you need, relying on the optimizer to do its job; however, even simple queries can sometimes be inefficient, depending on how they're coded. In addition to learning SQL, learn whatever tool your RDBMS offers to analyze query access paths.

You've merely scratched the surface of the many, many facilities SQL offers for coding complex, highly sophisticated queries. Let's now look at the most (but far from only) important one.

Joins

Most queries require information from more than one table. A *join* is a relational database operation that produces a table by retrieving data from two (not necessarily distinct) tables and matching their rows according to a *join specification*.

Different types of joins exist, which you'll look at individually, but keep in mind that every join is a *binary* operation; that is, one table is joined to another, which may be the same table since tables can be joined to themselves. The join operation is a rich and somewhat complex topic. The next sections will cover the basics, using the Northwind database.

Inner Joins

An inner join is the most frequently used join. It returns only rows that satisfy the join specification. Although in theory any relational operator (such as > or <) can be used in the join specification, almost always the equality operator (=) is used. Joins using the equality operator are called *natural joins*.

The basic syntax for an inner join is as follows:

```
select
    <select list>
from
    left-table INNER JOIN right-table
    ON
    <join specification>
```

Notice that INNER JOIN is a binary operation, so it has two operands, left-table and right-table, which may be base tables or anything (for example, a table produced by a subquery or by another join) that can be queried. The ON keyword begins the join specification, which can contain anything that could be used in a WHERE clause.

Let's look at an example, where you retrieve a list of orders, the IDs of the customers who placed them, and the last name of the employees who took them.

Try It Out: Writing an Inner Join

To write an inner join, do this:

1. Enter the following query into the QueryProcessor application, and execute it. You should see the results as in Figure 13-14.

```
select
    orders.orderid,
    orders.customerid,
    employees.lastname
from
    orders inner join employees
    on
    orders.employeeid = employees.employeeid
```

Figure 13-14. *Coding an inner join*

How It Works

Let's start with the select list.

```
select
    orders.orderid,
    orders.customerid,
    employees.lastname
```

Since you're selecting columns from two tables, you need to identify which table a column comes from, which you do by prefixing the table name and a dot (.) to the column name.

This is known as *disambiguation*, or removing ambiguity so the database manager knows which column to use. Though this has to be done only for columns that appear in both tables, best practice is to qualify all columns with their table names.

The following FROM clause specifies both the tables you're joining and the kind of join you're using:

```
from
    orders inner join employees
    on
    orders.employeeid = employees.employeeid
```

It specifies an inner join of the Orders and Employees tables.

```
orders inner join employees
```

It also specifies the criteria for joining them.

```
on
orders.employeeid = employees.employeeid
```

The inner join on EmployeeID produces a table composed of three columns: OrderID, CustomerID, and LastName. The data is retrieved from rows in Orders and Employees where their EmployeeID columns have the same value. Any rows in Orders that don't match rows in Employees are ignored and vice versa. (This isn't the case here, but you'll see an example soon.) An inner join always produces only rows that satisfy the join specification.

Note Columns used for joining don't have to appear in the select list. In fact, EmployeeID isn't in the select list of the example query.

Joins can be quite complicated. Let's revise this one to simplify things a bit.

Try It Out: Writing an Inner Join Using Correlation Names

To write an inner join using correlation names, do this:

1. Enter the following query into the QueryProcessor application, and execute it. You should see the results as in Figure 13-15.

```
select
    o.orderid,
    o.customerid,
    e.lastname
from
    orders o inner join employees e
    on
    o.employeeid = e.employeeid
```

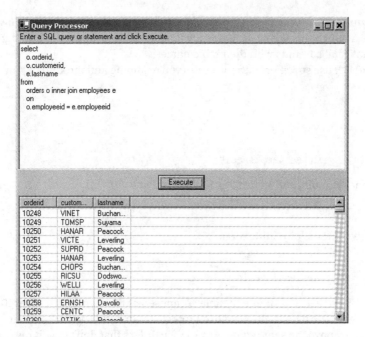

Figure 13-15. *Coding an inner join using correlation names*

How It Works

You've simplified the table references by providing a *correlation name* for each table. (This is somewhat similar to providing column aliases, but correlation names are intended to be used as alternative names for tables. Column aliases are used more for labeling than for referencing columns.) You can now refer to Orders as o and to Employees as e. Correlation names can be as long as table names and can be in mixed case, but obviously the shorter they are, the easier they are to code.

```
from
    orders o inner join employees e
```

You used the correlation names in both the select list and the ON clause.

```
select
    o.orderid,
    o.customerid,
    e.lastname
from
    orders o inner join employees e
on
    o.employeeid = e.employeeid
```

Let's do another variation, so you can see how to use correlation names and aliases together.

Try It Out: Writing an Inner Join Using Correlation Names and Aliases

To write an inner join using correlation names and aliases, do this:

1. Enter the following query into the QueryProcessor application, and execute it. You should see the results as in Figure 13-16.

```
select
    o.orderid    OrderID,
    o.customerid CustomerID,
    e.lastname   Employee
from
    orders o join employees e
    on
    o.employeeid = e.employeeid
```

Figure 13-16. *Coding an inner join using correlation names and aliases*

How It Works

You simply add aliases for each column in the select list. This produced more customized column headings. It has no effect on the rest of the query.

```
select
    o.orderid    OrderID,
    o.customerid CustomerID,
    e.lastname   Employee
```

You also remove the keyword INNER from the join operator, just to see that it's optional. It's better practice to use it, since it clearly distinguishes inner joins from *outer joins*, which you'll look at soon.

```
from
    orders o join employees e
```

As the next example of inner joins, you'll look at their original—but deprecated—syntax. You may see this frequently in legacy code, and it still works with most RDBMSs, but the SQL standard may not allow it in the future.

Try It Out: Writing an Inner Join Using Original Syntax

To write an inner join using the original syntax, do this:

1. Enter the following query into the QueryProcessor application, and execute it. You should see the results as in Figure 13-17.

    ```
    select
        o.orderid    OrderID,
        o.customerid CustomerID,
        e.lastname   Employee
    from
        orders o, employees e
        where
            o.employeeid = e.employeeid
    ```

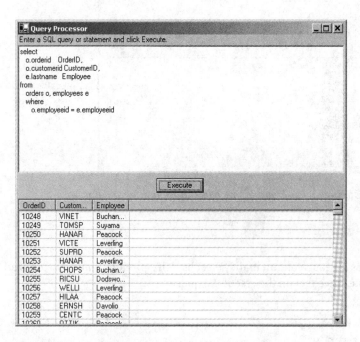

Figure 13-17. *Coding an inner join using original syntax*

How It Works

Note the differences in how you specify the join operator with a comma, instead of INNER JOIN, and how you used a WHERE, instead of an ON, clause.

```
from
    orders o, employees e
    where
        o.employeeid = e.employeeid
```

This syntax was the only one available until the 1992 SQL standard. Any number of tables could be specified, separated by commas. All join predicates had to be specified in a single WHERE clause. Although you haven't seen an example, in the new syntax each join is a distinct operation on two tables and has its own ON clause, so joining more than two tables requires multiple join operators, each with its own ON clause. The new syntax is not only preferred because the old may someday be unsupported, but also because it forces you to specify precisely (and think clearly about) what joins you need.

As the final inner join example, you'll see how to perform joins on more than two tables with the new syntax.

Try It Out: Writing an Inner Join of Three Tables

You'll replace the customer ID with the customer name. To get it, you have to access the Customers table. Enter the following query into the QueryProcessor application, and execute it. If you widen the CustomerName column, you should see the results in Figure 13-18.

```
select
    o.orderid      OrderID,
    c.companyname  CustomerName,
    e.lastname     Employee
from
    orders o
    inner join
    employees e
    on
        o.employeeid = e.employeeid
    inner join
    customers c
    on
        o.customerid = c.customerid
```

Figure 13-18. *Coding an inner join of three tables*

How It Works

First, you modified the select list, replacing CustomerID from the Orders table with CompanyName from the Customers table.

```
select
    o.orderid     OrderID,
    c.companyname CustomerName,
    e.lastname    Employee
```

Second, you added a second inner join, as always with two operands: the table produced by the first join and the base table Customers. You reformatted the first join operator, splitting it across three lines simply to make it easier to distinguish the tables and joins. You can also use parentheses to enclose joins, and you can make them clearer when you use multiple joins. (Further, since joins produce tables, their results can also be associated with correlation names for reference in later joins and even in the select list, but such complexity is beyond the scope of this discussion.)

```
from
    orders o
    inner join
    employees e
    on
        o.employeeid = e.employeeid
    inner join
    customers c
    on
        o.customerid = c.customerid
```

What's happens is this: The result of the first join, which matched orders to employees, is matched against the Customers table from which the appropriate customer name is retrieved for each matching row from the first join. Since referential integrity exists between Orders and both Employees and Customers, all Orders rows have matching rows in the other two tables.

How the database actually satisfies such a query depends on a number of things, but joins are such an integral part of relational database operations that query optimizers are themselves optimized to find efficient access paths among multiple tables to perform multiple joins. However, the fewer joins needed, the more efficient the query, so plan your queries carefully. Usually you have several ways to code a query to get the same data, but almost always only one of them is the most efficient.

Now you know how to retrieve data from two or more tables—when the rows match. What about rows that don't match? That's where outer joins come in.

Outer Joins

Outer joins return *all* rows from (at least) one of the joined tables even if rows in one table don't match rows in the other. Three types of outer joins exist: left outer join, right outer join, and full outer join. The terms *left* and *right* refer to the operands on the left and right of the join operator. (Refer to the basic syntax for the inner join, and you'll see why we called the operands left-table and right-table.) In a left outer join, all rows from the left table will be retrieved whether they have matching rows in the right table. Conversely, in a right outer join, all rows from the right table will be retrieved whether they have matching rows in the left table. In a full outer join, all rows from both tables are returned.

■**Tip** Left and right outer joins are logically equivalent. It's always possible to convert a left join into a right join by changing the operator and flipping the operands or a right join into a left with a similar change. So, only one of these operators is actually needed. Which one you choose is basically a matter of personal preference, but a useful rule of thumb is to use either left or right, but not both in the same query. The query optimizer won't care, but humans find it much easier to follow a complex query if the joins always go in the same direction.

When is this useful? Quite frequently. In fact, whenever a parent-child relationship exists between tables, despite the fact that referential integrity is maintained, some parent rows may not have related rows in the child table. (And, though we didn't mention it earlier, child rows may be allowed to have null foreign key values and, therefore, not match any row in the parent table.) This situation doesn't exist in the original Orders and Employees data, so you'll have to add some data before you can see the effect of outer joins.

You need to add an employee so you have a row in the Employees table that doesn't have related rows in Orders. To keep things simple, you'll provide data only for the columns that aren't nullable.

Try It Out: Adding an Employee with QueryProcessor

To add an employee with QueryProcessor, do this:

1. Enter the following SQL into the QueryProcessor application, and execute it. You should see the results as in Figure 13-19.

```
insert into employees
(
firstname,
lastname
)
values ('Judith', 'Gregory')
```

Figure 13-19. *Adding an employee with* QueryProcessor

How It Works

Although QueryProcessor isn't really designed to handle SQL statements, it submits them to the database. Since statements don't return result sets, you have no output to display. You submit a single INSERT statement, providing the two required columns. The first column, EmployeeID, is an IDENTITY column, so you can't provide a value for it, and the rest are nullable, so you don't need to provide values for them.

```
insert into employees
(
firstname,
lastname
)
values ('Judith', 'Gregory')
```

You now have a new employee, Judith Gregory, who has never taken an order.

Now, let's say you want a list of all orders taken by all employees—but this list must include *all* employees, even those who haven't taken any orders.

Try It Out: Using LEFT OUTER JOIN

To use LEFT OUTER JOIN, do this:

1. Enter the following SQL into the QueryProcessor application, and execute it. Scroll down to the row for Judith Gregory, and you should see the results as in Figure 13-20.

```
select
    e.firstname,
    e.lastname,
    o.orderid
from
    employees e
    left outer join
    orders o
    on
    e.employeeid = o.employeeid
order by
    2, 1
```

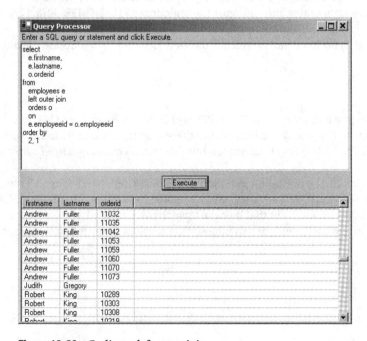

Figure 13-20. *Coding a left outer join*

How It Works

Had you used an inner join you would have missed the row for the new employee. (Try it to see for yourself.) The only new SQL in the FROM clause is the join operator itself.

```
from
    employees e
    left outer join
    orders o
    on
    e.employeeid = o.employeeid
```

You also added an ORDER BY clause, to sort the result set by first name within last name, to see that the kind of join has no effect on the rest of the query, and to see an alternate way to specify columns, by position number within the select list rather than by name. This technique is convenient (and may be the only way to do it for columns that are produced by expressions, for example, by the SUM function).

```
order by
    2, 1
```

Note that the OrderID column for the new employee is blank. This is because the column is NULL, since no value exists for it. The same holds true for any columns from the table that don't have matching rows (in this case, the right table).

You can obtain the same result by placing the Employees table on the right and the Orders table on the left of the join operator and changing the operator to RIGHT OUTER JOIN. (Try it!) Remember to flip the correlation names, too.

The keyword OUTER is optional and is typically omitted. Left and right joins are *always* outer joins.

Other Joins

The SQL standard also provides for FULL OUTER, UNION, and CROSS JOINs (and even NATURAL JOIN, basically an inner join using equality predicates), but these are much less used and beyond the scope of this book. We won't provide examples, but this section contains a brief summary of them.

A FULL OUTER join is like a combination of both the LEFT and RIGHT OUTER joins. All rows from both tables will be retrieved, even if they have no related rows in the other table.

A UNION join is unlike outer joins in that it doesn't match rows. Instead, it creates a table that has all the rows from both tables. For two tables, it's equivalent to the following query:

```
select
    *
from
    table1
union all
select
    *
from
    table2
```

The tables must have the same number of columns, and the data types of corresponding columns must be compatible (able to hold the same types of data).

A CROSS join combines all rows from both tables. It doesn't provide for a join specification, since this would be irrelevant. It produces a table with all columns from both tables and as many rows as the product of the number of rows in each table. The result is also known as a *Cartesian product*, since that's the mathematical term for associating each element (row) of one set (table) with all elements of another set. For example, if there are five rows and five columns in table A and ten rows and three columns in table B, the cross join of A and B would produce a table with fifty rows and eight columns. This join operation is not only virtually inapplicable to any real-world query, but it's also a potentially very expensive process for even small real-world databases. (Imagine using it for a production tables with thousands or even millions of rows.)

Summary

In this chapter, you learned how to construct more sophisticated queries using the following SQL features:

- The DISTINCT keyword to eliminate duplicates from the result set

- Subqueries, which are queries embedded in other queries

- The IN predicate, using lists of literals and lists returned by subqueries

- Aggregate functions such as MIN, MAX, SUM, and AVG

- The GROUP BY clause for categorizing aggregates

- CASE expressions for providing column values based on logical tests

- Functions for accessing the components of the datetime data type

- Inner, outer, and other joins

In the next chapter, you'll learn about two other important database objects: views and stored procedures.

CHAPTER 14

■ ■ ■

Using Views and Stored Procedures

In this chapter you'll learn about *views* and *stored procedures*. Views are named queries that produce *viewed tables* (to use the standard SQL definition) that can be used in much the same way as the tables (or other views) on which they're based. Stored procedures are routines known to the database manager that allow you to package SQL in an optimal fashion for reuse.

Both have many advantages. In this chapter, you'll look at the following:

- What a view is and how to create one

- What a stored procedure is and how to create one

- How to provide input to and handle output from a stored procedure

- How to use views and stored procedures in C# programs

Using Views

Views are often used for security to limit access to data. You can create views that don't include columns (and rows) containing sensitive information, thereby hiding the data from users. This is important, but it's only one aspect of the view concept.

The fundamental purpose of views is to provide convenient perspectives on data, minimizing what users need to know to get the information they want. Views allow you to hide not just data but database complexity. Since they're queries, and queries are operations on tables that produce a single table, you can specify whatever complicated operations you need (for example, joining tables and performing calculations) yet present the end results as just another (viewed) table. Unlike a base table, a view doesn't actually contain data. For this reason views are often called *virtual tables*.

The following are some common uses for views:

- **Joining multiple tables so they look like a single table**: You can use views to join both tables and other views. Querying against such views is much simpler than working with the base tables themselves.

- **Restricting users to specific rows**: Views can be highly selective. Users can be restricted to only those views that expose the data they're allowed to see.

- **Restricting users to specific columns**: Only the columns in a view's select list are exposed. Even the column names can be changed so the nature of the underlying data is clarified or disguised.

- **Aggregating information**: Views can summarize data, thus providing more precise information while hiding details.

Let's look at the views that are already in the Northwind database. In Server Explorer, expand the Views node. You'll see the views in Figure 14-1.

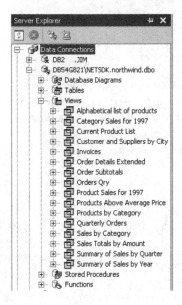

Figure 14-1. Northwind *views*

You can open a view by right-clicking it and selecting Retrieve Data from View. You can see the query behind the view by right-clicking the view and selecting Design View.

You can create views in an MSDE database in two ways.

- Using Server Explorer

- Executing the CREATE VIEW statement

If you're using a full SQL Server instance, you can also use its Query Analyzer to execute the CREATE VIEW statement or its Enterprise Manager to create views. In any case (or database), you can write a C# program to execute the CREATE VIEW statement.

Since you're using MSDE, you'll look at using Server Explorer first, before looking at the CREATE VIEW statement itself.

Try It Out: Creating and Using a View from Server Explorer

Let's create a simple view and use it in Server Explorer. Since, as explained before, a view is a saved query, you'll define a query involving the Employees and Orders tables.

1. In Server Explorer, right-click the Views node and select New View.

2. A dialog will pop up and list all the tables in the database. Select the Orders and Employees tables, and then click Add and then click Close. The tables that are selected will be placed in a diagram pane. Check the boxes next to EmployeeID, LastName, and FirstName in Employees and OrderID in Orders. As you check the columns, notice that they're added to the query in the third pane. Right-click anywhere outside the diagram components, and select Run. The screen should appear as in Figure 14-2.

Figure 14-2. *Creating a view with Server Explorer*

3. Save the view by clicking the Save icon. A window will pop up asking you to name the view. Name it EmployeesAndOrders, and then click OK. Behind the scenes a CREATE VIEW statement is executed to create the view.

How It Works

The dialog box is divided into four panes. The Diagram pane shows the tables, their columns, and the relationship between the tables. In this case, a one-to-many relationship exists between Employees and Orders.

The second pane is called the Grid pane, and it shows the columns selected in the query. Since you checked `EmployeeID`, `LastName`, `FirstName`, and `OrderId`, they appear in the column headed `Column`, with their tables in the column headed `Table`. Notice that the `Output` column is checked; this means that the corresponding column in the table will be listed in the query output.

The third pane is the Query pane. It shows the SQL representing the query that makes up the view. As you add or remove tables or columns, this pane will display the modified SQL. You can also directly modify the SQL, and the Diagram and Grid panes will automatically reflect the changes.

The fourth pane shows the result of the query and is called the Results pane. You can see the data in the view by right-clicking any of the panes and selecting Run.

Let's see how to use the `EmployeesAndOrders` view to obtain information for the employee with ID 1 only.

Try It Out: Creating a View Using Another View

Expanding on the previous example, let's create a view that uses another view as though it were a table. You'll use the `EmployeesAndOrders` view but select only orders for employee 1.

1. In Server Explorer, right-click the Views node and select New View.

2. When the Add Table dialog appears, click Close. Don't select any tables.

3. In the Query pane, replace the SQL with the following query:

```
select
    *
from
    employeesandorders
where
    employeeid = 1
```

4. Right-click in the Query pane, and select Run. Notice (in Figure 14-3) that only orders for employee 1 are returned.

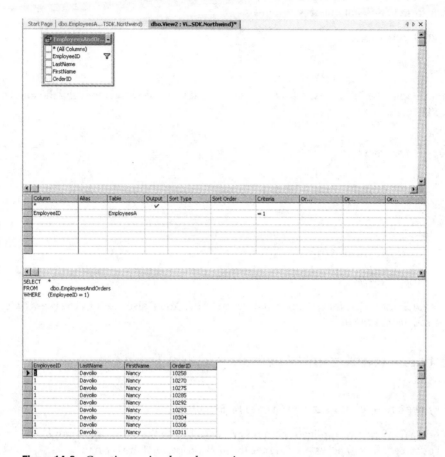

Figure 14-3. *Creating a view based on a view*

5. Save the view as `EmployeesAndOrders_1`. You can use this view like a table. Double-click it in Server Explorer, and observe that the results are always displayed for employee 1.

How It Works

You used the `EmployeesAndOrders` view to create another view. While the `EmployeesAndOrders` view gets all orders taken by all employees, the `EmployeesAndOrders_1` view selects only orders taken by employee 1.

You can also create ad hoc queries (that is, queries that aren't saved) using `EmployeesAndOrders` to obtain information about other employees as well, but only with the information for the columns that are in the view.

Creating a View Using C#

When you create a view in Server Explorer, a CREATE VIEW statement is run behind the scenes. The basic form of this statement is as follows:

```
CREATE VIEW <view name>
AS
<query>
```

For example, the EmployeesAndOrders_1 view could have been created using the following CREATE VIEW statement:

```
CREATE VIEW
    EmployeesAndOrders_1
AS
SELECT
    EmployeeId,
    LastName,
    FirstName,
    OrderId
FROM
    EmployeesAndOrders
```

Now you'll use a custom C# program to create views. You'll also see how to access a view from C# and display the results.

Try It Out: Creating and Accessing a View from C#

Follow these steps:

1. Create a new solution named Chapter14_Examples.

2. Add a C# Windows application named ViewsAndSPs to the solution. Rename Form1.cs to ViewsAndSPs.cs. Change the Text property of the form to Views and Stored Procedures.

3. Add a TabControl control, and click the *Add Tab* link in the Properties pane twice to create two tab pages. Change their text to Views and StoredProcedures.

4. To the Views page add buttons, text boxes, and a list view, as shown in Figure 14-4. Name the controls and set their properties as in Table 14-1. (You'll design the Stored Procedures page later in the chapter.)

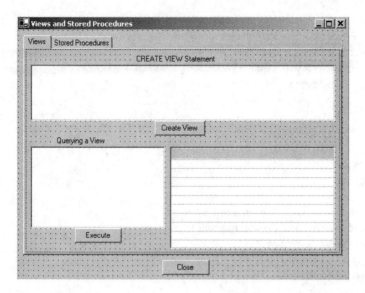

Figure 14-4. ViewsAndSPs *tab page layout*

Table 14-1. Views *Tab Page Attributes*

Control	Name	Remarks
TabControl	tabControl1	Add two pages to the TabPages property, and specify the Text property as Views and Stored Procedures, respectively.
Label	label1	Text: CREATE VIEW statement.
TextBox	txtCreateView	To type in the SQL statement to create a view. Set the Multiline property to True.
Button	cmdCreateView	Text: Create View. To execute the statement in txtCreateView.
TextBox	txtSQL	For queries against views. Set the Multiline property to True.
ListView	lvwViewRS	To show the data retrieved by the view. Set the GridLines property to True and View property to Details.
Button	cmdExecuteView	Text: Execute. To execute the query typed in txtSQL.
Button	cmdClose	Text: Close. To close the form.

5. Add a using directive for the SQL Server data provider to the ViewsAndSPs.cs file.

```
using System.Data.SqlClient;
```

6. Double-click the Create View button, and enter the following code in its click event handler.

```csharp
//Create connection
SqlConnection conn = new SqlConnection(@"
    data source = (local)\netsdk;
    integrated security = sspi;
    database = northwind
");

try
{
    //Open connection
    conn.Open();

    //Create command with SQL entered by user
    SqlCommand cmd = conn.CreateCommand();
    cmd.CommandText = txtSQL.Text;

    //Execute command
    cmd.ExecuteNonQuery();

    // Display success message.
    MessageBox.Show("View was created successfully.");
}
catch (System.Data.SqlClient.SqlException  ex)
{
    // Display error message.
    MessageBox.Show(
        "Could not create the view.\nError Message: " + ex.Message);
}
finally
{
    // Close connection.
    conn.Close();
}
```

7. Double-click the Execute button, and enter the following code in its click event handler:

```csharp
//Create connection
SqlConnection conn = new SqlConnection(@"
    data source = (local)\netsdk;
    integrated security = sspi;
    database = northwind
");

try
{
    //Clear the list view header and items
    lvwViewRS.Columns.Clear() ;
    lvwViewRS.Items.Clear();
```

```csharp
    //Open connection
    conn.Open();

    //Create command with SQL entered by user
    SqlCommand cmd = conn.CreateCommand();
    cmd.CommandText = txtSQL.Text;

    //Create a data reader
    SqlDataReader dr = cmd.ExecuteReader();

    //Put data reader column names into list view header
    for (int i=0; i< dr.FieldCount; i++)
    {
        ColumnHeader c = new ColumnHeader();
        c.Text = dr.GetName(i);
        lvwViewRS.Columns.Add(c);
    }

    //Put data reader rows into list view
    ListViewItem itmX;
    while (dr.Read())
    {
        //Create list view item
        itmX=new ListViewItem();

        //Specify text and subitems
        itmX.Text= dr.GetValue(0).ToString();
        for (int i=1 ; i< dr.FieldCount; i++)
        {
            itmX.SubItems.Add(dr.GetValue(i).ToString());
        }

        //Add item to list view Items collection
        lvwViewRS.Items.Add(itmX);
    }

    //Close data reader
    dr.Close();
}
catch ( System.Data.SqlClient.SqlException ex)
{
    // Display error message
    MessageBox.Show ("There was an error in executing the query. " +
        "Error Message:" + ex.Message);
}
finally
{
    // Close connection.
    conn.Close();
}
```

8. Build and run the project with Ctrl+F5. In the text box below CREATE VIEW statement, enter the following statement, and click Create View:

```
create view EmployeesAndOrders_2
as
select
    e.EmployeeID,
    e.LastName,
    e.FirstName,
    o.OrderID
from
    employees e
    inner join
    orders o
    on
        e.employeeid = o.employeeid
where
    e.employeeid = 2
```

You'll get a confirmation message saying the view was created successfully.

9. In Server Explorer, refresh the Views node and you'll see EmployeesAndOrders_2 listed.

10. Now let's test the view itself. Recollect that a view can be queried like a table. In the text box captioned *Querying a View*, enter the following query, and click the Execute button:

```
select
    *
from
    employeesandorders_2
```

You'll see the result of the query as in Figure 14-5.

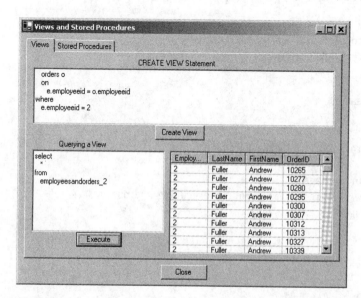

Figure 14-5. *Querying* EmployeesAndOrders_2

How It Works

Since most of the code should be familiar to you by now from discussions in previous chapters, we'll go over only the main points here. First, you coded a CREATE VIEW statement, which defined a view containing EmployeeID, LastName, FirstName, and OrderID. When you clicked the Create View button, the statement was submitted by the ExecuteNonQuery method and the view was created.

```
//Create command with SQL entered by user
SqlCommand cmd = conn.CreateCommand();
cmd.CommandText = txtSQL.Text;

//Execute command
cmd.ExecuteNonQuery();

// Display success message.
MessageBox.Show("View was created successfully.");
```

After creating the view, you tested it by coding a query against it and clicking the Execute button. Since queries return datasets, you used the ExecuteReader method to get a data reader.

```
//Create command with SQL entered by user
SqlCommand cmd = conn.CreateCommand();
cmd.CommandText = txtSQL.Text;

//Create a data reader
SqlDataReader dr = cmd.ExecuteReader();
```

You populated the list view header with the data reader column names and then looped through the rows in the data reader and displayed them, closing the data reader at the end of the loop. Since the EmployeesAndOrders_2 view filters the data, only rows for employee 2 are displayed.

```
//Put data reader column names into list view header
for (int i=0; i< dr.FieldCount; i++)
{
   ColumnHeader c = new ColumnHeader();
   c.Text = dr.GetName(i);
   lvwViewRS.Columns.Add(c);
}

//Put data reader rows into list view
ListViewItem itmX;
while (dr.Read())
{
   //Create list view item
   itmX=new ListViewItem();
```

```
    //Specify text and subitems
    itmX.Text= dr.GetValue(0).ToString();
    for (int i=1 ; i< dr.FieldCount; i++)
    {
        itmX.SubItems.Add(dr.GetValue(i).ToString());
    }

    //Add item to list view Items collection
    lvwViewRS.Items.Add(itmX);
}

//Close data reader
dr.Close();
```

You've seen how to create views and use them in queries, but there's more to views that's beyond our concern in this book. For example, some views are updatable, and others aren't. Also, some views enforce constraints, but others don't. Unless you're performing updates, you typically don't have to know whether you're accessing data through a table or view. Even then you don't need to know as long as the view is updateable.

Using Stored Procedures

Stored procedures are callable modules executed by the database manager. Most RDBMSs have supported them for years, but many required they be written in a language (C and Java are the most common) other than SQL. Today, the SQL standard and most RDBMSs support stored procedures coded purely in SQL and have enhanced SQL to include procedural statements, such as IF and WHILE, and even structured exception handling. With this added functionality, stored procedures have become an extremely important part of database programming. Providing reusable, optimized code, they can significantly improve system performance and reliability while reducing the time and cost of both development and operation.

Stored procedures can have *parameters* that can be used for input or output. They also return a single integer status code and can return one or more result sets. They can be called from client programs or other stored procedures. They are powerful, indeed, and are becoming the preferred mode of database programming, particularly for multitier applications and Web services, since (among their many benefits) they can dramatically reduce network traffic between clients and database servers.

You'll learn how to create different kinds of stored procedures using Server Explorer and then learn how to use them in C# applications. You'll begin by creating a stored procedure that has no parameters. This kind of stored procedure is most often used to execute predefined queries.

Try It Out: Creating and Executing a Stored Procedure with No Parameters

Suppose that you want a result set showing the employee ID and last name for all employees of Northwind Traders. Let's code a stored procedure to provide this. (You'll refine this stored procedure, adding parameters, later.)

■ Note To run this example, you must have Visual Studio .NET Professional or higher. If you have Visual C#
Standard Edition, skip to the next "Try It Out" section.

Follow these steps:

1. In Server Explorer, expand the Northwind connection, right-click the Stored Procedures
   node, and click New Stored Procedure.

2. You'll be presented with a window as in Figure 14-6.

```
Start Page | ViewsAndSPs.cs [Design] | ViewsAndSPs.cs | dbo.StoredPro...SDK.Northwind) |                    ◁ ▷ ✕
CREATE PROCEDURE dbo.StoredProcedure1
/*
    (
        @parameter1 datatype = default value,
        @parameter2 datatype OUTPUT
    )
*/
AS
    /* SET NOCOUNT ON */
    RETURN
```

Figure 14-6. *Stored procedure skeleton SQL*

The /* and */ symbols delimit comments and code inside them is ignored by the
database engine. They're used to comment out more than one line of code. (A pair of
dashes (--) is the standard SQL single-line comment delimiter. Anything from the
dashes through the end of the line is a comment and is ignored.)

Replace the skeleton with the following:

```
create procedure sp_Select_AllEmployees
as
    select
        employeeid,
        lastname
    from
        employees
    return
```

3. Save the stored procedure by clicking the Save icon. Notice that under the Stored Procedures node in Server Explorer, there's a new node for sp_Select_AllEmployees.

4. Now let's execute the stored procedure. Right-click the sp_Select_AllEmployees node in Server Explorer, and click Run Stored Procedure. An output window, as shown in Figure 14-7, will appear showing the results of the stored procedure execution. Scroll down to the bottom and notice that the last line says @RETURN_VALUE = 0. Stored procedures return a value of zero by default. But this can be changed, as you'll see in a later example.

```
Output                                                                          ×
Database Output                                                                 ▼
8           Callahan                                                            ▲
1           Davolio
9           Dodsworth
2           Fuller
10          Gregory
7           King
3           Leverling
4           Peacock
6           Suyama
No more results.
(10 row(s) returned)
@RETURN_VALUE = 0
Finished running dbo."sp_Select_AllEmployees".                                  ▼
◄                                                              ►
```

Figure 14-7. *Output from* sp_SelectAllEmployees

How It Works

This is a simple stored procedure. In a CREATE PROCEDURE statement, you specify the name of the stored procedure. Then the AS keyword separates the signature (the procedure's name and parameter list, but here you define no parameters) of the stored procedure from its body (the SQL that makes up the procedure).

```
create procedure sp_Select_AllEmployees
as
```

After AS, the procedure body has just two components, a query and a RETURN statement.

```
select
    employeeid,
    lastname
from
    employees
return
```

The RETURN statement signifies that the stored procedure has completed its work. That's it; after you saved the stored procedure, you executed it. It ran and produced a result set, the list of all employees, displayed in the Output window.

To modify an existing stored procedure, right-click its node, select Edit Stored Procedure, and then make changes in the editor that appears. Note that the ALTER PROCEDURE statement is used.

If you expand the new node, you'll see nodes for the two columns in its query's select list.

Note The prefix `sp_` is a Transact-SQL convention that typically indicates that the stored procedure is coded in SQL. The prefix `xp_` is also used to indicate that the stored procedure isn't written in SQL. (However, not all `sp_ stored` procedures provided by SQL Server are written in SQL.)

Try It Out: Using an Alternative Method for Creating a Stored Procedure

If you don't have Visual Studio .NET Professional, you can still use Server Explorer to create stored procedures, by submitting SQL as you did in Chapter 3. Let's walk through the steps briefly.

1. In Server Explorer, expand the connection to the Northwind database.

2. Double-click any table, for example, Employees. Once the data grid is displayed, click Show SQL Pane icon on the toolbar.

3. Replace the SQL with the following:

```
create procedure sp_Select_AllEmployees
as
    select
        employeeid,
        lastname
    from
        employees
    return
```

4. Click the Run Query icon to execute the CREATE PROCEDURE statement, and the new stored procedure is created. You'll get a small confirmation dialog box reporting success. Click OK.

5. Right-click the Stored Procedures node in Server Explorer, and click Refresh. A node for the new stored procedure will appear in the tree (see Figure 14-8).

6. Now let's execute the stored procedure. Right-click the sp_Select_AllEmployees node in Server Explorer, and click Run Stored Procedure. An output window (refer to Figure 14-7) appears, showing the results of the stored procedure execution. Scroll down to the bottom, and notice that the last line says @RETURN_VALUE = 0. Stored procedures return a value of zero by default. But you can change this, as you'll see in a later example.

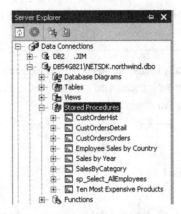

Figure 14-8. *Server Explorer tree including* `sp_SelectAllEmployees`

How It Works

All you did was execute a `CREATE PROCEDURE` statement. See the preceding "How It Works" for an explanation of what it does.

If you expand the new node, you'll see nodes for the two columns in its query's select list.

For each of the other stored procedures you create in this chapter, if you don't have Visual Studio .NET Professional, you'll need to follow these steps to create each new stored procedure, as the code in the later examples depends on them.

Let's move on to look at some more stored procedures.

Try It Out: Creating and Executing a Stored Procedure with a RETURN Value

In this example the stored procedure will return 1 if the number of orders is greater than 100 and 2 otherwise. An application calling this stored procedure could test the return value and display an appropriate message to the user. (Since there are more than 800 orders, you expect a return value of 1.)

1. Create a stored procedure with the following SQL:

```
create procedure sp_Orders_MoreThan100
as
    declare @orders int

    select
        @orders = count(*)
    from
        orders

    if @orders > 100
        return 1
    else
        return 2
```

2. If you try to run the stored procedure the same way you ran the first one, by right-clicking it in the Server Explorer tree and then clicking Run Stored Procedure, you won't get what you expect (see Figure 14-9).

Figure 14-9. *Trying to run* sp_Order_MoreThan100

3. Notice that you can't expand the stored procedure node in the tree. Unlike sp_Select_AllEmployees, it has no items for display, so the only output was the message that the procedure was running.

4. Open the Tables node in Server Explorer, and right-click Orders. Click the SQL icon and replace the code in the editor pane with the following:

```
declare @rc int
exec @rc = sp_orders_morethan100
select @rc
```

5. Click the ! icon to execute the stored procedure. You should get the same output as in Figure 14-10. The return value appears as though it were the first and only column in a single-row result set.

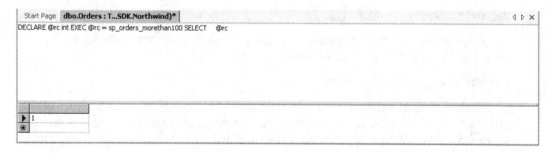

Figure 14-10. *Correctly displaying* sp_Order_MoreThan100 *output*

How It Works

You begin by creating a stored procedure called sp_Orders_MoreThan100 that has no parameters.

```
create procedure sp_Orders_MoreThan100
as
```

In the procedure body (following the AS keyword) you first declare an integer variable called @orders to hold the number of orders. (In Transact-SQL, local variable names begin with @.)

```
declare @orders int
```

Then, within a query select list, you assign a value to the variable with the COUNT function.

```
select
    @orders = count(*)
from
    orders
```

Finally, you code an IF statement that returns 1 if the value of the variable @Orders is greater than 100, and 2 if the value is less than or equal to 100.

```
if @orders > 100
    return 1
else
    return 2
```

Since the only item in the select list is a local variable, there are no columns per se for output, so you have to write some code to capture the return value and display it. The code is straightforward. First you declare a local variable to hold the return value after the procedure terminates.

```
declare @rc int
```

Then you execute the stored procedure with an EXECUTE (short form: EXEC) statement, assigning the return value to the local variable.

```
exec @rc = sp_orders_morethan100
```

Finally, you display the value of the local variable. (This use of SELECT is a Transact-SQL extension to standard SQL, a query requiring no FROM clause.) Note that since you're executing a query, you get a result set, here with only one value in it. That's why the output has one row with one column.

```
select @rc
```

Now let's now look at a stored procedure that accepts an input argument. Stored procedures that accept input are very useful.

■Note The term *parameter* refers to a variable declared between parentheses before the AS keyword in stored procedure declaration. An *argument* is a value passed as input to a procedure and stored in an *input parameter* for use within the procedure. Stored procedures can also declare *local variables* that aren't parameters and output parameters that aren't associated with arguments. Parameters and local variables exist only while the procedure is executing.

Try It Out: Creating and Executing a Stored Procedure with an Input Parameter

In the following example, the stored procedure accepts an employee number and returns a list of orders taken by that employee.

1. Create a stored procedure with the following SQL:

```
create procedure sp_Orders_ByEmployeeId
    @employeeid int
as
    select
        orderid,
        orderdate
    from
        orders
    where
        employeeid = @employeeid

return
```

2. Execute the procedure. Since it requires an EmployeeID as an input parameter, you'll be prompted for it (see Figure 14-11).

Figure 14-11. *Prompting for* sp_Orders_ByEmployeeID *input*

Observe the columns in Figure 14-11. The data type, direction, and name of the parameter are displayed. The direction In means the parameter is an input parameter. Enter 2 in the Value column, and click OK.

The stored procedure will return the output in Figure 14-12.

```
Output                                                                              ×
Database Output                                                                     ▼
  11015      4/10/1998                                                              ▲
  11020      4/14/1998
  11028      4/16/1998
  11032      4/17/1998
  11035      4/20/1998
  11042      4/22/1998
  11053      4/27/1998
  11059      4/29/1998
  11060      4/30/1998
  11070      5/5/1998
  11073      5/5/1998
No more results.
(96 row(s) returned)
@RETURN_VALUE = 0
Finished running dbo."sp_Orders_ByEmployeeId".
◄                                                                                  ►
```

Figure 14-12. *Output of* sp_Orders_ByEmployeeID *for employee 2*

How It Works

When you create the stored procedure, you specify an input parameter. Parameters are declared between the stored procedure name and the AS keyword (much like declaring C# method parameters). The line @employeeid int specifies the name of the parameter, @employeeid, and its data type, int. Parameters are local variables within procedures. In Transact-SQL they're preceded by @, just as declared local variables are. (Other SQL dialects use other conventions.) By default, a parameter is an input parameter.

```
@employeeid int
```

The body of the procedure comprises a query, using the parameter in the WHERE clause, and a RETURN statement. Notice that you don't specify a return value.

```
as
   select
      orderid,
      orderdate
   from
      orders
   where
      employeeid = @employeeid

return
```

In Transact-SQL, a stored procedure can have up to 2,100 parameters, but typically only a few are used.

The RETURN statement can return only a single integer value. What if you need to return more than one value or a value that's not an integer? You could use a result set, but the overhead of generating and processing it for only one row is likely to be less efficient than using output parameters.

Try It Out: Executing a Stored Procedure with Input and Output Parameters

Say you want to find the earliest date and the latest date that a given employee placed an order, as indicated by OrderDate in Orders. You could write a stored procedure that takes an employee ID as an input parameter and return the dates as columns in a query. But you can be a bit more efficient by using two output parameters.

1. Create a stored procedure with the following SQL:

```
create procedure sp_Dates_ByEmployeeId
   @employeeid int ,
   @edate      datetime = null output,
   @ldate      datetime = null output
as
  select
     @edate = min(orderdate),
     @ldate = max(orderdate)
  from
     orders
  where
     employeeid = @employeeid

  return
```

2. Run the stored procedure from the SQL pane as in the previous example but using the following SQL. You should see the result in Figure 14-13.

```
declare
   @earliest datetime,
   @latest   datetime

exec sp_dates_byemployeeid 2, @earliest output, @latest output

select @earliest, @latest
```

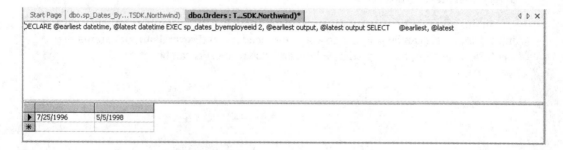

Figure 14-13. *Displaying output parameters*

How It Works

You specify one input parameter (@employeeid) of type int and two output datetime parameters (@edate and @ldate). You'll pass an employee ID to the stored procedure as an input argument and pass back the earliest and latest order dates for the employee in the output parameters. Though not absolutely required, you default the output parameters to nulls (= null) before you specify that they're output parameters (output). Parameters need to be initialized before use. By explicitly defaulting the output parameters to null, you make it somewhat easier to code and invoke the procedure. (Input parameters can also be given default values.)

```
create procedure sp_Dates_ByEmployeeId
    @employeeid int ,
    @edate       datetime = null output,
    @ldate       datetime = null output
as
```

In the body of the procedure, you assign values to the output parameters by using the MIN and MAX functions on OrderDate.

```
select
    @edate = min(orderdate),
    @ldate = max(orderdate)
from
    orders
where
    employeeid = @employeeid
```

You executed the procedure with a variation on the previous example, which captured and displayed the return code. You declared two local variables to hold the returned dates.

```
declare
    @earliest datetime,
    @latest   datetime
```

You executed the procedure, passing it an integer argument for the employee ID and specifying the local variables as the recipients of the two output parameters.

```
exec sp_dates_byemployeeid 2, @earliest output, @latest output
```

Finally, you displayed the results using the Transact-SQL extension to a standard SQL query.

```
select @earliest, @latest
```

In this example, two output values were returned. In a more complex problem, several input parameters can be supplied to a stored procedure, and several output parameters, a RETURN value other than zero (if needed), and also result sets can be returned.

■**Note** The syntax for creating and executing stored procedures differs slightly depending on what dialect of SQL an RDBMS supports. Even in Transact-SQL you'll have additional provisions for declaring and accessing parameters that may be useful to know about depending on what your procedures need to do. We've presented the most generic (and most often used) syntax, but consult your SQL documentation for the details of how best to define and call stored procedures.

Working with Stored Procedures in C#

You've learned about stored procedures using Server Explorer. Now you'll explore them using C#. You'll extend the ViewsAndSPs application you developed earlier in the chapter to handle stored procedures.

Try It Out: Setting Up a C# Project to Execute Stored Procedures

Follow these steps:

1. Earlier in this chapter, you created a form with two tabs, one for views and another for stored procedures. Select the Stored Procedures tab and add buttons, text boxes, and a list view as shown in Figure 14-14 and described in Table 14-2.

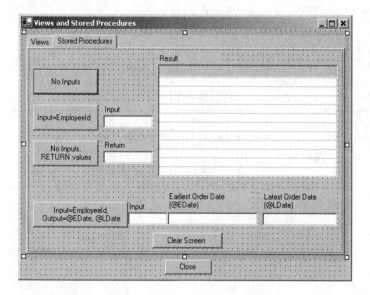

Figure 14-14. *Stored Procedures tab page layout*

Table 14-2. ViewsAndSPs *Tab Page Attributes*

Control	Name	Remarks
Label	label8	Text: Result.
ListView	LvwRS	To display results. Set the GridLines property to True and the View property to Details.
Button	cmdNoInput	Text: No-Input. To execute a stored procedure without any input parameters.
Button	cmdInput	Text: Input = EmployeeID. To execute a stored procedure by supplying one input parameter.
Label	label3	Text: Input
TextBox	txtEmpId1	To supply the employee ID argument.
Button	CmdReturn	Text: No-Input, RETURN values. To execute a stored procedure that returns values using the RETURN statement.
Label	label4	Text: Return.
TextBox	txtReturn	To display the value from the RETURN statement.
Button	cmdOutput	Text: Input = Employee ID, Output = @Edate, @Ldate. To execute a stored procedure that takes one input argument and returns two output parameters.
Label	label5	Text: Input.
TextBox	txtEmpId2	To supply the input.
Label	label6	Text: Earliest Order Date (@EDate).
TextBox	txtEDate	To display the earliest date.
Label	label7	Text: Latest Order Date (@Ldate).
TextBox	txtLDate	To display the latest date.
Button	cmdClear	Text: Clear Screen. To clear the list view and text boxes for the next execution.
Button	cmdClose	Text: Close. To close the form.

2. Build and run the solution with Ctrl+F5. Select the Stored Procedures tab. You should see the tab page in Figure 14-15.

Figure 14-15. *Stored Procedures tab page displayed*

Now let's try to execute the stored procedures one at a time.

Try It Out: Executing a Stored Procedure with No Input Parameters from C#

You want to execute sp_Select_AllEmployees, which takes no input and returns a list of all employees. You need to write code behind the cmdNoInput button to execute this stored procedure and display the results in the list view to its right.

1. Add the following code to the click event handler for the No Input button:

```
//Create connection
SqlConnection conn = new SqlConnection(@"
    data source=(local)\netsdk;
    integrated security = sspi;
    database=Northwind
");

try
{
    //Clear the list view
    lvwRS.Columns.Clear() ;
    lvwRS.Items.Clear();
```

```
//Create command
SqlCommand cmd= conn.CreateCommand();

//Specify the stored procedure to be executed
cmd.CommandType = CommandType.StoredProcedure;
cmd.CommandText ="sp_Select_AllEmployees";

//Open connection
conn.Open();

//Create data reader
SqlDataReader dr = cmd.ExecuteReader();

//Set up list view header
for (int i=0; i < dr.FieldCount; i++)
{
   ColumnHeader ch = new ColumnHeader();
   ch.Text=dr.GetName(i);
   lvwRS.Columns.Add(ch);
}

//Put data reader rows in the list view
ListViewItem itmX;
while (dr.Read())
{
   //create the list view item
   itmX = new ListViewItem();
   //Specify text and subitems
   itmX.Text = dr.GetValue(0).ToString();
   for (int i = 1 ; i< dr.FieldCount; i++)
   {
      itmX.SubItems.Add(dr.GetValue(i).ToString());
   }

   //Add item to list view Items collection
   lvwRS.Items.Add(itmX);
}

//Close reader
dr.Close();
}
catch ( System.Data.SqlClient.SqlException  ex)
{
   // Display the error message.
   MessageBox.Show(
       "There was an error in executing the SQL.\n"
     + "Error Message: " + ex.Message);
}
```

```
finally
{
    //Close connection
    conn.Close();
}
```

2. Build and run the solution with Ctrl+F5. Click the No-Input button to see the results as shown in Figure 14-16.

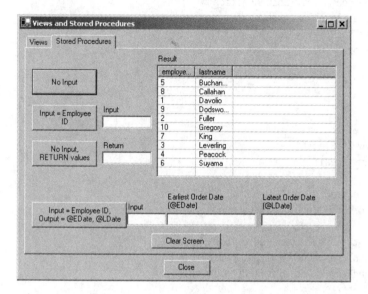

Figure 14-16. *Executing a stored procedure with no arguments*

How It Works

We'll explain only the code relevant to executing the stored procedure. The rest should be familiar by now.

You created a command a bit differently, specifying the CommandType property and using the stored procedure name rather than an SQL string as CommandText.

```
//Create command
SqlCommand cmd= conn.CreateCommand();

//Specify the stored procedure to be executed
cmd.CommandType = CommandType.StoredProcedure;
cmd.CommandText ="sp_Select_AllEmployees";
```

Since the stored procedure has no parameters, nothing more is required. You know that this stored procedure returns a data set, so you use a data reader to access it. Not all stored procedures, of course, return data sets; some return just a return value, and others return output parameters. Let's see how to deal with these cases.

You'll call a procedure that accepts one input argument and returns a result set.

Try It Out: Executing a Stored Procedure with One Input Parameter from C#

You'll call the sp_Orders_ByEmployeeId stored procedure, supplying the employee ID in a text box and displaying the result set in the list view.

1. Add the following code to the click event handler for the Input = Employee ID button:

```
//Create connection
SqlConnection conn = new SqlConnection(@"
    data source=(local)\netsdk;
    integrated security = sspi;
    database=Northwind
");

try
{
    //Clear the list view
    lvwRS.Columns.Clear();
    lvwRS.Items.Clear();

    //Create command
    SqlCommand cmd = conn.CreateCommand();

    //Specify the stored procedure to be executed
    cmd.CommandType = CommandType.StoredProcedure;
    cmd.CommandText = "sp_Orders_ByEmployeeId";

    //Create an input parameter
    SqlParameter parInput = cmd.Parameters.Add("@employeeid", SqlDbType.Int);
    parInput.Direction = ParameterDirection.Input;
    parInput.Value = Convert.ToInt32(txtEmpId1.Text);

    //Open connection
    conn.Open();

    //Execute the command and display the results
    //Create data reader
    SqlDataReader dr = cmd.ExecuteReader();

    //Set up list view header
    for (int i = 0; i < dr.FieldCount; i++)
    {
        ColumnHeader ch = new ColumnHeader();
        ch.Text = dr.GetName(i);
        lvwRS.Columns.Add(ch);
    }
```

```
        //Put data reader rows in the list view
        ListViewItem itmX;
        while (dr.Read())
        {
            //Create list view item
            itmX = new ListViewItem();
            //Specify text and subitems
            itmX.Text = dr.GetValue(0).ToString();
            for (int i = 1 ; i < dr.FieldCount; i++)
            {
                itmX.SubItems.Add(dr.GetValue(i).ToString());
            }
            //Add item to list view Items collection
            lvwRS.Items.Add(itmX);
        }
        //Close data reader
        dr.Close();
    }
    catch ( System.Data.SqlClient.SqlException  ex)
    {
        // Display error message.
        MessageBox.Show(
            "There was an error in executing the SQL Command.\n"
            + "Error Message:" + ex.Message);
    }
    finally
    {
        //Close connection
        conn.Close();
    }
```

2. Now, build and run the solution with Ctrl+F5. In the Input text box, type **2** to get the list of all orders placed by employee 2. Click the Input = Employee ID button to see results as shown in Figure 14-17.

Figure 14-17. *Executing a stored procedure with an input argument*

You can now experiment with different employee IDs.

How It Works

In this example, an employee ID is passed as a parameter. As in the previous example, the only significant change is in configuring the command. You specify that it's for a stored procedure as in the previous example.

```
//Create command
SqlCommand cmd = conn.CreateCommand();

//Specify the stored procedure to be executed
cmd.CommandType = CommandType.StoredProcedure;
cmd.CommandText = "sp_Orders_ByEmployeeId";
```

Then you create a command parameter (an instance of SqlParameter) so you can supply the input argument to the command. Each command has a collection named Parameters. You create command parameters by adding to this collection (there is no public constructor for SqlParameter), providing the parameter's name (note that they *aren't* case sensitive) as the first argument and its data type as the second. Once the command parameter has been created, you specify its direction and value.

```
//Create an input parameter
SqlParameter parInput = cmd.Parameters.Add("@employeeid", SqlDbType.Int);
parInput.Direction = ParameterDirection.Input;
parInput.Value = Convert.ToInt32(txtEmpId1.Text);
```

Note that you use a member of the System.Data.ParameterDirection enumeration to explicitly state that the parameter is an input parameter, but this was actually necessary since the default is Input.

```
parInput.Direction = ParameterDirection.Input;
```

The ParameterDirection enum can take four values: Input, Output, InputOutput, and ReturnValue. The meanings are self-evident. (SQL Server, unlike some other RDBMSs, doesn't support input/output parameters.)

Let's summarize what you've done here. To specify input to a stored procedure, you used a SqlParameter object, specified its direction as Input, and supplied a value for it. Then you simply called ExecuteReader to execute the stored procedure and get the data set it returns.

Now let's see how to handle a return value from a stored procedure in C#.

Try It Out: Handling a Stored Procedure Return Value

You'll call sp_Orders_MoreThan100 and capture its return value.

1. Add the following code to the click event handler for the RETURN button:

```
//Create connection
SqlConnection conn = new SqlConnection(@"
    data source=(local)\netsdk;
    integrated security = sspi;
    database=Northwind
");

try
{
    //Create command
    SqlCommand cmd = conn.CreateCommand();

    //Specify stored procedure that is to be executed
    cmd.CommandType= CommandType.StoredProcedure;
    cmd.CommandText="sp_Orders_MoreThan100";

    //Create return parameter
    SqlParameter parReturn =
        cmd.Parameters.Add("returnvalue", SqlDbType.Int);
    parReturn.Direction = ParameterDirection.ReturnValue ;

    //Open connection
    conn.Open();

    //Execute command and display return value
    cmd.ExecuteScalar();
    txtReturn.Text =
        Convert.ToString(cmd.Parameters["returnvalue"].Value);
}
```

```
catch ( System.Data.SqlClient.SqlException ex)
{
    // Display error message.
    MessageBox.Show(
        "There was an error in executing the SQL Command.\n"
    + "Error Message: " + ex.Message);
}
finally
{
    conn.Close();
}
```

2. Build and run with Ctrl+F5. Click the No-Input, RETURN values button and you'll see the display in Figure 14-18. A value of 1 is displayed in the text box adjacent to the button. Remember that this stored procedure returns 1 if there are more than 100 orders placed; other it returns 2.

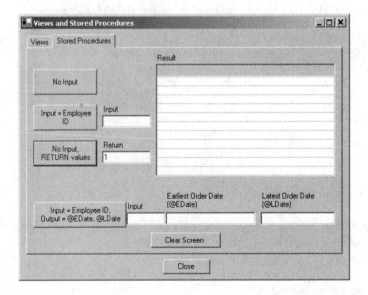

Figure 14-18. *Handling a stored procedure return value*

How It Works

This is similar to the prior example, except you don't need a data reader since no result set is returned. You create a command, and then you add a command parameter to it and configure the parameter to handle a return value.

```
//Create command
SqlCommand cmd = conn.CreateCommand();
```

```
//Specify stored procedure that is to be executed
cmd.CommandType= CommandType.StoredProcedure;
cmd.CommandText="sp_Orders_MoreThan100";

//Create return parameter
SqlParameter parReturn = cmd.Parameters.Add("returnvalue", SqlDbType.Int);
parReturn.Direction = ParameterDirection.ReturnValue ;
```

Now that you've specified the parameter that will hold the return value, you can execute the stored procedure. Since this stored procedure will return only one value, you call the ExecuteScalar method on the command object.

```
//Execute command and display return value
cmd.ExecuteScalar();
txtReturn.Text = Convert.ToString(cmd.Parameters["returnvalue"].Value);
```

The return value from the stored procedure will be placed in the Value property of the parReturn command parameter. You convert it to a string and place it in a text box.

```
txtReturn.Text = Convert.ToString(cmd.Parameters["returnvalue"].Value);
```

Stored procedures are often used to modify data. In these stored procedures you can check for a certain condition that would make it necessary to abort inserts, updates, or deletes and inform the user of the reason for the failure. In such cases you can use the RETURN statement in the stored procedure to inform the calling program of the reason, and the program can take the appropriate action based on the return value.

The final example is a stored procedure that accepts input and returns output in parameters to the calling program.

Try It Out: Executing a Stored Procedure with Both Input and Output Parameters

You'll call the sp_Dates_ByEmployeeId stored procedure from C# and display the earliest and the latest dates of the orders taken by an employee.

1. Add the following code to the click event handler for the cmdOutput button:

```
//Create connection
SqlConnection conn = new SqlConnection(@"
    data source=(local)\netsdk;
    integrated security = sspi;
    database=Northwind
");

try
{
    //Create command
    SqlCommand cmd = conn.CreateCommand();
```

```
        //Specify stored procedure that is to be executed
        cmd.CommandType= CommandType.StoredProcedure;
        cmd.CommandText="sp_Dates_ByEmployeeId";

        //Create input parameter
        SqlParameter parInput =
            cmd.Parameters.Add("@employeeid", SqlDbType.Int);
        parInput.Direction = ParameterDirection.Input;
        parInput.Value= Convert.ToInt32(txtEmpId2.Text);

        //Create output parameters
        SqlParameter parOutput1 =
            cmd.Parameters.Add("@edate",SqlDbType.DateTime);
        parOutput1.Direction = ParameterDirection.Output ;
        SqlParameter parOutput2 =
            cmd.Parameters.Add("@ldate",SqlDbType.DateTime);
        parOutput2.Direction = ParameterDirection.Output ;

        //Open connection
        conn.Open();

        //Execute command and display results
        cmd.ExecuteNonQuery();
        txtEDate.Text = Convert.ToString(parOutput1.Value);
        txtLDate.Text = Convert.ToString(parOutput2.Value);
    }
    catch ( System.Data.SqlClient.SqlException  ex)
    {
        // Display error message.
        MessageBox.Show(
            "There was an error in executing the SQL Command.\n"
          + "Error Message: " + ex.Message);
    }
    finally
    {
        conn.Close();
    }
```

2. Build and run with Ctrl+F5. Enter **3** in the Input text box, and click the button to its left as in Figure 14-19. Observe that the earliest date and latest date of orders taken by employee 3 are then displayed.

Figure 14-19. *Handling both input and output parameters*

Specify different employee IDs, and observe the results.

How It Works

You specify the sp_Dates_ByEmployeeId as the stored procedure to execute.

```
//Create command
SqlCommand cmd = conn.CreateCommand();

//Specify stored procedure that is to be executed
cmd.CommandType= CommandType.StoredProcedure;
cmd.CommandText="sp_Dates_ByEmployeeId";
```

You create a command parameter for @employeeid of type Int and specify its direction and value.

```
//Create input parameter
SqlParameter parInput = cmd.Parameters.Add("@employeeid", SqlDbType.Int);
parInput.Direction = ParameterDirection.Input;
parInput.Value= Convert.ToInt32(txtEmpId2.Text);
```

Then you create two output parameters to hold the earliest and latest dates. You call them parOutput1 and parOutput2 and for @edate and @ldate, respectively, and then specify their direction as Output.

```
//Create output parameters
SqlParameter parOutput1 = cmd.Parameters.Add("@edate",SqlDbType.DateTime);
parOutput1.Direction = ParameterDirection.Output ;
SqlParameter parOutput2 = cmd.Parameters.Add("@ldate",SqlDbType.DateTime);
parOutput2.Direction = ParameterDirection.Output ;
```

Since this stored procedure doesn't return a result set, you don't use the ExecuteReader method; and since it doesn't return only a return value, you don't use the ExecuteScalar method either. You use ExecuteNonQuery instead.

```
//Execute command and display results
cmd.ExecuteNonQuery();
```

You then place the earliest and latest dates in their text boxes.

```
txtEDate.Text = Convert.ToString(parOutput1.Value);
txtLDate.Text = Convert.ToString(parOutput2.Value);
```

That's it for the discussion of stored procedures. We could have written an entire book covering the creation and use of stored procedures, but these are the essentials that you should understand.

Summary

In this chapter you learned about views and stored procedures. First we discussed views, in particular how to create them and use them like tables. You used both Server Explorer and C# to experiment with views.

Most of the chapter was dedicated to stored procedures, the various ways they accept input and produce output, and how to call stored procedures and handle what they return in C#. In particular, you learned how to create appropriate command parameters and when to use the ExecuteReader, ExecuteScalar, and ExecuteNonQuery when dealing with stored procedures.

Along the way you practiced many techniques covered in earlier chapters. We didn't cover handling multiple result sets from stored procedures, because you use the same technique presented in Chapter 7. Applying this to a stored procedure would be an excellent exercise and really test your mastery of the concepts presented in this chapter.

Next we'll return to some database concepts: indexes and constraints.

CHAPTER 15

■ ■ ■

Using Indexes and Constraints

Indexes and constraints each offer different benefits. When used properly, indexes can dramatically improve performance, particularly for queries. Constraints enhance data integrity by defining data validation rules in the database itself rather than relying on applications to code them consistently and correctly. You first looked at constraints in Chapter 12, and we'll expand that knowledge here.

In this chapter, we'll cover the following:

- The advantages and disadvantages of indexing

- Choosing the best columns and data types for indexes

- Clustered and nonclustered indexes

- Using constraints to maintain database integrity

- Understanding UNIQUE, CHECK, DEFAULT, and NOT NULL constraints

Understanding Indexes

Relational databases use indexes to minimize the time it takes to find data. You may not have noticed it in the simple queries you've seen so far, but each query takes some time for the database to run it and return its results. This is more noticeable when running several complex queries against larger tables of data.

Note Neither creating nor dropping indexes requires changes to application code. The database engine uses indexes transparently.

A database engine uses an index in much the same way as a reader uses the index of a book. For example, if you wanted to find all references to INSERT statements in this book, you could begin on page 1 and scan each page of the book, marking each time you found the word until you reach the end of the book. This approach is time consuming and laborious. Alternatively, you can use the index in the back of the book to find the page number for each occurrence of an INSERT statement. This approach produces the same results, but it's much faster and easier.

When a table has no index, the result is similar to the reader who looks at every page; the database engine needs to look at every row. In other words, it performs a *table scan*. This isn't necessarily a problem for small tables, and it's sometimes unavoidable, even with indexes. However, as a table grows to thousands (or even millions) of rows, scans can become prohibitively expensive.

The following query on the Products table of the Northwind database retrieves products in a specific price range:

```
SELECT
    ProductID,
    ProductName,
    UnitPrice
FROM
    Products
WHERE
    (UnitPrice > 12.5) AND (UnitPrice < 14)
```

Currently you have no index on the Product table to help this query, so the database engine performs a table scan and examines each row to see if UnitPrice falls between 12.5 and 14. In Figure 15-1, the database search touches a total of 77 rows to find just three matches.

Figure 15-1. *Table scan of* Products

Suppose you created an index on the UnitPrice column. The index would contain a copy of each UnitPrice value and a reference (much like a page number in a book's index) to each row containing the value. The database keeps the index entries in ascending order and can quickly find the three rows to satisfy the query, without scanning every row in the table.

Caution In the "Try It Out" sections of this chapter, we'll use some features available only in the Architect and Professional versions of Visual Studio .NET. We'll also present the SQL you can use to produce the same results without these versions of Visual Studio.

Try It Out: Creating a Simple Index

To create a simple index, follow these steps:

1. In Server Explorer, right-click the Products table and select Design Table. The window shown in Figure 15-2 will appear.

Figure 15-2. Products *Design view*

2. Click the Manage Indexes and Keys icon to open the Property Pages dialog box for the Products table (see Figure 15-3).

Figure 15-3. *Property Pages dialog box for the* Products *table*

The dialog box displays an existing index on the Products table: the PK_Products index. In the "Maintaining Uniqueness" section, you'll see how primary keys are automatically indexed to enforce uniqueness.

3. Click the New button, and then replace the Index Name entry with IDX_UnitPrice.

4. Expand the column entry (see Figure 15-4), and select the UnitPrice column to include it in the index. Click Close. Server Explorer then creates the index.

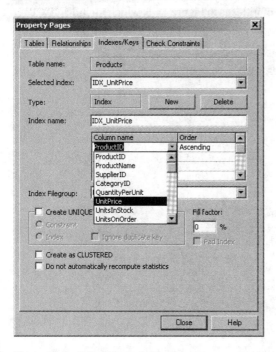

Figure 15-4. *Selecting index columns*

5. You can check that the index has been created in several ways. One is to run the built-in stored procedure `sp_helpindex` with the table name as its argument. For example, if you executed it with the `QueryProcessor` you built in Chapter 13 and widened the output columns, you'd see the list of indexes in Figure 15-5, which includes `IDX_UnitPrice`.

Figure 15-5. *Listing indexes with* `sp_helpindex`

How It Works

You could have created the same index with the following SQL:

```
CREATE INDEX IDX_UnitPrice
ON Products
(
   UnitPrice
)
```

The `CREATE INDEX` statement specifies the name of the index (`IDX_UnitPrice`), the table to be indexed (`Products`), and the column(s) to index on (`UnitPrice`). Server Explorer did this for you, and SQL Server created the index.

Let's take a look at what happened in more detail.

The database takes the key columns specified in `CREATE INDEX` and organizes their values into a special data structure known as a *B-tree*. A B-tree supports fast searches with a minimum amount of disk reads, allowing the database engine to quickly find the starting and ending points for a query.

Conceptually (physically, SQL Server and all RDBMSs build a somewhat more sophisticated structure), you can think of an index as shown in Figure 15-6. On the left, each index *node* contains the index key (UnitPrice) value. The index tree may have multiple levels of nodes, since each node has a maximum size and nodes *split* as the number of index entries increases. (B-trees split in a balanced way so that the number of levels is kept to a minimum in order to minimize input/output [I/O] in traversing the tree.) At the bottom level, *leaf nodes* have pointers to base table rows for a specific key value. Consequently, data can be accessed with minimal I/Os: to the index nodes and then directly to rows of the base table.

Figure 15-6. *Logical structure of a two-level B-tree index*

■**Note** Although all indexes are conceptually similar to the previous description, they can be configured (both logically and physically) in a variety of ways, and each RDBMS offers its own variations. Consult your database documentation to learn what your RDBMS provides, so you can wisely determine how best to define—and exploit—indexes.

Given this sketch of how indexes work, let's look at some scenarios to examine the benefits they provide.

Taking Advantage of Indexes

The database engine uses indexes to boost performance, often dramatically. All major RDBMSs have a component known as the *query optimizer*. The optimizer's job is to find the fastest and most resource-efficient means of executing queries. An important (perhaps the most important) part of this job is selecting the best index or indexes to use. In the following sections, you'll examine the types of queries that typically benefit the most from indexes.

Searching for a Row or Range of Rows

The most obvious use for an index is to find a row or set of rows that satisfies a WHERE clause or join (ON) predicate. If an index is ordered on the values in a particular column, it can be used to find values within a range as well as for a specific value.

For example, all the following SQL could benefit from an index on UnitPrice:

```
DELETE FROM Products
WHERE
    UnitPrice = 1

UPDATE Products
    SET Discontinued = 1
WHERE
    UnitPrice > 15

SELECT
    *
FROM
    Products
WHERE
    UnitPrice BETWEEN 14 AND 16
```

Note that you can use indexes for statements (here, DELETE and UPDATE) as well as for queries.

Sorting Rows

When you ask for a sorted result set, the database will try to find an index to avoid sorting the rows. Sorts most often occur to satisfy the ORDER BY clause, but the DISTINCT keyword and other query components can require internal sorting that may also cause an index to be used.

For example, the following query returns all products sorted by price:

```
SELECT
    *
FROM
    Products
ORDER BY
    UnitPrice ASC
```

Without an index on UnitPrice, the database must scan the Products table and then sort the rows to process the query. However, even though all rows must be accessed, the optimizer may choose to use the index if it estimates that the resource cost will be less than the combined scan and sort. Note that if only some rather than all rows were to be accessed based on UnitPrice, the probability that the index would be more cost effective would increase and the likelihood that it would be used would be greater.

You can use the same index for the following query, assuming the index is descending (not the case here, since by default SQL Server creates an ascending index), or the RDBMS can scan the index in reverse (SQL Server will but some RDBMSs can't, and some require you to explicitly provide for this when creating the index):

```
SELECT
    *
FROM
    Products
ORDER BY
    UnitPrice DESC
```

Note How the optimizer makes its choices depends on many factors. Don't assume that because *you* think an index will be used that the optimizer will agree. The rule of thumb is simple. If no index exists, the optimizer's choices are limited, so it's up to you to make sure that appropriate indexes exist. On the other hand, indexes take up space, and though they can dramatically enhance performance of queries (or any operation that needs to find a subset of rows), they can incur significant overhead since changes to data require indexes to be updated, too. Choose wisely which indexes to create, and the optimizer will be able to make wiser choices; however, never create an index without considering its potential costs as well as benefits.

Grouping Rows

As you saw in Chapter 13, you can use a GROUP BY clause to group rows and aggregate values, for example, counting the number of orders placed by a customer. To process a query with a GROUP BY clause, the database has to sort the rows on the columns on the grouping columns.

The following query counts the number of products by price:

```
SELECT
    Count(*),
    UnitPrice
FROM
    Products
GROUP BY
    UnitPrice
```

The database can use the IDX_UnitPrice index to retrieve the prices in order and count the number of products at each price quickly. Indexing a field used in a GROUP BY clause can often speed up a query. As always, whether such an index will be used is up to the optimizer.

Maintaining Uniqueness

Columns requiring uniqueness (such as primary keys) must have a *unique index* for the database to enforce this constraint (which we'll discuss soon). You have several methods for establishing a unique constraint. Defining a primary key will automatically (in SQL Server but not in all RDBMSs) cause a unique index to be created for the key. You can also explicitly create unique indexes, in addition to the one for the primary key. Let's do it.

Try It Out: Creating a Unique Index

To create a unique index, follow these steps:

1. In Server Explorer, right-click the `Products` table and select Design Table. The window in Figure 15-2 will appear. Click the Manage Indexes and Keys icon to open the Property Pages dialog box.

2. Click New, name the index `IDX_ProductName`, select the `ProductName` column as the key, and then check the Create UNIQUE check box. Click the Index radio button when it becomes enabled (see Figure 15-7). Click Close to create the index and close the dialog box.

Figure 15-7. *Defining a unique index*

Alternatively, you can create a unique index using the following SQL:

```
CREATE UNIQUE INDEX IDX_ProductName
ON Products
(
    ProductName
)
```

How It Works

The `UNIQUE` keyword specifies that the index will be unique. That doesn't mean the index key is the primary key for the table. Although the index uniquely identifies rows, just like a primary key, a table may have multiple unique indexes but only one primary key.

So far, you've seen why indexes are useful and where they're best applied. Now let's look at some options available when creating an index and some common rules of thumb for designing indexes.

Using Clustered Indexes

Earlier in the chapter we made an analogy between a database index and the index of a book. A book index stores words in order with a reference to the page numbers where the word is located. The corresponding type of index for a database is known as a *nonclustered index*: only the index key and a reference are stored.

In contrast, a *clustered index* maintains base table rows in the same physical sequence as the index key. A phone book is a good analogy. A phone book sorts entries physically in alphabetical order; once you find a name in a phone book, you have immediate access to the rest of the data for the name, such as the phone number and address.

▬**Note** A clustered index determines the physical ordering of the rows in a table. For this reason, a table can have only one clustered index, since it can have only one physical order.

In Figure 15-8, we searched using a clustered index on `UnitPrice`. Note how the rows are stored in index order. The three rows shown are all stored on the same physical database page.

Figure 15-8. *Clustered index data storage*

A clustered index is typically the most important index in terms of performance. Choosing what key to use is often not easy, since a clustered index doesn't need to be unique and several good candidates (often, but not necessarily the primary key) may exist for physical clustering. Almost any large table should be clustered. The performance benefits can be enormous. On the other hand, choosing the clustering key unwisely can lead to disastrous performance.

A DISADVANTAGE OF CLUSTERED INDEXES

If you update a row and change the value of a clustered index key, you may need to move the row physically to maintain clustering. This essentially turns an UPDATE into a DELETE followed by an INSERT, with an obvious impact on performance. It can also lead to *fragmentation* of storage for base table data, further slowing access and eventually requiring that storage be reorganized, which is often a time-consuming task.

Tip Don't define a clustered index on columns that are subject to frequent change.

To create a clustered index, simply use the CLUSTERED keyword in the CREATE INDEX statement (and note that a clustered index can also be unique, so CLUSTERED UNIQUE is valid). For example:

```
CREATE CLUSTERED INDEX IDX_SupplierID
ON Products
(
    SupplierID
)
```

Most of the tables in the Northwind database already have a clustered index. Since there can be only one clustered index per table, if you executed this statement you'd receive an error.

As a general rule of thumb, every table should have a clustered index. If you create only one index for a table, make it clustered. In SQL Server, creating a primary key will automatically create a clustered index (if none already exists) using the primary key as the index key. (Check your RDBMS documentation to see if it automatically defines a clustered index. Some do; others don't.)

Sometimes it's better to use a unique nonclustered index on the primary key and a clustered index on a column or group of columns more commonly used by queries. For example, if the majority of searches are for product price instead of product ID (the primary key), the clustered index could be more effective on the price column.

Using Composite Keys

A *composite key* is composed of two or more columns. Both clustered and nonclustered indexes can have composite keys, and composite keys don't necessarily have to be unique. Often, a primary key must be composite because no single column is unique. Sometimes, columns that aren't used to identify rows are included in keys that do, so the database can find data by searching only the index, without accessing the base table itself.

Note Before designing a composite key that has extra columns, to avoid accessing the base table, read your RDBMS documentation carefully. This may or may not enhance performance at a reasonable cost in extra storage, depending on both your data and your database manager.

Try It Out: Creating an Index with a Composite Key

Suppose the following query is the most popular query executed by your application, and you need to tune the database to support it:

```
SELECT
    ProductName,
    UnitPrice
FROM
    Products
ORDER BY
    UnitPrice
```

You can create a composite index by following these steps:

1. In Server Explorer, right-click the Products table and select Design Table. The window in Figure 15-2 will appear. Click the Manage Indexes and Keys icon to open the Property Pages dialog box. Specify two columns for the index, UnitPrice and ProductName, as in Figure 15-9.

Figure 15-9. *Defining a composite index*

2. Alternatively, you can execute the following equivalent SQL statement:

```
CREATE INDEX IX_UnitPrice_ProductName
ON Products
(
    UnitPrice,
    ProductName
)
```

How It Works

The index key has two columns. The query can now be satisfied purely from the index since the only columns it needs are in the index key. Figure 15-10 illustrates the index structure. Data from UnitPrice and ProductName make up the key, and only if you need other data, such as ProductID, do you have to access the base table.

Figure 15-10. *Conceptual view of an index with a composite key*

Learning Additional Index Guidelines

Choosing the correct columns and types for an index is only the first step in creating an effective index. In the following sections, we'll briefly explain the following two factors that deserve consideration:

- Index key length
- Index selectivity

Keeping Index Keys Short

The larger an index key is, the more storage it requires and the harder a database has to work to use the index. As a rule of thumb, limit index keys to as few columns as possible. While composite indexes are useful and can sometimes optimize performance, they're also larger and should be carefully planned before actually implemented. Using a smaller data type for an index key column—for example, a 4-byte rather than an 8-byte integer, or a 10-character fixed-length string rather than a 20-character variable-length one—is often well worth considering.

Finding Distinctive Keys

The most effective indexes are those with a small percentage of duplicate values. Think of having a phone book for a city where 75 percent of the population has the last name Smith. A phone book for this area may be easier to use if the entries were sorted by first name instead of last name. A good index will allow the database to disregard as many rows as possible during a search.

An index with a high percentage of unique values is sometimes called a *selective* index. Obviously, a unique index is the most selective of all, because it has no duplicate values. SQL Server and other RDBMSs can track statistics for indexes and ascertain how selective each index is. The query optimizer utilizes such statistics when selecting the best index to use.

Maintaining Indexes

You can remove indexes with the DROP INDEX statement. Since an index is a separate physical structure, dropping an index doesn't affect the data in the underlying base table. Once dropped, an index must be completely re-created. (This can be a relatively expensive process for large tables.)

If an index is dropped, the query optimizer will, of course, have to redetermine the access path to the table.

Understanding Constraints

The primary purpose of a constraint is to support data integrity. For instance, a foreign key constraint ensuring that all orders reference existing products maintains referential integrity of the data.

Data integrity is so important that relying on users and applications to enforce integrity rules is unwise; you must build these rules into the database. This part of the chapter will show what kinds of rules you can define and how to define them.

Understanding Data Integrity

Data integrity can be classified as follows:

- **Entity integrity**: Each row in a table is uniquely identifiable. You enforce entity integrity with a primary key constraint.

- **Referential integrity**: Relationships between tables are preserved as data is inserted, modified, and deleted. You enforce referential integrity with foreign key constraints.

- **Domain integrity**: Values aren't only of a given data type, but also conform to validity rules (range, format, consistency, and so on) for the real-world entity they represent.

Since we've already covered primary keys and foreign keys, we'll briefly discuss how to define them as constraints and then focus on other constraints that maintain domain integrity.

You can enforce domain integrity using a variety of techniques, including check constraints, unique constraints, and default constraints. These are the techniques we'll cover in this chapter, but other options are available to enforce domain integrity. Even selecting the data type for a column enforces domain integrity to some extent.

The following are some domain integrity constraints you may want to apply to a product table:

- An integer product ID is the primary key.

- A product name must be unique.

- A product name can't be null.

- The unit price must be greater than zero.

- The default unit price is $1.

Defining Constraints

Let's create a table with the previous constraints.

Try It Out: Defining Constraints

To define a constraint, follow these steps:

1. In Server Explorer, right-click Tables for the Northwind database, and then click New Table.

2. In the Design grid, define the primary key, ProductId as int (see Figure 15-11).

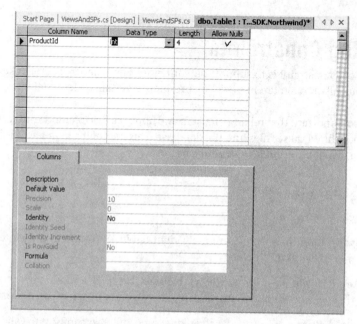

Figure 15-11. *Defining a column*

3. Click the Set Primary Key icon to designate this column as the primary key (see Figure 15-12). Note that the Allow Nulls column in the grid is automatically unchecked, since no part of a primary key can be null.

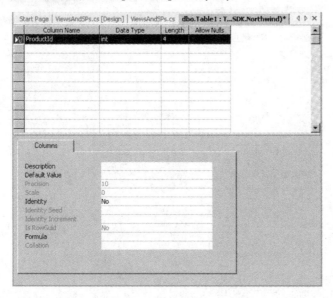

Figure 15-12. *Designating a column as a primary key*

4. Add a ProductName column as nvarchar with a length of 40. Uncheck the Allow Nulls column in the grid, as in Figure 15-13. (You'll make it unique later.)

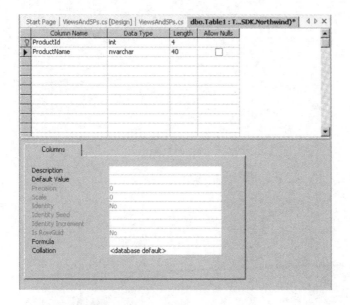

Figure 15-13. *Defining a column as* NOT NULL

5. Add a UnitPrice column as money and enter 1.00 as the Default Value in the Columns grid, as in Figure 15-14.

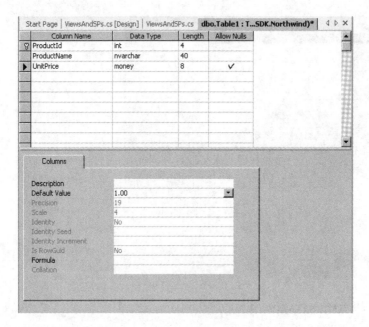

Figure 15-14. *Defining a column with a default value*

6. Click the Manage Check Constraints icon. This will open the Property Pages dialog box at the Check Constraints tab (see Figure 15-15). Enter `unitprice > 0.00` in the Constraint Expression text box, and then change the Constraint Name to UnitPriceNotZero. Click Close. The check constraint is added to the table definition.

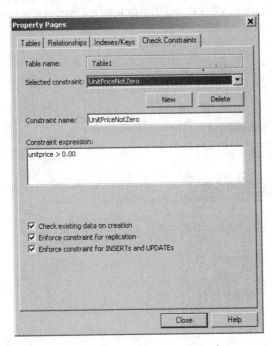

Figure 15-15. *Adding a check constraint*

7. Click the Manage Indexes and Keys icon. This will open the Property Pages dialog box at the Indexes/Keys tab (see Figure 15-16). Click New. Change Index name to IDX_ProductName. Select the ProductName column as the index key, and check the Create UNIQUE box. Note that when the radio buttons are enabled, you leave the default Constraint selected, unlike Figure 15-7, where you were defining a unique index rather than a unique constraint. Click Close. The unique constraint is added to the table definition.

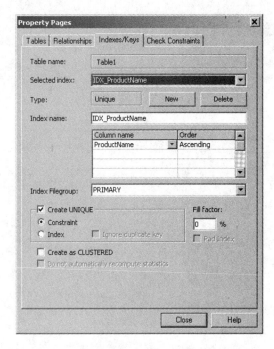

Figure 15-16. *Defining a unique constraint*

8. Click the Save icon, and name the table ProductsTest when prompted. Click OK. The new table is created in the Northwind database.

9. To see that the constraints have been added, execute the following query in the QueryProcessor application from Chapter 13. Widen the columns, and you should see the output as in Figure 15-17.

```
select
    constraint_name,
    constraint_type
from
    information_schema.table_constraints
where
    table_name = 'productstest'
```

Figure 15-17. *Querying the information schema for table constraints*

How It Works

Defining a table with the help of such a friendly visual tool was easy because it transparently generated a CREATE TABLE statement that included all the column and constraint definitions. It even created the primary key index as a clustered index and also a unique index in order to enforce the unique constraint on ProductName. The syntactical details are beyond the scope of this book, but rest assured that you could have done the same thing with SQL.

The most important thing to note is that you can define constraints in any order. You could have designated the primary key as your last act rather than doing it immediately after defining the column. (In fact, if the primary key were composite, you would have had to define all the columns for it before designating them as the key.)

Even after you've created a table, you can add constraints (with the ALTER TABLE statement, beyond this book's scope—and to be used sparingly and carefully). You'll now look at some of the things that need to be considered when adding constraints, especially if the table isn't empty when the constraint is added.

Using Check Constraints

You use *check constraints* to validate values and formats for a particular column. They're extremely useful for enforcing rules in the database. Check constraints contain an expression, which the database will evaluate when you modify or insert a row. If the expression evaluates to false, the database won't perform the operation.

Defining a check constraint is similar to coding a WHERE clause predicate, using relational operators (>, <, <=, >=, <>, =), BETWEEN, IN, LIKE, and IS NULL, as well as the AND and OR logical operators. We specified the check constraint on UnitPrice with this predicate:

```
unitprice > 0.00
```

■**Caution** Check constraints have performance implications since they're executed during data modifications. Too many constraints can slow down performance.

Check Constraints and Existing Values

If you add a check or unique constraint to a populated table, then you run a chance of failure, because the database will check existing data to see if it complies with the constraint. (This isn't optional behavior with a unique constraint—all the data must comply.) It's possible to *defer* (SQL Server also calls this *disabling* the constraint) testing the data when adding a check constraint, allowing you to define the constraint and handle possible exceptions later. Load utilities typically use this technique to expedite bulk insertions, particularly when a table has several constraints that would unacceptably slow down the load and for data that's expected to conform to the constraint. However, to ensure data integrity, the constraint should eventually be checked, and most RDBMSs (though not SQL Server) force this by making the table unavailable for processing until the constraint is checked.

It's also possible to defer constraint validation for INSERT and UPDATE statements and disable specific constraints, using the ALTER TABLE statement, but this practice isn't recommended and should be carefully planned beforehand. The various scenarios for enforcing constraints can be quite complicated. Choosing to temporarily not enforce them may be justified for performance but must always be implemented in a way that assures data integrity.

Check Constraints and NULL Values

We've said that the database will stop a data modification only when a check constraint is violated, that is, when the constraint expression evaluates to false. Note that the database allows the modification to take place if the expression is logically unknown because a NULL value is involved. For example, suppose you use the following INSERT statement on ProductsTest:

```
insert into productstest
(
    productid,
    productname,
    unitprice
)
values (99, 'Product 99', NULL)
```

Even with the constraint that UnitPrice must be greater than zero, the INSERT is successful. A NULL value doesn't allow the database to evaluate the expression as true or false, making the expression logically unknown.

Restrictions On Check Constraints

Although check constraints are by far the easiest way to enforce domain integrity in a database, they do have some limitations, namely:

- They can't reference a different row in a table.

- They can't reference a column in a different table.

For example, you can't define a check constraint on the Products table to test if a product name is unique, since a check constraint can't examine values in rows other than the row currently under examination. For this situation you'd use a unique constraint. Likewise, you can't define a check constraint on the Products table to test if a product's CategoryId is present in the Categories table, as a check constraint can't examine values in other tables. To do this, use a foreign key constraint.

■**Tip** You can, however, create a check constraint that references more than one column within the same row.

Using NULL Constraints

Although not strictly a constraint, whether to allow NULL values in a column is an important part of domain integrity.

When defining a column you can use NULL (the default) or NOT NULL to specify its *nullability*. Primary key columns can't be nullable.

Unique constraint key columns can be nullable; however, the constraint checking considers NULL values as equal, so only one row may have a NULL value for a nullable unique key column. In general, allowing NULL values for unique keys isn't a good idea.

Using Default Constraints

Default constraints aren't strictly constraints though some RDBMSs, including earlier versions of SQL Server, allow them to be named like true constraints. They supply a value for a column when an INSERT statement doesn't specify one. A default can assign a constant value, the value of a system function, or NULL to a column. In SQL Server you can use a default on any column except IDENTITY columns and columns of type timestamp.

Dropping Constraints

You can permanently remove any constraint from a table with the DROP CONSTRAINT clause of the ALTER TABLE statement.

Summary

We started this chapter with an explanation of indexes, showing what they are and the advantages and disadvantages of using them. While indexes can increase the performance of some queries, they can slow down the overall process of updating the database. Consequently, you need to think carefully when deciding whether to create an index. You also learned the difference between clustered and nonclustered indexes.

In the second part of the chapter, you learned how various constraints ensure data (entity, referential, and domain) integrity. You saw how to define unique, check, default, and nullability constraints and discussed their implications at runtime.

There's much more to both indexes and constraints, but we've covered the basics you'll use most often. Using them wisely is crucial for successful database operation. Now that you know the fundamentals, study your RDBMS documentation and experiment with various scenarios. Whether an index or a constraint is advisable is often not just a conceptual issue but one best resolved by actually testing one's assumptions.

In the next chapter you'll look at another integrity issue: authenticating and authorizing users.

Securing Your Database

You need to ask yourself the following two critical questions about database security:

- *Who* can access the database?

- *What* can they do with the database?

The first question involves *authentication*, which involves determining the identity of the user trying to access the database. The classic authentication approach requires a user name and password to prove the user's identity. The second question involves *authorization*. Users can perform only the actions they're allowed to perform, based on rights granted to them as individuals or groups.

Although many aspects of database security exist and each database system handles it in its own way, you should become familiar with some fundamental concepts and facilities.

In this chapter, we'll cover the following, using SQL Server terminology and techniques:

- Authentication modes

- Login and user management

- Database roles

- How to grant and revoke permissions

■Note Security is another area where database terminology is diverse. The SQL standard uses the term *privilege* for the authority granted to a specific user (or group) to perform a specific action on a database object (for example, tables, views, and indexes). Some RDBMSs distinguish between privileges and authorities. SQL Server calls privileges *permissions*.

Included in the code download for this chapter is a Windows Forms application named AdminHelp. This utility lets you view security-related SQL Server settings. Let's become familiar with the application before studying security topics.

Using the AdminHelp Utility

SQL Server provides a number of stored procedures to view and update security settings. While SQL Server provides a visual tool, Enterprise Manager, for administering security, MSDE doesn't. So, we've built our own little utility, AdminHelp, as a visual interface to make using the common stored procedures more convenient. Figure 16-1 shows the utility's main screen.

Figure 16-1. AdminHelp *main screen*

This utility is available as a project in the code download for this chapter. Copy the Chapter16_Examples directory to your working directory (we used C:\BegCSharpDb). Open the solution in Visual Studio, and execute it with Ctrl+F5 to see the screen shown in Figure 16-1. Before you can view any settings, you must connect to a database, which you can do by selecting File ➤ Connect to Database. Here's the code for the connection:

```
protected void GetNewConnection()
{
    string connString = @"
        server=(local)\netsdk;
        integrated security = sspi;
        database = northwind
    ";

    sqlConnection = new SqlConnection(connString);
    sqlConnection.Open();
}
```

If you want to use this utility to work with a different database, then simply change the parameters in the connection string.

Introducing Database Security

Before we dive into the details of database security, we'll first quickly overview the security process and how it works.

When dealing with Windows security, a system administrator typically places users into one or more groups to ease system management. In addition to built-in groups, such as Administrators and Guests, an administrator can create new groups.

For example, Joy, Tim, and Amy all work in human resources (HR). All three employees will probably need access to the same resources on a machine or network, such as a spreadsheet of employee salaries. An administrator could create a new group named HR and add each user to the group. The administrator then grants permissions for the salary spreadsheet to the group, instead of each user. As employees join or leave the HR department, it's easier to add or remove them from the HR group than to comb through each resource and grant or deny privileges at the user level.

Now suppose Joy needs to access an employee database to run a report. The first stage is to log into the database server. As you'll see shortly, the login may be authenticated by the SQL Server instance itself or managed separately by the Windows security system (if Joy has already been authenticated by a Windows domain server). Once the login is authenticated, she is logged into the database server but can't actually do anything. To be able to access a particular database, the login needs to be mapped to one of the user accounts managed by that database. The database then grants certain permissions to each user, which describe whether they can, for example, view a table or run a stored procedure. This process is known as *authorization*.

As with Windows, it can be difficult to manage all these permissions at the level of the individual user. For a database administrator, groups work equally well. It's likely that everyone in the HR department will need to run reports, so rather than add Joy, Tim, and Amy as individual database user accounts, you can just add the HR group as a whole. As employees join and leave the HR group, you wouldn't have to do anything to grant and deny the employees access.

Furthermore, the database supports *roles*, which work at both the server and the individual database level. Rather than grant permissions to individual users, you can add or remove users from roles. You'll see how all this works later in the "Managing Roles" section.

■**Tip** If you're logged into Windows as an administrator, a lot of this is sorted out under the hood for you, and you'll automatically have full administrative rights over any of the databases on the database server.

Throughout the rest of this chapter, you'll take a closer look at how all this works and at the various stored procedures provided by SQL Server to view and alter the security settings.

Understanding Authentication

The SQL Server database engine operates in one of two authentication modes. In Windows Authentication mode, the engine relies on the operating system to authenticate users. This is the mode we've been using throughout the book, specified by the `Integrated Security=SSPI` parameter in the connection string.

In Mixed Mode, the database engine can still use Windows Authentication but can also perform authentication itself by verifying a user's login and password credentials using SQL Server Authentication. We'll cover both of these modes in more detail in the following sections.

Windows Authentication

Windows Authentication is the preferred mode for SQL Server because of its tight integration with the more robust and manageable security features of the Windows operating system. Unless you're on a Windows 98 system, Windows Authentication is the default mode for installation.

Tip Windows 98 doesn't have the strong security system of Windows NT, 2000, and XP, so Windows Authentication isn't available with it. When we use the term *Windows security*, we're referring to Windows NT 4 or later.

In a typical forms-based data access application using Windows Authentication, a user will first log into a Windows machine. The local machine or a domain controller on the network will validate the user name and password supplied by the user. At this point, the user launches the application to connect to an MSDE or SQL Server instance. The connection string includes the following parameter:

```
Integrated Security=SSPI;
```

This parameter instructs the client-side database software to establish a *trusted connection*. This means that the SQL Server instance relies on Windows to authenticate the user who is connecting to the database. The client establishes the connection using a layer of Microsoft software known as the Security Support Provider Interface (SSPI).

Note Authentication allows a client to connect to an instance of the database engine but doesn't yet grant access to any databases managed by the instance. You'll see how this works in the "User Accounts" section when you learn how to map database user accounts to server logins.

Windows Authentication allows a database administrator to take advantage of the built-in security features of Windows. These features include (but are not limited to) the following:

- **Password expiration**: This forces users to change passwords after a set amount of time.

- **Account lock out**: This helps prevent malicious users from guessing a password by disabling an account after a set number of failed login attempts.

- **Strong passwords**: This prevents guessing passwords by enforcing a minimum length and preventing common words from being used as passwords.

In addition to providing a robust security infrastructure, Windows Authentication allows clients to use the same login and password to access resources on the local machine, the network, and the database server.

Mixed Mode Authentication

In Mixed Mode, the database engine can still perform Windows Authentication over trusted connections, but it also provides a second type of authentication: SQL Server Authentication.

In a typical Mixed Mode scenario, a user logs into a machine and launches a forms-based application that connects to a database. The connection string in this case would include the following parameters:

```
User ID=poonam;Password=picnic;
```

This connection string explicitly specifies a user name and password. The client will use a *nontrusted connection*, because no Windows credentials are associated with the connection. The database engine will check that the user ID exists and that the password is valid. The database server carries out the authentication process.

Mixed Mode Authentication places a greater burden on both the database and the database administrator to manage users and passwords. In addition, the security features aren't as robust. For these reasons, Windows Authentication is the preferred authentication mode.

Managing Users

Both of the authentication modes require valid login entries in the database server. To be authorized to access an individual database, however, a login must map to a database-specific user account. Authorization in MSDE revolves around database *users* and database *roles*, which are similar to the users and groups of Microsoft Windows but are specific to each database.

In the following sections, we'll cover how to manage user accounts and roles, but first we'll show how to view server login information and also how to add and remove users.

Database Logins

You can view the list of logins using the sp_helplogins stored procedure. When you execute this, it returns the following two result sets:

- The list of available logins

- Detailed information for each login, including the databases for which they're authorized

Although many query windows will show only one result set, you can use our `AdminHelp` application to view both result sets. Make sure you've established a connection, and then click the View Logins button to get a screen like the one shown in Figure 16-2.

Figure 16-2. *Viewing login information*

■**Note** Many of the queries in this chapter will return a column with a security identification number (SID). We won't make any special use of SIDs in this chapter. The database uses this number internally to uniquely identify each login name.

For now we want to concentrate on the first column (`LoginName`) of the first result set. You can see two valid logins for the database engine.

The first row is an entry for a Windows group. Users placed into the `Administrators` group have additional privileges to perform administrative tasks on a machine. Adding a group as a SQL Server login allows any of the users who are members of the group to log in. When adding a local built-in group such as `Administrators`, a special prefix (`BUILTIN`) is used instead of the computer or domain name used for individual users.

■**Note** By default, installing MSDE and SQL Server adds `BUILTIN\Administrators` as an available login.

With Windows Authentication, we recommend you manage database logins with groups instead of by individual Windows accounts. As you create database objects (tables, views, stored procedures, and so on), think about how the groups in your organization should be able to access these objects.

The second row is a SQL Server login. A client accessing the database using Mixed Mode Authentication can specify this login name as the user ID parameter in the connection string. In fact, the sa login is a special account: the system administrator login. You can use this all-powerful login to perform administrative tasks within SQL Server (members of group BUILTIN\Administrators have the same power). The sa login is created by default for use in Mixed Mode Authentication.

Note that the default password for the sa login is an empty string, which is a potentially disastrous security hole, so you should always explicitly provide a password for sa when installing SQL Server—and carefully secure it from those who don't need to know it.

Adding and Removing Login Entries

The stored procedure sp_grantlogin adds a Windows user or group as a login entry. Only a single argument is required: the user name or group name to add. As shown in the sp_helplogins output in Figure 16-2, you must precede a Windows group name with BUILTIN and a Windows user name with a computer name or domain name, separating the names with a backslash. For example, suppose you really do have a Windows group for human resources named HR. The following command would allow members of the HR group to log in:

```
exec sp_grantlogin 'ComputerName\HR'
```

You can grant a login to an individual user with the same stored procedure, like so:

```
exec sp_grantlogin 'ComputerName\Joy'
```

To remove a Windows user or group, use the sp_revokelogin stored procedure. This procedure also requires a user or group name in the same format as the previous one. For example, executing the following removes the HR group from the list of valid logins:

```
exec sp_revokelogin 'ComputerName\HR'
```

Joy, even if she is a member of the HR group, can still log into the database engine, since she was also added as an individual user with sp_grantlogin. Revoking login permissions for a group doesn't revoke login permissions for users within the group if they already have individual logins. Individual security specifications override those for a group.

As time passes, an administrator may remove users and groups from Windows, but the login permission remains in the database server. You should use the sp_validatelogins stored procedure to see a list of logins granted on the database server with no corresponding entry in Windows. You can also view this list in AdminHelp with the Validate Logins button. These logins should be unusable, so you should revoke them.

SQL Server Logins

Managing logins for SQL Server Authentication requires a different set of stored procedures. To add a SQL Server login, use the sp_addlogin stored procedure. While the only required parameter is a login name, we also recommend you supply a password as the second parameter. The following adds the login name Juan:

```
exec sp_addlogin 'Juan', 'Juanpassword'
```

With Windows Authentication, when users change passwords in the operating system, no additional work is required to synchronize a database password. The database relies on the operating system to validate the identity. With SQL Server Authentication, the password is stored in the database, not in Windows. To change a password for a SQL Server login, use the sp_password stored procedure. The parameters are the existing password, the new password, and the login name, like so:

```
exec sp_password 'Juanpassword', 'NewJuanpassword', 'Juan'
```

You can use the stored procedure sp_droplogin to remove a SQL Server login. The only parameter for this procedure is the login name. The next command will remove Juan from the list of available logins:

```
exec sp_droplogin 'Juan'
```

SQL Server will never confuse a Windows group or user name with a SQL Server login name. Windows groups and usernames always have a backslash (after the computer or domain name). The backslash is an illegal character for SQL Server login names.

It doesn't matter which particular database you're currently using when executing the previous stored procedures. You may be currently using the Northwind database or the master database. In either case, logins apply to the server instance, not to a specific database.

As we mentioned earlier, a login doesn't give a user access to any particular database on the server. For instance, you could apply security settings in the Northwind database that restrict access to administrators only. Other users could still log into the database server and perhaps use other databases. However, only members of the BUILTIN\Administrators group, or users logging in as sa, would have the ability to retrieve information from Northwind.

Special Users

SQL Server has the following two special users:

dbo: dbo is present in every database. This user is the database owner and has permission to perform any activity in a database. You can't delete the dbo user. Note that both the SQL Server sa login and the BUILTIN\Administrators group map to the dbo user in all databases.

guest: By default, the guest user isn't present when you create a new database. You can remove the guest user from a database (except the master and tempdb databases). The guest account allows users to access a database if they have valid logins to the database server but don't have their own user accounts for the database.

Figure 16-3 illustrates the process of mapping logins to user accounts using Windows Authentication. Three members of the HR group—Joy, Tim, and Amy—are using the guest account.

Figure 16-3. dbo *and* guest *login account mappings*

In this figure, we have logins available for the user Joy, the group HR, and the group
BUILTIN\Administrators. The engine maps administrators to the dbo user implicitly. Joy, Tim,
and Amy will all log into the Northwind database as the guest user since there's no user account
created explicitly for them. In the second database, no explicit user exists for Joy, Tim, and Amy,
and a guest account isn't present. The second database isn't available to the members of HR but
is available to administrators.

User Accounts

You must map server-level logins to user accounts in each database. Although you could use
the guest account to allow access to a database from any login (as shown in Figure 16-3), this
isn't best practice. Instead, you should add a user account into each database for every user
with a server login that needs to access it. A login can map to different user accounts in different databases; the names don't need to be the same. In the following sections, we'll discuss
how to add, delete, and view user accounts.

Adding a User Account

You can map a login to a user account in the current database using the sp_grantdbaccess stored procedure. The first parameter to the stored procedure is the login name, and the second parameter is the name of the user account to create and associate with the login. Assuming you're in the Northwind database as an administrator, you can map the HR login to a user account named HR with the following command:

```
exec sp_grantdbaccess 'ComputerName\HR', 'hr'
```

The user account name doesn't need to reflect the login name. For example, you could have also named the user account humanresources. One member of the HR group has her own login: Joy. You can associate Joy with a specific user account as follows:

```
exec sp_grantdbaccess 'ComputerName\Joy', 'joy'
```

When Joy logs in, she'll map to the user account specified for her login (joy), even though she's a member of the human resources group and can gain access via the hr user. The engine will always try to match an individual account first, before looking for a group of which the user is a member. You can use this behavior to assign the user different permissions based on the groups in which they belong.

After applying these new changes, you can reexamine the concepts in Figure 16-3. The result is Figure 16-4.

Figure 16-4. *User and group login account mappings*

Viewing User Accounts

You can view all the user accounts in a database using the system stored procedure
sp_helpuser. The AdminHelp application executes this stored procedure when you click View
Users in the main form. The output for the Northwind database looks like Figure 16-5.

Figure 16-5. *Viewing* Northwind *users*

Removing a User Account

You can remove a user account from a database using the system stored procedure
sp_revokedbaccess. The only parameter to this procedure is the user name. To remove the
user joy, you'd issue the following command:

```
exec sp_revokedbaccess 'joy'
```

In this case, however, Joy may still be able to log into the database if she is still a member
of the HR group under Windows.

■**Tip** As you can see, it makes more sense to handle user authorization at the group level rather than
the level of the individual user. If you make changes to a group, then you aren't left with the problem of
"dangling users."

Note that you can't remove the dbo user, and you can't remove a user who currently owns
an object in the database. If you need to revoke access for a user with objects in a database,
you can use the sp_changeobjectowner stored procedure first to change ownership.

Managing Roles

Database roles are similar to groups in Windows. You can use groups to collect users into
a single entity and manage permissions using the collection instead of a single entity. If you're
already creating logins based on Windows groups, you're already achieving this behavior.
However, database roles add an extra degree of flexibility.

The two types of role are as follows:

- **Fixed server roles**: These are built-in and apply at the server level. They can't be deleted or changed.

- **Database roles**: These apply at the individual database level. A set of fixed database roles is predefined for you, but you can also create your own custom roles.

You'll see in the "Creating Roles" section how to create your own application-specific roles. It's always worth taking a look at the built-in roles first, however, to see if they fit your needs.

We'll also begin to touch upon database permissions; for example, is a given user allowed to create a table or query against a table? Once you have a better understanding of roles, we'll cover specific permissions.

Fixed Server Roles

Adding a user to a fixed server role will grant the user all the permissions associated with the server role. Server roles are *fixed* because you can't add or remove these roles, and you can't modify the permissions assigned to them. Table 16-1 gives the name of each server role and a general description of the permissions associated with the role.

Table 16-1. *Fixed Server Roles*

Fixed Server Role	Users in This Role Are Allowed To...
bulkadmin	Perform bulk inserts to the database.
dbcreator	Add, modify, and remove databases.
diskadmin	Manage the physical disk files used by the server for data storage.
processadmin	Manage processes in the engine and, for example, kill a connection.
securityadmin	Manage logins and change passwords.
serveradmin	Modify configuration settings on the server and shut the server down.
setupadmin	Add and remove remote (linked) servers.
sysadmin	Perform any activity on the server. (The BUILTIN\Administrator group is a member of this role by default. This is the administrative role.)

To view the specific permissions assigned to each fixed server role, execute the sp_srvrolepermission stored procedure. You can use the Server Role Permissions button in AdminHelp to display the results of the stored procedure. The utility will first ask you to select the name of the server role to display. As an example, Figure 16-6 shows the permissions for the dbcreator role.

Figure 16-6. *Viewing permissions for role* dbcreator

You can add database users to a fixed server role with the sp_addsrvrolemember stored procedure. Since these are server-level roles, not database roles, you must add a login name, not a user name from a specific database. For example, if Joy still has a valid login, you could make Joy a member of the sysadmin group with the following:

```
exec sp_addsrvrolemember 'ComputerName\Joy', sysadmin
```

You can view members in each server role by executing sp_helpsrvrolemember. This is available from AdminHelp by clicking the Server Role Members button. The procedure returns a row for each member in each server role (see Figure 16-7).

Figure 16-7. *Viewing server role members*

To remove a user from the sysadmin server role, execute the sp_dropsrvrolemember procedure, using the login and the role name as parameters, like so:

```
exec sp_dropsrvrolemember 'ComputerName\Joy', sysadmin
```

Fixed Database Roles

Adding a user to a fixed database role will grant to the user all the permissions associated with the database role for the given database. These roles are fixed because you can't add or remove them from a database or modify the permissions assigned to them. Table 16-2 summarizes the fixed database roles.

Table 16-2. *Fixed Database Roles*

Fixed Database Role	Description
db_accessadmin	Can add or remove users in the database
db_backupoperator	Can perform backup and diagnostic operations
db_datareader	Can issue SELECT queries on any user table in the database
db_datawriter	Can modify the data in any user table (using INSERT, UPDATE, and DELETE SQL statements)
db_ddladmin	Can issue data definition language commands to create, drop, and alter objects
db_denydatareader	Can't select data
db_denydatawriter	Can't insert, update, or delete data
db_owner	Can perform any activity in the database
db_securityadmin	Can manage all permissions, roles, and role memberships

To view the specific permissions assigned to a fixed database role, use the sp_dbfixedrolepermission stored procedure, or click the Fixed Role Permissions button in AdminHelp. Figure 16-8 shows sample output for the db_datawriter role.

Figure 16-8. *Viewing permissions for fixed database role* db_datawriter

A member with the db_datawriter role can perform INSERT, UPDATE, and DELETE on any table in the database.

If an existing database role already has the required permission set for a user, the best solution is to use the fixed database role instead of creating a new role. To add a user to a role, execute the sp_addrolemember stored procedure, passing the database role and the user name, like so:

```
exec sp_addrolemember db_owner, joy
```

You can view a list of the roles and their members using the sp_helprolemember procedure. You can view these in AdminHelp by clicking the Role Members command button.

You can remove a user from a role with the sp_droprolemember procedure, like so:

```
exec sp_droprolemember db_owner, joy
```

The Public Role

Every database also contains a fixed role named `public`. Every user in a database is a member of the `public` role. You can't remove the `public` role, and you can't add or remove users from it. The permissions assigned to the public role become the default permissions for the database.

We'll now show how to create your own custom roles.

Creating Roles

You can create a custom role using the `sp_addrole` stored procedure, passing the role name as follows:

```
exec sp_addrole customrole
```

You can create roles only at the database level. The only server roles available are the fixed server roles created by default. Adding a user to a custom role uses the same `sp_addrolemember` procedure you used earlier.

```
exec sp_addrolemember customrole, hr
```

If you now look at the available roles and users for the database through `AdminHelp` (with the Role Members button), you should see the results in Figure 16-9.

Figure 16-9. *Viewing role members*

The dialog box shows only the roles currently populated with users. Even though other fixed database roles exist in `Northwind`, they don't have any members. The stored procedure will also not show the members of the `public` role, since all users (and even the other groups) are members of this role.

To remove a role, execute the `sp_droprole` stored procedure, passing the name of the role as a parameter. However, you need to remove all members of a role before the procedure returns successfully. You can remove a member from a role with the `sp_droprolemember` stored procedure, like so:

```
exec sp_droprolemember customrole, hr
exec sp_droprole customrole
```

With all the users and roles in place, you can finally begin to look at how to assign specific permissions to them.

Managing Permissions

You manage permissions by granting, denying, or revoking them for a user, group, or role. You can grant, revoke, and deny permissions for database objects (such as tables and stored procedures) and even for certain statements (such as CREATE TABLE).

The authority to manage permissions is restricted to a limited number of roles. You need to be a sysadmin, a db_owner, a db_securityadmin, or the owner (or creator) of a database object to manage permissions.

First, we'll cover the differences between granting, denying, and revoking permissions using a simple example. Second, we'll show how to change the authorization for users to select data from the Employees table of the Northwind database.

Revoking Permission

In the Northwind database, the public role has the ability to select from the Employees. Recall that every database user is a member of the public group, so any user has the ability to select from Employees. As the first restriction on Northwind, you'll remove this permission from the public role. You remove a permission with the REVOKE statement. For example:

```
REVOKE SELECT ON employees FROM public
```

The REVOKE statement for a database object (such as a table) requires you to specify the privilege(s) (here, SELECT), the object name (here, Employees), and the user or role (here, the public role) from which you're revoking the privilege. We'll take a closer look at available privileges later in the "Object Permissions" and "Statement Permissions" sections.

After an administrator has executed this REVOKE statement, no public users will be able to retrieve data from the table; however, users in certain fixed roles and the table owner still can. Remember, you can never adjust the permissions of fixed roles, such as the sysadmin and db_owner roles. Users in these roles will always have unrestricted access to objects in a database. However, the hr group has a user account in the database but belongs to no roles other than public. If a member of the hr group attempts to query Employees, they will receive the following error:

```
Msg 229, Level 14, State 5, Server <hostname>\NETSDK, Line 1
SELECT permission denied on object 'Employees', database 'Northwind', owner 'dbo'.
```

Tip Remember, you mapped the database account hr to the Windows group HR earlier in the chapter with sp_grantdbaccess, so the database user hr is an alias for the Windows group HR.

Granting Permission

Granting a permission enables a user or role to perform some activity. In the following SQL, we grant permission to the hr account to SELECT from the Employee table. The syntax is similar to REVOKE.

```
GRANT SELECT ON Employees TO hr
```

Here, you allow all three members of the HR group (Joy, Tim, and Amy) to select from the Employees table.

Denying Permission

Denying a permission explicitly prohibits a user or role from obtaining it. While REVOKE removes a previous permission, DENY ensures the permission can't be granted. Remember, a user may be a member of multiple groups or roles, and each may be granted different permissions. The only way to ensure a user or role never has a specific permission is to explicitly DENY the permission.

As an example, let's first add Tim as a user to the database, like so:

```
exec sp_grantdbaccess 'ComputerName\Tim', 'tim'
```

When Tim accesses the Northwind database, he'll do so as the user tim, instead of the user hr. Remember, the database engine is as selective as possible when mapping a login to a database user. Now explicitly DENY Tim's SELECT access to the Employees table, like so:

```
DENY SELECT On Employees TO tim
```

Although Tim was granted the permission to SELECT from Employees earlier as a member of the Windows group HR, you've now explicitly denied this privilege to tim, so he no longer has (or can have) this permission.

■Note A DENY takes precedence over any permissions a user, group, or role has been granted. Explicitly denying a permission ensures the permission is never inherited from another role or group. However, DENY doesn't work against a fixed server role.

You'll see a specific example of DENY in action in the "Object Permissions" section.

Resolving Permission Conflicts

We've changed a few of the permissions on the database now, so let's quickly review the actions on the Employees table to this point.

- You revoked SELECT from role public.

- You granted SELECT to group hr.

- You denied SELECT to user tim.

Now let's explicitly add Amy (the third member of the HR group) to the database with the following:

```
exec sp_grantdbaccess 'ComputerName\Amy', amy
```

Next, revoke Joy's permission to select from the Employees table with the following:

```
REVOKE SELECT ON employees FROM joy
```

At this point you have conflicting permissions. Amy is a member of the HR group, and since you granted this group SELECT permission, Amy can still SELECT from Employees. Then you revoked the permission for Joy. However, she is still a member of the HR group and inherits the permissions of HR. The HR permissions allow Joy to select from Employees. A REVOKE (unlike a DENY) won't take away permissions granted to a user by another role or group. For Tim, on the other hand, you explicitly denied the SELECT permission, and the database won't allow him to inherit this permission from the HR group of which he is a member. Figure 16-10 illustrates the behavior.

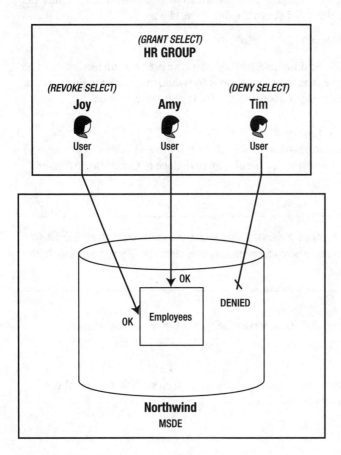

Figure 16-10. *A complex permissions scenario*

With a basic understanding of GRANT, DENY, and REVOKE, you'll now see other permissions you can manage with these statements.

Object Permissions

Object permissions are the permissions you can apply to objects, such as tables or stored procedures. So far, you've been looking at how to work with the SELECT permission in these examples. For tables and views, you can grant, deny, or revoke the following permissions:

- SELECT

- INSERT

- DELETE

- REFERENCES

- UPDATE

You can specify more than one permission in a GRANT, DENY, or REVOKE statement in a comma-separated list. For example, if you wanted to allow hr to retrieve, insert, and update (but not delete) rows in the Employees table, you could use the following:

```
GRANT SELECT, INSERT, UPDATE ON Employees TO hr
```

For SELECT and UPDATE statements, you can grant, deny, or revoke permissions on specific columns instead of the entire table. For example, if you wanted to remove Joy's ability to access the BirthDate and HireDate columns, you could use the following statement:

```
DENY SELECT (BirthDate, HireDate) ON Employees TO Joy
```

Notice you need to use a DENY statement instead of a REVOKE, because REVOKE won't take away the GRANT you gave to the HR group, of which Joy is a member. Joy can still update the table with the previous GRANT.

You use the REFERENCES permission to control the placement of foreign key constraints on a table. Foreign key constraints have an obvious impact on INSERT, UPDATE, and DELETE logic for a table, as well as performance implications. You could remove the permission from the public role like this:

```
REVOKE REFERENCES ON Employees FROM public
```

Stored procedures have only one permission: EXECUTE. This permission controls the ability to invoke a stored procedure. You could revoke the permission to execute the CustOrderHist stored procedure from the public role like this:

```
REVOKE EXECUTE ON CustOrderHist FROM public
```

Finally, you can use the following shortcut to modify all permissions for a given object at once, using the ALL keyword:

```
REVOKE ALL ON Employees FROM public
```

This statement removes any permissions the public role has on the Employees table.

Statement Permissions

You also have the ability to grant, deny, or revoke permissions on a select list of statements at the database level. These permissions relate to the kinds of things you can do in terms of the actual structure of the database rather than simply the data it contains. The statements include the following:

- BACKUP DATABASE

- BACKUP LOG

- CREATE DATABASE

- CREATE DEFAULT

- CREATE FUNCTION

- CREATE PROCEDURE

- CREATE RULE

- CREATE TABLE

- CREATE VIEW

By default, only members of the sysadmin, db_owner, and ddl_admin roles have the ability to create a table. You can give Joy the permission to create tables in the Northwind database with the following statement:

```
GRANT CREATE TABLE TO Joy
```

Notice that many statements aren't in this list (for example, DROP TABLE and ALTER TABLE). Permissions for these statements are implicitly given to the owner of a database object (and, of course, system administrators and database owners, who have full control). If Joy has permission to create a table, then she is authorized to change or delete any table she creates.

Viewing Permissions

You can view permissions using the stored procedure sp_helprotect. This procedure allows you to view all the permission settings in the database or to view just the settings regarding a specific object or user.

The AdminHelp utility provides an interface to the sp_helprotect procedure. The All Permissions button will list all the permission settings in the current database. As you can see by the scroll bar in Figure 16-11, listing all the permission settings in a database can produce many rows.

Figure 16-11. *Viewing all permissions*

You can also view the permissions assigned to a specific user or role by clicking the Permissions by User/Role button. A dialog box will pop up asking you to select the user or role to view. Figure 16-12 shows sample permissions for hr.

Figure 16-12. *Permissions for* hr

Finally, you can view the permissions assigned to a specific object using the Permissions by Object button. You can then select a table, stored procedure, view, or statement to see the permissions on it. Figure 16-13 shows sample permissions on the Employees table.

Figure 16-13. *Permissions on the* Employees *table*

The sp_helprotect stored procedure provides output only for explicit permissions. The permissions given to fixed roles (such as sysadmin or db_owner) are implicit, unchangeable, and not listed in the output.

AdminHelp and Viewing Object Permissions

You've seen a few examples now of using AdminHelp when a parameter is required for the query. In these cases, AdminHelp uses a form named PickOne to allow the user to select a parameter from a ComboBox control, shown in Figure 16-14.

Figure 16-14. PickOne *combo box*

The combo box is populated by one of the following overloaded AppendListContents methods. The PickOne form maintains an ArrayList as a data source for the combo box. Items are added to the ArrayList from a SqlDataReader or from a string array.

```
public void AppendListContents(
   SqlDataReader sqlDataReader,
   string fieldName)
{
   while(sqlDataReader.Read())
   {
      list.Add(sqlDataReader[fieldName]);
   }
   PickList.DataSource = list;
}

public void AppendListContents(string[] items)
{
   for(int i = 0; i < items.Length; i++)
   {
      list.Add(items[i]);
   }
   PickList.DataSource = list;
}
```

The reason you have two methods to populate the ComboBox is that some of the queries build the parameter list from hard-coded values as well as from a database query. For example, the last query we demonstrated called sp_helpprotect to view the permissions on a database object. You want to populate the list with the names of the tables, stored procedures, and views in the database, which you keep in an array.

```
private void PermissionObject_Click(object sender, System.EventArgs e)
{
    CheckConnection();
    if (sqlConnection != null)
    {
        PickOne pickOne = new PickOne("Select an object or statement");

        SqlCommand sqlCommand = GetUserObjectsCommand();
        SqlDataReader sqlDataReader = sqlCommand.ExecuteReader();

        pickOne.AppendListContents(sqlDataReader, "name");

        sqlDataReader.Close();

        string [] statementPermissions = {
            "CREATE DATABASE",  "CREATE DEFAULT",   "CREATE FUNCTION",
            "CREATE PROCEDURE", "CREATE RULE",      "CREATE TABLE",
            "CREATE VIEW",      "BACKUP DATABASE", "BACKUP LOG"
        };

        pickOne.AppendListContents(statementPermissions);

        if (pickOne.ShowDialog() == DialogResult.OK)
        {
            sqlCommand = GetPermissionsCommand();
            SqlParameter sqlParameter =
                new SqlParameter("@name", pickOne.Selected);
            sqlCommand.Parameters.Add(sqlParameter);

            QueryForm queryForm = new QueryForm(sqlCommand);
            queryForm.ShowDialog();
        }
    }
}
```

When the user picks one of the objects or statements from the PickOne dialog box, you add a parameter to the command's Parameter collection and pass the command to QueryForm for execution and display.

Implementing Security

Implementing a security design requires you to analyze how all your users are going to use your databases and applications. Typically, users will fall into one of the following groups (although larger applications and larger organizations may well require more fine-grained control):

- Users who require full control of the database application

- Users who perform a handful of administrative tasks, such as backing up the database

- Typical application users, who can query a majority of the tables but may have restrictions placed on certain objects

- Special application users, who have the all the abilities of typical application users, plus additional rights

Remember, first you need to grant login rights to the server for any users or Windows groups requiring access. For example, imagine you have a customer service forms–based application and the Windows users and groups in Table 16-3.

Table 16-3. *Hypothetical Windows Users and Groups*

Account	Description
APRESS\dbas	Database administrator group
APRESS\netoperations	Network operations, responsible for backups and other maintenance duties
APRESS\customerservice	Customer service employees, who require read and update permission on all the tables with the exception of a few tables and fields with sensitive information
APRESS\Jill	A customer service manager, who will have all the permissions of the customer service group and the additional capability to view and modify sensitive information

You could add the APRESS\dbas group to the sysadmin fixed server role, giving members control over each database on the server. Recall that you also can use the fixed database role, db_owner, if you want to restrict the highest level of control to a single database, instead of all databases on the server.

By adding the APRESS\netoperations group to the db_backupoperator fixed role in the database, you can enable the network operations group to perform backups of the database.

You can grant permissions to nonsensitive database objects directly to the customerservice group and then grant additional permissions to Jill. Ideally, Jill would belong to a Windows group that identifies her as a customer service manager. However, if she doesn't, instead of granting access to sensitive areas of the database directly to Jill, you could create a new role in the database, named managers (for example), assign Jill to the role, and grant the additional permissions to this role. This provides an extra layer of indirection, in case you need to grant new privileges to others.

This is just one example of an application with simple security requirements. More complex applications will require additional planning with additional custom roles. In fact, planning and administering security for an enterprise database system is often a challenging full-time task for a security administrator.

Summary

In this chapter we covered the basic security concepts and facilities for MSDE and SQL Server.

- Using Windows and Mixed Mode Authentication

- Mapping server logins to database accounts

- Grouping users into custom roles, fixed server roles, and fixed database roles

- Setting permissions and granting, revoking, and denying them on database objects and statements

Other RDBMSs provide similar facilities, and all of them support standard SQL's GRANT and REVOKE statements. However, the specifics differ, so consult your database documentation when planning and implementing database security.

Using XML and ADO.NET

XML is a language for organizing data into documents that are readable by humans and have a hierarchical structure. The self-describing nature of XML documents makes them convenient for exchanging information between systems.

The use of XML is so widespread that .NET has, from the start, provided extensive support for it. In fact, XML is one of the core technologies underlying .NET. While the intent of this chapter isn't to delve deeply into XML, we'll discuss the basics and how you can use XML in C# applications.

Specifically, we'll cover the following topics:

- The advantages and disadvantages of XML

- The structure of an XML document

- ADO.NET support for XML

- Experimentation with XML in C#

The Pros and Cons of XML

XML is a formal standard (called a *recommendation*) of the World Wide Web Consortium (W3C) and has become the de facto industry standard for data exchange. It's easy to use and it's flexible. Here's an XML snippet that defines a simple XML document:

```
<book>
  <title>Title1</title>
  <author>Author1</author>
  <copyright date=2004 />
</book>
```

This XML document contains four *elements*: book, title, author, and copyright. It has the *root element* (also called the *document element*) book, which is delimited by a *start tag* (`<book>`) and an *end tag* (`</book>`). This element has content; here, the content is one occurrence of each of the other elements. The title and author elements also have content, but they contain data rather than other elements. The copyright element is *empty*. Note that this is indicated by an *empty-element tag*, which ends with a slash, as opposed to an end tag, which starts with a slash. The date=2004 part of the copyright tag is called an *attribute*. (Nonempty elements can also have attributes.) This hierarchical structure, where elements nest but never overlap, is required for *well-formed* XML.

You'll examine the structure more in the "Understanding the Structure of an XML Document" section. For now, let's consider some of the important advantages of using XML documents.

- XML is a text-based format containing data and a semantic description of that data. This format is readable by both machines and humans. Its hierarchical structure makes it effective for representing data and relationships.

- XML is a platform-independent standard. This makes it an excellent format for exchanging data between applications, even on different operating systems. This is perhaps the main reason it has been deeply integrated into the .NET Framework.

- XML is at the heart of Web services—a way of programmatically accessing functionality over the Internet. Discovery documents (which are used to locate available Web services, configuration files for Web servers, and many other kinds of information resources) are stored in the XML format.

- XML parsing is well defined and widely implemented, making it possible to retrieve information from XML documents in a variety of environments. Using schemas (themselves a specialized form of XML document), you can validate the structure and meaning of XML data before acceptance and use.

- XML supports the Unicode character encoding, which maps virtually all the characters of all human languages, making it easy to create internationalized documents.

- In SQL Server 2000 (and most other major RDBMSs), you can obtain query results as XML documents.

- You can document C# (and other computer language) source code with XML, and you can easily convert this documentation into an Extensible HTML (XHTML) file for display and distribution.

- You can transfer XML documents via HTTP, so they can pass over the Internet (and through firewalls) more easily than binary data.

Of course, XML has a few drawbacks as well. Its text-based format means the following:

- Data stored as XML will take up more space than the binary representation of the same data.

- XML parsing can be slower than parsing highly optimized binary formats and can require more memory.

XML's flexibility and human readability, as well as that it's an open standard adopted by all major vendors and available on any platform, almost always outweigh its potential disadvantages. Let's now look at the basic structure of an XML document in more detail and create one in Visual Studio.

Tip You don't need Visual Studio .NET (or any other IDE) to create XML documents. Any text editor will do, since XML documents contain only Unicode text (and ASCII is a subset of Unicode). So, if you don't have Visual Studio, you can use Notepad or WordPad instead. Of course, IDEs are easier to work with, especially for complex or multiple XML documents.

Understanding the Structure of an XML Document

An XML document can be any textual object, a file on disk, a string in memory, or even a stream from some data source. We'll use text files here. Here's a minor variation on the earlier XML document, adding a new first line:

```xml
<?xml version="1.0" encoding="utf-8" ?>
<book>
  <title>Title1</title>
  <author>Author1</author>
  <copyright date=2004 />
</book>
```

The document begins with the following *XML declaration*:

```xml
<?xml version="1.0" encoding="utf-8" ?>
```

This specifies the XML version and character encoding of the document. Though not required, the XML declaration is recommended by the World Wide Web Consortium (W3C) XML specification.

Next, the XML document comprises one or more elements. As you saw before, each element has a start tag, content (if any), and an end tag. Elements can contain other elements. In this XML document, the title and author elements are contained in the book element.

Each element can also have attributes. For example, the copyright element has one attribute, date, with a *value* of 2004.

```xml
<copyright date=2004 />
```

XML is called *extensible* because you can define your own tags, as long as they're constructed properly. Properly constructed XML files are well-formed. How do you know if an XML document is well-formed? Well-formedness has many rules, but the following two are always required:

- Every document must have a single root element.

- Elements can't overlap.

A document object model (XML-DOM) accesses the different parts of an XML document. XML-DOM refers to elements, attributes, and textual content as *nodes*. The .NET Framework namespace System.Xml contains classes that implement XML-DOM and provides methods for navigating XML documents.

Let's create a simple XML document in Visual Studio .NET. You'll represent two books, their titles, their authors, and the authors' ages. After creating the document, you'll view it and modify it.

Try It Out: Creating an XML Document in Visual Studio .NET

To create an XML document in Visual Studio .NET, follow these steps:

1. Create a new chapter solution, and call it Chapter17_Examples.

2. Add a C# Windows application named XmlDemo.

3. Right-click the project in Solution Explorer, select Add and Add New Item…, and then select the XML File template. Accept the default filename, XMLFile1.xml, as in Figure 17-1. Then click Open.

Figure 17-1. *Adding an XML file to a project*

4. Double-click the file in Solution Explorer to open it in Code view, and then add the following code to it:

```
<books>
  <book>
    <title>Title1</title>
    <author>
      <name>Author1</name>
      <age>34</age>
    </author>
  </book>
  <book>
    <title>Title2</title>
    <author>
      <name>Author2</name>
      <age>24</age>
    </author>
  </book>
</books>
```

5. Right-click in Code view, and select View Data. Even though the XML file is in a hierarchical text format, you can view it in the familiar grid format. You should see the XML data as in Figure 17-2.

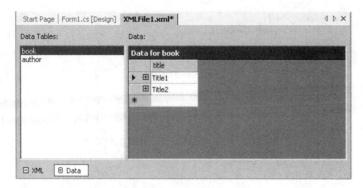

Figure 17-2. *XML data displayed in Visual Studio*

6. Click the plus signs to expand Title1 and Title2, and click the *book author* link to see the author information for each title. As you can see, even though the data was described in a hierarchical XML document, Visual Studio .NET displays it as a table—in fact, as nested tables. You can view the data in either data format by clicking the XML and Data buttons at the bottom of the window.

7. Now let's try to add a new title in Data view and see if the XML source changes to reflect this. Select the row marked with an asterisk below Title2 and name it Title3. Then expand the node, click the *book author* link, and name it Author3 and 53, for its name and age, respectively (see Figure 17-3).

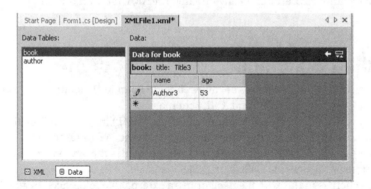

Figure 17-3. *Adding data to an XML document in Data view*

8. Click the XML button at the bottom of the window. You'll see that the XML document has been changed, as in Figure 17-4.

```
Start Page | Form1.cs [Design] | XMLFile1.xml*                          ◁ ▷ ×
     1    <?xml version="1.0" encoding="utf-8" ?>                            ▲
     2    <books>
     3       <book>
     4          <title>Title1</title>
     5          <author>
     6             <name>Author1</name>
     7             <age>34</age>
     8          </author>
     9       </book>
    10       <book>
    11          <title>Title2</title>
    12          <author>
    13             <name>Author2</name>
    14             <age>24</age>
    15          </author>
    16       </book>
    17       <book>
    18          <title>Title3</title>
    19          <author>
    20             <name>Author3</name>
    21             <age>53</age>
    22          </author>
    23       </book>
    24    </books>                                                          ▼
  ◀                                                                    ▶
 ⊞ XML   ⊟ Data
```

Figure 17-4. *XML document changed after changes in Data view*

How It Works

As you can see, Visual Studio .NET automatically updated the XML file with the data you added in Data view.

Understanding Schemas

You can define what elements and attributes are allowed to do in an XML document in two ways: Document Type Definitions (DTDs) and XML Schemas.

DTDs are part of Standard Generalized Markup Language (SGML) from which XML derives, but because they use non-XML syntax, they aren't used much in the .NET Framework. XML Schemas, on the other hand, are XML documents, and .NET provides the System.Xml.Schema namespace to support the XML Schema Definition (XSD) language.

You can include schemas in the XML file itself or in an external file referenced by the XML document. Let's create a schema from an XML file using Visual Studio .NET.

Try It Out: Creating an XML Schema in Visual Studio .NET

To create an XML Schema in Visual Studio .NET, follow these steps:

1. In XML view, right-click the XMLFile1.xml you created in the previous exercise. Select Create Schema.

2. A file called XMLFile1.xsd is immediately created and added to the project, as shown in Figure 17-5.

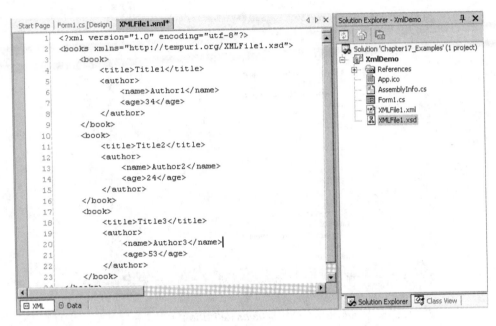

Figure 17-5. *Creating an XML Schema (.xsd file)*

3. In XMLFile1.xml, notice that an XML namespace attribute (xmlns) has been added to the root element to reference the schema.

```
<books xmlns="http://tempuri.org/XMLFile1.xsd">
```

Now, the XML file is restricted to only the elements defined in the schema. Let's try to violate the schema definition and see what happens.

4. In XMLFile1.xml, insert a new element, salary, into Author1, as in Figure 17-6.

```
Start Page | Form1.cs [Design] | XMLFile1.xml*                           ◁ ▷ ×
   1   <?xml version="1.0" encoding="utf-8" ?>
   2   <books xmlns="http://tempuri.org/XMLFile1.xsd">
   3      <book>
   4         <title>Title1</title>
   5         <author>
   6            <name>Author1</name>
   7            <age>34</age>
   8            <salary>10000</salary>
   9         </author>
  10      </book>
  11      <book>
  12         <title>Title2</title>
  13         <author>
  14            <name>Author2</name>
  15            <age>24</age>
  16         </author>
  17      </book>
  18      <book>
  19         <title>Title3</title>
  20         <author>
  21            <name>Author3</name>
  22            <age>53</age>
  23         </author>

⊞ XML   ⊟ Data
```

Figure 17-6. *Violating an XML Schema definition*

5. Notice that the editor marks it with a red wavy underline, and the tooltip says that the active schema doesn't support the salary element. This warning shows you that the schema specified in the XSD file is controlling the XML document. (Observe that the salary element is ignored in Data view.)

6. Double-click XMLFile1.xsd in Solution Explorer. You'll see the window in Figure 17-7.

Figure 17-7. *XML Schema graphic display*

7. Notice how the hierarchy (books have titles and authors; authors have names and ages) is represented as though it were composed of two tables. You can see the actual XML code in the XSD file by clicking the XML button (see Figure 17-8).

```
Start Page | Form1.cs [Design] | XMLFile1.xml* | XMLFile1.xsd                        ◄ ▷ ✕
 1  <?xml version="1.0"?>
 2  <xs:schema id="books" targetNamespace="http://tempuri.org/XMLFile1.xsd" xmlns
 3    <xs:element name="books" msdata:IsDataSet="true" msdata:EnforceConstraints=
 4      <xs:complexType>
 5        <xs:choice maxOccurs="unbounded">
 6          <xs:element name="book">
 7            <xs:complexType>
 8              <xs:sequence>
 9                <xs:element name="title" type="xs:string" minOccurs="0" />
10                <xs:element name="author" minOccurs="0" maxOccurs="unbounded">
11                  <xs:complexType>
12                    <xs:sequence>
13                      <xs:element name="name" type="xs:string" minOccurs="0" />
14                      <xs:element name="age" type="xs:string" minOccurs="0" />
15                    </xs:sequence>
16                  </xs:complexType>
17                </xs:element>
18              </xs:sequence>
19            </xs:complexType>
20          </xs:element>
21        </xs:choice>
22      </xs:complexType>
23    </xs:element>
24  </xs:schema>
◄                                                                                    ▷
□ DataSet   ⊞ XML
```

Figure 17-8. *XSD source generated by Visual Studio .NET*

How It Works

XSD is a language of its own, beyond the scope of this book. It's enough for your purposes simply to know how to create an XSD file from an XML file in VS.NET. In fact, so many facilities of .NET and Visual Studio make using XML transparent that you no longer need to know much at all about XML to be highly productive (though, of course, the more you know, the more you'll understand, and the even more productive you'll be).

Writing Valid XML

An XML file that has an associated schema is considered *valid* when the structure and content of the XML file is consistent with the schema. The elements in the XML document must appear in the structure defined in the schema, and the content of individual elements must conform to the elements and character data specified for them in the schema.

Note that XML documents can be well-formed but not valid. A document that isn't well-formed will raise errors with a parser and can't be validated. A document that's well-formed is valid if it complies with an associated schema (or DTD).

You can use Visual Studio .NET to verify that XML files are both well-formed and valid. Let's try it on XMLFile1.xml.

Try It Out: Validating an XML Document

To validate an XML document, follow these steps:

1. Open XMLFile1.xml in XML view. (It should still have the salary element underlined, as in Figure 17-6. If not, reenter the erroneous line.) Select XML ➤ Validate XML Data. A Task List window will appear as in Figure 17-9, listing errors.

Figure 17-9. *Task List window displaying XML validation errors*

2. Remove the erroneous line, and try again. The status bar at the bottom of the screen should report "No validation errors were found."

How It Works

Visual Studio validates your XML document and reports any errors.

Using XML with ADO.NET

You've seen that XML organizes data in a hierarchy. You also know that ADO.NET views data in relational fashion, as tables with rows and columns. The .NET Framework Class Library (FCL) unifies these two models.

XML support (in `System.Xml` and related namespaces) is tightly integrated with ADO.NET (in `System.Data` and related namespaces). The `DataSet` class in `System.Data` represents a relational data source, and the `XmlDocument` class in `System.Xml` represents an XML document and derives from `System.Xml.XmlNode`, which provides methods for using XML-DOM to access the elements of an XML document.

Further, `System.Xml.XmlDataDocument`, derived from `XmlDocument`, maps hierarchical data to `DataSets`, thus transparently unifying ADO.NET and XML for you.

The `System.Data.DataSet` class has extensive support for XML (in fact, the data in datasets is stored internally in XML format), including methods for reading and writing XML data and schemas. The SQL Server data provider supports XML with a variety of methods. For example, `SqlCommand` has an `ExecuteXMLReader` method that creates a `System.Xml.XmlReader` object that is analogous to relational data readers but accesses XML data instead of database tables.

Let's read data from an XML document into a dataset and write data from a dataset into an XML document.

Try It Out: Reading an XML Document into a Dataset

To read an XML document into a dataset, follow these steps:

1. Add three buttons and a data grid to your `XmlDemo` project's `Form1.cs`. Name the buttons `btnReadXml`, `btnWriteXml`, and `btnConfigXml`. Change the form's caption (the `Text` property) to `XML Demo`. The layout should appear as in Figure 17-10.

Figure 17-10. `XmlDemo` *layout*

2. Add the following to the Click event handler for btnReadXml:

```
DataSet ds = new DataSet();
ds.ReadXml(
    @"c:\BegCSharpDb\Chapter17_Examples\XmlDemo\XMLFile1.xml",
    XmlReadMode.InferSchema
);
dataGrid1.SetDataBinding(ds, "book");
```

3. Build and run with Ctrl+F5. Click the Read XML button. You'll see that the XML file has been read and the data grid has been populated, as shown in Figure 17-11 (after the title entries have been expanded). You can follow the *book author* links to see name and age.

Figure 17-11. *Reading an XML document in an application*

How It Works

First you create a dataset.

```
DataSet ds = new DataSet();
```

Then you call the dataset's ReadXML method, passing the file path and XML read mode.

```
ds.ReadXml(
    @"c:\BegCSharpDb\Chapter17_Examples\XmlDemo\XMLFile1.xml",
    XmlReadMode.InferSchema
);
```

The ReadXML method is overloaded and takes several combinations of parameters. The one you use accepts a string, identifying the XML file to read, and a member of the System.Data.XmlReadMode enumeration, indicating how to read the data and schema into the dataset. InferSchema means that the schema for this document must be inferred from the XML document itself, not from its XSD file.

Finally, you bind the table in the DataSet to the data grid. Here, book is the name of the data table, and ds is the dataset that contains it.

```
dataGrid1.SetDataBinding(ds, "book");
```

Now let's change the dataset's data and write the changes back to the XML file.

Try It Out: Writing a Dataset to an XML File

To write a dataset to an XML file, follow these steps:

1. Add the following to the Click event handler for btnWriteXml:

```
DataSet ds = (DataSet) dataGrid1.DataSource[0];
ds.WriteXml(
    @"c:\BegCSharpDb\Chapter17_Examples\XmlDemo\XMLFileOut.xml",
    XmlWriteMode.IgnoreSchema
);
```

2. Build and run with Ctrl+F5.

3. Click the ReadXML button to populate the data grid.

4. Click the *book author* link for Title2. The screen in Figure 17-12 will appear. Change the age of the author to 44.

Figure 17-12. *Changing XML data in an application*

5. Click the WriteXML button. The XMLFileOut.xml file will be created in the XmlDemo project folder, but it isn't automatically added to the project. Close the application, and add the file to the project by right-clicking the project in Solution Explorer, selecting Add ➤ Add Existing Item..., selecting All Files (when the dialog box opens), and double-clicking XMLFileOut.xml.

6. Double-click the XMLFileOut.xml item in Server Explorer to open it in XML view, and observe that the age for Author2 is 44. Switch to Data view, drill down to the age for Author2, and you'll see again that it's 44.

7. Experiment using other values and writing them back out.

How It Works

You first create a DataSet object, casting the data grid's data source (of C# object type) to the DataSet type.

```
DataSet ds = (DataSet) dataGrid1.DataSource[0];
```

Note that you've already changed the author's age in the data grid, changing the contents of the dataset.

Then you call the dataset's WriteXML to write the contents of the dataset to the file. The XMLWriteMode.IgnoreSchema member of the System.Data.XmlWriteMode enumeration indicates to write the contents of the dataset, without an XSD schema.

```
ds.WriteXml(
    @"c:\BegCSharpDb\Chapter17_Examples\XmlDemo\XMLFileOut.xml",
    XmlWriteMode.IgnoreSchema
);
```

As you can see, reading and writing XML files is easy thanks to the XML support in ADO.NET. Now let's look at another use of XML: defining application configuration files.

Defining Application Configuration Using XML

Applications typically need some initialization values. For example, database applications need a connection string to connect to the database. Instead of hard-coding this string into the application, if you can store it in a file and read it at runtime, then you can change the connection string (perhaps to point to a backup database should the primary database go down) without changing application source code. You can conveniently store such configuration data in XML files. An application can interrogate the specific section of an XML file where a required item is specified. Prior to XML configuration files, connection strings and other startup information were generally stored in the Windows registry, but this method wasn't nearly as user-friendly—or robust—as XML configuration files.

The .NET Framework supports the configuration of applications, machine, security settings, and so on, using the System.Configuration namespace. Configuration is a big and complex topic, and a detailed discussion is beyond the scope of this book. You'll learn only how to access a connection string stored in an XML file, but this is a useful thing to know how to do and a good basis for understanding how applications and XML configuration files work together.

XML configuration files have a .config extension, and they must have the same name as the assembly. For example, if chapter17.exe is the name of the executable assembly, then the name of the configuration file must be chapter17.exe.config. The config file must be in the same folder as the assembly or in the Global Assembly Cache. Depending on what you're trying to configure, the config file can implement one of several schemas available—for example, a Startup Settings schema, a Network Setting schema, or a Configuration Sections schema. Each schema has a specific set of elements. The Configuration Sections schema provides XML elements that can be used to specify custom application settings, such as the connection string. So, now let's create an XML file called chapter17.exe.config and access the connection string therein from a C# application.

Try It Out: Creating an Application Configuration File

To create an application configuration file, follow these steps:

1. Right-click the XmlDemo project item in Solution Explorer, select Add ➤ Add New Item..., select XML File, name it XmlDemo.exe.config, and click Open.

2. Add the following to the XML file:

```
<configuration>
  <appSettings>
    <add
      key="cnnorthwind"
      value="
        data source = (local)\netsdk;
        integrated security = sspi;
        database = northwind"
    />
  </appSettings>
</configuration>
```

3. Notice that a schema file isn't referenced here. It isn't necessary to do so, because the .NET Framework recognizes the elements you used.

4. In the form, add the following using directives (for ADO.NET, for accessing the config file, and for working with XML, respectively):

```
using System.Data.SqlClient;
using System.Configuration;
using System.Xml;
```

5. Add the following to the Click event handler for btnConfigXml:

```
// Get connection string from.config file
    string connString = ConfigurationSettings.AppSettings["cnnorthwind"];

    // Create connection
    SqlConnection conn = new SqlConnection(connString);

    // Create command to retrieve all employees in XML format
    SqlCommand cmd = new SqlCommand();
    cmd.Connection = conn;
    cmd.CommandText = @"
        select
            employeeid,
            lastname
```

```
    from
        employees
    for xml auto
";

try
{
    // Open connection
    conn.Open();

    // Get XML reader
    XmlReader xmlrdr = cmd.ExecuteXmlReader();

    // Create a dataset
    DataSet ds = new DataSet();

    // Read the XmlReader object into the dataset
    ds.ReadXml(xmlrdr,XmlReadMode.InferSchema);

    // Bind the dataset to the datagrid
    dataGrid1.DataSource=ds;
}
catch (SqlException ex)
{
    MessageBox.Show (ex.Message);
}
finally
{
    conn.Close();
}
```

6. Build and run the solution with Ctrl+F5. Copy the XmlDemo.exe.config file to the Chapter17_Examples\XmlDemo\bin\Debug folder (where the XmlDemo.exe file is placed by the compiler).

7. Now click the Config button. Click the plus button inside the data grid, and then click the *employees* link. You'll see the grid open as in Figure 17-13.

Figure 17-13. *Accessing a database specified in an XML configuration file*

How It Works

In the XmlDemo.exe.config file, you use the appSettings element to specify the application-specific settings you want for the configuration.

```
<configuration>
  <appSettings>
    <add
      key="cnnorthwind"
      value="
        data source = (local)\netsdk;
        integrated security = sspi;
        database = northwind"
    />
  </appSettings>
</configuration>
```

Within appSettings, you include an element named add that specifies a key-value pair to include in the application settings. Note that this element is empty. Its related information is given as two attributes: key and value.

You retrieve the connection string from the application settings by using the property's indexer with the key cnnorthwind.

```
// Get connection string from.config file
string connString = ConfigurationSettings.AppSettings["cnnorthwind"];
```

After creating a connection using the retrieved connection string, you create a command to retrieve data from the Employees table.

```
// Create command to retrieve all employees in XML format
SqlCommand cmd = new SqlCommand();
cmd.Connection = conn;
cmd.CommandText = @"
   select
      employeeid,
      lastname
   from
      employees
   for xml auto
";
```

Notice that the query has an extra clause. FOR XML AUTO is a Transact-SQL extension that instructs the database to return the results in XML format rather than as a tabular result set. (It's also possible to insert, update, and delete records in a database using XML with the OPENXML Transact-SQL statement.) Since the query will return an XML document, you can't store it in a data reader as you have so far throughout the book. Instead, you use the ExecuteXmlReader method to store the result in an XmlReader object, which is an instance of the System.Xml.XmlReader class, not an ADO.NET class but one tightly integrated with it. You use the ReadXml method to read the contents with the XML reader.

```
// Get XML reader
XmlReader xmlrdr = cmd.ExecuteXmlReader();

// Create a dataset
DataSet ds = new DataSet();

// Read Xml data into dataset
ds.ReadXml(xmlrdr, XmlReadMode.InferSchema);
```

Finally, you bind the dataset to the data grid.

```
// Bind dataset to data grid
dataGrid1.DataSource = ds;
```

Try changing the value properties in the configuration file to an invalid machine or database, and click the buttons to see what error messages result.

Summary

This chapter began with a quick overview of XML and its advantages and disadvantages. Then, after analyzing the basic elements of an XML document, you used Visual Studio .NET to construct an XML document and generate its schema automatically. Next, we discussed support for XML in ADO.NET; you read an XML document into a DataSet and wrote an XML document from a DataSet. Finally, you looked at application configuration files, an important application of XML in database programs.

XML is a huge topic and we've just skimmed the surface here. But this chapter is a good foundation from which you can develop your experience with this standard for describing and storing data.

In the next chapter, you'll look at handling errors arising from ADO.NET code and the database itself.

CHAPTER 18

■ ■ ■

Handling Exceptions

Up to now we've been rather relaxed in our handling of potential database exceptions. Robust database applications demand more careful attention to this important issue.

In this chapter, we'll cover what exceptions can arise when using ADO.NET. We'll focus on the SQL Server data provider, since we're using MSDE, but exception handling isn't RDBMS specific, so the same techniques are applicable to whatever database you use.

Specifically, we'll cover the following:

- Understanding C# exception handling in general

- Handling ADO.NET exceptions

- Handling database exceptions

Let's start with a quick review of C#'s exception-handling facilities.

Handling Exceptions C#

The CLR supports *structured exception handling*. The three basic C# facilities for handling exceptions are as follows:

- The try statement

- System.Exception and its derived classes

- The throw statement

The following sections cover each of these techniques briefly.

Using the try Statement

C# provides the try statement to support structured exception handling. Its basic syntax is as follows:

```
try {
    // Code that may throw an exception
}
catch (<ExceptionType> e) {
    // Code to handle an exception of a specific type
}
finally {
    // Code that always executes
}
```

The catch and finally clauses are optional, but you must use at least one. You can have any number of specific catch clauses. You must declare them so that derived types appear before base types. You can have, at most, one general catch clause—in other words, one that doesn't specify an exception variable. If used, it must be the last catch clause. You can have, at most, one finally clause.

In principle, any code that may throw an exception should be contained in a try block so that exceptions can be caught. In practice, not every exception necessarily requires handling, but it's always important to make sure you handle all exceptions that can negatively affect your program's performance and reliability.

Sometimes you may want to handle an exception that's thrown internally by executing code that records the exception and then moves forward. Alternatively, you may want to display a useful message to the user. Otherwise, any code that throws an exception will present the user with a gray box of unintelligible error details.

If no exception occurs in the code in the try block, then execution will move to the finally block if it exists. It isn't mandatory to provide a finally block; however, they're useful places for closing connections and other cleanup code. The code in the finally block will always be executed, regardless of whether a catch block was entered.

You can also nest try statements. In this scenario, catch blocks relate only to the try statement to which they belong.

If code outside a try block generates an exception, the runtime will move up the call stack and look for an appropriate catch clause in a calling method. If none is found, the program will be terminated and a message box displayed that identifies the error. So, at the uppermost level of code, it's important to catch all errors that may arise. The basic idea is to prevent users from seeing messages they won't understand. Typically, you can best handle such errors by logging them for later reference and providing users with a polite alert that doesn't leave them wondering what to do next.

Using Class System.Exception

System.Exception is the base class for all exceptions. Two basic kinds of exceptions exist: *system exceptions* (instances of System.SystemException) for CLR-thrown exceptions, and *application exceptions* (instances of System.ApplicationException) for user-defined exceptions. They both provide properties and methods for determining precise information about an exception, and you'll use a variety of them in later examples.

Using the throw Statement

Exceptions are *thrown* with the throw statement. Its syntax is as follows:

```
throw <object>
```

Any type of object can be thrown, but in practice only. For example, if a method receives an invalid argument, you can throw a System.ArgumentException with the following:

```
throw new System.ArgumentException
```

When this statement is used, the corresponding catch block (if it exists) or a generic catch block will come into play and handle the exception.

Structured exception handling is both elegant and robust. It's of particular importance in database programming, where errors come from three sources: application programs, ADO.NET, and databases. With this in mind, let's look at exceptions thrown by ADO.NET and databases.

Handling ADO.NET Exceptions

First, let's see how to handle exceptions thrown by ADO.NET. In the following example, you'll try to execute a stored procedure without specifying the CommandText property. You'll first use no exception handling, and then you'll add it.

Try It Out: Handling an ADO.NET Exception (Part 1)

To handle an ADO.NET exception, follow these steps:

1. Create a new solution named Chapter18_Examples.

2. Add a C# Windows application named AdoNetExceptions.

3. Change the Text property of Form1 to ADO.NET Exceptions.

4. Add a tab control to the form. Add a tab page to this, and change its Text property to ADO.NET. Add a button to the tab page, and change its Text property to ADO.NET Exception-1. Add a label to the right of this button, and change its Text property to Incorrect ADO.NET code will cause an exception. Add a second button to the tab page, and change its Text property to ADO.NET Exception-2. Add a label to the right of this button, and change its Text property to Accessing a nonexistent column will cause exception.

5. Add a second tab page, and change its Text property to Database. The layout should look like Figure 18-1.

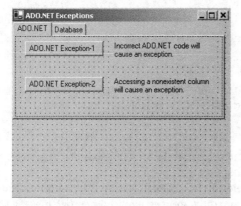

Figure 18-1. AdoNetExceptions *layout*

6. Add the following using directive for the SQL Server data provider namespace:

```
using System.Data.SqlClient;
```

7. Add the following code to the click event handler for button1. This will provide the first exception.

```
// Create connection
SqlConnection conn = new SqlConnection(@"
    data source = (local)\netsdk;
    integrated security = sspi;
    database = northwind
");

// Create command
SqlCommand cmd = conn.CreateCommand();

// Specify that a stored procedure is to be executed
cmd.CommandType = CommandType.StoredProcedure;

// Deliberately fail to specify the procedure
// cmd.CommandText = "sp_Select_AllEmployees";

    // Open connection
    conn.Open();
    // Create data reader
    SqlDataReader dr = cmd.ExecuteReader();
    // Close reader
    dr.Close();
```

```
if (conn.State == ConnectionState.Open)
{
    MessageBox.Show ("Finally block closing the connection", "Finally");
    conn.Close();
}
```

8. Run the program with Ctrl+F5. Click the ADO.NET Exception-1 button, and you'll see the message box in Figure 18-2.

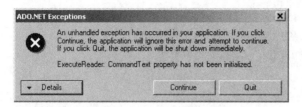

Figure 18-2. *ADO.NET unhandled exception*

9. Modify the button1_Click event handler as shown with the following bold code:

```
// Create connection
SqlConnection conn = new SqlConnection(@"
    data source = (local)\netsdk;
    integrated security = sspi;
    database = northwind
");

// Create command
SqlCommand cmd = conn.CreateCommand();

// Specify that a stored procedure is to be executed
cmd.CommandType = CommandType.StoredProcedure;

// Deliberately fail to specify the procedure
// cmd.CommandText = "sp_Select_AllEmployees";

try
{
    // Open connection
    conn.Open();
    // Create data reader
    SqlDataReader dr = cmd.ExecuteReader();
    // Close reader
    dr.Close();
}
```

```
catch (System.Data.SqlClient.SqlException ex)
{
  string str;
  str = "Source:" + ex.Source;
  str += "\n" + "Exception Message:" + ex.Message;
  MessageBox.Show (str, "Database Exception");
}
catch (System.Exception ex)
{
  string str;
  str = "Source:" + ex.Source;
  str += "\n" + "Exception Message:" + ex.Message;
  MessageBox.Show (str, "Non-Database Exception");
}
finally
{
    if (conn.State == ConnectionState.Open)
    {
       MessageBox.Show ("Finally block closing the connection", "Finally");
       conn.Close();
    }
}
```

10. Run the program with Ctrl+F5. Click the ADO.NET Exception-1 button, and you'll see the message box in Figure 18-3.

Figure 18-3. *ADO.NET handled exception*

How It Works

It'd be unusual to miss setting the CommandText property. However, this was an expedient way to cause an exception. When you call the ExecuteReader method, you get an exception, since the stored procedure to call hasn't been specified.

```
// Deliberately fail to specify the procedure
// cmd.CommandText = "sp_Select_AllEmployees";

   // Open connection
   conn.Open();
   // Create data reader
   SqlDataReader dr = cmd.ExecuteReader();
```

After seeing what happens without handling the exception, you execute the call from a try block. To catch the exception and prevent the program from crashing, you code two catch clauses.

```
catch (System.Data.SqlClient.SqlException ex)
{
  string str;
  str = "Source:" + ex.Source;
  str += "\n" + "Exception Message:" + ex.Message;
  MessageBox.Show (str, "Database Exception");
}
catch (System.Exception ex)
{
  string str;
  str = "Source:" + ex.Source;
  str += "\n" + "Exception Message:" + ex.Message;
  MessageBox.Show (str, "Non-Database Exception");
}
```

In the first catch clause, you specify a database exception type. The second catch block, which produced this message box, is a generic block that catches all types of exceptions. Note the caption of the message box in this catch block. It says *Non-Database Exception*. Although you may think that what you've received is a database exception, it's actually a client-side exception; in other words, this error is trapped before it gets to the database server.

When the button is clicked, since the CommandText property wasn't specified, an exception is thrown and caught by the second catch clause. Even though a catch clause for SqlException was provided, the exception was a System.InvalidOperationException, a common exception thrown by the CLR, not a database exception.

The exception message indicates where the problem occurred: in the ExecuteReader method. The finally block checks if the connection is open and, if it is, closes it and gives a message.

```
finally
{
  if (conn.State == ConnectionState.Open)
  {
    MessageBox.Show ("Finally block closing the connection", "Finally");
    conn.Close();
  }
}
```

Try It Out: Handling an ADO.NET Exception (Part 2)

Let's try another example of an ADO.NET exception. You'll execute a stored procedure and then reference a nonexistent column in the returned dataset. This will throw an ADO.NET exception. This time, you'll use a specific catch clause to trap the exception.

1. You'll use the sp_Select_AllEmployees stored procedure you created in Chapter 14. If you haven't already created it, please go to Chapter 14 and follow the steps in the "Try It Out: Creating and Executing a Stored Procedure with No Parameters" section.

2. Replace the code in the body of the button2_Click method with the following code:

```
// Create connection
SqlConnection conn = new SqlConnection(@"
   data source = (local)\netsdk;
   integrated security = sspi;
   database = northwind
");

// Create command
SqlCommand cmd = conn.CreateCommand();

// Specify stored procedure to be executed
cmd.CommandType = CommandType.StoredProcedure;
cmd.CommandText = "sp_Select_AllEmployees";

try
{
   // Open connection
   conn.Open();

   // Create data reader
   SqlDataReader dr = cmd.ExecuteReader();

   // Access nonexistent column
   string str = dr.GetValue(20).ToString();

   // Close data reader
   dr.Close();
}
catch (System.InvalidOperationException ex)
{
   string str;
   str = "Source:" + ex.Source;
   str += "\n" + "Message:"+ ex.Message;
   str += "\n" + "\n";
   str += "\n" + "Stack Trace :" + ex.StackTrace;
   MessageBox.Show (str, "Specific Exception");
}
catch (System.Data.SqlClient.SqlException ex)
{
   string str;
   str = "Source:" + ex.Source;
   str += "\n" + "Message:" + ex.Message;
   MessageBox.Show (str, "Database Exception");
}
```

```
catch (System.Exception ex)
{
   string str;
   str = "Source:" + ex.Source;
   str += "\n"+ "Message:" + ex.Message;
   MessageBox.Show (str, "Generic Exception");
}
finally
{
   if ( conn.State == ConnectionState.Open)
   {
      MessageBox.Show (
            "Finally block closing the connection",
            "Finally"
      );
      conn.Close();
   }
}
```

■Tip Testing whether a connection is open before attempting to close it isn't actually necessary. The `Close` method doesn't throw any exceptions, and calling it multiple times on the same connection, even if it's already closed, causes no errors.

3. Run the program with Ctrl+F5. Click the ADO.NET Exception-2 button, and you'll see the message box in Figure 18-4.

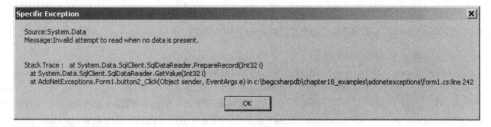

Figure 18-4. *Handling a specific ADO.NET exception*

4. For a quick comparison, we'll now demonstrate a SQL Server exception, an error that occurs within the database. Alter the name of the stored procedure in the code to a name that doesn't exist within the Northwind database. For example:

```
// Specify stored procedure to be executed
cmd.CommandType = CommandType.StoredProcedure;
cmd.CommandText = "sp_Select_NoEmployees";
```

5. Run the program with Ctrl+F5. Click the ADO.NET Exception-2 button, and you'll see the message box in Figure 18-5.

Figure 18-5. *Handling a database exception*

How It Works

First you create the data reader and try to access an invalid column, so an exception is thrown.

```
// Create data reader
SqlDataReader dr = cmd.ExecuteReader();

// Access nonexistent column
string str = dr.GetValue(20).ToString();
```

Here you tried to get the value of column 20, which doesn't exist. You add a new catch clause to handle this kind of ADO.NET error.

```
catch (System.InvalidOperationException ex)
{
    string str;
    str = "Source:" + ex.Source;
    str += "\n" + "Message:"+ ex.Message;
    str += "\n" + "\n";
    str += "\n" + "Stack Trace :" + ex.StackTrace;
    MessageBox.Show (str, "Specific Exception");
}
```

When an exception of type System.InvalidOperationException is thrown, this catch clause will execute, displaying the source, message, and stack trace for the exception. Without this specific catch clause, the generic catch block would have trapped the exception. Try commenting out this catch block and executing the code to see which catch clause traps the exception.

Next, you run the program for a nonexistent stored procedure.

```
// Specify stored procedure to be executed
cmd.CommandType = CommandType.StoredProcedure;
cmd.CommandText = "sp_Select_NoEmployees";
```

You catch your first database exception with the following:

```
catch (System.Data.SqlClient.SqlException ex)
{
    string str;
    str = "Source:" + ex.Source;
    str += "\n" + "Message:" + ex.Message;
    MessageBox.Show (str, "Database Exception");
}
```

This leads into the next topic: handling exceptions thrown by the database manager.

Handling Database Exceptions

An exception of type System.Data.SqlClient.SqlException is thrown when the SQL Server database returns a warning or error. This class is derived from System.SystemException and is sealed so it can't be inherited, but it has several useful members that can be interrogated to obtain valuable information about the exception.

An instance of SqlException is thrown whenever the .NET data provider for SQL Server encounters an error or warning from the database. Table 18-1 describes the properties of this class that provide information about the exception.

Table 18-1. SqlException *Properties*

Property Name	Description
Class	Gets the severity level of the error returned from the SqlClient data provider. The severity level is a numeric code that's used to indicate the nature of the error. Levels 1 to 10 are informational errors; 11 to 16 are user-level errors; and 17 to 25 are software or hardware errors. At level 20 or greater, the connection is usually closed.
Errors	Contains one or more SqlError objects that have detailed information about the exception. This is a collection that can be iterated through.
HelpLink	The help file associated with this exception.
InnerException	Gets the exception instance that caused the current exception.
LineNumber	Gets the line number within the Transact-SQL command batch or stored procedure that generated the exception.
Message	The text describing the exception.
Number	The number that identifies the type of exception.
Procedure	The name of the stored procedure that generated the exception.
Server	The name of the computer running the instance of SQL Server that generated the exception.
Source	The name of the provider that generated the exception.
StackTrace	A string representation of the call stack when the exception was thrown.
State	Numeric error code from SQL Server that represents an exception, warning, or "no data found" message. For more information, see SQL Server Books Online.
TargetSite	The method that throws the current exception.

When an error occurs within SQL Server, it uses a Transact-SQL RAISERROR statement to raise an error back to the calling program. A typical error message looks like the following:

```
Server: Msg 2812, Level 16, State 62, Line 1
Could not find stored procedure 'sp_DoesNotExist'
```

In this message, 2812 represents the error number, 16 represents the severity level, and 62 represents the state of the error.

You can also use the RAISERROR statement to display specific messages within a stored procedure. The RAISERROR statement in its simplest form takes three parameters. The first parameter is the message itself that needs to be shown. The second parameter is the severity level of the error. Any users can use severity levels 11 through 16. They represent messages that can be categorized as information, software, or hardware problems. The third parameter is an arbitrary integer from 1 through 127 that represents information about the state or source of the error.

Let's see how a SQL error, raised by a stored procedure, is handled in C#. You'll use the following Transact-SQL to raise an error when the number of orders in the Orders table exceeds ten.

```
if @orderscount > 10
    raiserror (
        'Orders Count is greater than 10 - Notify the Business Manager',
        16,
        1
    )
```

Note that in this RAISERROR statement, you specify a severity level of 16, an arbitrary state number of 1, and a message string. When a RAISERROR statement that you write contains a message string, the error number is given automatically as 50000. When SQL Server raises errors using RAISERROR, it uses a predefined dictionary of messages to give out the corresponding error numbers. (See SQL Server Books Online to learn how to add your own messages to SQL Server's predefined messages.)

Try It Out: Handling a Database Exception (Part 1): RAISERROR

Follow these steps:

1. To the Database tab page, add a button to the tab page and change its Text property to Database Exception-1 (RAISERROR). Add a label to the right of this button, and change its Text property to Calls a stored procedure that uses RAISERROR.

2. Add a second button to the tab page, and change its Text property to Database Exception-2 (SP Error). Add a label to the right of this button, and change its Text property to Calls a stored procedure that encounters an error.

3. Add a third button to the tab page, and change its Text property to Database Exception-3 (Errors Collection). Add a label to the right of this button, and change its Text property to Multiple SqlError objects created. The layout should look like Figure 18-6.

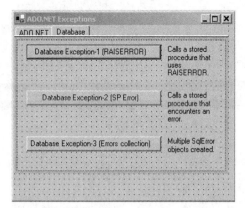

Figure 18-6. *Database tab page layout*

4. Using Server Explorer, create a stored procedure named sp_DbException_1, as follows:

```
create procedure sp_DbException_1
as
set nocount on

declare @orderscount int

select
    @orderscount = count(*)
from
    orders

if @orderscount > 10
    raiserror (
        'Orders Count is greater than 10 - Notify the Business Manager',
        16,
        1
    )

return
```

5. Add the following code to the button3_Click method:

```
// Create connection
SqlConnection conn = new SqlConnection(@"
    data source = (local)\netsdk;
    integrated security = sspi;
    database = northwind"
);
```

```csharp
// Create command
SqlCommand cmd = conn.CreateCommand();

// Specify stored procedure to be executed
cmd.CommandType = CommandType.StoredProcedure;
cmd.CommandText = "sp_DBException_1";

try
{
    // Open connection
    conn.Open();

    // Execute stored procedure
    cmd.ExecuteNonQuery();
}
catch (System.Data.SqlClient.SqlException ex)
{
    string str;
    str = "Source:"+ ex.Source;
    str += "\n"+ "Number:"+ ex.Number.ToString();
    str += "\n"+ "Message:"+ ex.Message;
    str += "\n"+ "Class:"+ ex.Class.ToString ();
    str += "\n"+ "Procedure:"+ ex.Procedure.ToString();
    str += "\n"+ "Line Number:"+ex.LineNumber.ToString();
    str += "\n"+ "Server:"+ ex.Server.ToString();

    MessageBox.Show (str, "Database Exception");
}
catch (System.Exception ex)
{
    string str;
    str = "Source:"+ ex.Source;
    str += "\n"+ "Error Message:"+ ex.Message;
    MessageBox.Show (str, "General Exception");
}
finally
{
    if (conn.State == ConnectionState.Open)
    {
        MessageBox.Show (
            "Finally block closing the connection",
            "Finally"
        );
        conn.Close();
    }
}
```

6. Run the program with Ctrl+F5, and then click the RAISERROR button. You'll see the message box in Figure 18-7.

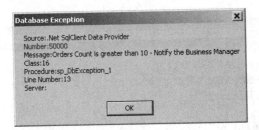

Figure 18-7. *Handling a raised database exception*

Observe the caption and contents of the message box. The source, message, name of the stored procedure, exact line number where the error was found, and name of the machine are all displayed. You obtain this detailed information about the exception from the SqlException object.

How It Works

In the sp_DBException_1 stored procedure, you first find the number of orders in the Orders table and store the number in a variable called @orderscount. Then, if @orderscount is greater than ten, you raise an error using the RAISERROR statement.

```
select
    @orderscount = count(*)
from
    orders

if @orderscount > 10
    raiserror (
        'Orders Count is greater than 10 - Notify the Business Manager',
        16,
        1
    )
```

Then within a try block you execute the stored procedure using the ExecuteNonQuery method.

```
// Execute stored procedure
cmd.ExecuteNonQuery();
```

When the stored procedure is executed, the RAISERROR statement raises an error. This is trapped by the following catch clause:

```
catch (System.Data.SqlClient.SqlException ex)
{
    string str;
    str = "Source:"+ ex.Source;
    str += "\n"+ "Number:"+ ex.Number.ToString();
    str += "\n"+ "Message:"+ ex.Message;
    str += "\n"+ "Class:"+ ex.Class.ToString ();
    str += "\n"+ "Procedure:"+ ex.Procedure.ToString();
    str += "\n"+ "Line Number:"+ex.LineNumber.ToString();
    str += "\n"+ "Server:"+ ex.Server.ToString();

    MessageBox.Show (str, "Database Exception");
}
```

Try It Out: Handling a Database Exception (Part 2): Stored Procedure

Now let's see what happens when a statement in a stored procedure encounters an error. You'll now create a stored procedure that attempts an illegal INSERT, and then you'll extract information from the SqlException object.

1. Using Server Explorer, create a stored procedure named sp_DbException_2, as follows:

```
create procedure sp_DBException_2
as
set nocount on

insert into employees
(
    employeeid,
    firstname
)
values (50, 'Cinderella')

return
```

2. Add the following code to the button4_Click method:

```
// Create connection
SqlConnection conn = new SqlConnection(@"
    data source = (local)\netsdk;
    integrated security = sspi;
    database = northwind"
);

// Create command
SqlCommand cmd = conn.CreateCommand();
```

```csharp
// Specify stored procedure to be executed
cmd.CommandType = CommandType.StoredProcedure;
cmd.CommandText = "sp_DBException_2";

try
{
    // Open onnection
    conn.Open();

    // Execute stored procedure
    cmd.ExecuteNonQuery();
}
catch (System.Data.SqlClient.SqlException ex)
{
    string str;
    str = "Source:"+ ex.Source;
    str += "\n"+ "Number:"+ ex.Number.ToString();
    str += "\n"+ "Message:"+ ex.Message;
    str += "\n"+ "Class:"+ ex.Class.ToString ();
    str += "\n"+ "Procedure:"+ ex.Procedure.ToString();
    str += "\n"+ "Line Number:"+ex.LineNumber.ToString();
    str += "\n"+ "Server:"+ ex.Server.ToString();

    MessageBox.Show (str, "Database Exception");
}
catch (System.Exception ex)
{
    string str;
    str = "Source:"+ ex.Source;
    str += "\n"+ "Error Message:"+ ex.Message;
    MessageBox.Show (str, "ADO.NET Exception");
}
finally
{
    if (conn.State == ConnectionState.Open)
    {
        MessageBox.Show (
                "Finally block closing the connection",
                "Finally"
        );
        conn.Close();
    }
}
```

3. Run the program with Ctrl+F5, and then click the SP Error button. You'll see the message box in Figure 18-8.

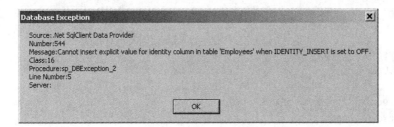

Figure 18-8. *Handling a database exception*

How It Works

The stored procedure tries to insert a new employee into the Employees table.

```
insert into employees
(
    employeeid,
    firstname
)
values (50, 'Cinderella')
```

However, since the EmployeeID column in the Employees table is an IDENTITY column, you can't explicitly assign a value to it.

■**Tip** Actually, you can—as the message indicates—if you use SET IDENTITY_INSERT employees OFF in the stored procedure before you attempt the INSERT. This would allow you to insert explicit EmployeeID values, but this seldom is, or should be, done.

When this SQL error occurs, the specific SqlException catch clause traps it and displays the information. The finally block then closes the connection.

It's possible for stored procedures to encounter several errors. You can trap and debug these using the SqlException object, as you'll see next.

Try It Out: Handling a Database Exception (Part 3): Errors Collection

The SqlException class has an Errors collection property. Each item in the Errors collection is an object of type SqlError. When a database exception occurs, the Errors collection is populated. For the example, let's try to establish a connection to a nonexistent database and investigate the SqlException's Errors collection.

1. Add the following code to the button5_Click method. Note that we've intentionally misspelled the database name.

```
// Create connection
SqlConnection conn = new SqlConnection(@"
    data source = (local)\netsdk;
    integrated security = sspi;
    database = northwnd"
);

// Create command
SqlCommand cmd = conn.CreateCommand();

// Specify stored procedure to be executed
cmd.CommandType = CommandType.StoredProcedure;
cmd.CommandText = "sp_DBException_2";

try
{
    // Open onnection
    conn.Open();

    // Execute stored procedure
    cmd.ExecuteNonQuery();
}
catch (System.Data.SqlClient.SqlException ex)
{
    string str ="";
    for (int i = 0; i < ex.Errors.Count; i++)
    {
        str += "\n" + "Index #" + i + "\n" +
               "Exception : " + ex.Errors[i].ToString() + "\n" +
               "Number:" + ex.Errors[i].Number.ToString() + "\n"
        ;
    }
    MessageBox.Show (str, "Database Exception");
}
catch (System.Exception ex)
{
    string str;
    str = "Source:"+ ex.Source;
    str += "\n"+ "Error Message:"+ ex.Message;
    MessageBox.Show (str, "ADO.NET Exception");
}
finally
```

```
        {
            if (conn.State == ConnectionState.Open)
            {
                MessageBox.Show (
                    "Finally block closing the connection",
                    "Finally"
                );
                conn.Close();
            }
        }
    }
```

2. Run the program with Ctrl+F5, and then click the Errors Collection button. You'll see the message box in Figure 18-9.

Figure 18-9. *Handling multiple database errors*

Observe that two items are found in the Errors collection, and their error numbers are different.

How It Works

In the connection string, you specify a database that doesn't exist on the server; here you misspell Northwind as Northwnd.

```
// Create connection
SqlConnection conn = new SqlConnection(@"
    data source = (local)\netsdk;
    integrated security = sspi;
    database = northwnd"
);
```

When you try to open the connection, an exception of type SqlException is thrown.

```
catch (System.Data.SqlClient.SqlException ex)
{
    string str ="";
    for (int i = 0; i < ex.Errors.Count; i++)
    {
        str += "\n" + "Index #" + i + "\n" +
                "Exception : " + ex.Errors[i].ToString() + "\n" +
                "Number:" + ex.Errors[i].Number.ToString() + "\n"
        ;
    }
    MessageBox.Show (str, "Database Exception");
}
```

You then loop through the items of the Errors collection and get each Error object using its indexer.

This example shows that the SqlException object carries detailed information about every SQL error in its Errors collection.

Summary

We began this chapter by reviewing C#'s structured error handling. Then we discussed the sources of exceptions in ADO.NET database applications.

You saw how to handle exceptions thrown by the CLR and by the database. In particular, you learned how to handle both single and multiple database exceptions with the System.Data.SqlClient.SqlException class.

In the next chapter, you'll look at transactions and how to maintain database integrity when multiple users are working concurrently.

CHAPTER 19

■■■

Using Transactions

A *transaction* is a set of operations that's performed so the operations are guaranteed to succeed or fail as one unit.

A common example of a simple transaction is transferring money from a checking account to a savings account. This involves two operations: deducting money from the checking account and adding it to the savings account. Both must succeed together and be *committed* to the accounts, or both must fail together and be *rolled back* so that the accounts are maintained in a consistent state. Under no circumstances should money be deducted from the checking account but not added to the savings account (or vice versa). By using a transaction, both operations can be guaranteed to succeed or fail together.

Transactions may comprise many individual operations and even other transactions. Transactions are essential for maintaining data integrity, both for multiple related operations and when multiple users update the database *concurrently*.

In this chapter, we'll cover the following topics:

- When to use transactions

- The ACID properties of a transaction

- How to code transactions

When to Use Transactions

You should use transactions when several operations must succeed or fail as a unit. The following are some frequent scenarios where you must use transactions:

- In batch processing, where multiple rows must be inserted or deleted as a single unit

- Whenever a change to one table requires that other tables be kept consistent

- When modifying data in two or more databases, concurrently

- In distributed transactions, where data is manipulated in databases on different machines

When you use transactions, you place locks on data pending permanent change to the database. No other operations can take place on locked data until you lift the lock. You could lock anything from a single row up to the whole database. This is called *concurrency*; that is, concurrency is how the database handles multiple updates at one time.

In the bank example, locks ensure that two separate transactions don't access the same accounts at the same time. If they did, either deposits or withdrawals could be lost.

■Note It's important to keep transactions pending for the shortest period of time. A lock stops others from accessing the locked database resource. Too many locks, or locks on frequently accessed resources, can seriously degrade performance.

Understanding ACID Properties

A transaction is characterized by four properties, often referred to as the *ACID properties*: atomicity, consistency, isolation, and durability.

Atomicity: A transaction is atomic if it's regarded as a single action rather than a collection of separate operations. So then, only when all the separate operations succeed does a transaction succeed and is committed to the database. On the other hand, if a single operation fails during the transaction, everything is considered to have failed and must be undone (rolled back) if it has already taken place. In the case of the order-entry system of the Northwind database, when you enter an order into the Orders and Order Details tables, data will be saved together in both tables, or it won't be saved at all.

Consistency: The transaction should leave the database in a consistent state—whether or not it completed successfully. The data modified by the transaction must comply with all the constraints placed on the columns in order to maintain data integrity. In the case of Northwind, you can't have rows in the Order Details table without a corresponding row in the Orders table, as this would leave the data in an inconsistent state.

Isolation: Every transaction has a well-defined boundary. One transaction shouldn't affect other transactions running at the same time. Data modifications made by one transaction must be isolated from the data modification made by all other transactions. A transaction sees data in the state it was in before another concurrent transaction modified it, or it sees the data after the second transaction has completed, but it doesn't see an intermediate state.

Durability: Data modifications that occur within a successful transaction are kept permanently within the system regardless of what else occurs. Transaction logs are maintained so that should a failure occur, the database can be restored to its original state before the failure. As each transaction is completed, a row is entered in the database transaction log. If you have a major system failure that requires the database to be restored from a backup, you could then use this transaction log to insert (roll forward) any successful transactions that had taken place.

Every database server that offers support for transactions enforces these four properties automatically. All you need to do is create the transactions in the first place, which is what you'll look at next.

How to Code Transactions

The following three statements control transactions in SQL Server:

- **BEGIN TRANSACTION**: This marks the beginning of a transaction.

- **COMMIT TRANSACTION**: This marks the successful end of a transaction. It signals the database to save the work.

- **ROLLBACK TRANSACTION**: This denotes that a transaction hasn't been successful and signals the database to roll back to the state it was in prior to the transaction.

Coding Transactions in SQL

Let's code some simple transactions to see how the transaction control statements work.

Try It Out: Rolling Back a Transaction

This example shows how to safely delete a sales order in the Northwind database. As you know, an order has a header row in the Orders table and detail rows in the Order Details table. When you delete an order, you need to delete both header and details or nothing. You have several ways to achieve this. In this example, you'll do it with a stored procedure.

1. In Server Explorer, expand the Northwind node, right-click the Stored Procedures node, and then click New Stored Procedure.

2. Replace the code with that in Listing 19-1.

Listing 19-1. `sp_TransTest1`

```
CREATE PROCEDURE sp_TransTest1(@OrderId as integer)
AS
DECLARE @Err int

BEGIN TRANSACTION

-- Delete the order
DELETE FROM Orders
WHERE OrderId = @OrderId

-- Save @@ERROR in local variable @Err
SET @Err = @@ERROR

-- If error number is not zero, roll back
IF @Err <> 0
BEGIN
   ROLLBACK TRANSACTION
   RETURN @Err
END

-- Delete the order details
DELETE [Order Details]
WHERE OrderId = @OrderId
```

```
-- Save @@ERROR number in local variable @Err
SET @Err = @@ERROR

-- If error number is not zero, roll back
IF @Err <> 0
BEGIN
   ROLLBACK TRANSACTION
   RETURN @Err
 END

-- If no error, commit the transaction
COMMIT TRANSACTION
RETURN
```

3. Click the Save icon. This will run the CREATE PROCEDURE statement.

4. Before running the stored procedure, you need to make sure that the relationship between Orders and Order Details doesn't cascade deletes.

   In Server Explorer, right-click the Database Diagrams node, and then click New Diagram. In the Add Table window, select Orders and Order Details, and then click Add. Click Close to view the diagram. Right-click the relationship, and select Property Pages. Select the Relationships tab, and then uncheck the Cascade Delete Related Records check box (see Figure 19-1). Click Close.

Figure 19-1. *Suppressing cascade of deletes*

5. Run the procedure in Server Explorer by right-clicking its node and selecting Run Stored Procedure. When prompted, enter 10260 for @OrderId. You'll see the error message in the output window shown in Figure 19-2. Its full text is as follows:

```
Running dbo."sp_TransTest1" ( @OrderId = 10260 ).

DELETE statement conflicted with COLUMN REFERENCE constraint
'FK_Order Details_Orders'.
The conflict occurred in database 'Northwind', table
'Order Details', column 'OrderID'.
Running dbo."sp_TransTest1_SQL" ( @OrderId = 10260 ).
```

Figure 19-2. *Violating referential integrity*

How It Works

You want to delete the rows for a given OrderId from the Orders and Order Details tables in a transaction. You begin by declaring @OrderId as an input parameter for the stored procedure and a local variable @Err, which you use to hold the error number should one occur.

```
CREATE PROCEDURE sp_TransTest1(@OrderId as integer)
AS
DECLARE @Err int
```

You begin the transaction with the BEGIN TRANSACTION statement.

```
BEGIN TRANSACTION
```

Next you try to delete the row for a specified order from the Orders table.

```
-- Delete the order
DELETE FROM Orders
WHERE OrderId = @OrderId
```

Error handling is important at all times in SQL Server, and it's never more so than inside transactional code. When you issue the DELETE statement, you have a possibility that it may not succeed for whatever reason. If an error occurs, a variable built into SQL Server called @@ERROR will store the error's number. If an error doesn't occur, the value of @@ERROR is 0.

@@ERROR is reset to 0 after every Transact-SQL statement is executed, so before it's reset you store its current value for the DELETE statement in @Err for checking. Unlike C#, Transact-SQL doesn't support structure exception handling, so you have to check manually for each error.

```
-- Save @@ERROR in local variable @Err
SET @Err = @@ERROR
```

If @Err is any value other than 0, an error has occurred, and you must roll back the transaction. You also include PRINT and RAISERROR statements to tell you that a rollback has occurred.

```
-- If error number is not zero, roll back
IF @Err <> 0
BEGIN
    ROLLBACK TRANSACTION
    RETURN @Err
END
```

Note Technically, you didn't need to roll back the transaction since the DELETE statement failed and no data was actually changed in the database.

If all goes well, you try to delete the corresponding rows from Order Details for this @OrderId. As before, you save @@ERROR in the local variable @Err and use it to determine if you should roll back the transaction.

```
-- Delete the order details
DELETE [Order Details]
WHERE OrderId = @OrderId

-- Save @@ERROR number in local variable @Err
SET @Err = @@ERROR

-- If error number is not zero, roll back
IF @Err <> 0
BEGIN
    ROLLBACK TRANSACTION
    RETURN @Err
 END
```

If the stored procedure still hasn't encountered any errors, you issue the COMMIT TRANSACTION statement to commit the deletions. By default, if no expression is used after RETURN, a value of 0 is returned.

```
-- If no error, commit the transaction
COMMIT TRANSACTION
RETURN
```

Try It Out: Committing a Transaction

In this example, you'll modify the stored procedure by flipping the DELETE statements so that the Order Details rows are deleted before the Orders rows.

1. In Server Explorer, expand the Northwind node, right-click the Stored Procedures node, and then click New Stored Procedure.

2. Replace the code with that in Listing 19-2.

Listing 19-2. sp_TransTest2

```
CREATE PROCEDURE sp_TransTest2(@OrderId as integer)
AS
DECLARE @Err int

BEGIN TRANSACTION

-- Delete the order details
DELETE [Order Details]
WHERE OrderId = @OrderId

-- Save @@ERROR number in local variable @Err
SET @Err = @@ERROR

-- If error number is not zero, roll back
IF @Err <> 0
BEGIN
   ROLLBACK TRANSACTION
   RETURN @Err
 END

-- Delete the order
DELETE FROM Orders
WHERE OrderId = @OrderId

-- Save @@ERROR in local variable @Err
SET @Err = @@ERROR

-- If error number is not zero, roll back
IF @Err <> 0
BEGIN
   ROLLBACK TRANSACTION
   RETURN @Err
END

-- If no error, commit the transaction
COMMIT TRANSACTION
RETURN
```

3. Click the Save icon. This will run the CREATE PROCEDURE statement.

4. Run the procedure in Server Explorer by right-clicking its node and selecting Run Stored Procedure. When prompted, enter 10260 for @OrderId. You'll see the output window shown in Figure 19-3. No errors occur, and both the order and its details are deleted.

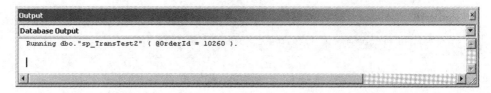

Figure 19-3. *Successful completion of a transaction*

How It Works

The new stored procedure differs from the first only in the order of the DELETE statements, which have been reversed. When you execute the stored procedure, a transaction begins, and the rows are deleted from the Order Details table first and then from Orders. This ensures that the foreign key constraint isn't violated and no error is generated. With both deletions having been successfully carried out, you then commit the transaction.

ADO.NET Transactions

In ADO.NET, a *transaction* is an instance of a class that implements the interface System.Data.IDbTransaction. Like a data reader, a transaction has no constructor of its own but is created by calling another object's method—in this case, a connection's BeginTransaction method. Commands are associated with a specific transaction for a specific connection, and any SQL submitted by these commands is executed as part of the same transaction.

Try It Out: Working with ADO.NET Transactions

In this ADO.NET example, you'll code a C# equivalent of sp_TransTest2.

1. Create a new solution called Chapter19_Examples.

2. Add a C# Windows application named Transactions. Rename Form1.cs to Transactions.cs.

3. Add a label, a text box, and two buttons as shown in Figure 19-4.

Figure 19-4. Transactions *layout*

4. Add a using directive to Transactions.cs.

```
using System.Data.SqlClient;
```

5. Double-click the Delete Order (Roll Back) button, and add the following code to its click event handler:

```
// Create connection
SqlConnection cn =
    new SqlConnection(
        @"Data Source = (local)\NETSDK;" +
         "Integrated Security=SSPI;database=Northwind"
    );

// Open connection
cn.Open();

// Begin transaction
SqlTransaction objTrans = cn.BeginTransaction();

try
{
    // Create command
    SqlCommand cmd = cn.CreateCommand();
    cmd.CommandType = CommandType.Text;
    cmd.Transaction = objTrans;

    // Delete order
    cmd.CommandText = "DELETE Orders WHERE OrderId = " +
        Convert.ToString(textBox1.Text);
    cmd.ExecuteNonQuery();
```

```
    // Commit transaction
    objTrans.Commit();

    // No exception, transaction committed, give message
    MessageBox.Show(
        "Transaction Committed\n" +
        "Order and Order Details " +
        "have been successfully deleted.",
        "Commit Transaction");
}
catch (System.Data.SqlClient.SqlException ex)
{
    // Roll back transaction
    objTrans.Rollback();

    MessageBox.Show(
        "Error - TRANSACTION ROLLED BACK\n" + ex.Message,
        "Rollback Transaction"
    );
}
catch (System.Exception ex)
{
    MessageBox.Show("System Error\n" + ex.Message, "Error");
}
finally
{
    // Close connection
    cn.Close();
}
```

6. Double-click the Delete Order (Commit) button, and add the following code to its click event handler:

```
// Create connection
SqlConnection cn =
    new SqlConnection(
        @"Data Source=(local)\NETSDK;" +
        "Integrated Security=SSPI;database=Northwind"
    );

// Open connection
cn.Open();

// Begin transaction
SqlTransaction objTrans = cn.BeginTransaction();
```

```
try
{
    // Create command
    SqlCommand cmd = cn.CreateCommand();
    cmd.CommandType = CommandType.Text;
    cmd.Transaction = objTrans;

     //Delete order details
     cmd.CommandText = "DELETE [Order Details] WHERE OrderId = " +
         Convert.ToString(textBox1.Text);
     cmd.ExecuteNonQuery();

     //Delete order
     cmd.CommandText="DELETE Orders WHERE OrderId = " +
         Convert.ToString(textBox1.Text);
     cmd.ExecuteNonQuery();

     //Commit transaction
     objTrans.Commit();

     // No exception, transaction committed, give message
     MessageBox.Show(
         "Transaction Committed\n" +
         "Order and Order Details " +
         "have been successfully deleted.",
         "Commit Transaction");
}
catch (System.Data.SqlClient.SqlException  ex)
{
     //Roll back transaction
     objTrans.Rollback();

     MessageBox.Show(
         "Error - TRANSACTION ROLLED BACK\n" + ex.Message,
         "Rollback Transaction"
     );
}
catch (System.Exception ex)
{
     MessageBox.Show("System Error\n" + ex.Message, "Error");
}
finally
{
     // Close connection
     cn.Close();
}
```

7. Build and run the solution with Ctrl+F5. Enter 10249 for Order ID, and click Delete Order (Roll Back). As expected, an error message box appears as in Figure 19-5.

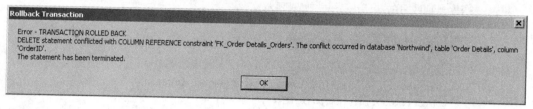

Figure 19-5. *Rolling back a transaction*

8. Now click Delete Order (Commit). As expected, a message box appears confirming that the transaction is successful, as in Figure 19-6.

Figure 19-6. *Committing a transaction*

How It Works

Both event handlers work in basically the same way. First you open a connection, and second you create a transaction for it.

```
// Open connection
cn.Open();
```

```
// Begin transaction
SqlTransaction objTrans = cn.BeginTransaction();
```

Note that transactions are connection specific. You can't create a second transaction for the same connection before committing or rolling back the first one. Though the method implies it begins a transaction, the transaction itself performs no work until the first SQL is executed by a command.

You then create a command, specify that it will execute SQL rather than call a stored procedure (CommandType defaults to Text, by the way), and specify the transaction within which the command will execute. Any SQL you later associate with the command will execute as part of this transaction.

```
// Create command
SqlCommand cmd = cn.CreateCommand();
cmd.CommandType = CommandType.Text;
cmd.Transaction = objTrans;
```

In the first event handler, you execute only one SQL statement—to delete an order. You then call the transaction's Commit method to commit the data. Note that, unlike in the stored procedures, you *don't* execute the SQL COMMIT statement. ADO.NET handles transactions differently than SQL does. The details are beyond the scope of this book, but rest assured that both ADO.NET and SQL transactions guarantee all operations will succeed or fail as a unit. Just remember to use Commit rather than COMMIT in C# programs.

```
// Delete order
cmd.CommandText = "DELETE Orders WHERE OrderId = " +
    Convert.ToString(textBox1.Text);
cmd.ExecuteNonQuery();

// Commit transaction
objTrans.Commit();
```

In the second event handler, you execute two SQL statements—to delete order details before deleting an order. Note that for each statement, you first assign the SQL to CommandText and then submit it to the database with ExecuteNonQuery. Only after both statements have executed do you call the transaction's Commit method. Had you called Commit after the first DELETE, the order details would have been deleted and stayed deleted even if the delete of the order failed. Commit, just like COMMIT, makes changes permanent and ends the current transaction.

```
//Delete order details
cmd.CommandText = "DELETE [Order Details] WHERE OrderId = " +
    Convert.ToString(textBox1.Text);
cmd.ExecuteNonQuery();

//Delete order
cmd.CommandText = "DELETE Orders WHERE OrderId = " +
    Convert.ToString(textBox1.Text);
cmd.ExecuteNonQuery();

//Commit transaction
objTrans.Commit();
```

If an error is encountered, a catch block calls the transaction's Rollback method. This undoes any changes for all SQL operations performed within the transaction (in other words, since the most recent call to Commit or Rollback).

```
catch (System.Data.SqlClient.SqlException  ex)
{
    //Roll back transaction
    objTrans.Rollback();

    MessageBox.Show(
        "Error - TRANSACTION ROLLED BACK\n" + ex.Message,
        "Rollback Transaction"
    );
}
```

Suggestions for Further Study

You've seen only the tip of the transaction iceberg in this chapter. Though the basic techniques remain the same and you can write many real-world programs with what you've learned, you have a great deal more to learn about how both ADO.NET and RDBMSs manage transactions. Some important topics include the following:

Isolation levels: The BeginTransaction method is overloaded and accepts an argument specifying how the transaction is isolated from other concurrent transactions. What isolation levels are available depends on the RDBMSs. For example, SQL Server supports six isolation levels, DB2 and MySQL support four, and Oracle supports three. The SQL standard itself defines four. Further, the default isolation level is RDBMS specific. Study the documentation for both your database and data provider before choosing an isolation level. The actual choice also depends on just what your program does and what kind of performance it seeks to achieve.

Nested transactions: Transactions can be nested. In general, commits and rollbacks are local to the nested transaction, but, again, consult your RDBMS documentation for specifics.

Savepoints: Savepoints are defined by the SQL standard and supported by most RDBMSs. They allow you to roll back part of a transaction without terminating the entire transaction.

Summary

In this chapter you learned what transactions are and when to use them. You learned about the ACID properties of transactions. You then learned how to code transactions in SQL.

The next chapter presents the fundamentals of event handling.

CHAPTER 20

■ ■ ■

Working with ADO.NET Events

ADO.NET objects (such as connections and datasets) can fire events when a property has changed. For example, you can make a connection that notifies you when it opens or closes. Similarly, you can create a dataset object that notifies you when a column value is changed or when a row is deleted.

In this chapter, we'll discuss the following topics about events:

- What events and delegates are and how they're useful

- Different types of events supported by ADO.NET objects

- How to add and remove event handlers

Understanding Events and Delegates

An *event* is a class member (of the `delegate` type) that enables a class or object to provide notifications by invoking methods on other objects that signal the occurrence of an action. The action could be user interaction, such as mouse clicks, or operations carried out by a program. The object that triggers the event is the *event source*. The object that captures the event and responds to it is the *event consumer* (or *client*). The method that handles the event is the *event handler*.

The event source doesn't care what objects consume its events. The consumers give it delegates; that is, they give it a mapping to methods that the source will execute when the event occurs.

Delegates encapsulate an invocation list of one or more methods. A delegate is an object that can be sent to multiple sources, so a single delegate can handle multiple events. For example, a button-click event and a menu command–click event can both invoke the same delegate, which then calls a single method to handle these separate events the same way.

The binding mechanism used with delegates is dynamic; in other words, a delegate can be bound at runtime to any method whose signature matches that of the event handler. This feature allows you to set up or change the bound method depending on a condition and to attach dynamically an event handler to a control.

When an event is raised, the code within the event handler is executed. Each event handler provides two parameters that help handle the event correctly. The first parameter, the sender, provides a reference to the object that raised the event. The second parameter is an object specific to the event that's being handled. By referencing the object's properties (and sometimes its methods), you can obtain detailed information about the event. Typically each event has an event handler with a different event-object type for the second parameter.

This event-handling process applies to all events in the .NET Framework. Consequently, ADO.NET objects, such as connections, data adapters, and datasets, all raise events that can be handled using the same process. We'll discuss the events raised by ADO.NET objects in detail throughout this chapter, but for now, let's get a feel for how all the different pieces of this process work.

Connections support two events, InfoMessage and StateChange, as shown in Figure 20-1.

Figure 20-1. *Connection events*

The declaration of the delegate that binds the StateChange event to an event handler looks like this:

```
public delegate void StateChangeEventHandler(
    object sender,
    StateChangeEventArgs e
);
```

The code to bind the StateChange event to an event handler named CnStateChange looks like this (note the += operator):

```
cn.StateChange += new StateChangeEventHandler(CnStateChange);
```

The event handler itself, which will execute after the event is raised, looks like this:

```
private void CnStateChange(object sender, StateChangeEventArgs ev)
{
    // Event handler code
}
```

Note the parameters of the event handler, which are the same as the parameters of the delegate declaration. The following sections cover all these in more detail. You'll now look at the syntax of adding and removing event handlers.

Adding and Removing Event Handlers

In C#, you specify a delegate by using the += operator. For example, you can bind the StateChange event of the connection object called cn to the CnStateChange method (which you write yourself) by activating a delegate called StateChangeEventHandler (which is provided for you by .NET). The StateChange event of the connection object fires whenever the connection state changes to open or closed.

```
cn.StateChange += new StateChangeEventHandler(CnStateChange);
```

Similarly, you can deactivate a delegate by removing it with the -= operator, as follows:

```
cn.StateChange -= new StateChangeEventHandler(CnStateChange);
```

Once deactivated, when the StateChange event fires, it won't be handled by the CnStateChange event handler. This process of activating and deactivating a delegate can take place as needed in code.

In this chapter, we'll discuss the events raised by ADO.NET objects and how to handle them. While events can be raised and handled by non-ADO.NET objects as well, this chapter pertains only to the ADO.NET objects.

Raising and Handling ADO.NET Events

You can handle the events raised by ADO.NET objects using appropriate delegates. These events are raised when a certain property of the object changes. Although these objects raise several events, we'll discuss only a few, because all can be handled in the same fashion. You'll use the System.Data.SqlClient .NET data provider, but all data providers handle events in a similar way.

Working with Connection Object Events

The connection object has two events: StateChange and InfoMessage. Let's look at these in more detail.

Using the StateChange Event

The connection object raises the StateChange event when the state of the connection changes. The event handler receives a StateChangeEventArgs object, which you can examine for detailed information about the event. For example, it has OriginalState and CurrentState properties that you can access to find out the state of the connection object before and after a change.

Try It Out: Writing the Connection.StateChange Event

You'll now see how this event is handled. You'll open a connection to the Northwind database, retrieve one row from the Customers table, and close the connection. Then you'll write an event handler to notify you of when the connection state changes.

1. Create a new solution called Chapter20_Examples.

2. Add a C# Windows application named Events.

3. Add four buttons, a label, and a list box as shown in Figure 20-2.

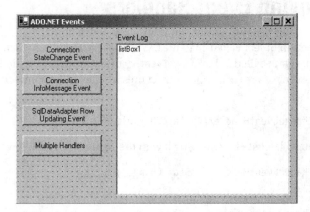

Figure 20-2. Events *layout*

4. Add a using directive for the System.Data.SqlClient namespace.

5. In the click event handler for the first button, add the following code:

```
// Create connection
SqlConnection cn = new SqlConnection(@"Data Source=(local)\NETSDK;" +
  "Integrated Security=SSPI;database=Northwind");

// Create command
SqlCommand cmd = new SqlCommand();
cmd.CommandText = "SELECT TOP 1 CustomerId, CompanyName FROM Customers";
cmd.Connection = cn;

// Delegate the StateChange event to the CnStateChange function
cn.StateChange += new StateChangeEventHandler(CnStateChange);

try
{
    listBox1.Items.Clear();

    //Open connection - CnStateChange event will be fired.
    cn.Open();

    // Create data reader
    SqlDataReader dr = cmd.ExecuteReader();
```

```
    // Display the rows in list box
    while(dr.Read())
    {
        listBox1.Items.Add(dr.GetString(0) + "-" + dr.GetString(1));
    }
}
catch(SqlException e1)
{
    MessageBox.Show (e1.Message);
}
finally
{
    //Close connection - CnStateChange event will be fired.
    cn.Close();
}
```

6. Add the following method:

```
private void CnStateChange(object sender, StateChangeEventArgs ev)
{
    // Event handler for the StateChange Event
    listBox1.Items.Add("-----------------------------");
    listBox1.Items.Add("Entering StateChange EventHandler");
    listBox1.Items.Add("Sender = " + sender.ToString());
    listBox1.Items.Add("Original State = " + ev.OriginalState.ToString());
    listBox1.Items.Add("Current State = " + ev.CurrentState.ToString());
    listBox1.Items.Add("Exiting StateChange EventHandler");
    listBox1.Items.Add("-----------------------------");
}
```

7. Build and run the solution with Ctrl+F5. Click the Connection StateChange Event button. You'll see the results in Figure 20-3.

Figure 20-3. *Displaying* StateChange *event information*

Notice the values of the Original State and Current State properties before and after the data displays. This example shows that as the connection state changes the event handler takes over and handles the event.

How It Works

You use a query that selects one row from the Customers table.

```
// Create command
SqlCommand cmd = new SqlCommand();
cmd.CommandText = "SELECT TOP 1 CustomerId, CompanyName FROM Customers";
cmd.Connection = cn;
```

Next, you specify the event handler for the StateChange event using the += operator.

```
// Delegate the StateChange event to the CnStateChange function
cn.StateChange += new StateChangeEventHandler(CnStateChange);
```

The location where you specify the event handler is important. In this case, since you want to capture the connection's StateChange event, you specify the delegate before you actually open the connection.

You then write the event handler. Earlier, you specified CnStateChange as the name of the method that will handle the event. The StateChangeEventHandler delegate provides objects with information about the event: the sender object and the StateChangeEventArgs object. The declaration of this event handler must have the same parameters as the StateChangeEventHandler delegate declaration. In the C# documentation, if you search for StateChangeEventHandler, you'll see the following declaration for the delegate:

```
private void CnStateChange(object sender, StateChangeEventArgs ev)
{
    // Event handler for the StateChange Event
    listBox1.Items.Add("-----------------------------");
    listBox1.Items.Add("Entering StateChange EventHandler");
    listBox1.Items.Add("Sender = " + sender.ToString());
    listBox1.Items.Add("Original State = " + ev.OriginalState.ToString());
    listBox1.Items.Add("Current State = " + ev.CurrentState.ToString());
    listBox1.Items.Add("Exiting StateChange EventHandler");
    listBox1.Items.Add("-----------------------------");
}
```

As you can see, the two parameters are sender and StateChangeEventArgs. The StateChange event provides the delegate with these objects, and the delegate gives the event handler these objects so the event handler can handle the event appropriately. That's why the CnStateChange event handler has the same parameters as the StateChangeEventHandler delegate described previously. You also capture the sender object's identity with sender.ToString().

This makes it clear when the execution enters and leaves the event handler. You can also see that the sender object is the connection. When the connection is opened, its current state is Open and its original state is Closed. When the connection is closed, the current state is Closed and the original state is Open.

This example runs pretty well, and you can see what's happening, but in a real-life application why would users care to be notified if a connection is open or closed? All they need is to see the data. One way to use the StateChange event is to keep track of how many times connections are established and keep a running total. Based on this, you can charge users a fee per connection. (Of course, this is a rudimentary way of charging a fee, and you'll have to figure in other factors.) Another way to use this event would be to keep track of how much time a user has had a connection open and charge based on this.

Using the InfoMessage Event

The InfoMessage event is raised by the connection when the database gives out information messages. Information messages aren't error messages from the database. They're warning and informational messages issued by the database. In the case of SQL Server, any message with a severity of ten or less is considered informational and would be captured with the InfoMessage event.

The InfoMessage event handler receives an InfoMessageEventArgs object that contains a collection of the messages from the data source in its Errors collection property. The Error objects in this collection are of type SqlError and can be queried for information such as the number, the source, the message, and the exact line number in the stored procedure where this message originated from, among others. Let's run a query and a Transact-SQL PRINT statement. You'll capture this event and query the information in the Errors collection.

Try It Out: Writing the Connection.InfoMessage Event

To write the Connection.InfoMessage event, follow these steps:

1. In Design view, double-click the Connection InfoMessage Event button. Add the following code to the click event handler:

```
// Create connection
SqlConnection cn = new SqlConnection(@"Data Source=(local)\NETSDK;" +
    "Integrated Security=SSPI;database=Northwind");

// Delegate the InfoMessage event to the CnInfoMessage method
cn.InfoMessage += new SqlInfoMessageEventHandler(CnInfoMessage);

// Delegate the StateChange event to the CnStateChange function
cn.StateChange += new StateChangeEventHandler(CnStateChange);

// Create command
SqlCommand cmd = new SqlCommand();
cmd.CommandText = "SELECT TOP 2 CustomerId FROM Customers";
cmd.Connection = cn;

try
{
    // Clear list box
    listBox1.Items.Clear();
```

```
    //Open connection
    cn.Open();

    // Create data reader
    SqlDataReader dr = cmd.ExecuteReader();

    while(dr.Read())
    {
        listBox1.Items.Add(dr.GetString(0));
    }

    dr.Close();

    // Execute a PRINT statement
    cmd.CommandText = "PRINT 'Get CustomerId for all customers'";
    cmd.ExecuteNonQuery();
}
catch(SqlException ex)
{
    MessageBox.Show (ex.Message);
}
finally
{
    //Close connection
    cn.Close();
}
```

2. Add the following method:

```
private void CnInfoMessage(object sender, SqlInfoMessageEventArgs ev)
{
    foreach (SqlError err in ev.Errors)
    {
        listBox1.Items.Add("-------------------------------");
        listBox1.Items.Add("Entering InfoMessage Event Handler");
        listBox1.Items.Add("Source- " + err.Source);
        listBox1.Items.Add("State- " + err.State);
        listBox1.Items.Add("Number- " + err.Number);
        listBox1.Items.Add("Procedure- " + err.Procedure);
        listBox1.Items.Add("Server- " + err.Server);
        listBox1.Items.Add("Message- " + err.Message);
        listBox1.Items.Add("Exiting InfoMessage Event Handler");
        listBox1.Items.Add("-------------------------------");
    }
}
```

3. Build and run the solution with Ctrl+F5. Click the Connection InfoMessage Event button. You'll see the results in Figure 20-4.

Figure 20-4. *Displaying* InfoMessage *event information*

How It Works

After creating a connection object, you specify the CnInfoMessage function as the EventHandler for the InfoMessage event.

```
// Delegate the InfoMessage event to the CnInfoMessage method
cn.InfoMessage += new SqlInfoMessageEventHandler(CnInfoMessage);
```

You also capture the StateChange event by using the same EventHandler you used before.

```
// Delegate the StateChange event to the CnStateChange function
cn.StateChange += new StateChangeEventHandler(CnStateChange);
```

Then you execute a query and get the CustomerIds of two employees and add them to the list box.

```
// Create command
SqlCommand cmd = new SqlCommand();
cmd.CommandText = "SELECT TOP 2 CustomerId FROM Customers";
cmd.Connection = cn;
```

Now, you execute a PRINT statement against the database. You use the ExecuteNonQuery() method of the command object since the PRINT statement doesn't return any rows.

```
// Execute a PRINT statement
cmd.CommandText = "PRINT 'Get CustomerId for all customers'";
cmd.ExecuteNonQuery();
```

The EventHandler method cnInfoMessage is written with the same signature as the delegate SqlInfoMessageEventHandler. The two arguments are the sender object and the SqlInfoMessageEventArgs object, which contains information about the event. You then loop through the Errors collection of the object and list several pieces of information about the message itself.

```
private void CnInfoMessage(object sender, SqlInfoMessageEventArgs ev)
{
    foreach (SqlError err in ev.Errors)
    {
        listBox1.Items.Add("-----------------------------");
        listBox1.Items.Add("Entering InfoMessage Event Handler");
        listBox1.Items.Add("Source- " + err.Source);
        listBox1.Items.Add("State- " + err.State);
        listBox1.Items.Add("Number- " + err.Number);
        listBox1.Items.Add("Procedure- " + err.Procedure);
        listBox1.Items.Add("Server- " + err.Server);
        listBox1.Items.Add("Message- " + err.Message);
        listBox1.Items.Add("Exiting InfoMessage Event Handler");
        listBox1.Items.Add("-----------------------------");
    }
}
```

Working with Row Update Events

So far you've seen the connection events. ADO.NET supports a wide variety of other events for the purpose of aiding in data validation. For example, a data adapter serves as a bridge between a dataset and a database. When the data adapter is ready to update the changes in the dataset, it raises predefined events. You can code handlers for these events to find more information about the status of the update. Table 20-1 lists some of the common events raised when data is manipulated in ADO.NET objects. The table presents the object that raises the event, the event name, the name of the delegate, and the EventArgs object received by the event handler. The object received by the event handler itself has several properties you can use to take appropriate action.

Table 20-1. *Common ADO.NET Events*

Object	Event	Delegate	Remarks
SqlDataAdapter	RowUpdating	SqlRowUpdatingEventHandler	Raised before the row is updated in the database. The event handler receives a SqlRowUpdatingEventArgs object.
SqlDataAdapter	RowUpdated	SqlRowUpdatedEventHandler	Raised after a row is updated in the database. The event handler receives a SqlRowUpdatedEventArgs object.
SqlDataAdapter	FillError	FillErrorEventHandler	Raised when the Fill method is called. The event handler receives a FillErrorEventArgs object.
DataTable	ColumnChanging	DataColumnChangeEventHandler	Raised when the data in a data column is changing. The handler receives a DataColumnChangingEventArgs object.

Table 20-1. *Common ADO.NET Events*

Object	Event	Delegate	Remarks
DataTable	ColumnChanged	DataColumnChangeEventHandler	Raised after value has been changed for the specified data column in a data row. The handler receives a DataColumnChangedEventArgs object.
DataTable	RowChanging	DataRowChangeEventHandler	Raised when a data row is changing. The event handler receives a DataChangeEventArgs object.
DataTable	RowChanged	DataRowChangeEventHandler	Raised after a data row has changed. The event handler receives a DataChangeEventArgs object.
DataTable	RowDeleting	DataRowChangeEventHandler	Raised before a data row is deleted. The event handler receives a DataRowChangeEventArgs object.
DataTable	RowDeleted	DataRowChangeEventHandler	Raised after a data row is deleted. The event handler receives a DataRowchangeEventArgs objects.

Try It Out: Using RowUpdating and RowUpdated Events

Let's experiment with the SQL Server data adapter's RowUpdating and RowUpdated events; in this example, you'll see how they're fired and handled when a value in a dataset changes.

1. In Design view, double-click the SqlDataAdapter RowUpdating Event button. Add the following code to the click event handler:

```
// Clear list box
listBox1.Items.Clear();

// Create connection
SqlConnection cn = new SqlConnection(@"Data Source=(local)\NETSDK;" +
  "Integrated Security=SSPI;database=Northwind");

try
{
    //Open connection
    cn.Open();

    // Create data adapter
    SqlDataAdapter da = new SqlDataAdapter("SELECT * FROM Customers", cn);
```

```
    // Build command
    SqlCommandBuilder cb = new SqlCommandBuilder(da);

    // Create and fill dataset (select only first row)
    DataSet ds = new DataSet();
    da.Fill(ds, 0, 1, "Customers");

    // Add handlers
    da.RowUpdating += new SqlRowUpdatingEventHandler(OnRowUpdating);
    da.RowUpdated += new SqlRowUpdatedEventHandler(OnRowUpdated);

    // Modify DataSet
    DataTable dt = ds.Tables["Customers"];
    dt.Rows[0][1] = "The Volcano Corporation";

    // Update - this operation fires two events (RowUpdating/RowUpdated).
    da.Update(ds, "Customers");

    // Remove handlers
    da.RowUpdating -= new SqlRowUpdatingEventHandler(OnRowUpdating);
    da.RowUpdated -= new SqlRowUpdatedEventHandler(OnRowUpdated);
}
catch (SqlException ex)
{
    MessageBox.Show(ex.Message);
}
finally
{
    //Close connection
    cn.Close();
}
```

2. Add the following method to handle the RowUpdating event:

```
// Event Handler for RowUpdating event
private void OnRowUpdating(object sender, SqlRowUpdatingEventArgs e)
{
    DisplayEventArgs(e);
}
```

3. Add the following method to handle the RowUpdated event:

```
// Event Handler for RowUpdated event
private void OnRowUpdated(object sender, SqlRowUpdatedEventArgs e)
{
    DisplayEventArgs(e);
}
```

4. Add the following overloaded `DisplayEventArgs` methods:

```
private void DisplayEventArgs(SqlRowUpdatingEventArgs args)
{
    listBox1.Items.Add("OnRowUpdating event");
    if (args.Status != UpdateStatus.Continue)
        listBox1.Items.Add("RowStatus = " + args.Status.ToString());
}

private void DisplayEventArgs(SqlRowUpdatedEventArgs args)
{
    listBox1.Items.Add("OnRowUpdated event");
    listBox1.Items.Add("Records Affected = " + args.RecordsAffected);
}
```

5. Build and run the solution with Ctrl+F5. Click the SqlDataAdapter RowUpdating Event button. You'll see the results in Figure 20-5.

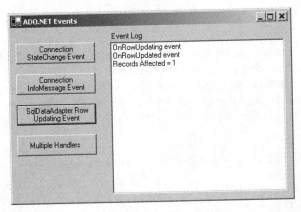

Figure 20-5. *Displaying* RowUpdating *and* RowUpdated *event information*

6. Click the button again. You'll see the results in Figure 20-6.

Figure 20-6. *Displaying only* RowUpdating *event information*

How It Works

Note that the first time the button is clicked, the RowUpdating and RowUpdated events fired. But the second time, the RowUpdated event doesn't fire, and the RowStatus is SkipCurrentRow.

What you've essentially done in this example is retrieve one row from the Customer table, update it to get the RowUpdating and RowUpdated events to fire, and handle the events. You create and initialize a data adapter and a command builder as follows:

```
// Create data adapter
SqlDataAdapter da = new SqlDataAdapter("SELECT * FROM Customers", cn);
```

```
// Build command
SqlCommandBuilder cb = new SqlCommandBuilder(da);
```

Then you create a dataset and use the Fill method to fill it with one row of data.

```
// Create and fill dataset (select only first row)
DataSet ds = new DataSet();
da.Fill(ds, 0, 1, "Customers");
```

Then you add handlers for the RowUpdating and RowUpdated events using the += operator as follows:

```
// Add handlers
da.RowUpdating += new SqlRowUpdatingEventHandler(OnRowUpdating);
da.RowUpdated += new SqlRowUpdatedEventHandler(OnRowUpdated);
```

You now modify the dataset. You change the name of the company to "The Volcano Corporation."

```
// Modify DataSet
DataTable dt = ds.Tables["Customers"];
dt.Rows[0][1] = "The Volcano Corporation";
```

You now update the database by sending the dataset changes to it. At this moment, the RowUpdating event and the RowUpdated event fire.

```
// Update - this operation fires two events (RowUpdating/RowUpdated).
da.Update(ds, "Customers");
```

Finally, you remove the handlers. It isn't necessary in this example, but we've shown it for demonstration purposes. As mentioned earlier in the chapter, the location in code where handlers are added and removed is important and will affect whether events are handled, even if event handlers are present. Notice that you use the -= operator to remove the handlers.

```
// Remove handlers
da.RowUpdating -= new SqlRowUpdatingEventHandler(OnRowUpdating);
da.RowUpdated -= new SqlRowUpdatedEventHandler(OnRowUpdated);
```

Both the OnRowUpdating and OnRowUpdated event handlers call a method named DisplayEventArgs. The OnRowUpdating event handler receives the SqlRowUpdatingEventArgs object, and the OnRowUpdated event handler receives the SqlRowUpdatedEventArgs object. As these two events are different, the delegates of these events pass slightly different information to the handler.

```
// Event Handler for RowUpdating event
private void OnRowUpdating(object sender, SqlRowUpdatingEventArgs e)
{
    DisplayEventArgs(e);
}

// Event Handler for RowUpdated event
private void OnRowUpdated(object sender, SqlRowUpdatedEventArgs e)
{
    DisplayEventArgs(e);
}
```

The overloaded DisplayEventArgs method adds an item to the list box to indicate that the executing code has entered it. It also uses the argument passed to it and checks Status. Status is an enumeration of type UpdateStatus. If Status isn't UpdateStatus.Continue, the status is written to the list box. When a row is in the process of being updated, if a change has been made to the row, the status of the row will be marked as Continue and the RowUpdated event will fire for the row. If the status isn't UpdateStatus.Continue, then the RowUpdated event won't fire.

```
private void DisplayEventArgs(SqlRowUpdatingEventArgs args)
{
    listBox1.Items.Add("OnRowUpdating event");
    if (args.Status != UpdateStatus.Continue)
        listBox1.Items.Add("RowStatus = " + args.Status.ToString());
}
```

If the row can be updated, the RowUpdated event will fire, which will be handled by the OnRowUpdated event handler, which in turn will pass the execution to the version of DisplayEventArgs function that takes the SqlRowUpdatedEventArgs object as the parameter.

This object carries with it information about how many rows were updated in the RecordsAffected property, which is displayed in the list box.

```
private void DisplayEventArgs(SqlRowUpdatedEventArgs args)
{
  listBox1.Items.Add("OnRowUpdated event");
  listBox1.Items.Add("Records Affected = " + args.RecordsAffected);
}
```

The first time the button is clicked, the company name changes to "The Volcano Corporation." This raises both the RowUpdating and the RowUpdated events. The second time the button is clicked, since the company name is already "The Volcano Corporation," only the RowUpdating event is raised, and the row's UpdateStatus is marked as SkipCurrentRow. So the RowUpdated event doesn't fire.

Working with Multiple Handlers

It's also possible to have the same event call multiple handlers. You can do this in two ways. You can individually bind the event to two different event handlers; alternatively, you can use a *multicast delegate* where you specify a list of event handlers, and, when the event is fired, all the listed handlers will be invoked successively. You'll use the first alternative in the following example.

Try It Out: Using Multiple Handlers for the Same Event

Follow these steps:

1. Double-click the Multiple Handlers button. Add the following code to the click event handler:

```
// Create connection
SqlConnection cn = new SqlConnection(@"Data Source=(local)\NETSDK;" +
    "Integrated Security=SSPI;database=Northwind");

// Delegate the StateChange event to two handlers
cn.StateChange += new StateChangeEventHandler(CnStateChange);
cn.StateChange += new StateChangeEventHandler(CnStateChange2);

// Create command
SqlCommand cmd = new SqlCommand();
cmd.CommandText = "SELECT TOP 1 CustomerId, CompanyName FROM Customers";
cmd.Connection = cn;

try
{
    listBox1.Items.Clear();
    // Open connection
    cn.Open();
    // Create data reader
    SqlDataReader dr = cmd.ExecuteReader();
```

```
    while(dr.Read())
    {
        listBox1.Items.Add(dr.GetString(0) + "-" + dr.GetString(1));
    }
}
catch(SqlException ex)
{
    MessageBox.Show (ex.Message);
}
finally
{
    //Close connection
    cn.Close();
}
```

2. Add a second event handler for the StateChange event as follows:

```
private void CnStateChange2(object sender, StateChangeEventArgs ev)
{
    // Second Event handler for the StateChange Event
    listBox1.Items.Add("-----------------------------");
    listBox1.Items.Add("Entering Second StateChange EventHandler");
    listBox1.Items.Add("Sender = " + sender.ToString());
    listBox1.Items.Add("Original State = " + ev.OriginalState.ToString());
    listBox1.Items.Add("Current State = " + ev.CurrentState.ToString());
    listBox1.Items.Add("Exiting Second StateChange EventHandler");
    listBox1.Items.Add("-----------------------------");
}
```

3. Build and run the solution with Ctrl+F5. Click the SqlDataAdapter RowUpdating Event button. You'll see the results in Figure 20-7.

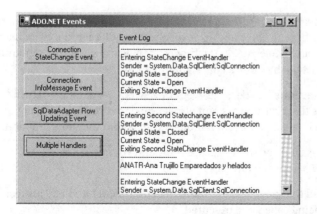

Figure 20-7. *State change events*

Observe that the event log in Figure 20-7 shows that the first StateChange event handler was invoked and then the second StateChange event handler was invoked. You can code these two handlers to perform different actions, of course.

How It Works

You bind the StateChange event to two different handlers separately.

```
// Delegate the StateChange event to two handlers
cn.StateChange += new StateChangeEventHandler(CnStateChange);
cn.StateChange += new StateChangeEventHandler(CnStateChange2);
```

Notice that in the second instance, you bind it to the CnStateChange2 method, which is the same as CnStateChange except for its enter and exit messages.

```
private void CnStateChange2(object sender, StateChangeEventArgs ev)
{
    // Second Event handler for the StateChange Event
    listBox1.Items.Add("------------------------------");
    listBox1.Items.Add("Entering Second StateChange EventHandler");
    listBox1.Items.Add("Sender = " + sender.ToString());
    listBox1.Items.Add("Original State = " + ev.OriginalState.ToString());
    listBox1.Items.Add("Current State = " + ev.CurrentState.ToString());
    listBox1.Items.Add("Exiting Second StateChange EventHandler");
    listBox1.Items.Add("------------------------------");
}
```

Summary

This chapter discussed the basics of handling ADO.NET events. You saw what events are and how to use delegates to bind them to event handlers. Specifically, you learned and tried the following features:

- You learned that a connection's StateChange event fires when the state changes from Open to Closed or from Closed to Open. You wrote an event handler for this event using the StateChangeEventHandler delegate. In the process, you learned that the signature of the event handler must be the same as the signature of the delegate.

- You learned that a connection's InfoMessage event fires when the database returns informational messages that aren't errors. You also learned that you can bind any number of events to their respective event handlers from within the same function.

- You then saw how to use a data adapter's RowUpdating and RowUpdated events to determine the status of a row before and after it's updated.

- You also saw how to bind the same event to more than one event handler. This resulted in each event handler being called and executed.

In the next chapter, you'll learn how to store and retrieve binary and text data.

Working with Text and Binary Data

Some kinds of data have special formats, are very large, or vary greatly in size. In this chapter, you'll learn techniques for working with text and binary data, including the following:

- What data types to use

- How to load, retrieve, and display image data

- How to work with headers in binary data

- How to work with data too large to fit easily into memory

- How to retrieve and store text data

We'll use the .NET data provider for SQL Server, but the concepts are basically the same for other .NET data providers. We'll start by covering what data types support these kinds of data.

Understanding SQL Server Text and Binary Data Types

SQL Server provides the types CHAR, NCHAR, VARCHAR, NVARCHAR, BINARY, and VARBINARY for working with text and binary data. You can use these with text (character) data up to a maximum of 8,000 bytes (4,000 bytes for Unicode data, NCHAR, and NVARCHAR, which use 2 bytes per character).

For larger data, SQL Server provides the TEXT, NTEXT, and IMAGE data types. TEXT and NTEXT are for large character data (NTEXT is for Unicode characters), and IMAGE is for storing anything else. The SQL Server designers must have decided IMAGE was more intuitive than BLOB, as the most common use for large binary data is pictures. However, IMAGE is usable for any type of binary data—video, sound, documents, or anything else you may store in a file.

Note DB2, MySQL, Oracle, and the SQL standard call such data types *large objects* (LOBs); specifically, they're binary large objects (BLOBs) and character large objects (CLOBs).

Within your C# program, binary data types map to an array of bytes (byte[]), and character data types map to string or character arrays (char[]). Table 21-1 summarizes the characteristics of these data types.

Table 21-1. *Large Data Type Mappings*

SQL Server Data Type	C# Data Type	Maximum Size
CHAR, VARCHAR	string, char[]	8,000 characters
NCHAR, NVARCHAR	string, char[]	4,000 2-byte (Unicode) characters
BINARY, VARBINARY	byte[]	8,000 bytes
TEXT	string, char[]	2,147,483,647 characters
NTEXT	string, char[]	1,073,741,823 2-byte (Unicode) characters
IMAGE	byte[]	2,147,483,647 bytes

An alternative to using these data types is to not store the data itself in the database but instead define a column containing a path that points to where the data is actually stored. This can be more efficient for accessing large amounts of data, and it can save resources on the database server by transferring the demand to a file server. It does require more complicated coordination and has the potential for database and data files to get out of sync. We won't use this technique in this chapter.

IMAGE is almost always going to be the best choice for binary data, because it's rare that you can guarantee that the size of a binary data item is always going to be less than 8,000 bytes. Even small pictures or sound files often exceed this size.

IMAGE is stored as a "pointer" within the table that points to another location within the SQL Server database that stores the data, so there's some slight overhead for IMAGE data compared to BINARY and VARBINARY, but for binary data this is typically not a significant performance consideration.

You implement NTEXT and TEXT in a similar way to IMAGE—as pointers to the data. In this case, however, the overhead is worth thinking about in choosing between these types and NVARCHAR or VARCHAR. It depends on your application needs. Many applications have a "notes" or other similar column for text that can be relatively long, but on average you can accommodate 2,000 characters a page for several pages of text in 8,000 characters.

The choice between NTEXT and TEXT depends on whether you want text to be stored as Unicode 2-byte characters or 1-byte ASCII/ANSI characters. The native character type in C# and the .NET Framework is Unicode, so the text will be converted to 2-byte characters when received from a database. If your application will be used internationally, with different languages and character sets, then it makes sense to use Unicode data types. If this isn't the case, then it may be wasteful to double the storage requirement. But storage continually gets cheaper, so flexibility may outweigh this consideration; however, with multimegabyte data, it's worth careful thought.

CHAR, NCHAR, and BINARY are fixed-length data types directly stored in database tables; they always take up the size specified when creating the table, even if the actual size of the data value is shorter. You use this when the data is mostly the same average length close to the specified size. For example, if your table stored icons where the binary size was small and every icon was the same size, then BINARY may well be the best data type to use. Most character data larger than a few hundred characters varies significantly in length, so fixed-length CHAR or NCHAR data types become less appropriate as the data length increases.

NVARCHAR, VARCHAR, and VARBINARY accommodate varying-length data so they don't waste space in the database. Very small bitmaps or sound files that will always be less than 8,000 bytes can be stored as VARBINARY. As mentioned previously, you can store text data a few paragraphs or pages in length and always less than 8,000 bytes in length as VARCHAR or NVARCHAR.

Storing Images in a Database

Let's start by creating a database table for storing images and then loading some images into it. We'll use some images from the ASP.NET QuickStart, located in C:\Program Files\ Microsoft Visual Studio .NET 2003\SDK\v1.1\QuickStart\aspplus\images. We'll use small images that can fit in any of the data types we've discussed.

Try It Out: Loading Image Binary Data from Files

In this example, you'll write a program that creates a database table and then stores milk carton images in it.

1. Create a new solution named Chapter21_Examples, and add a C# console application named LoadImages.

2. Rename Class1.cs to LoadImages.cs, and replace its code with the code in Listing 21-1.

Listing 21-1. LoadImages.cs

```
using System;
using System.Data;
using System.Data.SqlClient;
using System.IO;

namespace LoadImages
{
    class LoadImages
    {
        string imageFileLocation =
            @"C:\Program Files\Microsoft Visual Studio .NET 2003\"
            + @"SDK\v1.1\QuickStart\aspplus\images\";

        string imageFilePrefix = "milk";
        int numberImageFiles = 8;
        string imageFileType = ".gif";
        int maxImageSize = 10000;
        SqlConnection conn = null;
        SqlCommand cmd = null;
```

```csharp
static void Main()
{
    LoadImages loader = new LoadImages();

    try
    {
        // Open connection
        loader.OpenConnection();
        // Create command
        loader.CreateCommand();
        // Create table
        loader.CreateImageTable();
        // Prepare insert
        loader.PrepareInsertImages();
        // Insert images
        int i;
        for (i = 1; i <= loader.numberImageFiles; i++)
        {
            loader.ExecuteInsertImages(i);
        }
    }
    catch (SqlException ex)
    {
        Console.WriteLine(ex.ToString());
    }
    finally
    {
        loader.CloseConnection();
    }
}

void OpenConnection()
{
    // Create connection
    conn = new SqlConnection(@"
        server = (local)\netsdk;
        integrated security = sspi;
        database = tempdb
    ");
    // Open connection
    conn.Open();
}
```

```csharp
void CloseConnection()
{
   // Close connection
   conn.Close();
   Console.WriteLine("Connection Successfully Closed!");
}

void CreateCommand()
{
   cmd = new SqlCommand();
   cmd.Connection = conn;
}

void ExecuteCommand(string cmdText)
{
   int cmdResult;
   cmd.CommandText = cmdText;
   Console.WriteLine("Executing command:");
   Console.WriteLine(cmd.CommandText);
   cmdResult = cmd.ExecuteNonQuery();
   Console.WriteLine("ExecuteNonQuery returns {0}.", cmdResult);
}

void CreateImageTable()
{
   ExecuteCommand(@"
      create table imagetable
      (
         imagefile nvarchar(20),
         imagedata image
      )
   ");
}

void PrepareInsertImages()
{
   cmd.CommandText = @"
      insert into imagetable
      values (@ImageFile, @ImageData)
   ";
   cmd.Parameters.Add("@ImageFile", SqlDbType.NVarChar);
   cmd.Parameters.Add("@ImageData", SqlDbType.Image);
}
```

```
void ExecuteInsertImages(int imageFileNumber)
{
    string imageFileName = null;
    byte[] imageImageData = null;

    imageFileName =
        imageFilePrefix + imageFileNumber.ToString() + imageFileType;
    imageImageData =
        LoadImageFile(imageFileName, imageFileLocation, maxImageSize);

    cmd.Parameters["@ImageFile"].Value = imageFileName;
    cmd.Parameters["@ImageData"].Value = imageImageData;

    ExecuteCommand(cmd.CommandText);
}

byte[] LoadImageFile(
    string fileName,
    string fileLocation,
    int maxImageSize
)
{
    byte[] imagebytes = null;
    string fullpath = fileLocation + fileName;
    Console.WriteLine("Loading File:");
    Console.WriteLine(fullpath);
    FileStream fs = new FileStream(fullpath, FileMode.Open);
    BinaryReader br = new BinaryReader(fs);
    imagebytes = br.ReadBytes(maxImageSize);

    Console.WriteLine(
        "Imagebytes has length {0} bytes.",
        imagebytes.GetLength(0)
    );

    return imagebytes;
}
}
}
```

3. Run the program with Ctrl+F5. You should see the output in Figure 21-1. It displays the operations performed, their statuses, and the size of each of the eight images.

```
Executing command:

        create table imagetable
        (
            imagefile nvarchar(20),
            imagedata image
        )

ExecuteNonQuery returns -1.
Loading File:
C:\Program Files\Microsoft Visual Studio .NET 2003\SDK\v1.1\QuickStart\aspplus\i
mages\milk1.gif
Imagebytes has length 6553 bytes.
Executing command:

        insert into imagetable
        values (@ImageFile, @ImageData)

ExecuteNonQuery returns 1.
Loading File:
C:\Program Files\Microsoft Visual Studio .NET 2003\SDK\v1.1\QuickStart\aspplus\i
mages\milk2.gif
Imagebytes has length 5970 bytes.
Executing command:

        insert into imagetable
        values (@ImageFile, @ImageData)

ExecuteNonQuery returns 1.
Loading File:
C:\Program Files\Microsoft Visual Studio .NET 2003\SDK\v1.1\QuickStart\aspplus\i
mages\milk3.gif
Imagebytes has length 5046 bytes.
Executing command:

        insert into imagetable
        values (@ImageFile, @ImageData)

ExecuteNonQuery returns 1.
Loading File:
C:\Program Files\Microsoft Visual Studio .NET 2003\SDK\v1.1\QuickStart\aspplus\i
mages\milk4.gif
Imagebytes has length 7854 bytes.
Executing command:

        insert into imagetable
        values (@ImageFile, @ImageData)

ExecuteNonQuery returns 1.
Loading File:
C:\Program Files\Microsoft Visual Studio .NET 2003\SDK\v1.1\QuickStart\aspplus\i
mages\milk5.gif
Imagebytes has length 8664 bytes.
Executing command:

        insert into imagetable
        values (@ImageFile, @ImageData)

ExecuteNonQuery returns 1.
Loading File:
C:\Program Files\Microsoft Visual Studio .NET 2003\SDK\v1.1\QuickStart\aspplus\i
mages\milk6.gif
Imagebytes has length 8174 bytes.
Executing command:

        insert into imagetable
        values (@ImageFile, @ImageData)

ExecuteNonQuery returns 1.
Loading File:
C:\Program Files\Microsoft Visual Studio .NET 2003\SDK\v1.1\QuickStart\aspplus\i
mages\milk7.gif
Imagebytes has length 8394 bytes.
Executing command:

        insert into imagetable
        values (@ImageFile, @ImageData)

ExecuteNonQuery returns 1.
Loading File:
C:\Program Files\Microsoft Visual Studio .NET 2003\SDK\v1.1\QuickStart\aspplus\i
mages\milk8.gif
Imagebytes has length 8307 bytes.
Executing command:

        insert into imagetable
        values (@ImageFile, @ImageData)

ExecuteNonQuery returns 1.
Connection Successfully Closed!
Press any key to continue_
```

Figure 21-1. *Loading image data*

How it Works

The `Main` method does three major things: it creates a table to hold images, it prepares a command to insert images, and it loops through the image files and inserts them.

```
try
{
    // Open connection
    loader.OpenConnection();
    // Create command
    loader.CreateCommand();
    // Create table
    loader.CreateImageTable();
    // Prepare insert
    loader.PrepareInsertImages();
    // Insert images
    int i;
    for (i = 1; i <= loader.numberImageFiles; i++)
    {
        loader.ExecuteInsertImages(i);
    }
}
```

Note that you connect to `tempdb`, the temporary database that's created when SQL Server starts. The tables in this database are temporary; that is, they're always deleted when SQL Server stops. This is ideal for these examples, but remember to not use `tempdb` for any data that needs to be persistent.

```
void OpenConnection()
{
    // Create connection
    conn = new SqlConnection(@"
        server = (local)\netsdk;
        integrated security = sspi;
        database = tempdb
    ");
    // Open connection
    conn.Open();
}
```

Next, you create the table itself, a simple one containing the image filename and the image. (Note that you use the `IMAGE` data type for the `imagedata` column.)

```
void CreateImageTable()
{
    ExecuteCommand(@"
        create table imagetable
```

```
    (
        imagefile nvarchar(20),
        imagedata image
    )
");
}
```

You then configure the command to perform an INSERT statement and map two parameters to the SqlDbType enumeration members that provide an exact match between the C# variables and the database data types.

```
void PrepareInsertImages()
{
    cmd.CommandText = @"
        insert into imagetable
        values (@ImageFile, @ImageData)
    ";
    cmd.Parameters.Add("@ImageFile", SqlDbType.NVarChar);
    cmd.Parameters.Add("@ImageData", SqlDbType.Image);
}
```

The executeInsertImages method accepts an integer to use as a suffix for the image filename, calls loadImageFile to get a byte array containing the image, assigns the filename and image to their corresponding command parameters, and then executes the command to insert the image.

```
void ExecuteInsertImages(int imageFileNumber)
{
    string imageFileName = null;
    byte[] imageImageData = null;

    imageFileName =
        imageFilePrefix + imageFileNumber.ToString() + imageFileType;
    imageImageData =
        LoadImageFile(imageFileName, imageFileLocation, maxImageSize);

    cmd.Parameters["@ImageFile"].Value = imageFileName;
    cmd.Parameters["@ImageData"].Value = imageImageData;

    ExecuteCommand(cmd.CommandText);
}
```

The loadImageFile method reads the image file, displays the number of bytes in the file, and returns the image as a byte array. C# file I/O is beyond the scope of this book, but it's straightforward here, simply reading a file stream in binary mode to fill a byte array.

```
byte[] LoadImageFile(
    string fileName,
    string fileLocation,
    int maxImageSize
)
{
    byte[] imagebytes = null;
    string fullpath = fileLocation + fileName;
    Console.WriteLine("Loading File:");
    Console.WriteLine(fullpath);
    FileStream fs = new FileStream(fullpath, FileMode.Open);
    BinaryReader br = new BinaryReader(fs);
    imagebytes = br.ReadBytes(maxImageSize);

    Console.WriteLine(
        "Imagebytes has length {0} bytes.",
        imagebytes.GetLength(0)
    );

    return imagebytes;
}
```

Rerunning the Program

Since the program always creates the imagetable table, you must cycle (stop and restart) SQL Server before rerunning it to re-create an empty tempdb database. (See Chapter 1 if you've forgotten how to stop and start MSDE.)

Using a Different SQL Data Type

To see what happens when you specify a data type with small length restrictions, modify createImageTable to use varbinary(8000) instead of image.

```
void CreateImageTable()
{
    ExecuteCommand(@"
        create table imagetable
        (
            imagefile nvarchar(20),
            imagedata varbinary(8000)
        )
    ");
}
```

This works for the first couple images, and then an exception appears, as shown in Figure 21-2.

```
C:\BegCSharpDb\Chapter21_Examples\LoadImages\bin\Debug\LoadImages.exe"          _ □ ×
Loading File:
C:\Program Files\Microsoft Visual Studio .NET 2003\SDK\v1.1\QuickStart\aspplus\i
mages\milk5.gif
Imagebytes has length 8664 bytes.
Executing command:

            insert into imagetable
            values (@ImageFile, @ImageData)

System.Data.SqlClient.SqlException: String or binary data would be truncated.
The statement has been terminated.
   at System.Data.SqlClient.SqlCommand.ExecuteReader(CommandBehavior cmdBehavior
, RunBehavior runBehavior, Boolean returnStream)
   at System.Data.SqlClient.SqlCommand.ExecuteNonQuery()
   at LoadImages.LoadImages.executeCommand(String cmdText) in c:\begcsharpdb\cha
pter21_examples\loadimages\loadimages.cs:line 83
   at LoadImages.LoadImages.executeInsertImages(Int32 imageFileNumber) in c:\beg
csharpdb\chapter21_examples\loadimages\loadimages.cs:line 121
   at LoadImages.LoadImages.Main() in c:\begcsharpdb\chapter21_examples\loadimag
es\loadimages.cs:line 39
Connection Successfully Closed!
Press any key to continue_
```

Figure 21-2. *Exceeding column size*

You can see that the size restrictions of BINARY/VARBINARY aren't adequate, even when working with small images such as these.

Retrieving Images from a Database

Now that you've stored some images, you'll see how to retrieve and display them. Of course, in order to display them, you'll have to switch to a Windows Forms application.

Try It Out: Displaying Stored Images

To display stored images, follow these steps:

1. Add a C# Windows application named DisplayImages to your solution. Rename Form1.cs to DisplayImages.cs.

2. Add text box, button, and picture box controls to the form as in Figure 21-3.

Figure 21-3. DisplayImages *layout*

3. Add a new class named Images to the project. Replace the code in Images.cs with the
code in Listing 21-2.

Listing 21-2. Images.cs

```
using System;
using System.Data;
using System.Data.SqlClient;
using System.Drawing;
using System.IO;

namespace DisplayImages
{
   public class Images
   {
      string imageFilename = null;
      byte[] imageBytes = null;

      SqlConnection imageConnection = null;
      SqlCommand imageCommand = null;
      SqlDataReader imageReader = null;

      // Constructor
      public Images()
      {
         imageConnection = new SqlConnection(@"
            data source = (local)\netsdk;
            integrated security = sspi;
            initial catalog = tempdb;
         ");

         imageCommand = new SqlCommand(@"
            select
               imagefile,
               imagedata
            from
               imagetable
         ", imageConnection);

         // Open connection and create data reader
         imageConnection.Open();
         imageReader = imageCommand.ExecuteReader();
      }

      public Bitmap GetImage()
      {
         MemoryStream ms = new MemoryStream(imageBytes);
         Bitmap bmap = new Bitmap(ms);
```

```
        return bmap;
    }

    public string GetFilename()
    {
        return imageFilename;
    }

    public bool GetRow()
    {
        if (imageReader.Read())
        {
            imageFilename = (string) imageReader.GetValue(0);
            imageBytes = (byte[]) imageReader.GetValue(1);

            return true;
        }
        else
        {
            return false;
        }
    }

    public void EndImages()
    {
        // Close the reader and the connection.
        imageReader.Close();
        imageConnection.Close();
    }
}
}
```

4. Add the instance variable images of type Images to DisplayImages.cs.

```
public class DisplayImages : System.Windows.Forms.Form
{
    private System.Windows.Forms.TextBox textBox1;
    private System.Windows.Forms.Button button1;
    private System.Windows.Forms.PictureBox pictureBox1;
    private Images images;
```

5. Add the following bold code to the DisplayImages constructor after the call to InitializeComponent:

```
public DisplayImages()
{
    //
    // Required for Windows Form Designer support
    //
    InitializeComponent();
```

```
images = new Images();

if (images.getRow())
{
    this.textBox1.Text = images.GetFilename();
    this.pictureBox1.Image = (Image)images.GetImage();
}
else
{
    this.textBox1.Text = "DONE";
    this.pictureBox1.Image = null;
}
}
```

6. Just to be complete, you should also clean up after yourself in the Dispose method by adding the following bold line:

```
protected override void Dispose( bool disposing )
{
    images.EndImages();
    if( disposing )
    {
        if (components != null)
        {
            components.Dispose();
        }
    }
    base.Dispose( disposing );
}
```

7. Double-click the Next button, and insert the following code into the event handler:

```
if (images.GetRow())
{
    this.textBox1.Text = images.GetFilename();
    this.pictureBox1.Image = (Image)images.GetImage();
}
else
{
    this.textBox1.Text = "DONE";
    this.pictureBox1.Image = null;
}
```

8. Make the project the startup project, and run the program with Ctrl+F5. You should see the output in Figure 21-4. Click Next to see all the milk carton images; when the end is reached, the word *DONE* will appear in the text box. Since you didn't add an Exit button, just close the window to exit.

Figure 21-4. *Displaying image data*

How It Works

You declare a type, Images, to access the database and provide methods for the form components to easily get and display images. In its constructor, you connect to the database and create a data reader to handle the result set of a query that retrieves all the images you stored earlier.

```
// Constructor
public Images()
{
    imageConnection = new SqlConnection(@"
        data source = (local)\netsdk;
        integrated security = sspi;
        initial catalog = tempdb;
    ");

    imageCommand = new SqlCommand(@"
        select
            imagefile,
            imagedata
        from
            imagetable
    ", imageConnection);

    // Open connection and create data reader
    imageConnection.Open();
    imageReader = imageCommand.ExecuteReader();
}
```

When the form is initialized, the new code creates an instance of Images, looks for an image with GetRow, and, if one is found, assigns the filename and image to the text box and picture box with the GetFilename and GetImage methods, respectively.

```
images = new Images();

if (images.getRow())
{
    this.textBox1.Text = images.getFilename();
    this.pictureBox1.Image = (Image)images.getImage();
}
else
{
    this.textBox1.Text = "DONE";
    this.pictureBox1.Image = null;
}
```

You use the same if statement in the Next button's click event handler to look for the next image. If none is found, you display the word *Done* in the text box.

```
if (images.getRow())
{
    this.textBox1.Text = images.getFilename();
    this.pictureBox1.Image = (Image)images.getImage();
}
else
{
    this.textBox1.Text = "DONE";
    this.pictureBox1.Image = null;
}
```

You call the endImages method when the form terminates to close the connection. (Had you used a dataset instead of a data reader, you could have closed the connection in the Images instance immediately after the images were retrieved, which would be a good exercise for you to attempt.)

```
protected override void Dispose( bool disposing )
{
    images.endImages();
    if( disposing )
    {
        if (components != null)
        {
            components.Dispose();
        }
    }
    base.Dispose( disposing );
}
```

The image is returned from the database as an array of bytes. The `PictureBox` control Image property can be a `Bitmap`, `Icon`, or `Metafile` (all derived classes of Image). `Bitmap` supports a variety of formats including BMP, GIF, and JPG. The `getImage` method, shown here, returns a `Bitmap` object:

```
public Bitmap getImage()
{
    MemoryStream ms = new MemoryStream(imageBytes);
    Bitmap bmap = new Bitmap(ms);

    return bmap;
}
```

`Bitmap`'s constructor doesn't accept a byte array, but it will accept a `MemoryStream` (which is effectively an in-memory representation of a file), and `MemoryStream` has a constructor that accepts a byte array. So, you create a memory stream from the byte array and then create a bitmap from the memory stream.

Does this result in a lot of extra memory usage? It does a bit, though you can minimize this by calling the `Dispose` method on each object as soon as that stage of the conversion is complete. You'll now look at a technique that helps minimize memory usage when reading large text objects.

Working with Text Data

Handling text is similar to handling images except for the data type used for the database column.

Try It Out: Loading Text Data from a File

Follow these steps:

1. Add a C# console application named `LoadText` to the solution.

2. Rename `Class1.cs` to `LoadText.cs`, and replace the code with that in Listing 21-3.

   Listing 21-3. `LoadText.cs`

```
using System;
using System.Data;
using System.Data.SqlClient;
using System.Data.SqlTypes;
using System.IO;
namespace LoadText
{
    class LoadText
    {
        static string fileName =
            @"c:\begcsharpdb\chapter21_examples\loadimages\loadimages.cs";
```

```csharp
SqlConnection conn = null;
SqlCommand cmd = null;

static void Main()
{
    LoadText loader = new LoadText();
    try
    {
        // Get text file
        loader.GetTextFile(fileName);
        // Open connection
        loader.OpenConnection();
        // Create command
        loader.CreateCommand();
        // Create table
        loader.CreateTextTable();
        // Prepare insert command
        loader.PrepareInsertTextFile();
        // Load text file
        loader.ExecuteInsertTextFile(fileName);
        Console.WriteLine(
            "Loaded {0} into texttable.", fileName
        );
    }
    catch (SqlException ex)
    {
        Console.WriteLine(ex.ToString());
    }
    finally
    {
        loader.CloseConnection();
    }
}

void CreateTextTable()
{
    ExecuteCommand(@"
        if exists
          (
            select
                table_name
            from
                information_schema.tables
            where
                table_name = 'texttable'
          )
        drop table texttable
    ");
```

```
    ExecuteCommand(@"
        create table texttable
        (
            textfile varchar(255),
            textdata text
        )
    ");
}

void OpenConnection()
{
    // Create connection
    conn = new SqlConnection(@"
        data source = (local)\netsdk;
        integrated security = sspi;
        initial catalog = tempdb;
    ");

    // Open connection
    conn.Open();
}

void CloseConnection()
{
    // Close connection
    conn.Close();
}

void CreateCommand()
{
    cmd = new SqlCommand();
    cmd.Connection = conn;
}

void ExecuteCommand(string commandText)
{
    int commandResult;
    cmd.CommandText = commandText;
    Console.WriteLine("Executing command:");
    Console.WriteLine(cmd.CommandText);
    commandResult = cmd.ExecuteNonQuery();
    Console.WriteLine("ExecuteNonQuery returns {0}.", commandResult);
}
void PrepareInsertTextFile()
{
    cmd.CommandText = @"
        insert into texttable
        values (@TextFile, @TextData)
```

```
                    ";
            cmd.Parameters.Add("@TextFile", SqlDbType.NVarChar);
            cmd.Parameters.Add("@TextData", SqlDbType.Text);
        }

        void ExecuteInsertTextFile(string textFile)
        {
            string textData = GetTextFile(textFile);
            cmd.Parameters["@TextFile"].Value = textFile;
            cmd.Parameters["@TextData"].Value = textData;
            ExecuteCommand(cmd.CommandText);
        }

        string GetTextFile(string textFile)
        {
            string textBytes = null;
            Console.WriteLine("Loading File: " + textFile);

            FileStream fs = new FileStream(textFile, FileMode.Open);
            StreamReader sr = new StreamReader(fs);
            textBytes = sr.ReadToEnd();

            Console.WriteLine("TextBytes has length {0} bytes.",
                textBytes.Length);

            return textBytes;
        }
    }
}
```

3. Make the project the startup project, and run the program with Ctrl+F5. You should see the output in Figure 21-5.

Figure 21-5. *Loading a text file into a database*

How It Works

You simply load the source code for the LoadImages program into a table, texttable, that you create in the temporary database.

```
static string fileName =
    @"c:\begcsharpdb\chapter21_examples\loadimages\loadimages.cs";

    ExecuteCommand(@"
    create table texttable
    (
        textfile varchar(255),
        textdata text
    )
");
```

The ExecuteInsertTextFile method accepts a filename, calls GetTextFile to retrieve the text data, assigns the filename and file contents two command parameters, and executes the command to insert a new row.

```
void ExecuteInsertTextFile(string textFile)
{
    string textData = GetTextFile(textFile);
    cmd.Parameters["@TextFile"].Value = textFile;
    cmd.Parameters["@TextData"].Value = textData;
    ExecuteCommand(cmd.CommandText);
}
```

Instead of the BinaryReader you used for images, GetTextFile uses a StreamReader (derived from System.IO.TextReader) to read the contents of the file into a string.

```
string GetTextFile(string textFile)
{
    string textBytes = null;
    Console.WriteLine("Loading File: " + textFile);

    FileStream fs = new FileStream(textFile, FileMode.Open);
    StreamReader sr = new StreamReader(fs);
    textBytes = sr.ReadToEnd();

    Console.WriteLine("TextBytes has length {0} bytes.",
        textBytes.Length);

    return textBytes;
}
}
```

Otherwise, the processing logic is basically the same as you've seen many times through-out the book: open a connection, access a database, and then close the connection.

Now let's retrieve the text you just stored.

Retrieving Data from Text Columns

Retrieving data from TEXT columns is just like retrieving it from the smaller character data types. You'll now write a simple console program to show how this works.

Try It Out: Retrieving Text Data

Follow these steps:

1. Add a C# console application named RetrieveText to the solution.

2. Rename class1.cs to RetrieveText.cs, and replace the code with that in Listing 21-4.

Listing 21-4. RetrieveText.cs.

```
using System;
using System.Data;
using System.Data.SqlClient;

namespace RetrieveText
{
    public class RetrieveText
    {
        string textFile = null;
        char[] textChars = null;
        SqlConnection conn = null;
        SqlCommand cmd = null;
        SqlDataReader dr = null;
```

```csharp
public RetrieveText()
{
   // Create connection
   conn = new SqlConnection(@"
      data source = (local)\netsdk;
      integrated security = sspi;
      initial catalog = tempdb;
   ");

   // Create command
   cmd = new SqlCommand(@"
      select
         textfile,
         textdata
      from
         texttable
   ", conn);

   // Open connection
   conn.Open();

   // Create data reader
   dr = cmd.ExecuteReader();
}

public bool GetRow()
{
   long textSize;
   int bufferSize = 100;
   long charsRead;
   textChars = new Char[bufferSize];

   if (dr.Read())
   {
      // Get file name
      textFile = dr.GetString(0);
      Console.WriteLine("------ start of file:");
      Console.WriteLine(textFile);
      textSize = dr.GetChars(1, 0, null, 0, 0);
      Console.WriteLine("--- size of text: {0} characters -----",
         textSize);
      Console.WriteLine("--- first 100 characters in text -----");
      charsRead = dr.GetChars(1, 0, textChars, 0, 100);
      Console.WriteLine(new String(textChars));
      Console.WriteLine("--- last 100 characters in text -----");
      charsRead = dr.GetChars(1, textSize - 100, textChars, 0, 100);
      Console.WriteLine(new String(textChars));
```

```
          return true;
      }
      else
      {
          return false;
      }
  }

  public void endRetrieval()
  {
      // Close the reader and the connection.
      dr.Close();
      conn.Close();
  }

  static void Main()
  {
      RetrieveText rt = null;
      try
      {
          rt = new RetrieveText ();

          while (rt.GetRow() == true)
          {
              Console.WriteLine("----- end of file:");
              Console.WriteLine(rt.textFile);
              Console.WriteLine("=====================================");
          }
      }
      catch (SqlException ex)
      {
          Console.WriteLine(ex.ToString());
      }
      finally
      {
          rt.endRetrieval();
      }
  }
}
}
```

3. Make the project the startup project, and run the program with Ctrl+F5. You should see the output in Figure 21-6.

Figure 21-6. *Retrieving text*

How It Works

After querying the database, you get the filename from the table with GetString and print it to see which files are displayed. You then call GetChars with a null character array to get the size of the TEXT column.

```
// Get filename
textFile = dr.GetString(0);
Console.WriteLine("------ start of file:");
Console.WriteLine(textFile);
textSize = dr.GetChars(1, 0, null, 0, 0);
Console.WriteLine("--- size of text: {0} characters -----",
    textSize);
```

Rather than print the whole file, you display the first 100 bytes, using GetChars to extract a substring.

```
Console.WriteLine("--- first 100 characters in text -----");
charsRead = dr.GetChars(1, 0, textChars, 0, 100);
Console.WriteLine(new String(textChars));
Console.WriteLine("--- last 100 characters in text -----");
charsRead = dr.GetChars(1, textSize - 100, textChars, 0, 100);
Console.WriteLine(new String(textChars));
```

You do the same thing with the last 100 characters.

```
Console.WriteLine("--- last 100 characters in text -----");
charsRead = dr.GetChars(1, textSize - 100, textChars, 0, 100);
Console.WriteLine(new String(textChars));
```

Otherwise, this program is like any other that retrieves and displays character data.

Summary

In this chapter, you learned how to store and retrieve binary and text data. You stored such data in a database and then retrieved and displayed it.

You have more to learn about large objects, particularly about database-specific issues that affect performance, but, whatever RDBMS you use, these are the fundamental C# techniques. In fact, these techniques will take you a long way.

That completes our coverage of C# and databases using ADO.NET 1.1. The next (and final) chapter will present information about ADO.NET 2.0.

■ ■ ■

Using ADO.NET 2.0

As this book goes to press, Microsoft is about to release new versions of ADO.NET, C#, Visual Studio, and SQL Server, all of which are now in beta releases. All these products have been significantly enhanced in many ways, but the changes don't deprecate anything you've learned so far. The majority of changes, particularly to ADO.NET, involves internal and infrastructure issues beyond the scope of this book and largely transparent to all developers.

In this chapter, you'll play with a few new features of ADO.NET that are related to topics we've already covered. You'll see that unless you choose to use new features, no new programming is required. C# programs that use ADO.NET 1.1 will work, without changes, with ADO.NET 2.0. Likewise, C# programs written for .NET Framework 1.1 require no change to run in .NET Framework 2.0. Of course, to use the latest versions of .NET components, you must rebuild your projects with the latest class and runtime libraries.

Many new features offer exciting development and performance benefits. Though you don't have to, you may find it worth the effort to modify programs to take advantage of the new features. We'll show you how to use three of them.

In this chapter, we'll cover the following:

- How to convert ADO.NET 1.1 programs to ADO.NET 2.0

- How to load data tables with data readers

- How to extract XML data more compactly

- How to update data more efficiently

Converting ADO.NET 1.1 Programs to ADO.NET 2.0

Visual Studio 2005 provides a somewhat different interface than Visual Studio 2003. We'll cover it as we prove our assertion that ADO.NET 1.1 programs can run without changes using ADO.NET 2.0. Let's rebuild the ComplexBinding project from Chapter 9.

Try It Out: Rebuilding an ADO.NET 1.1 Project for ADO.NET 2.0

To rebuild an ADO.NET 1.1 project for ADO.NET 2.0, follow these steps:

1. Open Visual Studio 2005, and select File ➤ New ➤ Project.... This opens the window in Figure 22-1.

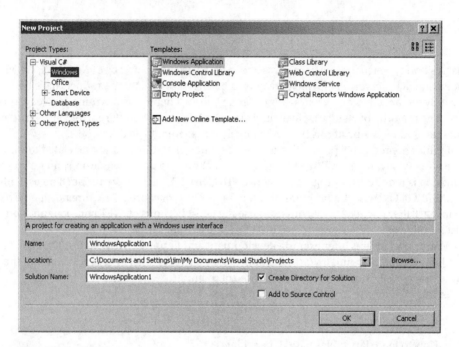

Figure 22-1. *New Project window*

2. Expand the Other Project Types node, and select Visual Studio Solutions. Select Blank Solution, name it Chapter22_Examples, and place it in the C:\BegCSharpDb directory, as shown in Figure 22-2. Then click OK.

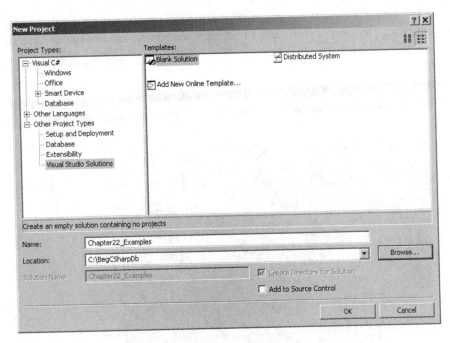

Figure 22-2. *Creating the* `Chapter22_Examples` *solution*

3. In Solution Explorer, right-click the solution and select Add ➤ Existing Project.... When the Add Existing Project window opens, navigate to the `ComplexBinding` project in the `Chapter9_Examples` solution, and then double-click the `ComplexBinding.csproj` file. This starts the Visual Studio Conversion Wizard, as shown in Figure 22-3. Click Next.

Figure 22-3. *Starting the Visual Studio Conversion Wizard*

4. The next screen (see Figure 22-4) asks if you want to create a backup. After you've decided, click Next. If you create a backup, it will be stored in the Backup folder of the solution folder.

Figure 22-4. *Specifying a backup for a converted project*

5. When the next screen (see Figure 22-5) appears, click Finish.

Figure 22-5. *Converting an existing project*

6. If, as it should, all goes well, you'll see the screen in Figure 22-6. Click Close. The ComplexBinding project now appears in Solution Explorer.

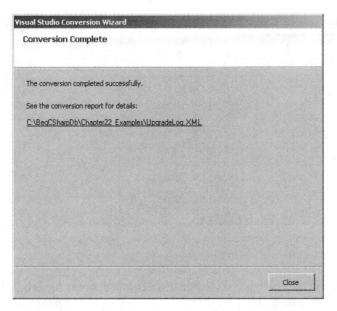

Figure 22-6. *Successful conversion of an existing project*

7. Run the project with Ctrl+F5. Data should appear, as shown in Figure 22-7.

	CustomerID	CompanyNa	ContactName	ContactTitle	Address	City	Region	Posta
►	ALFKI	The Volcano	Maria Anders	Sales Repres	Obere Str. 57	Berlin	(null)	1220!
	ANATR	Ana Trujillo E	Ana Trujillo	Owner	Avda. de la C	México D.F.	(null)	0502
	ANTON	Antonio More	Antonio More	Owner	Mataderos 2	México D.F.	(null)	0502
	AROUT	Around the H	Thomas Hard	Sales Repres	120 Hanover	London	(null)	WA1
	BERGS	Berglunds sn	Christina Ber	Order Admini	Berguvsväge	Luleå	(null)	S-95
	BLAUS	Blauer See D	Hanna Moos	Sales Repres	Forsterstr. 57	Mannheim	(null)	6830
	BLONP	Blondesddsl	Frédérique Ci	Marketing Ma	24, place Klé	Strasbourg	(null)	6700
	BOLID	Bólido Comid	Martín Somm	Owner	C/ Araquil, 67	Madrid	(null)	2802
	BONAP	Bon app'	Laurence Leb	Owner	12, rue des B	Marseille	(null)	1300
	BOTTM	Bottom-Dollar	Elizabeth Lin	Accounting M	23 Tsawasse	Tsawassen	BC	T2F 8
	BSBEV	B's Beverage	Victoria Ashw	Sales Repres	Fauntleroy Ci	London	(null)	EC2 5
	CACTU	Cactus Comi	Patricio Simp	Sales Agent	Cerrito 333	Buenos Aires	(null)	1010

Figure 22-7. *Running the converted project*

8. To prove that you're actually using ADO.NET 2.0, open the References node, right-click System.Data, and click Properties. Note that the Runtime Version property of the ADO.NET assembly (System.Data.dll) is 2.0.40607 (see Figure 22-8).

Figure 22-8. System.Data.dll *is for ADO.NET 2.0.*

How It Works

Totally transparently, without your changing anything, Visual Studio converts the original ADO.NET 1.1 project to use ADO.NET 2.0.

Yes, Visual Studio 2005 looks a bit different from Visual Studio 2003, but it still has the Conversion Wizard. All you basically have to do is request the project be added to the solution.

Loading Data Tables with Data Readers

Datasets are powerful but relatively expensive resources. Prior to ADO.NET 2.0, a data table had to be associated with a dataset so it could be loaded with a data adapter. Now, both System.Data.DataSet and System.Data.DataTable have been enhanced with Load methods that use data readers directly instead of relying on data adapters (which use data readers of their own). In cases where you don't need the overhead of a dataset, you can now simply use data tables.

Try It Out: Loading a Data Table with a Data Reader

In this example, you'll modify ComplexBinding to use a data table, loaded by a data reader, instead of a dataset loaded by an adapter.

1. Open the Form1.cs file in Code view.

2. Replace the code in the Form1_Load method with the following line:

```
dataGrid1_Navigate(sender, null);
```

3. Replace the code in the dataGrid1_Navigate method with the following:

```
string connString = @"
    server = (local)\netsdk;
    integrated security = sspi;
    database = northwind
";

string sql = @"
    select
        *
    from
        customers
";

// Create connection
SqlConnection conn = new SqlConnection(connString);

// Create command
SqlCommand cmd = new SqlCommand(sql, conn);

// Open connection
conn.Open();

// Load data table with data reader
SqlDataReader dr = cmd.ExecuteReader();
DataTable dt = new DataTable("customers");
dt.Load(dr);

// Bind data table to data grid
dataGrid1.DataSource = dt;

// Close reader and connection
dr.Close();
conn.Close();
```

4. Run it with Ctrl+F5. You should see the same output as in Figure 22-7.

How It Works

The first thing you do is simplify things. The code in Form1_Load is the same as in dataGrid1_Navigate, so you now call the latter method directly and have to change things in only one place.

```
dataGrid1_Navigate(sender, null);
```

In dataGrid1_Navigate, you use the same connection string, query, and connection as before. The big difference comes next, when you replace these three statements:

```
SqlDataAdapter da = new SqlDataAdapter(sql, conn);
DataSet ds = new DataSet();
da.Fill(ds, "customers");
```

with the following five statements:

```
// Create command
SqlCommand cmd = new SqlCommand(sql, conn);

// Open connection
conn.Open();

// Create data reader
SqlDataReader dr = cmd.ExecuteReader();

// Create data table and load with data reader
DataTable dt = new DataTable("customers");
dt.Load(dr);
```

Instead of creating a data adapter, passing its constructor the query and connection, you create a command with the same information. Then, since you won't have an adapter to open the connection implicitly when it fills a dataset, you explicitly open the connection. You create a data reader instead of a data adapter, create a data table instead of a dataset, and then load the data table with the data reader by calling its Load method and passing the data reader to use.

As in the original program, you bind the data grid to the data table, but instead of using the data grid's SetDataBinding method, like so:

```
dataGrid1.SetDataBinding(ds, "customers");
```

you use the data grid's DataSource property, like so:

```
dataGrid1.DataSource = dt;
```

SetDataBinding requires both a dataset and data table, and you don't have (or need) a dataset.

Finally, since you no longer have an adapter to automatically close the connection, you should explicitly close the reader and the connection.

```
// Close reader and connection
dr.Close();
conn.Close();
```

Note DataTable's Load method is overloaded. You can optionally specify a member of the System.Data.LoadOption enumeration to control how newly retrieved rows will affect the rows in a data table that's already populated. DataSet's Load method *always* requires that a load option be specified.

Serializing Data More Compactly

In Chapter 8 you serialized (extracted) a dataset to an XML file. The technique used was appropriate for relatively small amounts of data but produced XML files that weren't as compact as possible. For larger datasets, and especially for data intended to be shared over networks, smaller files can significantly enhance performance. Let's modify the `WriteXml` project from the `Chapter8_Examples` solution to use a more compact ADO.NET 2.0 serialization method.

Try It Out: Serializing a Dataset to a Binary File

To serialize a dataset to a binary file, follow these steps:

1. Following a procedure similar to the earlier "Try It Out: Rebuilding an ADO.NET 1.1 Project for ADO.NET 2.0" section, add the `WriteXML` project from the `Chapter8_Examples` solution to the `Chapter22_Examples` solution.

2. Open the `Class1.cs` file in Code view, and change the folder for the output file as follows:

```
// Extract dataset to XML file
ds.WriteXml(
    @"c:\begcsharpdb\chapter22_examples\productstable.xml"
);
```

3. Make this the startup project, and run it with Ctrl+F5. It will create a `productstable.xml` file in the solution directory.

4. The original program doesn't extract much data, so change the query in `Class1.cs` to retrieve all data from the `Orders` table.

```
// Query
string qry = @"
    select
        *
    from
        orders
";
```

5. Add the following code after the statement that creates the connection to create an output file for the binary data:

```
// Create file stream
FileStream fs = new FileStream(
    @"c:\begcsharpdb\chapter22_examples\orderstable.bin",
    FileMode.Create
);
```

6. Change the name of the XML output file.

```
// Extract dataset to XML file
ds.WriteXml(
    @"c:\begcsharpdb\chapter22_examples\orderstable.xml"
);
```

7. Add the following code to the try block after the call to WriteXml:

```
// Create binary formatter
BinaryFormatter bf = new BinaryFormatter();
// Specify binary serialization for dataset
ds.RemotingFormat = SerializationFormat.Binary;
// Output dataset
bf.Serialize(fs, ds);
```

8. Add the following statement to the finally block:

```
fs.Close();
```

9. Add the following using directives:

```
using System.IO;
using System.Runtime.Serialization.Formatters.Binary;
```

10. Make this the startup project, and run it with Ctrl+F5. This creates two files. The file orderstable.xml should be about 488 kilobytes (KB) and look like Figure 22-9. The file orderstable.bin should be about 138KB and look like Figure 22-10.

Figure 22-9. *Text XML document*

Figure 22-10. *Binary XML document*

How It Works

Though it takes ten steps, you don't really do much work. The first three steps simply convert the original program to ADO.NET 2.0. Step 4 merely changes the query to get more data, so the difference in extracted file size is more obvious. Step 6 just changes the directory for the output file. Let's look at the other steps.

The original program uses the dataset's `WriteXML` method, which implicitly performs I/O to a specified file. However, `WriteXml` doesn't provide for compaction, so you need to explicitly create an output file, and you do so in step 5. Even if you're not familiar with C# file I/O, this is straightforward. You simply create a file stream for the `orderstable.bin` file. The `FileMode.Create` argument means that a new file will be created, overwriting an existing one, if necessary.

```
// Create file stream
FileStream fs = new FileStream(
    @"c:\begcsharpdb\chapter22_examples\orderstable.bin",
    FileMode.Create
);
```

In step 7, you add the compaction logic. A binary formatter can serialize or deserialize an object or a collection of related objects. It's not new to .NET 2.0 or part of ADO.NET, but for database applications that pass data over networks, it's often an important alternative to ADO.NET's XML methods. Here, you create a binary formatter, specify that the dataset will be serialized in binary, rather than XML format, and call the binary formatter's `Serialize` method, passing it the file stream to write to and the dataset to format.

```
// Create binary formatter
BinaryFormatter bf = new BinaryFormatter();
// Specify binary serialization for dataset
ds.RemotingFormat = SerializationFormat.Binary;
// Output dataset
bf.Serialize(fs, ds);
```

From an ADO.NET perspective, the second statement is the most interesting. In ADO.NET 2.0, both DataSet and DataTable have a new property, RemotingFormat, which can have one of two values from the new System.Data.SerializationFormat enumeration: Binary or Xml. The default is SerializationFormat.Xml, so you set it to Binary before serializing the dataset. Unfortunately, though the serialization format for datasets and data tables can now be specified in ADO.NET, somewhat inexplicably, WriteXml ignores it, forcing you to use a binary formatter instead to achieve compaction.

Step 8 isn't absolutely required, but as with any external resource, you should close open files when done.

```
fs.Close();
```

Step 9 makes the file I/O and serialization namespaces available.

Whether you need to use this technique instead of calling WriteXml depends on your performance constraints, but it's so easy to do that it may be a good idea to always use it, choosing the Binary or Xml modes to suit your needs.

Tip The Xml serialization format produces a file somewhat smaller than the text file output by WriteXml, but it's not at all as easy for a human to read; therefore, if readability is important, use WriteXml.

Updating in Batches

Prior to ADO.NET 2.0, when a data adapter performed updates, it passed every INSERT, UPDATE, or DELETE statement separately to the database manager. This can be quite expensive over network connections, and is still the default behavior, but a new property UpdateBatchSize has been added to the data adapters for SQL Server (System.Data.SqlClient.DataAdapter) and for the Microsoft-supplied Oracle data provider (System.Data.OracleClient.DataAdapter).

Try It Out: Specifying Batch Updates

To specify batch updates, follow these steps:

1. Following a procedure similar to the earlier "Try It Out: Rebuilding an ADO.NET 1.1 Project for ADO.NET 2.0" section, add the DataGridUpdate project from the Chapter9_Examples solution to the Chapter22_Examples solution.

2. Open the Form1.cs file in Code view, and add a single line of code to the buttonUpdate_Click method. Place it before the call to the data adapter's Update method.

```
da.UpdateBatchSize = 10;
```

3. Make this the startup project, and run it with Ctrl+F5. The window in Figure 22-11 appears. Change some data, and click Update to test that the program still works.

Figure 22-11. *Batch updating*

How It Works

You simply set the data adapter's batch size to a number greater than the default of 1. That's all there is to it. Just make sure you do it before calling the Update method; otherwise you'll use the default.

Summary

In this chapter, you examined several new features of ADO.NET 2.0. It has many more enhancements; in fact, it has so many that several books could probably be written on how best to exploit them, especially in concert with enhancements to SQL Server itself. But the fundamentals of using C# to access databases that you've learned in this book are still the ones you most need to understand.

The ADO.NET architecture has expanded and now offers even more powerful and convenient ways to process database data, but ADO.NET still comes down to connections, commands, and data providers that pass results to data readers either explicitly or implicitly.

Well, that's it. By now you should feel confident and competent in C# database programming. You're no longer just a beginner. We hope you enjoyed our book and found it helpful in your work. Most of all, we hope you'll have as much fun using C# and ADO.NET as we do for real-world programming!

■ ■ ■

Creating the
SQL Tool Application

In Chapter 3, we discussed various ways to execute SQL, including using `osql` and using the Visual Studio .NET SQL tool. You used a custom application to execute queries and statements. Because our tool is a simple C# project to access databases, we're including instructions for how to create it in this appendix.

The utility as implemented here isn't very powerful and doesn't have all the bells and whistles even a small application needs to be ready for production, but you can easily expand it and make it robust enough to suit your needs.

Let's build it!

Try It Out: Building a Custom Query Tool

The tool is a standard C# Windows Forms application, so open Visual Studio .NET and follow these steps:

1. Create a new solution called `AppendixA_Examples`.

2. Create a new C# project within this solution by right-clicking the solution, selecting Add ➤ New Project…, and creating a new C# Windows application called `SqlTool`.

3. Click the form, and set the properties as shown in Table A-1 using the Properties window.

   Table A-1. Form Properties

Property	Value
Text	SQL Tool
WindowState	Maximized

4. Drag and drop a `RichTextBox` control from the Toolbox onto the form.

5. Using the Properties window, set its properties per Table A-2. (Set the font by clicking the (...) button to the right of the `Font` property in the panel and selecting the font name and size.)

Table A-2. RichTextBox *Properties*

Property	Value
(Name)	rtfSql
Dock	Top
Text	[Clear this property]
Font	Courier New
FontSize	10

6. Drag and drop a Splitter control from the Toolbox onto the form. This handy control latches onto the last control placed on a form with a specific value set for the Dock property. You want to be able to change the size of the RichTextBox, so you just need to change a single property on the splitter (see Table A-3).

Table A-3. Splitter *Properties*

Property	Value
Dock	Top

Your form should now look like Figure A-1.

Figure A-1. Splitter attached to RichTextBox

7. Drag and drop a ListView control from the Toolbox onto the form.

8. Set the properties of the list view as in Table A-4.

Table A-4. List View Properties

Property	Value
(Name)	listViewResult
Dock	Fill
GridLines	True
View	Details

9. Double-click a MainMenu control in the Toolbox. This will place a mainMenu1 object in the component tray.

10. Create a menu with four items. Click the Type Here box on the form, and then enter the menu name &Actions. In the Type Here box beneath it, enter the first menu item name &Execute and then the other menu items shown in Table A-5 in each succeeding Type Here box beneath it.

Table A-5. Menu Item Names

Property	Value
Text	&Actions
Text	&Execute
Text	&Format statements
Text	
Text	E&xit

11. The menu items need to have some properties set. Select the &Execute item, and set the properties as shown in Table A-6.

Table A-6. &Execute Item Properties

Property	Value
(Name)	menuItemExecute
Shortcut	F5

12. Select the &Format statements item, and set the properties as in Table A-7.

Table A-7. &Format statements Item Properties

Property	Value
(Name)	menuItemFormat
Shortcut	F12

13. Select the E&xit item, and set the property as in Table A-8.

Table A-8. E&xit *Item Property*

Property	Value
(Name)	menuItemExit

The form should now look something like Figure A-2.

Figure A-2. Menu and menu items

14. Right-click the form, and select View Code.

15. After the other using directives, add the following line:

```
using System.Data.SqlClient;
```

16. Add the lines in bold from Listing A-1 to the Form1 class after the menuItemExit field.

Listing A-1. *Declaring Application Work Fields*

```
private System.Windows.Forms.MenuItem menuItemExit;
private SqlConnection mConnection;
private SqlCommand mCommand;
private string[] mSqlKeyWords = new string[] {
    "select",
    "from",
    "where",
    "in",
    "between",
    "is",
    "null",
    "not",
```

```
    "order by",
    "asc",
    "desc",
    "insert",
    "into",
    "values",
    "update",
    "set",
    "delete",
    "truncate",
    "table",
    "join",
    "on",
    "create",
    "drop"
};
```

17. Add the lines in bold from Listing A-2 to the form's constructor.

Listing A-2. *Initializing the Connection String*

```
public Form1()
{
    InitializeComponent();

    mConnection = new SqlConnection(@"
        data source=(local)\netsdk;
        database=northwind;
        integrated security=sspi
    ");
}
```

18. Return to Design view, click the menu, and then double-click the &Execute item. Insert the lines in bold from Listing A-3, taking care to insert those that don't belong to the event handler *after* the end of the menuItemExecute_Click method.

Listing A-3. *Implementing the* Execute *Item Click Event Handler*

```
private void menuItemExecute_Click(object sender, System.EventArgs e)
{
    string selectedText = rtfSql.SelectedText;

    // First get the text to use. If the user has selected part of the text,
    // we use only the selection
    if (selectedText.Length == 0)
        selectedText = rtfSql.Text;
```

```
        // Check to see if the SELECT keyword exists in the text. If it does we
        // treat the text as a query.
        if (selectedText.ToLower().IndexOf("select", 0) >= 0)
            ExecuteSelect(selectedText);
        else
            ExecuteNonQuery(selectedText);
}

private void ExecuteSelect(string pText)
{
    try {
        bool first = true;
        ListViewItem lvi = null;

        // create a command object. Pass to its constructor the
        // SQL (pText) and the connection (mConnection)
        mCommand = new SqlCommand(pText, mConnection);

        // Open the connection
        mConnection.Open();

        // Execute the query and get a SqlDataReader returned
        SqlDataReader dr = mCommand.ExecuteReader();

        // Check to see if the DataReader was returned
        if (dr == null)
            return;

        // We've got a valid DataReader, use it
        while (dr.Read()) {
            // If this is the first loop, create column headers
            // in the list view.
            if (first) {
                listViewResult.Items.Clear();
                listViewResult.Columns.Clear();
                for (int i = 0; i < dr.FieldCount; i++)
                    listViewResult.Columns.Add(
                        dr.GetName(i).ToString(),
                        100,
                        HorizontalAlignment.Left
                    );
                first = false;
            }
            // Add the row to the list view
            for (int i = 0; i < dr.FieldCount; i++) {
                if (i == 0)
                    lvi = listViewResult.Items.Add(dr.GetValue(i).ToString());
```

```csharp
                else
                    lvi.SubItems.Add(dr.GetValue(i).ToString());
            }
        }
    }
    catch (System.Exception err) {
        // If an error is caught, display it to the user
        MessageBox.Show(err.Message);
    }
    finally {
        // Ensure that the connection is always closed when we
        // leave this method.
        mConnection.Close();
    }
}


private void ExecuteNonQuery(string pText)
{
    try {
        int rowsAffected = 0;

        // Create the command. pText is the text to use and mConnection is the
        // connection object.
        mCommand = new SqlCommand(pText, mConnection);

        // Open the connection
        mConnection.Open();

        // Execute the statement
        rowsAffected = mCommand.ExecuteNonQuery();

        // Clear the list view
        listViewResult.Columns.Clear();
        listViewResult.Items.Clear();

        // Display the number of rows affected.
        MessageBox.Show(rowsAffected + " row(s) affected");
    }
    catch (System.Exception err) {
        // If an error is caught, display it to the user.
        MessageBox.Show(err.Message);
    }
    finally {
        // Ensures the connection is closed when we leave this method
        mConnection.Close();
    }
}
```

19. Return to Design view, and double-click the &Format statements item. Insert the lines in bold from Listing A-4.

Listing A-4. *Implementing the* Format *statements* *Item Click Event Handler*

```csharp
private void menuItemFormat_Click(object sender, System.EventArgs e)
{
    for (int i = 0; i < 23; i++) {
        int index = 0;
        while (
                (index = rtfSql.Find(
                    mSqlKeyWords[i],
                    index,
                    RichTextBoxFinds.WholeWord
                  )
                ) >= 0
              ) {
            index++;
            rtfSql.SelectionColor = Color.Blue;
            rtfSql.SelectedText = mSqlKeyWords[i].ToUpper();
        }
    }
}
```

20. Return to Design view, and double-click the E&xit item. Enter the bold line from Listing A-5.

Listing A-5. *Implementing the* Exit *Item Click Event Handler*

```csharp
private void menuItemExit_Click(object sender, System.EventArgs e)
{
    Application.Exit();
}
```

21. Run the application. You should get a window that looks like Figure A-3 (after clicking the window's Restore Down box).

Figure A-3. SQL Tool application start

Chapter 3 contains examples using the application.

How It Works

This simple application allows you to enter SQL and send it to a database. You enter the SQL in the RichTextBox control at the top of the window and get the results back in the list view below it. You can change the size of the RichTextBox and list view by clicking the splitter bar between them and dragging it to the desired position.

Let's look briefly at the code. The first interesting place in the code is the constructor, where you create the connection and initialize it with a connection string.

```
mConnection = new SqlConnection(@"
    data source=(local)\netsdk;
    database=northwind;
    integrated security=sspi
");
```

If you're using a different database instance/server, you need to change the data source parameter appropriately.

The next interesting place in the code is the ExecuteSelect method. This method is called whenever the SQL contains the word *select*. The code that retrieves the data from the database is as follows:

```
// Create a command object. Pass to its constructor the SQL (pText)
// and the connection (mConnection)
mCommand = new SqlCommand(pText, mConnection);
```

```
// Open the connection
mConnection.Open();

// Execute the query and get a SqlDataReader returned
SqlDataReader dr = mCommand.ExecuteReader();
```

You first create a command object and instantiate it with the SQL you want to send to the database and the database connection. You then open the connection and call the ExecuteReader method on the command object. This method returns another object, which is a SqlDataReader, that allows you to read data returned from the query.

The following lines of code, down to the catch clause, concern themselves with inserting the data in the list view. The catch and finally clauses are interesting because you use them to perform two critical tasks: to inform the user of errors and to make absolutely sure that the connection is closed when you leave the method.

```
catch (System.Exception err) {
    // If an error is caught, display it to the user.
    MessageBox.Show(err.Message);
}
finally {
    // Ensure that the connection is closed when we leave this method
    mConnection.Close();
}
```

Remember that the finally clause of a try statement is always executed, no matter how the try block is exited.

The other method that's used to pass SQL to the database is ExecuteNonQuery. This method sends statements to the database and doesn't return any rows. The method is therefore somewhat less complex than the ExecuteReader method. The code that interacts with the database is almost identical to the ExecuteReader code.

```
int rowsAffected = 0;

// Create the command. pText is the SQL and mConnection is the
// connection object.
mCommand = new SqlCommand(pText, mConnection);

// Open the connection
mConnection.Open();

// Execute the statement
rowsAffected = mCommand.ExecuteNonQuery();
```

Note the final line. Instead of calling the ExecuteReader method on the command object, you call the ExecuteNonQuery method instead. You do so because you're executing a statement instead of a query, so no rows will be returned. ExecuteNonQuery returns an integer that indicates how many rows were affected by the statement.

The final method of interest doesn't actually do anything against the database. The method `menuItemFormat_Click` simply runs through the SQL in the `RichTextBox` control, coloring the keywords and changing them to uppercase. (This is entirely cosmetic, and many SQL keywords aren't on the list.)

Summary

We've demonstrated how to develop a simple yet general-purpose database application. Of course, you could enhance the application in many ways, but all we were interested in here was executing SQL. As you progress in C# database programming, modifying this project to perform more sophisticated actions would be a convenient way to practice your new skills.

For example, the tool connects only to the database specified in its hard-coded connection string. Changing it to provide for dynamic database selection would be a straightforward programming exercise. If you really want to stretch yourself, extending it to provide the same features as the `osql` utility would be an ambitious project—and a *very* nice visual tool for the MSDE environment. The only limitations are your time and imagination.

■■■

XML Primer

Developed in 1996 by the World Wide Web Consortium (W3C), Extensible Markup Language (XML) was first released to the public in 1998. Its most recent version is 1.1, but this offers only minor (albeit important) changes to version 1.0, which is the one we'll discuss since it's the one currently supported by Visual Studio .NET.

A *markup language* provides instructions for humans or machines that read or process them. XML is a subset of the Standard Generalized Markup Language (SGML) developed in the late 1960s and used for complex document definition and publishing. Like SGML, XML is a *meta language* for defining other markup languages. In fact, every time you define an XML document, you're actually defining a small language for formatting and managing it.

XML is much simpler than SGML, but it's an extraordinarily sophisticated and powerful language, with almost all the power of SGML but much less of the complexity. We can't cover every detail here, but XML is essentially straightforward; and since Visual Studio .NET and ADO.NET provide so many facilities for handling XML transparently, most of the time you don't require much beyond basic knowledge of XML. We'll give you enough to be quite effective.

XML has become the single most used and most important data transfer technology in modern computing. It's a core technology that underlies the .NET Framework. Understanding its basics is vital for any .NET programmer.

Understanding XML Documents

Data in XML is contained in *XML documents*. An XML document could be a physical file on your computer, a data stream over a network, or just a string in memory. It has to be complete in itself, however, and must obey certain rules. An XML document basically comprises a hierarchy of *elements* whose names, attributes, and contents are defined with XML to organize data.

XML Elements

XML elements can have *content* (data or other elements) or can be *empty*. An element that has content is delimited by a *start tag* and an *end tag*. An empty element is indicated by an *empty-element tag*.

Tags are formed with angle brackets (< >) and slashes (/). For example:

```
<book>Beginning C# Databases</book>
```

This example defines an element named book, with the start tag <book>, the end tag </book>, and the content Beginning C# Databases. (XML element names are case sensitive, so book isn't the same element as Book.)

A more detailed book element could include a copyright date, and it could be defined as follows (several alternatives exist):

```
<book>
  <title>Beginning C# Databases</title>
  <publisher>Apress</publisher>
  <copyright date="2005" />
</book>
```

In this example, the book element contains three elements instead of data. Its first element, title, contains data, so it's delimited by the start tag <title> and the end tag </title>. Its second element, publisher, also contains data and is delimited by start and end tags (<publisher> and </publisher>). Its third element, copyright, is empty, and it's composed entirely of an empty-element tag.

■**Note** The slash in an empty-element tag comes immediately *before* the closing angle bracket, but the slash in an end tag comes immediately *after* the opening angle bracket.

If you already know some Hypertext Markup Language (HTML) or Extensible HTML (XHTML), you may be thinking that this looks similar—and you're right! In fact, HTML, XHTML, and XML share much of the same syntax. The big difference is that XML doesn't have any predefined elements—you choose the names of your own elements, so there's no limit on the number of elements you can have. The most important point to remember is that XML is a meta language for defining markup languages, each of which has its own distinct vocabulary: a specific set of elements and the structure the elements are allowed to take in a particular document.

XML documents must be *well-formed*. At its simplest, this means that overlapping elements aren't allowed, so you must close all *child* elements before the end tag of their *parent* elements. This means, for example, that you can't do this:

```
<book>
  <title>Beginning C# Databases
  <publisher>Apress
  </title>
  </publisher>
  <copyright date="2005" />
</book>
```

This is illegal syntactically, because the publisher element starts within the title element, but the </title> end tag comes before the </publisher> end tag. It's also wrong semantically, since publisher is supposed to be a child of book, not a child of title, even if the elements didn't overlap.

An alternative syntax for empty elements exists. For example:

```
<copyright date="2005"></copyright>
```

This is equivalent to the following:

```
<copyright date="2005" />
```

Attributes

In addition to content, elements can have attributes, which are defined within the start or empty-element tags. Attributes have the following form, where the value of the attribute must be enclosed in either single or double quotes:

```
name="value"
```

For example:

```
<book title="Beginning C# Databases"></book>
```

And for example:

```
<book title='Beginning C# Databases'></book>
```

These are both legal, but the following isn't:

```
<book title=Beginning C# Databases></book>
```

At this point, you may be wondering why you need both these ways of storing data in XML. Take, the following, for instance:

```
<book>
  <title>Beginning C# Databases</title>
</book>
```

What's the difference between it and the following listing?

```
<book title="Beginning C# Databases"></book>
```

Many XML experts argue over this, but no definitive answer exists. Attributes are less favored in general, since the essential purpose of an XML document is to organize data, which is much more flexibly done with elements than with attributes, particularly since a specific attribute may be used only once for a single element. Attributes do consume less bandwidth if the document is sent over a network without compression (with compression there's not much difference). Probably the best course is to consider using elements first, since they map much more easily to relational data. The choice can be subtle (and difficult), and no hard-and-fast rules exist.

The XML Declaration

Besides elements and attributes, XML documents can have other parts (called *entities*), but most of them are important only if you really need to delve deeply into XML. One part, however, is optional but should be included in almost every XML document. This is the *XML declaration*. If used, it must occur before the first element in an XML document.

The XML declaration is similar in format to an element, but it has question marks immediately next to the angle brackets. It always has the name xml, and it always has an attribute named version; currently, this has two possible values: "1.0" and "1.1". The simplest form of an XML declaration is as follows:

```
<?xml version="1.0" ?>
```

A couple other attributes are defined but aren't required, and you'll usually include only the version attribute in your own XML.

Structure of an XML Document

Each XML document has a single *root element* (also called the *document element*), within which all other elements and data are contained. If more than one element exists at the top level of the document, the document isn't well-formed XML. So, the following is a well-formed XML document, since it nests book elements within the single book root element:

```
<?xml version="1.0" ?>
<books>
  <book>Beginning C# Databases</book>
  <book>Beginning C# Objects</book>
</books>
```

The following, however, isn't, since it has two book root elements:

```
<?xml version="1.0" ?>
<book>Beginning C# Databases</book>
<book>Beginning C# Objects</book>
```

Under the root element, you can flexibly structure data in a hierarchical fashion. You can even use XML to structure documents that aren't essentially for data storage, for example. XML has become a popular alternative to both HTML and XHTML for defining Web pages as well as traditional and hypertext documents.

Using XML Namespaces

Just as anyone can define C# classes, anyone can define XML elements. But how do you know which elements belong to which vocabulary? Just as you declare namespaces to organize C# types, you use XML namespaces to declare XML vocabularies. This allows you to include elements from a number of different vocabularies within a single XML document, without the risk of misinterpreting elements, for example, if two different vocabularies define a customer element.

XML namespaces can be quite complex, so we won't go into great detail here, but the basic syntax is simple. You associate specific elements or attributes with a specific namespace using a prefix, followed by a colon. For example, <apress:book> represents a book element that resides in the apress namespace. But how do you know what namespace apress represents? For this approach to work, you need to be able to guarantee that every namespace is unique. The easiest way to do this is to map the prefixes to something that's already known to be unique. This is exactly what happens: somewhere in the XML document, you need to associate namespace prefixes with a unique identifier. The most common approach is to use a uniform resource identifier (URI). URIs come in several flavors, but the most common type is simply a Web address, such as `"http://www.apress.com"`.

To identify a prefix with a specific namespace, use the `xmlns:<prefix>` attribute, setting its value to the unique URI that identifies the namespace. You can then use the prefix anywhere within that element, including any nested (child) elements. For example:

```
<?xml version="1.0" ?>
<books>
  <book xmlns:apress="http://www.apress.com">
    <apress:title>Beginning C# Objects</apress:title>
    <apress:author>Jacquie Barker</apress:author>
  </book>
</books>
```

Here you can use the `apress:` prefix with the `title` and `author` elements, because they're within the `book` element, where the prefix is defined. If you tried to add this prefix to the `books` element, however, the XML would be illegal, as the prefix isn't defined for this element.

You can also define a default namespace for an element using the `xmlns` attribute.

```
<?xml version="1.0" ?>
<books>
  <book xmlns="http://www.apress.com">
    <apress:title>Beginning C# Objects</apress:title>
    <apress:author>Jacquie Barker</apress:author>
    <html:img src="begcsharpobj.gif"
      xmlns:html="http://www.w3.org/1999/xhtml" />
  </book>
</books>
```

Here, the default namespace for the `book` element is `"http://www.apress.com"`. Everything within this element will, therefore, belong to this namespace, unless you explicitly request otherwise by adding a different namespace prefix, as for the `img` element (we set it to the namespace used by XML-compatible HTML documents).

Understanding Well-Formed and Valid XML

XML distinguishes between two forms of correctness. Documents that obey all the rules required by the XML standard are said to be *well-formed*. If an XML document isn't well-formed, parsers will be unable to interpret it correctly and will reject the document. To be well-formed, a document must at least do the following:

- Have only one root element

- Not have any overlapping elements (all child elements must be fully nested within their parents)

- Enclose all attribute values in quotes

This isn't a complete list by any means, but it highlights the most common pitfalls for programmers who are new to XML.

XML documents can obey all these rules, however, and still not be *valid*. Remember what we said earlier that XML is a meta language for defining markup languages. These languages define specific *document types*. Well-formed XML documents simply comply with the XML standard; to be valid, they also need to conform to any rules specified for the XML application. Not all parsers check whether documents are valid; those that do are called *validating parsers*. To check whether a document complies with an XML document type, you need a way of specifying what the document type is.

Validating XML Documents

XML supports two ways of defining which elements and attributes can be placed in a document and in what order: Document Type Definitions (DTDs) and XML Schemas. DTDs use a non-XML syntax inherited from SGML (the parent of XML) and are gradually being replaced by schemas. DTDs don't allow you to specify the data types of your elements and attributes, so they're relatively inflexible and not used that much in the context of the .NET Framework. Schemas, on the other hand, are flexible. They allow you to specify data types and are written in an XML syntax. However, schemas can be complex, and different formats exist for defining them—even within the .NET world!

Schemas

.NET supports two separate formats for schemas: XML Schema Definition (XSD) language and XML Data Reduced (XDR) schemas. These formats are mutually incompatible, and you really need to be familiar with XML before you attempt to write in either one, so we won't go into great detail here.

You can include schemas either within an XML document or in an external file. Let's look at sample XSD and XDR schemas for the following simple XML document, which contains basic details about an Apress C# book:

```
<?xml version="1.0" ?>
<books>
  <book>
    <title>Beginning C# Objects</title>
    <author>Jacquie Barker</author>
    <code>4982</code>
  </book>
</books>
```

XSD Schemas

Elements in XSD schemas must belong to the namespace "http://www.w3.org/2001/XMLSchema". If this namespace isn't included, the schema elements won't be recognized.

To associate the earlier XML document with an XSD schema in another file, you need to use a schemalocation element in the root element.

```
<?xml version="1.0" ?>
<books schemalocation="file://C:/BegCSharpDB/XML/books.xsd">
   ...
</books>
```

Now look at the following example XSD schema:

```
<schema xmlns="http://www.w3.org/2001/XMLSchema">
  <element name="books">
    <complexType>
      <choice maxOccurs="unbounded">
        <element name="book">
          <complexType>
            <sequence>
              <element name="title" />
              <element name="author" />
              <element name="code" />
            </sequence>
          </complexType>
        </element>
      </choice>
      <attribute name="schemalocation" />
    </complexType>
  </element>
</schema>
```

The first thing to notice here is that you set the default namespace to the XSD namespace. This tells the parser that all the elements in the document belong to the schema. If you don't specify this namespace, the parser will think that the elements are just normal XML elements and won't realize it needs to use them for validation.

The entire schema is contained within an element called schema (with a lowercase *s*— remember, case is important!). Each element that can occur within the document must be represented by an element element. This element has a name attribute that indicates the name of the element. If the element is to contain nested child elements, you must include the tags for them within a complexType element. Inside this, you specify how the child elements must occur. For example, you use a choice element to specify that any selection of the child elements can occur, or you use a sequence element to specify that the child elements must appear in the same order as they're listed in the schema. If an element can appear more than once (as the book element does), you need to include a maxOccurs attribute within its parent element. Setting this to "unbounded" means that the element can occur as often as you like. Finally, any attributes must be represented by attribute elements, including this schemalocation attribute, which tells the parser where to find the schema. You place this after the end of the list of child elements.

XDR Schemas

To attach an external XDR schema to an XML document, you specify a namespace for the document with the value "x-schema:<*schema_filename*>".

```xml
<?xml version="1.0" ?>
<books xmlns="x-schema:books.xdr">
   ...
</books>
```

The following schema is the XDR equivalent of the XSD schema you just saw. As you can see, it's very different.

```xml
<Schema xmlns="urn:schemas-microsoft-com:xml-data">
  <ElementType name="title" content="textOnly" />
  <ElementType name="author" content="textOnly" />
  <ElementType name="code" content="textOnly" />
  <ElementType name="book" content="eltOnly">
    <group order="seq">
      <element type="title" />
      <element type="author" />
      <element type="code" />
    </group>
  </ElementType>
  <ElementType name="books" content="eltOnly">
    <element type="book" />
  </ElementType>
</Schema>
```

Again, you set the default namespace to tell the parser that all the elements in the document belong to the schema definition; this time you set it to "urn:schemas-microsoft-com:xml-data". Notice that (unlike XSD schemas) this is a proprietary format, so it won't work with non-Microsoft products. In fact, XDR schemas are particularly useful when working with SQL Server, Microsoft's database server, because it has built-in support for XDR.

This time the root element is Schema with a capital *S*. This root element again contains the entire schema definition (remember that XML documents must have a single root element). After this, though, you have a big difference—the elements that will appear in the document are defined *in reverse order*! The reason for this is that each element in the document is represented in the schema by an ElementType element, and this contains an element element (note the lowercase *e* here) for each child element. Within the element tags, you set the type attribute to point to an ElementType element—and this must have been declared already. If you want to restrict how child elements can appear, you can use a group element within the ElementType and set its order attribute. In this case, you set it to "seq" to specify that the elements occur in the same sequence as in the schema—just like the sequence element in the XSD schema!

Try It Out: Creating an XML Document in Visual Studio .NET

Now that we've covered the basic syntax of XML, you can create an XML document. Fortunately, Visual Studio .NET does a lot of the hard work for you and will even create an XSD schema based on the XML document, without having to write a single line of code!

1. Open Visual Studio, and create a new solution called AppendixB_Examples. Right-click the solution, select Add ➤ Add New Item..., select XML File, and name it GhostStories.xml as in Figure B-1. Then click Open.

Figure B-1. *Adding an XML file to a solution*

2. Visual Studio opens the file in XML view. Notice how Visual Studio added the XML declaration, complete with an encoding attribute (see Figure B-2).

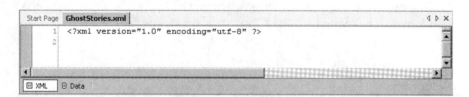

Figure B-2. *XML declaration generated by Visual Studio*

3. Move the cursor to the line underneath the XML declaration, and enter <stories>. Notice how Visual Studio automatically generates the end tag as soon as you close the start tag (see Figure B-3).

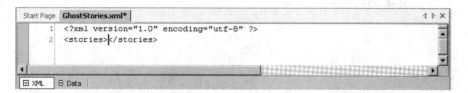

Figure B-3. *Visual Studio generating an end tag*

4. Add the following content to the stories element:

```
<story>
  <title>A House in Aungier Street</title>
  <author>
    <name>Sheridan Le Fanu</name>
    <nationality>Irish</nationality>
  </author>
  <rating>eerie</rating>
</story>
<story>
  <title>The Signalman</title>
  <author>
    <name>Charles Dickens</name>
    <nationality>English</nationality>
  </author>
  <rating>atmospheric</rating>
</story>
<story>
  <title>The Turn of the Screw</title>
  <author>
    <name>Henry James</name>
    <nationality>American</nationality>
  </author>
  <rating>a bit dull</rating>
</story>
```

5. Click the Data tab to switch to Data view, and double-click the separator between the title and rating column headings. You should see the display in Figure B-4.

Figure B-4. *XML data displayed*

6. You can actually edit the data in this table, so you can modify your XML document here without even having to type the tags. In the empty row at the bottom of the grid, enter Number 13 in the title column. Now, move to the rating box beside it, and enter mysterious. This enters a new story, but you still need to enter the author. To do this, click the plus sign next to the new row. This will open a link (story author) for the author element (see Figure B-5).

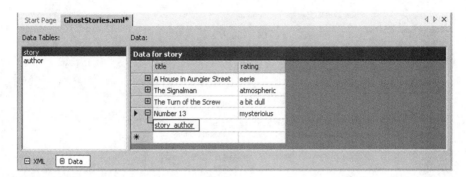

Figure B-5. *Adding an element to an XML file*

7. Click this link, and another table will be displayed so you can enter the name and nationality of the author. Enter MR James and English in the columns, and then press Enter (see Figure B-6).

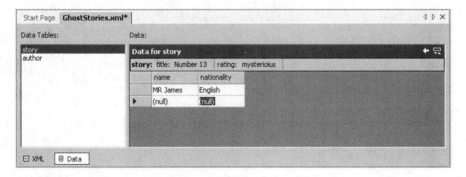

Figure B-6. *Adding nested element information*

8. Now click the XML tab at the bottom of the window to view the XML source again. A new `story` element should have been added just before the `</stories>` end tag (see Figure B-7).

```
Start Page   GhostStories.xml*                                              ◁ ▷ ✕
     1  <?xml version="1.0" encoding="utf-8" ?>
     2  <stories>
     3     <story>
     4        <title>A House in Aungier Street</title>
     5        <author>
     6           <name>Sheridan Le Fanu</name>
     7           <nationality>Irish</nationality>
     8        </author>
     9        <rating>eerie</rating>
    10     </story>
    11     <story>
    12        <title>The Signalman</title>
    13        <author>
    14           <name>Charles Dickens</name>
    15           <nationality>English</nationality>
    16        </author>
    17        <rating>atmospheric</rating>
    18     </story>
    19     <story>
    20        <title>The Turn of the Screw</title>
    21        <author>
    22           <name>Henry James</name>
    23           <nationality>American</nationality>
    24        </author>
    25        <rating>a bit dull</rating>
    26     </story>
    27     <story>
    28        <title>Number 13</title>
    29        <rating>mysterioius</rating>
    30        <author>
    31           <name>MR James</name>
    32           <nationality>English</nationality>
    33        </author>
    34     </story>
    35  </stories>

 ⊞ XML    ⊟ Data
```

Figure B-7. *XML after new* story *element added*

9. Now you'll get Visual Studio to create an XSD schema for this XML document. Go back to Data view. Right-click the grid, and select Create Schema. Visual Studio will create an XSD schema and also a diagram to represent it visually (see Figure B-8).

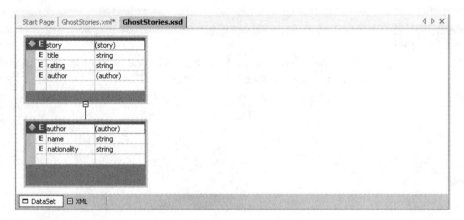

Figure B-8. *XML schema diagram*

10. To view the actual schema, right-click the diagram and select View XML Source (see Figure B-9).

```
Start Page | GhostStories.xml* | GhostStories.xsd
 1  <?xml version="1.0"?>
 2  <xs:schema id="stories" targetNamespace="http://tempuri.org/GhostStories.xsd
 3    <xs:element name="stories" msdata:IsDataSet="true" msdata:EnforceConstrai
 4      <xs:complexType>
 5        <xs:choice maxOccurs="unbounded">
 6          <xs:element name="story">
 7            <xs:complexType>
 8              <xs:sequence>
 9                <xs:element name="title" type="xs:string" minOccurs="0" />
10                <xs:element name="rating" type="xs:string" minOccurs="0" />
11                <xs:element name="author" minOccurs="0" maxOccurs="unbounded":
12                  <xs:complexType>
13                    <xs:sequence>
14                      <xs:element name="name" type="xs:string" minOccurs="0"
15                      <xs:element name="nationality" type="xs:string" minOccu
16                    </xs:sequence>
17                  </xs:complexType>
18                </xs:element>
19              </xs:sequence>
20            </xs:complexType>
21          </xs:element>
22        </xs:choice>
23      </xs:complexType>
24    </xs:element>
25  </xs:schema>
 DataSet   XML
```

Figure B-9. *XML schema for* stories *document*

How It Works

Visual Studio provides a convenient environment for editing and maintaining XML source and schemas.

Summary

This appendix is far from a complete guide to XML, but it's a good beginning. We hope you'll be confident about using and creating XML in Visual Studio .NET.

Index